Exodus

Westminster Bible Companion

Series Editors

Patrick D. Miller
David L. Bartlett

Exodus

J. GERALD JANZEN

Westminster John Knox Press
Louisville, Kentucky

Book design by Publishers' WorkGroup
Cover design by Drew Stevens

First edition
Published by Westminster John Knox Press
Louisville, Kentucky

This book is printed on acid-free paper that meets the American National Standards Institute Z39.48 standard. ♾

PRINTED IN THE UNITED STATES OF AMERICA

97 98 99 00 01 02 03 04 05 06 — 10 9 8 7 6 5 4 3 2 1

Library of Congress Cataloging-in-Publication Data

Janzen, J. Gerald, date.
    Exodus / J. Gerald Janzen. — 1st ed.
        p.   cm.—(Westminster Bible companion)
    Includes bibliographical references.
    ISBN 0-664-25255-9 (alk. paper)
    1. Bible. O.T. Exodus—Commentaries. I. Title. II. Series.
BS1245.3.J36 1997
221'. 12077—dc21   97-23711

To Pershing E. MacAllister
and C. Richard Petticrew,

trustees in faith

Contents

Series Foreword   xi

Introduction   1
    The Exodus: Whose Story?   1
    Reading Exodus as a Story   5
    Exodus as a Story in Two Acts   8

1. Oppression, Redemption, Covenant   13
    Exodus 1—24

    A Home Away from Home (1:1–7)   14
    A Wisdom Grounded in Ignorance and Fear (1:8–10)   16
    Oppressive Wisdom versus Redemptive Wisdom (1:11–22)   19
    True Wisdom's Midwives and the Child of Hope (2:1–10)   20
    Failed Rescue and Flight (2:11–15)   23
    Another Home Away from Home (2:15–22)   24
    The Cry of the Oppressed and the Ears That Hear (2:23–25)   26
    A Bush Aflame with Tongues of Fire (3:1–6)   27
    God Comes Down in Moses' Call (3:7–10)   29
    Moses' Doubt and the Sign of His Call (3:11–12)   30
    What's in a Name? (3:13–15)   31
    Moses' Commission in God's Name (3:16–22)   35
    Doubting Moses (4:1)   37
    Further Signs of Moses' Call (4:2–9)   38
    Final Doubts and God's Prevailing Call (4:10–17)   39
    Blessed Departure from a Home Away from Home (4:18–20)   41
    Problematic Departure from a Home Away from Home (4:21–23)   43
    Mortal Danger at a Rest Stop (4:24–26)   44
    Family Reunion and Rebirth of Hope (4:27–31)   45
    A First Skirmish with Pharaoh (5:1–3)   46

Moses and Aaron as "Outside Agitators" (5:4–9)   47
Making Bricks without Straw (5:10–21)   49
Moses Recalled and Renewed (5:22–6:9)   50
Genealogy and Community Morale (6:10–27)   55
Sending Moses Again to Pharaoh (6:28–7:7)   58
Pharaoh's Hard Heart, God's Harder Plagues
    (7:8–11:10; 12:29–36)   60
The First Passover (12:1–28)   79
Future Passovers (12:43–49)   87
Unleavened Bread and Consecration of Firstborn (13:1–16)   90
The Ambiguity of the Old in the New (12:33–36)   95
Flight in Haste and Hot Pursuit (12:37–14:9)   96
A Way through the Waters (14:10–31)   99
The Singing Sound of Deliverance (15:1–18)   104
Miriam as Israel's Song Leader (15:19–21)   108
Bitter Water Made Sweet (15:22–27)   111
Bread from Heaven and the Sabbath (16:1–36)   113
Water from Horeb/Sinai (17:1–7)   118
The Secret of Victory against Amalek (17:8–16)   121
Jethro's Feast (18:1–12)   125
Jethro's Advice (18:13–27)   129
Eagles' Wings and a Priestly Kingdom (19:1–9a)   132
Preparing to Meet God (19:9b–25)   137
The Ten Commandments (20:1–17)   139
The People's Response to God's Voice (20:18–21)   158
The Book of the Covenant (20:22–22:17)   159
Cultic Regulations and Social Justice (22:18–23:19)   172
Epilogue: Forewarned Is Forearmed (23:20–33)   176
Covenant and Consummation (24:1–11)   184
With God in Glory (24:12–18)   188

2. Planning a Place for Presence   191
    Exodus 25—31

The Tabernacle: A Home Away from Home (25:1–9)   191
The Ark (25:10–22)   194
The Table for the Bread of the Presence (25:23–30)   197
The Lampstand (25:31–40)   198
The Tabernacle (26:1–27:21)   200
Vestments for the Priesthood (28:1–43)   204
The Ordination of the Priests (29:1–37)   211
Concluding Instructions (29:38–31:18)   213

3. Sin, Redemption, Covenant 226
Exodus 32—34

The Golden Calf (32:1–6) 226
God's Wrath (32:7–10) 230
Moses' Intercession (32:11–14) 231
Moses' Wrath (32:15–20) 235
Aaron's Excuse (32:21–24) 237
Judgment on the Ringleaders (32:25–29) 239
Moses' Self-Offering in Atonement (32:30–35) 241
Resuming the Journey (33:1–6) 242
Parenthesis: Moses and God in the Tent (33:7–11) 244
Further Intercession (33:12–16) 245
Glory Hidden in Mercy (33:17–23) 246
Starting Over (34:1–4) 250
What's Hidden in a Name? (34:5–7) 251
Final Intercession (34:8–9) 256
God's Awesome Covenant (34:10) 257
Commandments and Forewarnings Renewed (34:11–28) 259
Moses' Shining Face (34:29–35) 261
Recurring Themes 263

4. Preparing a Place for Presence 269
Exodus 35—40

Works Cited 273

Series Foreword

This series of study guides to the Bible is offered to the church and more specifically to the laity. In daily devotions, in church school classes, and in listening to the preached word, individual Christians turn to the Bible for a sustaining word, a challenging word, and a sense of direction. The word that scripture brings may be highly personal as one deals with the demands and surprises, the joys and sorrows, of daily life. It also may have broader dimensions as people wrestle with moral and theological issues that involve us all. In every congregation and denomination, controversies arise that send ministry and laity alike back to the Word of God to find direction for dealing with difficult matters that confront us.

A significant number of lay women and men in the church also find themselves called to the service of teaching. Most of the time they will be teaching the Bible. In many churches, the primary sustained attention to the Bible and the discovery of its riches for our lives have come from the ongoing teaching of the Bible by persons who have not engaged in formal theological education. They have been willing, and often eager, to study the Bible in order to help others drink from its living water.

This volume is part of a series of books, the Westminster Bible Companion, intended to help the laity of the church read the Bible more clearly and intelligently. Whether such reading is for personal direction or for the teaching of others, the reader cannot avoid the difficulties of trying to understand these words from long ago. The scriptures are clear and clearly available to everyone as they call us to faith in the God who is revealed in Jesus Christ and as they offer to every human being the word of salvation. No companion volumes are necessary in order to hear such words truly. Yet every reader of scripture who pauses to ponder and think further about any text has questions that are not immediately answerable simply by reading the text of scripture. Such questions may be about historical and geographical details or about words that are obscure or so loaded with meaning that one cannot tell at a glance what is at stake. They may be about the fundamental meaning of a passage or about what connection a particular text might have to our contemporary world. Or a teacher preparing for a church school class may simply want to know: What should I say about this biblical passage when I have to teach it next Sunday? It is our hope that these volumes, written by teachers and pastors with long experience studying and teaching the Bible in the church, will help members of the church who want and need to study the Bible with their questions.

The New Revised Standard Version of the Bible is the basis for the interpretive comments that each author provides. The NRSV text is presented at the beginning of the discussion so that the reader may have at hand in a single volume both the scripture passage and the exposition of its meaning. In some instances, where inclusion of the entire passage is not necessary for understanding either the text or the interpreter's discussion, the presentation of the NRSV text may be abbreviated. Usually, the whole of the biblical text is given.

We hope this series will serve the community of faith, opening the Word of God to all the people, so that they may be sustained and guided by it.

Introduction

THE EXODUS: WHOSE STORY?

The book of Exodus is literally a story about "going out." As such, it touches on something all of us have in common. No matter who we are, where we live, or what our occupations and our circumstances, our lives are marked by all kinds of "goings out" and "comings in," together with the "goings on" that happen in between. These verbs can be used of an individual day (Psalm 104:22–23), or of the beginning and the end of any undertaking (Deut. 28:6; Josh. 14:11). As the use of Psalm 121 at funerals shows, they can even be applied to the whole of one's life as a "going out" and a "coming in" that God will "keep."

In between the ordinariness of daily life and the momentousness of a total life span, these verbs can also describe going out in battle and returning victorious (Numbers 15—17; 1 Sam. 18:16). Or, as in the case of Jacob, they can describe a flight from danger, an interim period filled with the unknown, and a concern for re-entry in safety (Gen. 28:10, 15, 20–21). The human concern that Jacob expresses, and the reassurance that God gives him, is summed up in one of the most encompassing sentences in the whole Bible: "For from him and through him and to him are all things" (Rom. 11:36).

The Bible's capacity to touch us and to move us in life-changing ways arises in large measure because it is filled with all kinds of stories of goings out, risky goings on, and finally (in spite of all sorts of interim dead ends), successful comings in or at least their promise and hope. The most dramatic "out-through-in" story in the Old Testament takes its beginning in the book of Exodus. The exodus from Egypt starts a story line whose continuation and completion help later Israel interpret other "out-through-in" stages of its life. This is true also in the New Testament, where the first followers of Jesus frequently draw on the images and themes of the book of Exodus to understand who Jesus is and to interpret their own experiences.

This "out-through-in" story stretches from Exodus to Joshua, but it is summarized in a number of places, as though its basic lesson cannot be too often repeated. In Deuteronomy 6:20–25, the movement is from Egypt and its *oppressive laws* to a land where Israel is given *laws for the people's good*. In Deuteronomy 26:5–11, the movement is from *famine* in Canaan through a period of Egyptian oppression, back into "a land *flowing with milk and honey*." In Joshua 24, the movement is from *serving other gods* (vv. 2, 14) to the promised land where Joshua calls them to "choose this day whom you will serve, . . . but as for me and my household, *we will serve the LORD*" (v. 15). These three summaries show how the one basic story of "out-through-in" deals with a variety of issues: the need for food, the need for just laws, and the impulse to worship whatever is understood to be the divine source of all human needs.

In all three summaries, the pivotal "movement out" is the exodus from Egypt. Likewise, all three in one way or another presuppose another prominent part of the book of Exodus, the covenant making at Mount Sinai (Exodus 19—40). The laws in Deuteronomy 6:20–25 are those given at Mount Sinai and restated or re-interpreted in Deuteronomy. The Feast of First Fruits in Deuteronomy 26:5–11 is first mandated in Exodus 23:19 and 34:22, 26. Joshua's call to turn from other gods and worship Yahweh who is "a jealous God" presupposes the Mount Sinai covenant (Exod. 20:3–6; 23:23–33; 34:12–16). So while the book of Exodus often points forward to the "going in" (3:8, 17; 6:8; 23:23–33; 34:12–16), it concentrates primarily on the two themes of "going out" from Egypt and "going through" the wilderness to Mount Sinai.

Another theme appears in our three summaries that may look like nothing more than a narrative backdrop but, in fact, is crucial to the story. It is the theme of Israel's ancestors, whose story is told in Genesis 12—50. This theme runs like a scarlet thread through Exodus and, in similar fashion, appears over thirty times throughout Deuteronomy. In Exodus 6:3–8, where we have another "out-through-in" summary, the theme of the ancestors is of great importance. For one thing, it emphasizes how the story of the exodus through to entry into the land occurs in fulfillment of God's promise to the ancestors. For another, it focuses on how this story brings with it understandings of God that are new and yet continuous with the understandings that the ancestors had come to. As I shall try to show at various points in the chapters that follow, the ancestral stories in Genesis 12—50 are not just a backdrop or prologue to the story of the exodus and entry into the land. Rather, they are foundational in such a way that, when the later story threatens to lose its way or come to a dead end, it is by appeal to God's relation to the ancestors that the later story is enabled to continue until it reaches its goal.

In connecting the story of the exodus with general human experiences of going out and coming in, I have implied that the exodus story is of interest for all people in all times and places. The question arises, however, whether in doing this I improperly "hijack" a story that properly belongs to a particular people with a particular history. In his book, *The Death and Resurrection of the Beloved Son,* the Jewish scholar Jon Levenson writes,

> In modern times, the tendency is to see the Exodus from Egypt as rooted in God's principled opposition to slavery. In point of fact, however, there is no such opposition in the Hebrew Bible or the New Testament, and the motivation for the Exodus actually lies in the special relationship of Israel to God. . . . It is the special status of Israel . . . that explains why the Exodus is not a story of universal liberation at all but only of one nation's release. (pp. 37–38)

Again, he writes,

> What motivates the Exodus is not God's identification with the oppressed, . . . nor is it his passion for justice. Rather, it is the covenant with the Patriarchs, a central feature of which . . . was the grant of the land of Canaan. (p. 96)

As an example of his point that the story of the exodus is "not a story of universal liberation at all but only of one nation's release," Levenson goes on to contrast the figures of Moses and Hagar (Sarah's slave girl whose story is told in Genesis 16 and 21): "YHWH's revelation to Moses, who, fleeing injustice, has escaped to the desert, stands in marked contrast to his unfeeling order to Hagar in very similar circumstances: 'Go back to your mistress, and submit . . . to her harsh treatment'" (Gen. 16:9).

Levenson's objection should be taken very seriously. In this book, I have tried my best to honor his concern for the "particularity" of the exodus story and the Jewish people, both ancient and modern, who are at its center. The importance of such an attempt is at least twofold. Any story about others should be read first in terms of their own particularity and only afterward in terms of how it may relate to, or shed light on, the story of our own lives. Moreover, the Christian church's relation to the Jews over the past many centuries has too often involved denigration of their status as children of Abraham and adherents of God's covenant given at Mount Sinai, even while we appropriate as the first part of our scripture the text they hold most sacred as their scripture. Such denigration of the particularity of the Jews and their traditions of chosenness is reflected, unfortunately, in the following verse by Ogden Nash: "How odd / Of God / To choose / The Jews." A colleague who is deeply involved in Jewish-Christian dialogue suggests that the appropriate response can be put this way: "But not as odd / As those who choose / The Jewish God / But not the Jews." In affirming the Old Testament as an integral part of our scripture, we Christians affirm that the God whom we worship is the God who led Israel out of Egypt in faithfulness to the promises made to the ancestors. If that is so, then, like Paul in Romans 11:28, we should be ready to affirm that, as regards chosenness, the Jews remain beloved of God for the sake of these same ancestors. This means that, unless we are to be odder than the God who chose the Jews, we will do well to take with utmost seriousness Jon Levenson's concern for the particularity of the exodus story.

Nevertheless, I offer two observations that justify reading the exodus story *both* as the story of a particular people *and* as a revelation of God's concern for the liberation and redemption of all people. First, I note that God's promise to the ancestors includes the prospect and intention that through these ancestors "all the families of the earth shall bless themselves" (Gen. 12:3 following NRSV footnote; also 18:18; 22:18; 26:4; 28:14; Ps. 47:8–9; 72:17). To be sure, when the descendants of Abraham and Sarah arrive at Sinai, they covenant with God to become "a priestly kingdom and a holy nation" (Exod. 19:3–6) and as such become "distinct . . . from every people on the face of the earth" (33:16). The question remains, how these covenanted descendants will become a means of blessing to all people. May it not be, in part, through the way their story can shed light on the stories of other peoples? Even though God can later say to Israel, "You only have I known of all the families of the earth" (Amos 3:2a), through the same prophet God can also say, "Are you not like the Ethiopians to me, / O people of Israel? . . . / Did I not bring Israel up from the land of Egypt, / and the Philistines from Caphtor / and the Arameans from Kir?" (Amos 9:7).

Second, the case of Hagar may work against Levenson's interpretation. God directs her to return and submit herself to the harsh treatment from which she had escaped, yet nevertheless God directs her also to name her son "Ishmael," meaning that God has heard her cry. She receives a promise that echoes the wording of God's promise to the ancestors (Gen. 16:10; 17:20; compare 15:1–5), and she is assured that her son will be a free man (Gen. 16:11–14). In naming God (v. 13), she does something no Israelite has the honor of doing. And twice, in Genesis 16 and 21, God rescues her from death by providing water in the wilderness—similar to how God "keeps" Israel in its wilderness trek from Egypt to Canaan. Indeed, as I have tried to show elsewhere (see bibliography), the Hagar story can be read as a miniature version of Israel's exodus story. Its importance lies in the way it shows that even the community of promise (Abraham and Sarah) can become the context of another's oppression. It shows also that while God's concern for liberation embodies itself definitively in Israel's exodus from Egypt (and, Christians affirm, in the liberation and redemption offered the world in Jesus Christ), it cannot be confined to Israel's (or the church's) own communal history.

READING EXODUS AS A STORY

One obvious question that we bring to any text is, "What does this mean?" Another question that we should ask is, "*How* does this mean?" That may sound like an odd question, but it is an important one. The late American poet and essayist John Ciardi wrote a book called *How Does A Poem Mean?* With copious examples from English and American poetry, he explored the different ways poets use to catch meaning in the nets of words that we call poems. Poems, of course, are a form of art and therefore a form of beauty, and they give a particular form of aesthetic pleasure. But poetry also has to do with meaning and with truth. Unlike the recipes in a cookbook or the instructions in an elementary arithmetic book, there are meanings and truths that simply are not sayable in a series of simple sentences. Indeed, the richer the meanings, and the more important the truths, the more difficult it is to say them simply in the spirit of "one plus one equals two."

Therefore, poets, and storytellers, too, resort to a variety of strategies for using words in ways that will catch and embody meanings and truths that we may all have felt and believed to be real, or at least have hoped against hope might be so, but find it difficult to express. Archibald MacLeish has put the matter this way, in his poem "Hypocrite Auteur": "An Age becomes an age, all else beside, / When sensuous poets in their pride invent / Emblems for the soul's consent / That speak the meanings men will never know, / But man-imagined images can show." What poetry and stories manage to do (supremely so the stories and the poetry of the Bible) is to shape and show a world of meaning that gains our soul's consent at a level that involves our "knowing" but goes much deeper, to a level of trust, commitment, and willingness to go along with the story and the God who is its central figure.

The strategies that poets and storytellers use in showing their meanings are so numerous and varied that lifelong students of these strategies cannot provide a full inventory of them. Fortunately, we do not need to be veteran students of these strategies to begin to enjoy a good story or poem. In the next few paragraphs, I want simply to remind the reader of a few basic things to keep in mind in the reading of Exodus.

First of all, in good storytelling the choice of the right words is important. An old cartoon illustrates this. Panel one: Someone tells a one-liner: "He fell down notwithstanding." Panel two: Everybody laughs. Panel three: One of the listeners tells it to his wife at home, this way: "He fell down nevertheless." Panel four: Seeing her straight face, he says, "How come nobody laughs when I tell a joke?" This cartoon also illustrates how plays on words and turns of phrase cannot be translated or explained; they can be enjoyed only by "getting inside them." In the pages that follow, I at times pause to consider the Hebrew words that underlie our English text, so that we may explore more fully how the choice of words contributes to *how* the story means.

Second, like a lengthy piece of music that introduces a theme early on and after that sounds the theme with variations at intervals throughout the piece, lengthy narratives build up their accumulating meanings and knit their various parts together by repetition, echo, and allusion. So we should be sensitive to the recurrence of terms and images, or of whole scenes, and we should feel free to let such connections play back and forth unhurriedly as we read and reread. Let me give a few examples.

First, at the level of repeated words and images, the story in Exodus is among other things a story of the people's struggle with belief. Moses raises the question at the burning bush when he says, "they do not believe me or listen to me" (4:1). When he first tells them of his call, they believe, and when they hear that God has seen their affliction they bow their heads and worship (4:31). After Pharaoh intensifies their burdens, they lose heart; when Moses tells them that God has appeared again to him to reassure him and them of liberation, they do not listen because they are so discouraged (6:9). Then, when the night of deliverance comes and Moses gives the people God's instructions for the celebration of the Passover, the people again bow their heads in worship (12:27).

Yet when they find themselves with the sea in front of them and Pharaoh's army behind them, they are afraid (14:10–12); and it is only when they see God's defeat of Pharaoh's army at the sea that they "believed in the LORD and in his servant Moses" (14:31). Several times in the wilderness they repeat their desire to return to Egypt, until finally, at

Mount Sinai, God says to Moses, "I am going to come to you in a dense cloud, in order that the people may hear when I speak with you and so believe in [Hebrew; NRSV, "trust"] you ever after" (19:9). A good example of a basic image repeated in different forms is God's reference to Israel as "my firstborn son" (4:22) and God's portrayal of that relationship in the image of an eagle and its young (19:4). As I shall try to show, the climactic portrayal of God in 34:6–7 also draws on descriptive words that are most "at home" in family relations.

Repetition can also come at the level of whole sentences. When God's proclamation of the divine name in 33:19 echoes the earlier proclamation in 3:14, this invites us to compare how these two proclamations function in their respective contexts. (In the following section, I will suggest how this particular repetition helps us to recognize the overall shape of the whole book.)

Moreover, repetition can come at the level of whole scenes. When Moses flees into the wilderness from Pharaoh's wrath, he comes to a well where he helps seven sisters water their livestock (Exod. 2:15–22). We have here a scene that we already have encountered twice in Genesis. In Genesis 24, Abraham's servant meets Rebekah at a well, and after watering his camels she goes home to tell her family about him. Later she becomes Isaac's wife, and much, much later she becomes the woman through whom God fulfills the promise of a child to Abraham. In Genesis 29, Jacob, fleeing the wrath of Esau, meets Rachel at a well, and after he helps her water her sheep, she goes home to tell her family about him. Later she becomes his wife, and much, much later she gives birth to Joseph, the son through whom God will keep the whole of Jacob's family alive in Egypt in time of famine (Gen. 50:19–26).

So when we read the story in Exodus 2:15–22, immediately our expectations should be aroused that the God of Abraham, Isaac, and Jacob is about to act providentially and that Israel's problematical story is about to take a turn for the better. Sometimes two passages that are reminiscent of one another also display striking contrasts. The similarities between Hagar's story and the story of the exodus are a good illustration of how this narrative strategy catches the complexities of life and prevents us from drawing simple conclusions about this or that individual or group of people.

Finally, I would like to draw attention to a structuring device that operates frequently in scripture from the scale of the most minute portion of text (say, three or four sentences) to whole passages and even whole books. This device involves the use of patterns of repetition. This pattern may take one of two basic forms (and from there can take on other variations):

The first form is A B A1 B1, where two elements of the text are simply repeated in the same pattern (for example, Ps. 27:1; 35:26). The second form,
which is equally common, involves inverting the order: A B B1 A1 (for example, Prov. 23:15–16). An example of an A B B1 A1 pattern in prose is
Exodus 14:13–14. In 20:22–26 the "concentric" pattern becomes A B C B1
A1 (see my analysis at those points). I shall highlight other examples at various points later.

Recognizing such patterns contributes to our enjoyment of the artistic
quality of the narrative, but it can also contribute to our understanding of
what is being communicated to us. A good example may be found in the
body of laws in 20:22–23:33. It is commonly held that in places this section looks rather loosely put together, without much apparent concern for
order or sequence. I shall summarize the results of a recent study that tries
to show how, in this section, various laws or groups of laws are organized
in concentric patterns. Not only does recognition of this organization enable us to understand the laws more clearly but also, by the way law is presented in artistic form, we are invited to engage the laws imaginatively and
not simply with flat-footed literalism.

The book of Exodus as a whole displays the pattern A B A1 B1. As I shall
try to show in the next section, recognizing this pattern helps us to appreciate some very important things about different aspects of human evil and
correspondingly different ways God goes about redeeming us from evil.

EXODUS AS A STORY
IN TWO ACTS

In pondering the shape of the book of Exodus as a whole, you may wonder why the content of chapters 25—31 is repeated so fully in chapters
35—40. This repetition looks like a spendthrift use of space and labor in a
day when texts were hand-copied onto long (and no doubt expensive)
leather scrolls. So why was it done? Can it be that this repetition is important to the message of the book? Is it possible that 25—31 and 35—40
are an instance of B B1, inviting us to read chapters 1—24 and 32—34 as
a (less obvious) instance of A A1? The more one studies these two long
narratives, the more one is struck with how they appear to tell two closely
related stories of evil, plight, and deliverance. What is particularly interesting is that each story traces in Old Testament terms what one or another part of the church has long held, or now holds, to be the core of the
gospel of Jesus Christ. Most interesting of all, the way these two stories are

interrelated in Exodus suggests how the church needs to hold together these two aspects of the core of its gospel.

The following outline shows how I understand the shape of the book of Exodus: I see it as comprising two main sections (1—31; 32—40), each with two subsections (A and B; A1 and B1):

A	1—24	Oppression, Redemption, Covenant
B	25—31	Planning a Place for Presence
A1	32—34	Sin, Redemption, Covenant
B1	35—40	Preparing a Place for Presence

As this outline indicates, the book of Exodus moves toward a place (B B1) in which God and people may be present to one another. This place is depicted as a new world or "new creation," of which the tabernacle is the architectural symbol and first expression. To arrive at this mutual presence, God acts (A A1) to deliver the people from the evil under which they suffer and to draw them into a covenant relationship. In A, that evil takes the form of Israel's oppression under the Egyptians. In A1, it takes the form of Israel's sin in making and using the golden calf in worship.

The following outline shows how these two groups of chapters, 1–24 and 32–34, trace a similar yet distinguishable story of evil, plight, and deliverance.

1 A *Israel comes under dire threat.*
   a. It is posed by the ruling power of Egypt (1:9–11).
   b. It arises through a change in Egypt ("a new king arose over Egypt, who did not know Joseph"; 1:8).
   c. The people's plight is innocent oppression (1:13–14).
   d. God hears the people's voice in their plight (2:23–25).

1 A1 *Israel comes under dire threat.*
   a. It is posed by the wrath of Yahweh (32:10).
   b. It arises through a change in the people (who corrupt the covenant relation with the calf; 32:1–7).
   c. The people's plight is guilty covenant violation (32:1–6).
   d. Moses hears the people's voice in their guilt (32:17–19).

2 A *Someone intercedes with the one who will effect redemption.*
  a. Yahweh intercedes with Moses, who after some reluctance
     agrees to go and bring Israel out of Egypt (3:7–4:17).
  b. God intervenes as remembering the covenant with the ances-
     tors (2:24; 3:6, 15, 16; 4:5; 6:3–8).
  c. The divine name Yahweh is interpreted to mean "I will be who
     I will be" (3:14); in this name lies the divine will and ability to
     save.

2 A1 *Someone intercedes with the one who will effect redemption.*
  a. Moses intercedes with Yahweh, to change his mind and turn
     from divine wrath (32:11–13).
  b. God changes his mind and turns from wrath, to remember the
     covenant with the ancestors (32:14; see 33:1).
  c. The divine name Yahweh is interpreted to mean "I will be gra-
     cious to whom I will be gracious, and I will show mercy to
     whom I will show mercy" (33:19); in this name lies the divine
     will and ability to forgive.

3 A *The redemption is followed by covenanting.*
  a. The covenant (24:8) rests on God's self-identification as "the
     LORD your God, who brought you out of the land of Egypt,
     out of the house of slavery" (20:2).
  b. The Decalogue (20:1–17) includes prohibitions against idols
     and against injustices and is augmented by other social, eco-
     nomic, and cultic laws (20:21–23:33).

3 A1 *The redemption is followed by covenanting.*
  a. The covenant (34:10) rests on God's self-identification as "the
     LORD, the LORD, a God merciful and gracious, slow to anger,
     and abounding in steadfast love and faithfulness (34:6–7)
  b. The Decalogue (in view of the idolatry of the calf) now be-
     comes largely a ritual Decalogue (34:11–26).

4 A *The narrative rings changes on the motif of seeing God.*
  a. Moses hides his face for fear of looking at God (3:6); the peo-
     ple are warned not to come up the mountain lest they gaze on
     God and many of them perish (19:21); yet after the mutual
     blood oath (24:8), Moses and several others go up the moun-
     tain, see God and eat and drink, and God does not lay a hand
     on them (24:8–11).

b. When the God who must not (yet) be seen speaks to the people (20:1–17), they are afraid and ask Moses to speak to them on God's behalf (20:18–20).

4 A1 *The narrative rings changes on the motif of seeing God.*

a. Moses climaxes his mediation of the broken covenant relation by asking to see God's glory (as though seeking a personal recapitulation of 24:9–11 to signal full restoration), but God indicates its impossibility under the circumstances and instead offers the reinterpreted divine name (33:19–23).

b. When Moses comes down with the tablets of the covenant, his face shines so brightly with God's light that the people are afraid to come near him until he calls to them (34:29–35).

This comparison gives only a bare outline of the major similarities and differences between chapters 1—24 and 32—34. My comments on the text will from time to time point out others. Now I want to suggest the importance of this kind of analysis.

In my own Christian tradition, I came to understand the problem of evil in human society as one of individual "sin," the failings by which we all "fall short of the glory of God" (Rom. 3:23). Redemption is thus a process involving confession and repentance on our part and the provision of atonement and forgiveness on God's part. Then in seminary I read a small but powerful book, *Christus Victor*, in which the author, Gustav Aulen, argued that such an emphasis is largely a development in Western Christendom, especially since the time of St. Anselm, archbishop of Canterbury in the eleventh century. In Aulen's analysis, the New Testament and early Christian tradition identify the human plight primarily as oppression by and bondage under the personified powers of sin, death, and hell. God's redemption comes through the power of Christ to conquer these evil powers and to set us free from their captivity.

Since Aulen wrote this book, a good deal of liberation theology has been based on a similar analysis of the biblical traditions. In that analysis, evil and redemption are not primarily issues of individual "falling short" and setting right through God's atoning forgiveness. Rather, evil is primarily a social structure of power by which the powerful and privileged oppress and marginalize the powerless and the lowly. Correspondingly, God's redemption is embodied in processes by which evil power structures are dissolved, dismantled, or overthrown, and humane structures are raised in their place. Of course, earlier Western understandings are still very prominent. But, as a general statement and at the risk of oversimplifying, we may

say that Christians in the West are divided into two camps, one emphasizing individual sin and the call to individual repentance, forgiveness, and
salvation, the other emphasizing corporate structures of evil and the call
to structural change and the liberation of oppressed groups.

The analysis of the narrative shape of Exodus I have offered suggests that
these two forms of evil and of divine redemption are distinguishable but in-
tegrally related. There are two keys to both the differences and the connections. First, the golden calf is the key to the connection between evil as
oppression and evil as the sin of covenant betrayal. The calf is a common ancient Near Eastern image of divine power, at home in Egypt as well as
Canaan and Mesopotamia. As such, the calf in Egypt would have symbolized the state power under which the Hebrews suffered. When they make a
calf for use in the worship of Yahweh (32:5), they show that they seek to worship the same kind of power under which they had suffered, but this time
having that power on their side instead of against them. In our own day, we
are learning how the abused becomes an abuser. Through this example, we
see that the different forms of evil in 1—24 and 32—34 are really different
aspects of the same fundamental evil. Second, God's interpretation of the divine name is the key to the connection between redemption as liberation and
redemption as forgiveness. In the face of Israel's oppression in Egypt, God,
who up to now has been a God of conception, birth, and nurture, now becomes a warrior who can save from oppressive political power (15:3). This
is possible because "I will be who I will be." In the face of Israel's sin of
covenant betrayal, God who is understandably angry now shows that (however it may be with humans) God is not in the grip of that anger; for in these
circumstances, "I will be who I will be" means "I will be gracious to whom
I will be gracious, and I will show mercy to whom I will show mercy."

The lessons of Exodus are thus both encouraging and sobering. They are
encouraging because they hold out hope for all who are oppressed by forces
over which they have no control. They are sobering because they caution
communities of the liberated not to perpetuate the very evils under which
they had been suffering. The fact that, in spite of the people's idolatry, the
instructions for the tabernacle (B) are repeated so fully in the *preparation* of
the tabernacle (B1), and that when it is finished God's glory fills it, means
that when all due weight has been given to the sobering story of the idolatry, the last word is one of encouragement. It testifies to the conviction expressed in Psalm 121:8, "The LORD will keep your going out and your
coming in from this time on and forevermore," and to Paul's conviction in
Romans 11:36, "from him and through him and to him are all things."

1. Oppression, Redemption, Covenant
Exodus 1—24

The title of a well-known introduction to the Bible several years ago described the Bible as *The Book of the Acts of God*. However, as the book of Exodus opens, the actors in the story are primarily Egyptians and Israelites, and God is hardly mentioned.

The signs of God's presence and activity in the world are like all signs: They are signs only to those who have learned how to recognize them as signs. To a gnat lighting on the page of a letter I am writing, the wet ink is only something to be smelled and possibly tasted, like any other wet substance. To the addressee, that same ink conveys a wealth of meaning. To a person from Mars, baseball makes no sense until it is explained that, for example, you may foul off any number of two-strike pitches and remain at the plate, except if you bunt foul in that situation you are out. To my niece, a professional scriptwriter and film director, the presence and activity of the director are both recognizable and describable in what she sees on the screen, but to me, knowing nothing of these things, the director is invisible and, for all I know, could be nonexistent. I do not know what to look for nor how to interpret it.

So it is with Exodus 1—2. If we are accustomed to look for God primarily in signs and wonders like those in Exodus 3—15 (or Psalm 78:43–55; 105:27–44), we may rightly conclude that God is *hidden* in chapters 1—2, and we may conclude further that God is *absent*. But if our eyes are trained by Genesis 12—50 to trace the marks of God's activity in human life, then Exodus 1—2 is charged with God's hidden presence working in and through the apparently primary actors there, in particular through the women. We shall have occasion later to reflect on the meaning and significance of the names of God in Genesis and Exodus. For now, I suggest that in Exodus 1—2 the God who is not hidden *away* from Israel, but *within* Israel's day-to-day experiences, goes by the name of "El Shaddai," a name associated with the sort of divine concern and activity traced in Genesis

17:1–22; 28:1–4; 35:9–12; 43:1–14; 48:1–4; and especially 49:25, and customarily translated as "God Almighty" (e.g., Exod. 6:3).

A HOME AWAY FROM HOME
Exodus 1:1–7

> 1:1 **These are the names of the sons of Israel who came to Egypt with Jacob, each with his household:** 2 **Reuben, Simeon, Levi, and Judah,** 3 **Issachar, Zebulun, and Benjamin,** 4 **Dan and Naphtali, Gad and Asher.** 5 **The total number of people born to Jacob was seventy. Joseph was already in Egypt.** 6 **Then Joseph died, and all his brothers, and that whole generation.** 7 **But the Israelites were fruitful and prolific; they multiplied and grew exceedingly strong, so that the land was filled with them.**

To begin reading the book of Exodus without having just read Genesis is like tuning in to the fourth episode of a season-long TV serial. You're grateful for the series host who gives an introductory summary of preceding episodes. In Exodus 1:1–7, however, the narrator does not summarize the plot of Genesis but presents its leading themes and God's purposes implicit in them. These themes set the background for all that follows in Exodus. Since we shall want to keep these themes in mind throughout Exodus and refer explicitly to them from time to time, we shall review the themes that are implicit in these simple, seemingly dry opening verses.

Exodus 1:1–7 sounds two leading themes: children and land. These themes have to do with our fundamental concern to find and remain within a place where we can flourish and extend ourselves into the future. These themes originate with the very beginning of the biblical story, in the Garden of Eden (Genesis 2—3) and especially in the story of creation (Genesis 1). God creates the earth to be a fruitful place (Gen. 1:9–13), and creates birds and sea creatures, animals and humans, to "be fruitful and multiply" and to "fill" the regions they inhabit (Gen. 1:20–23, 28). Again (Genesis 2), God creates the garden as a fruitful place for human habitation. But human sin leads to alienation from that place and renders problematical the related human vocations to reproduce and to till and care for the earth (Genesis 3). Genesis 4—11 traces the complications of these themes on the broad canvas of early human experience generally as sin abounds. The story of the flood in Genesis 6—9 presents an overwhelming natural catastrophe as God's judgment on massive human evil. The result is the twin calamities of the almost total end of all life and the destruction of the earth as a fruitful place. The flood is followed by a "new creation" partly like and partly unlike Genesis 1. This new creation is again rendered problematical by the particular way in which humankind attempts to secure its own place and assure its own future on the earth—by erecting a massive fortified city and a fearsome reputation to go with it (Gen. 11:1–9). (Royal inscriptions from ancient Babylonia typically assert the everlastingness of the city of Babylon and its ruling dynasty.) The story of Israel's ancestors that begins in Genesis 12:1–3 is, then, another "new beginning" on the twin themes of land and human reproduction. Confounding conventional wisdom, God chooses for this new beginning a couple who are both childless and landless, promises them children and a place to live, and calls on them to live as though such promises are trustworthy.

So, then, when Exodus 1:1–7 lists the names of the twelve sons of Jacob and gives the total number of their group as seventy (we shall encounter these two numbers again in Exodus), that simple and seemingly dry piece of information should vividly recall for the reader the dramatic process by which, in various ways and by a variety of timetables, God's promise of children has already been made good to several successive generations of initially childless couples. In doing so, these verses encourage us to recognize God's presence in the basic human processes of conception, birth, and nurture and in family relations governed by the virtues of "steadfast love" (or "kinship loyalty," Hebrew *hesed*, often in Genesis 12—50) and "mercy" (or "compassion," Hebrew *rahamim*, as in Genesis 43:14, and in 43:30 where NRSV has "affection").

But if 1:1–7 shows God making good on the promise of children, the promise of land seems further off than ever before. In Genesis 12:1–3, it was simply "the land that I will show you," but by Genesis 12:5–7 it became specifically the land of Canaan. In the past, when Israel's ancestors had to leave this land, they themselves had returned to it: Abraham and Sarah sojourned briefly in Egypt (Gen. 12:10–20); Isaac would have done the same, had God not commanded him to stay put (Gen. 26:1–2); Jacob had spent twenty years in exile in Paddan-aram before returning home (Genesis 28—35). But now, everyone who comes down to Egypt dies there (Exod. 1:6). God's trustworthiness concerning the promise of children was frequently tested in Genesis 12—50 but now is evident in Jacob's seventy descendants. But God's trustworthiness concerning the promise of land seems to be tested more severely with every successive move away from that land.

Yet a people so tested is given reassurance. If in Egypt they are far from the land of promise, this place of exile becomes a home away from home, where the descendants of Abraham and Sarah are able to fulfill God's intent in creation (Gen. 1:28): they are fruitful and prolific; they multiply and grow exceedingly strong, so that the "land" (the same word is translated "earth" in Gen. 1:28) is filled with them. If this says something about the manner of God's trustworthiness, it also says something about Egypt that we should not overlook. Much of the time, the Old Testament presents "Egypt" in negative terms as a symbol of oppression and opposition to the people of God. It is important, therefore, to observe that, at this point in the biblical story, Egypt is presented positively, practicing the law of hospitality. It makes room for these foreigners to live and prosper in its midst (compare Gen. 47:5–6), so that through Egypt's hospitality these people are able to fulfill in their own lives God's intention for all humankind (Exod. 1:7; Gen. 1:28; compare Deut. 23:7b).

Centuries later, Israel is again called upon to make its place of exile in Babylon a home away from home. While false prophets proclaim God's imminent liberation of the exiles, God through Jeremiah calls on the exiles: "Build houses and live in them; plant gardens and eat what they produce. Take wives and have sons and daughters; take wives for your sons, and give your daughters in marriage, that they may bear sons and daughters; multiply there, and do not decrease. But seek the welfare [*shalom*] of the city where I have sent you into exile, and pray to the LORD on its behalf, for in its welfare you will find your welfare" (Jer. 29:5–7). In Egypt or in Babylon, faith says with the psalmist, "My times [and, we may add, my places] are in your hand" (Psalm 31:15).

A WISDOM GROUNDED IN IGNORANCE AND FEAR
Exodus 1:8–10

> 1:8 **Now a new king arose over Egypt, who did not know Joseph.** 9 **He said to his people, "Look, the Israelite people are more numerous and more powerful than we.** 10 **Come, let us deal shrewdly with them, or they will increase and, in the event of war, join our enemies and fight against us and escape from the land."**

Nowadays the word "hospitality" has a wide range of meanings and can mean simply having friends or neighbors over for a meal. In traditional societies, hospitality governs specifically how one is to treat strangers in one's midst when they are few in number and in need of food and shelter. Thus, in Psalm 105:12–15, God calls on the nations to be hospitable toward Israel's ancestors; as we have seen, Egypt did that for a long time.

Now two things have changed. On the one side, the Israelites (Semites) now are so numerous as to be thought to pose a potential national security threat to their Egyptian (Hamitic) host country. The stage is thus partly set for the sort of ethnic and religious troubles that in our time have torn Bosnia apart. On the other side, a new dynasty comes to rule Egypt, different from the one that welcomed Joseph's family to Egypt. This new dynasty does not "know Joseph." Perhaps this means that, unlike the earlier dynasty, this new dynasty adopts an attitude of nonrecognition toward these aliens. (In 1995, a new Speaker of the U.S. Congress proposed to review the access of "resident aliens" to Social Security and Medicare benefits even if they paid social security and income taxes all their working lives.)

Not knowing Joseph could also have another meaning. Joseph was celebrated for a wisdom that saved not only his family but also Egypt and surrounding peoples in time of great famine (Genesis 39 and 41; Psalm 105:16–22). That wisdom led to a peaceful accommodation between Egyptians and the Semites in their midst. In "not knowing" Joseph, then, this new ruler either does not remember or does not credit Joseph's kind of wisdom and, in face of the new social situation, adopts a different kind of wisdom. (While NRSV has him say, "let us deal shrewdly with them," the King James Version translates Pharaoh's words literally: "let us deal wisely with them.") He and his counselors are going to apply the best social thinking they can draw on to deal with what is perceived as a threat to national security. But any problematic situation can be analyzed and dealt with from within one or another social or political philosophy or "wisdom." In our own day, we are familiar with think tanks informed by different philosophies—conservative, liberal, radical (not to mention groups informed by ideologies on the extreme right and left)—as to what genuinely constitutes the public good and how to achieve it. Given the "wisdom" or overall philosophy with which it is working, the new dynasty in Egypt is sincerely persuaded of the rightness of its assessments and policies, both in terms of the national interest and in terms of what the gods call for (see Exod. 12:12).

Egypt's search for wisdom is driven by fear. Now, fear in itself can be a good thing. It alerts us to situations in which we need to take special measures—perhaps unprecedented measures—to assure our well-being. But, like Cain in Genesis 4:7, we must find what it means to "do well" in the new situation, for what appears to be a door of opportunity may, instead, hide our own worst enemy. Like Cain, Egypt fails the challenge. Instead of searching for an inclusive wisdom that will embrace the legitimate interests of all, Egyptian and alien alike, the Pharaoh falls back into an "us versus them" wisdom.

In this connection, we may notice how Pharaoh's language echoes the language of those who built the fortified city of Babylon in Genesis 11:1–9. The expressions "Come, let us . . . or . . ." of Exodus 1:10 and "Come, let us . . . otherwise . . ." of Genesis 11:3–4 are identical in Hebrew and are the only two times these expressions occur in the Bible. (As a general principle, it is good to listen for how a passage we are reading finds echoes in other passages through similar phraseology or imagery or theme. In this way, the Bible as a whole becomes a guide to the interpretation of its individual passages.) In Genesis 11, the people fear that they might be "scattered" and lose their accustomed living space, in the Bible typically an outcome of war. This fear leads to the building of a fortified city. This intensifies an "us versus them" mentality, which then turns in on itself, dividing even this fortified city itself into "us versus them" parties unable to understand or trust one another. As a result, they are no longer able to hold together as one people in one place.

I suggested earlier that a fundamental human need (and, according to the Bible, a fundamental divine provision) is for space in which to live and grow toward a people's (and an individual's) future. Unlike plants, animals and humans are not rooted in one spot but may roam around within their supportive habitat. Yet we remain essentially connected to the earth for our nourishment and our shelter, and in our own way we do become "rooted" in a given place for reasons such as place of birth, economic interest, or meaningful experiences, to the point where being "uprooted" can be painful and even life-threatening. So we develop a vested interest in staying where we are and protecting our turf from "outsiders." NIMBY— "not in my back yard!"—is a suitable term for the new Pharaoh's wisdom.

In the Bible's wisdom, while all people have a God-given right to living space, no people has absolute or ultimate rights to a particular place. If "the earth is the LORD's," then the God who placed the first human within a fertile garden (Gen. 2:7–8), but then expelled the first couple for their embrace of false wisdom (Gen. 3:6), may likewise transplant people (Psalm 80:8–11; Isa. 5:1–2; also more generally Amos 9:7), and even drastically uproot and displace them (Jer. 1:10; 24:1–10). Like the builders of Babylon, the new Pharaoh and his counselors approach their own legitimate need for space with a wisdom that is divisive and becomes oppressive. It is a wisdom that is repeated again and again in the Bible, by Israelite as well as foreign rulers, until it reaches its climax (according to the New Testament) in the crucifixion when the "wisdom of this age [and] of the rulers of this age" encounters most dramatically the strange wisdom of the biblical God (1 Cor. 2:1–8).

OPPRESSIVE WISDOM
VERSUS REDEMPTIVE WISDOM
Exodus 1:11–22

1:11 **Therefore they set taskmasters over them to oppress them with forced labor. They built supply cities, Pithom and Rameses, for Pharaoh.** [12] **But the more they were oppressed, the more they multiplied and spread, so that the Egyptians came to dread the Israelites.** [13] **The Egyptians became ruthless in imposing tasks on the Israelites,** [14] **and made their lives bitter with hard service in mortar and brick and in every kind of field labor. They were ruthless in all the tasks that they imposed on them.**

[15] **The king of Egypt said to the Hebrew midwives, one of whom was named Shiphrah and the other Puah,** [16] **"When you act as midwives to the Hebrew women, and see them on the birthstool, if it is a boy, kill him; but if it is a girl, she shall live."** [17] **But the midwives feared God; they did not do as the king of Egypt commanded them, but they let the boys live.** [18] **So the king of Egypt summoned the midwives and said to them, "Why have you done this, and allowed the boys to live?"** [19] **The midwives said to Pharaoh, "Because the Hebrew women are not like the Egyptian women; for they are vigorous and give birth before the midwife comes to them."** [20] **So God dealt well with the midwives; and the people multiplied and became very strong.** [21] **And because the midwives feared God, he gave them families.** [22] **Then Pharaoh commanded all his people, "Every boy that is born to the Hebrews you shall throw into the Nile, but you shall let every girl live."**

Pharaoh's wisdom aims to kill two birds with one stone: Subjecting these aliens to forced labor will bring them under strict control, and it will provide cheap labor for building up Egypt's infrastructure, further strengthening the country against potential enemies. But the policy backfires. The Israelites become more numerous and take up even more space, to the point where the Egyptians "cannot stand the sight" of them ("dread" translates a Hebrew word that connotes "loathing, being sick of").

One who has read Genesis will see in this increase the continuing presence and activity of the God who made promises to Abraham, Sarah, and their descendants and who more generally has given humankind the mandate to "be fruitful, and multiply, and fill the earth" (Gen. 1:28). The Roman Catholic biblical scholar Norbert Lohfink argues that the command to "fill the earth" is not a mandate for unlimited exponential increase. Rather, the command is aimed at the community's survival in circumstances where its underpopulation renders it incapable of coping with natural and other challenges. In the context of Egyptian oppression, the instinctive response (and the divine presence working in that response) is to increase and, by that means, to enhance the odds of Israel's continuation as a people.

So the Egyptians modify their strategy in two ways. First, they subject the Israelites to grinding labor so hard that their lives become bitter to them (compare Job, in Job 3:11–26). Second, Pharaoh instructs the Hebrew midwives (whom the narrator takes care to identify by name) to kill all male newborns and to save the girls, presumably both to provide slave labor and to bear further laborers like themselves. But the midwives let the boys live like the girls. Why? Is it because of their religious convictions and commitments? Or is it because their own maternal instincts, their professional consciences, and their solidarity with their Hebrew sisters move them to oppose official policy and to do what they consider to be right? And does the narrator see that the "fear of God" is implicit in their actions whether or not it is their conscious motive?

When Pharaoh interrogates them, the midwives reply straight-facedly (but we may suspect them to be slyly scoring a point at Egyptian expense) that the Hebrew women are, literally, livelier than their Egyptian counterparts. It is as though their natural life force quickens under the threat of death to their newborns. Such fearless response to Pharaoh brings further success to the work of the midwives. Giving up on them, Pharaoh instructs his own people to throw all Hebrew male babies into the Nile. There is an old saying that "Egypt is the gift of the Nile," for the primary source of Egypt's life in ancient times was the Nile's annual flooding, which rendered the bordering land fertile. In that case, Pharaoh's instruction is both literally drastic and symbolically powerful. What gives life to Egypt is to bring death to the Hebrews. As we shall see, however, in at least one providential instance, the Nile joins the Hebrew midwives, Moses' mother and sister, and even Pharaoh's own daughter in defeating his aims.

TRUE WISDOM'S MIDWIVES AND THE CHILD OF HOPE
Exodus 2:1–10

> 2:1 Now a man from the house of Levi went and married a Levite woman. ² The woman conceived and bore a son; and when she saw that he was a fine baby, she hid him three months. ³ When she could hide him no longer she got a papyrus basket for him, and plastered it with bitumen and pitch; she put the child in it and placed it among the reeds on the bank of the river. ⁴ His sister stood at a distance, to see what would happen to him.

⁵The daughter of Pharaoh came down to bathe at the river, while her attendants walked beside the river. She saw the basket among the reeds and sent her maid to bring it. ⁶ When she opened it, she saw the child. He was crying, and she took pity on him, "This must be one of the Hebrews' children," she said. ⁷ Then his sister said to Pharaoh's daughter, "Shall I go and get you a nurse from the Hebrew women to nurse the child for you?" ⁸ Pharaoh's daughter said to her, "Yes." So the girl went and called the child's mother. ⁹ Pharaoh's daughter said to her, "Take this child and nurse it for me, and I will give you your wages." So the woman took the child and nursed it. ¹⁰ When the child grew up, she brought him to Pharaoh's daughter, and she took him as her son. She named him Moses, "because," she said, "I drew him out of the water."

In his conflict with the Israelites, Pharaoh has imposed oppressive slave labor on them all and has attempted to have all the Hebrew male children put to death. But the Hebrews continue to multiply. Now the conflict focuses on a specific instance. A Levite couple marry, and the wife bears a son. Her response in verse 2 (literally, "she saw that he was good") echoes Genesis 1:4, 10, 12, and so on. Imaging her creator, the mother takes steps to provide for the life she has brought forth. When she can no longer hide the child, she does a strange thing: She puts him in a watertight basket and sets it floating on the Nile. Is this an act of abandonment in despair (compare Isa. 49:15; Psalm 27:10), or is it a desperate commitment of the child into God's hands when all her own resources are at an end? The watch that the sister keeps (v. 4) suggests the latter, expressing a familial concern that extends beyond its ability to provide material care.

When Pharaoh's daughter sees the child and hears its cry, she is moved by feelings like those of a mother. When she identifies it as a Hebrew child, its sister subtly connects the child back to her ("get *you* . . . for *you*"), a connection she readily adopts. Then the sister's saving subterfuge (v. 7) places Moses back in his mother's care until he is weaned—in Hebrew culture a period of another three years or so.

Moses experienced maternal care that first nursed and protected him, then abandoned him to the care of God, and then received him back from the brink of death to nurse him again until his weaning. In this way, this child's earliest sense of life is shaped by experiences that are a miniature of the experiences of the Hebrew people as a whole. They were brought into existence through the birth narratives of the ancestors in Genesis, they now are going through a community crisis that threatens their existence, and they will shortly be rescued from the brink of that threat. If God's call for the man Moses to bring about that rescue will come explicitly at the burning bush, one may wonder whether the basis for that call is providentially laid in the infant's experiences narrated in these verses.

Finally, the child receives his name—not from his birth mother, as we might expect, but from his adoptive mother, who gives him a name common among Egyptian Pharaohs. Egyptian *mes* (as in "Rameses") means "child, son," and the Egyptian verb underlying the child's name (as in "Thutmose") means "to be born." In naming the child this way, she makes him her own; indeed, in her own way she has given him life, since, as she says, "I drew him out of the water."

The biblical narrator surely means for us to enjoy the ironies of the scene. Although the name in Egyptian means "son," in Hebrew the verb *mashah* means "to draw out"; if she names the child Moses because she drew him out of the water, then, whether she knows it or not, the form of the name in Hebrew, *mosheh*, identifies the child as "one who will draw out." Thus, she foreshadows the child's future and, by her naming, contributes to the providential basis for Moses' later call at the burning bush.

But the ironies cut both ways. If, on the one hand, she unwittingly serves God's purposes on behalf of the Hebrews, on the other hand, the Hebrews by this story are never allowed to forget that the leader who drew them out of Egypt was himself drawn forth from watery peril and cared for by an Egyptian woman who, as Pharaoh's daughter, could have had him put to death. If we wish to say that in acting this way she (unwittingly) acted in solidarity with the Hebrew women, we must resist the desire to co-opt her into the Israelite camp.

The issues here are delicate, complex, and difficult to distinguish and keep in proper balance. On the one hand, it is easy to lump people into one social group or another and then to characterize and value or devalue them simply on the basis of the group they belong to. Pharaoh's daughter should warn us against such a simplistic approach to intergroup conflict, for her actions do not conform to Pharaoh's policies. On the other hand, it is easy to ignore people's distinctive ethnic, economic, social, political, or religious identities and to assess and characterize them purely in terms of an abstract universal spiritual and ethical standard, in the course of which their concrete identities are bleached out or obscured. Again, Pharaoh's daughter should warn us against this, for in the narrative she remains Pharaoh's daughter.

There is a tension here between the particular agencies and identities through which God works in human affairs, and the universal solidarity in which all humankind is held through the one divine image that all people bear from creation (Gen. 1:27). If Pharaoh's daughter is not to be co-opted as an "anonymous Israelite," nevertheless the pity and the care she bestows on Moses resonate with the maternal care provided by his mother. This resonance calls on us to search for language that enables us to talk adequately about these two very different women, a language that both respects their differences and identifies what they hold in common.

FAILED RESCUE AND FLIGHT
Exodus 2:11–15

> 2:11 One day, after Moses had grown up, he went out to his people and saw their forced labor. He saw an Egyptian beating a Hebrew, one of his kinsfolk. 12 He looked this way and that, and seeing no one he killed the Egyptian and hid him in the sand. 13 When he went out the next day, he saw two Hebrews fighting; and he said to the one who was in the wrong, "Why do you strike your fellow Hebrew?" 14 He answered, "Who made you a ruler and judge over us? Do you mean to kill me as you killed the Egyptian?" Then Moses was afraid and thought, "Surely the thing is known." 15 When Pharaoh heard of it, he sought to kill Moses.

In his book *The Person*, psychologist Theodore Lidz explores the way each person is born *with* a biological heritage and *into* a cultural heritage, each heritage contributing to who we become. Other psychologists have explored the degree to which we understand ourselves in terms of how others see us. A recent course on the book of Exodus was frequently enriched by the comments of a class member who herself was given up for adoption and who has spent a good deal of her life wrestling with questions of family connection and personal identity. This student helped us to appreciate "from the inside" Moses' question, "Who am I?" (Exod. 3:11). In the present passage, Moses begins to explore that question.

If Moses' mother "saw" him as her own precious newborn and hid him, and if Pharaoh's daughter "saw" him crying and took pity on him, Moses begins to find out for himself who he really is when he "sees" an Egyptian beating one of his kinfolk. Moved to act on behalf of his kin, he kills the Egyptian. But when he sees two Hebrews fighting, he simply challenges the aggressor by an appeal to kin loyalty. The aggressor's retort (v. 14) is only the first of many Israelite challenges to his initiatives on their behalf. Rejected by kin and in danger from Pharaoh, he flees into the safety of the desert. Gail Sheehy, in her book *Passages*, coins the term "moratorium" for those times and places we withdraw to when we need to reassess our identity and our connections. Such a time and place is fittingly imaged by Moses' flight into the desolate desert, far from the marks and the patterns of activity that identified him in Egypt.

ANOTHER HOME AWAY FROM HOME
Exodus 2:15–22

> 2:15 But Moses fled from Pharaoh. He settled in the land of Midian, and sat down by a well. [16] The priest of Midian had seven daughters. They came to draw water, and filled the troughs to water their father's flock. [17] But some shepherds came and drove them away. Moses got up and came to their defense and watered their flock. [18] When they returned to their father Reuel, he said, "How is it that you have come back so soon today?" [19] They said, "An Egyptian helped us against the shepherds; he even drew water for us and watered the flock." [20] He said to his daughters, "Where is he? Why did you leave the man? Invite him to break bread." [21] Moses agreed to stay with the man, and he gave Moses his daughter Zipporah in marriage. [22] She bore a son, and he named him Gershom; for he said, "I have been an alien residing in a foreign land."

Literary critic Robert Alter, in *The Art of Biblical Narrative*, shows how "type scenes," whether in the Bible or in, for example, movie Westerns, follow such familiar plots that as soon as we spot the first clue to such a scene we know in a general way what to expect, even if in a given instance the scene takes an unexpected turn. The biblical example he chooses for study is "the encounter with the future betrothed at a well": Abraham's servant meets Rebekah there (Genesis 24); Jacob meets Rachel there (Genesis 29); even Tamar, hoping to have a child by Judah, waylays him by the entrance to Enaim, which means "twin wells," and as a result gives birth to twins. A well, whose water fertilizes the earth and sustains animal and human life, becomes a symbol of the children expected from a marriage (compare the Song of Sol. 4:15 with Prov. 30:15–16). Thus the well becomes a sign of hope and good news. So when we find Moses at a well where women come to water their flocks, our pulses should quicken with hope.

But, whereas in Genesis the repeated ancestral crisis was childlessness, in Exodus that is hardly the problem! Here, the crisis is deadly threat from a political oppressor. So how is the well relevant here, or that God whose presence and activity in Israel's life are symbolized by a well? By introducing into the familiar well scene a new element in the form of the hostile shepherds, the narrator connects this ancestral type scene to the present crisis in Egypt; for the shepherds are threatening this Midianite family at the very source of their continuing lives in an otherwise dry desert, just as the Egyptians are threatening the Hebrews at the source of their lives. So the recurrence of the well scene with this new twist suggests in its own way that the God of the ancestors may also be relevant to this new form of crisis. As for Moses, he intervenes vigorously as he had in 2:11–12, and this time he is successful. From this point on, the scene plays itself out as we would expect. Moses is taken home and marries Zipporah, whom he had met at the well.

What does this mean for Moses' identity? Will he now become an adoptive member of this Midianite family? When Zipporah bears a son, he names it Gershom. Since the play on the meaning of names is important to our understanding of some later passages in Exodus (as already in 2:10), a few words about the word-play will help in preparing for those passages. The name Gershom seems originally to be formed from the Hebrew verb *garash*, "to drive out, expel," perhaps indicating the hope that the bearer would be empowered to drive out and expel threats to the community. Indeed, the verb occurs in the present scene where the shepherds come and "drive away" (*garash*) the seven sisters from the well. But by playing on its similarity in sound with the phrase *ger-sham*, "an alien there," Moses gives it a new meaning: "I have been [or, I have become] an alien residing in a foreign land."

If our identity is in significant measure connected with our community and with our geographical place, then in both respects Moses by this name seems to express his sense of displacement. Yet his marriage and welcome into this Midianite family and the birth of his son there suggest that in the desert he has nevertheless found a home away from home.

For years, an African American storefront church near my seminary bore the name Gershom Church of God. It has been my practice, on the day before we study this passage, to ask students to study Exodus 2:22 in its biblical context for clues to the reason that this storefront congregation would name itself Gershom. In the New Testament, the first epistle of Peter (1:1) characterizes its readers as "exiles." As such, they would appreciate why this congregation would call itself Gershom. How close do Christians stand to Moses' part of the biblical story, if their situation as individuals or as a group never moves them to appreciate this name "from the inside"?

THE CRY OF THE OPPRESSED
AND THE EARS THAT HEAR
Exodus 2:23–25

2:23 **After a long time the king of Egypt died. The Israelites groaned under their slavery, and cried out. Out of the slavery their cry for help rose up to God.** 24 **God heard their groaning, and God remembered his covenant with Abraham, Isaac, and Jacob.** 25 **God looked upon the Israelites, and God took notice of them.**

Biblical scholar Donald Gowan, in *Theology in Exodus*, reads Exodus 1—2 on the analogy of the book of Job and Israel's psalms of complaint. Like those texts, he sees these opening chapters marked by the absence or hiddenness of God. The Israelites seem to be on their own under Egyptian oppression; their cries, in Gowan's view, run through these chapters until the climax of their intensity in 2:23–25. Yet, if our eyes have become trained by the creation stories of Genesis 1—2 and the ancestral stories in Genesis 12—50, surely we should see God present, if hidden, within the processes of birth and maternal care.

But Gowan still has a point. Even if God is present and active in these processes, that activity is finally eclipsed by the intensity of the people's oppression. In the face of such suffering, even the recollection of our birth, instead of giving reassurance and hope, can become a cause for questioning complaint. So Job, for example, wishes he had never been conceived, born, or nursed (Job 3). He can only ask in agony, "Why is light given to one in misery, / and life to the bitter in soul?" (3:20). Death would at least equalize the lot of the weary slave and the wicked taskmaster (3:17–19). Exodus 2:23–25 gathers up all the bewildered anguish of Job and the psalms of complaint, by the way it draws on four different words in the Hebrew vocabulary of complaint: "groaned," ('*anah* as in Job 3:24; Lam. 1:4, 8); "cried out" (*za'aq* as in Job 16:18; Hab. 1:2); "cry for help" (*sha'ah* as in Job 19:7; Hab. 1:2); and "groaning" (*na'aqah* as in Job 24:12; Judg. 2:18). To those who clamor in this way, God must surely seem absent or hidden.

But note how the narrator registers God's side of this situation. Two things stand out. First, in Hebrew prose as in our own, where several successive verbs have the same subject, usually that subject is indicated with a noun the first time and after that with pronouns. Here, the repeated noun subject, "God heard . . . God remembered . . . God saw . . . God knew," makes a fourfold emphasis on God that matches their fourfold cries. Second, if the first two mentions of their complaint make no reference to God, the last two draw back the veil to show us what is really happening all along: Every cry, with the individual throb of suffering it expresses, is falling, cry for cry, not on deaf ears, but on the heart of God. If God is hidden, God is hidden *within* the suffering.

Note the clause "God remembered his covenant with Abraham, Isaac, and Jacob." At key points in the Exodus narrative (and in the rest of the Old Testament and the New Testament as well), the covenant with the ancestors is presented as the basis of God's dealing with the people of God. This suggests that the character and identity of God as disclosed to the ancestors—a loyal and compassionate God who gives life and nurture and promises space to live—provide the continuing basis for hope in the face of all that threatens. Where oppression and suffering threaten to snuff out even that hope, it is because people feel their cry gains no hearing, finds no room, in the ears and hearts of those around them. It is the testimony of Scripture that, though no one else may provide that room by hearing, God does.

A BUSH AFLAME
WITH TONGUES OF FIRE
Exodus 3:1–6

> 3:1 **Moses was keeping the flock of his father-in-law Jethro, the priest of Midian; he led his flock beyond the wilderness, and came to Horeb, the mountain of God. ² There the angel of the LORD appeared to him in a flame of fire out of a bush; he looked, and the bush was blazing, yet it was not consumed. ³ Then Moses said, "I must turn aside and look at this great sight, and see why the bush is not burned up." ⁴ When the LORD saw that he had turned aside to see, God called to him out of the bush, "Moses, Moses!" And he said, "Here I am." ⁵ Then he said, "Come no closer! Remove the sandals from your feet, for the place on which you are standing is holy ground." ⁶ He said further, "I am the God of your father, the God of Abraham, the God of Isaac, and the God of Jacob." And Moses hid his face, for he was afraid to look at God.**

This is one of those passages (like Genesis 22, the Annunciation to Mary, and the Passion of Jesus) where perhaps we should simply take off our shoes, hide our face, and wait for God to speak. It is one of those texts in which the unfathomable reality of God has to be expressed within the limitations of human speech and the images of ordinary human experience. The following remarks, therefore, are offered with great diffidence.

First of all, the encounter comes in the midst of Moses' everyday activity as a shepherd. Presumably, he is conscious of nothing more than his flock scattered before him, grazing, looking for water, and needing protection from wild animals and guidance lest they stray too far from one another. Under a hot sun, the small bush in front of him shimmers in the heat that rises from the ground. Suddenly, this ordinariness turns into something extraordinary—a bush that is aflame and yet is not consumed. How can this be? He draws closer, and now the tongues of flame begin to whisper his own name. Like Abraham (Gen. 22:1), Jacob (Gen. 31:11), Joseph (Gen. 37:13), and Samuel (1 Sam. 3:4, 6, 8), he responds, "Here I am." In such contexts, this response is more than a simple "Speaking" (the way we might answer an unsolicited phone salesperson who greets us by name). It is a self-presentation, a self-offer, along the lines of a clerk's attentive "May I help you?" or a housekeeper's "You rang, madam?"

The voice now alerts Moses that he is in a presence that is not subject to his curiosity, investigation, or analysis. He is in the presence of the holy. He must not draw nearer but remove his sandals. Why this second injunction? Typically, religious expressions, symbols, and practices are rooted in everyday speech, images, and activities. Their religious use gives them a depth, intensity, and range of meaning that ordinary life is inadequate to account for. Yet the speech, images, and activities of ordinary life remain the starting point for our exploration of that further meaning.

So the questions are these: Where and why do we wear shoes? When and where do we take them off? Whatever we may do at home, we wear shoes out-of-doors so that we may step where we choose without fear of hurting our feet. The footwear may be cheap thongs to intercept sticky gum on a parking lot or hobnailed boots to tread on our victims and their territory. Footwear protects us from the ground, and it renders us insensitive to what our soles (and our souls!) might feel there. When we return home, our bare or stockinged feet enjoy the feel of smooth hardwood or a rug. It was the same in the ancient world. On entering one's tent or someone else's, one removed one's sandals to walk cleanly on the rug spread on the ground. A host's invitation to remove one's sandals (especially the offer to remove them and wash the feet, as in Gen. 18:4 and John 13) was an offer of hospitality—an offer of one's home as the visitor's home away from home. One accepted such hospitality by respecting the sanctity of the host's space and moving about in it courteously. If the God of the ancestors, whom contemporary scholars characterize as a family or clan God, could receive such hospitality at Abraham's hands (Gen. 18:1–8), it should not be surprising to find the same imagery used here, where Moses finds himself in the presence of that same God (Exod. 3:6)

What I am suggesting is that Moses finds himself in a presence that is unfathomably sacred, a presence that invites him to be at home at the same time that it claims his profound respect. He who has felt himself "an alien residing in a foreign land" (2:22) now finds himself a guest of God. As we shall shortly see, this encounter will raise to the most acute pitch the continuing question of his identity. Meanwhile, we note that Moses hides his face, afraid to look at God. Jean-Paul Sartre has reflected on the power of seeing as making us "monarch of all we survey." As we look around, we mentally identify and name what we see and put it in its place. A teacher can maintain classroom discipline with merely a look. One can feel very small in the eyes of one's enemy (Num. 13:33). Moses' initial curiosity led him to "turn aside and look at this great sight." Now curiosity gives way to humility and an awareness that any attempt to probe into this mystery and master it is totally inappropriate. In this situation, Moses is called upon not so much to know as to be known (Gal. 4:9).

The voice that addresses Moses identifies itself as "the God of Abraham, the God of Isaac, and the God of Jacob." This expression connects the scene at the burning bush in the closest way to the situation in Egypt as summarized in 2:23–25 and, further back, to the ancestral narratives themselves. As Moses hears it, he must find himself strangely reconnected with a past that he may have thought was only "history." One way we experience the faithfulness of God is through the way God enables us to connect the various parts of life together into a whole, when we have feared that it is being torn apart by what happens through the passage of time.

GOD COMES DOWN IN MOSES' CALL
Exodus 3:7–10

> 3:7 Then the LORD said, "I have observed the misery of my people who are in Egypt; I have heard their cry on account of their taskmasters. Indeed, I know their sufferings, 8 and I have come down to deliver them from the Egyptians, and to bring them up out of that land to a good and broad land, a land flowing with milk and honey, to the country of the Canaanites, the Hittites, the Amorites, the Perizzites, the Hivites, and the Jebusites. 9 The cry of the Israelites has now come to me; I have also seen how the Egyptians oppress them. 10 So come, I will send you to Pharaoh to bring my people, the Israelites, out of Egypt."

What God says to Moses in 3:7–8 is strikingly similar to what the narrator has reported in 2:23–25. Again, God sees, hears, and knows; only this time God does not remember but resolves to come down. Yet the resolve to bring the people out of Egypt and into "a good and broad land" arises out of that memory of the covenant made with the ancestors (compare Gen. 15:17–21). With us, faithful response is rooted in memory. Here it is suggested that the same holds true for God.

What God says to Moses in 3:9–10 may strike one at first as an unnecessary repetition of 3:7–8; and one way to analyze this passage is to attribute these two sets of verses to two different versions of the story joined by a later editor. But even if the text arose in this way, the result may suggest the dynamic process involved in Moses' dawning awareness of his call. At first, he becomes aware of *God's* concern for the Israelites and intention to "come down" and act on their behalf. Then he becomes aware that God wants to send *him* to Pharaoh to bring the people out. He who had been concerned only with the flock needing his shepherding attention now experiences God's concern for the "flock" of Israel (compare Psalm 77:20), and then God's concern becomes his own. Looking at the scene as a whole, we may say that God's way of "coming down" to deliver Israel is by entering Moses' everyday consciousness in such a way that the divine concern transforms Moses' shepherding concerns into a concern for the plight of his kin in their suffering.

Our sixth-grade son slept in on a Saturday morning. Finally coming into the kitchen, he opened the refrigerator door, looked briefly inside, slammed the door, and complained in a voice made grumpy by too much sleep, "Why isn't there anything for breakfast in this house?" His mother responded mildly, "Breakfast? It's almost time for lunch!" He responded, "Oh, well, in that case, I'll look again under a different pretext," and in a few minutes he was eating a Dagwood sandwich. If God's redemptive coming down into our lives can take the form of revelation, that revelation need not be a disclosure of other-worldly mysteries but simply God enabling us to look at our this-worldly situation "under a different pretext," the way God sees it. That "pretext" is the redemptive memory and compassionate faithfulness of God, into which revelation draws us and by which it sends us.

MOSES' DOUBT AND THE
SIGN OF HIS CALL
3:11–12

> 3:11 **But Moses said to God, "Who am I that I should go to Pharaoh, and bring the Israelites out of Egypt?"** [12] **He said, "I will be with you; and this**

shall be the sign for you that it is I who sent you: when you have brought the people out of Egypt, you shall worship God on this mountain."

Moses' "Who am I?" no doubt expresses his sense of inadequacy for what he is asked to do. That inadequacy may rest in part on the failure of his earlier efforts to intervene and the negative response of his Israelite kin (2:11–14). In part, it may rest on the sheer magnitude of the task. But God seizes on the opening provided by this rhetorical question and implicitly offers Moses a revised self-understanding (as though suggesting he think of himself "under a different pretext"). Whoever and whatever Moses may have thought himself to be, he is now to see himself as someone God is with. Moreover, God offers him a sign that it is indeed God who has sent him.

If NRSV correctly punctuates the text, God's sign is that, when Moses has brought the people out of Egypt, they will worship on this very mountain where Moses has had this encounter with God. But will the sign not be too late then? Does Moses not need a sign now? For this reason, some interpreters change the semicolon to a comma and the colon to a semicolon and thus take God's presence with Moses as the sign that God has sent him. In that case, what would be the sign that God is with him? I take NRSV to be correct, and I take the sign not to reassure Moses but eventually to persuade the people that God has sent Moses. He has already experienced rejection for his attempts to intervene ("Who made you a ruler and judge over us?"; 2:14), and he will experience more challenges. The sign and vindication of his leadership will be his success in leading the people out of Egypt in a deliverance that will move them to worship. Their own experience of liberation, and of the worship it moves them to, will verify to them that God has sent Moses. Meanwhile, all he will have to go on are his experience of God at the bush and the sense of calling and promise that experience has given him.

WHAT'S IN A NAME?
Exodus 3:13–15

3:13 **But Moses said to God, "If I come to the Israelites and say to them, 'The God of your ancestors has sent me to you,' and they ask me, 'What is his name?' what shall I say to them?"** 14 **God said to Moses, "I AM WHO I AM."** **He said further, "Thus you shall say to the Israelites, 'I AM has sent me to you.'"** 15 **God also said to Moses, "Thus you shall say to the Israelites, 'The**

LORD, the God of your ancestors, the God of Abraham, the God of Isaac, and
the God of Jacob, has sent me to you':
>   This is my name forever,
>   and this my title for all generations.

These verses have attracted a library of scholarly discussion, and there is
no space here to even begin to summarize the interpretations. The interested reader may pick up their trail in the commentaries by Brevard
Childs, John Durham, and Nahum Sarna. The interpretation presented
here involves the general question, "What's in a name?" To illustrate, we
may take the name Thatcher. Originally, it named someone skilled in
putting thatched roofs on houses. Likewise, Weaver named a person
skilled in weaving. For a new roof, one called on Thatcher; for a new linen
shirt, one called on Weaver. In time, however (if, say, the weaver's children kept the family name but went into a different trade), the name did
not necessarily correspond to a person's skills, but became simply a label
to identify and address a person and perhaps (as in marriage) to link that
person with others bearing it. If a Thatcher who was no longer a thatcher
became famous for doing something else that called for a high degree of
skill—if that Thatcher "made a name for herself"—the name "Thatcher"
would thereafter take on a new meaning. This change, in fact, happened
in the case of Margaret Thatcher as prime minister of Great Britain.
"Thatcherite" now names anyone who strives to embody and promote her
approach to government in that country. (In America, one can speak of
"Jeffersonian," "Jacksonian," and "Reagan" Democrats.) Now there are
those who hold that changing times call for different policies, however,
and among such people, Thatcherism is outdated.

With these things in mind, let us consider what Moses may be getting
at in his question in 3:13. God has said to him, "I am 'the God of your father'—the God of Abraham, the God of Isaac, and the God of Jacob" (3:6).
I have altered the punctuation of NRSV because the phrase "the God of
your father" in Genesis (e.g., 31:5, 29, 42, 53; 43:23; 46:1, 3; 50:17) and in
the ancient Near East generally was a generic term for deity. It was a way
of identifying a deity as having a specific character and sphere of concern,
activity, and, indeed, "skill" or wisdom. The expression "God of my/your/
their father" identifies God generically as a family or clan deity, specifically as divine parent of the clan. In addition to this generic label, the clan
deity may have a specific title or name. Such a God is known and named
in terms of the processes of human conception, gestation, birth, and nurture through the breast and the produce of the earth and in guidance, discipline, and protection through the gift of effective thinking, planning, and

inspiration. Since Abraham and descendants often find themselves among social groups of vastly greater numbers and strength (amid the city-states of Canaan and within the Egyptian empire), the protection God gives them comes largely in the form of cleverness in outwitting their enemies or generally pursuing their personal or family goals (e.g., Abraham in Gen. 12:10–20, Rebekah in Genesis 27, and Jacob in Gen. 30:25–31:5). We have seen this still in Exodus 1—2, in the resourceful activities of the midwives, Shiphrah and Puah, and of Moses' mother and sister.

But finally the resources derived from this family and clan God seem insufficient to protect the Israelites from the overwhelming force of Egyptian oppression, so that (2:23–25) they are reduced to the sort of complaint, doubt, and even despair expressed in the book of Job and the psalms of complaint. In this context, if Moses comes to these people and says to them, "the God of your ancestors [literally, "your fathers"] has sent me to you," the response "What is his name?" may not be a request for Moses to "give the [divine] password." It may be an expression of despairing irony— "What can our God do that he would not already have done if he could?"—in this way questioning the relevance of the God of the ancestors to this unprecedented kind of crisis. Whether Moses responds with the name "Yahweh" or "El Shaddai," or some other name familiar from the ancestral traditions, how is he to persuade them that such a name should inspire them with hope?

(In English translations of the Bible, the divine name that I have just referred to as "Yahweh" is commonly presented in capital letters as "the LORD," and on occasion in capital letters as "GOD." These terms represent the divine name whose consonants in Hebrew are YHWH. As the NRSV says in its preface to the reader, "[It] is almost if not quite certain that the Name was originally pronounced 'Yahweh.'" But in time Jewish readers came to hold this divine name as too sacred to be pronounced. So they added to the consonants YHWH the vowels for the word "Adonai," which in Hebrew means "Lord," or the vowels for the word "Elohim," which in Hebrew means "God." These vowels directed the reader to substitute "Lord" or "God" for the name YHWH. English translations of the Bible generally follow this substitution and indicate that they are doing so by putting the substituted word in capitals. In this companion to the book of Exodus, I sometimes use the term "the LORD" and sometimes "Yahweh." Both terms refer to the same divine name presented to Moses at the burning bush in Exodus 3:13–15 and again in 6:2–8.)

God responds with an answer that serves as a three-stage redefinition of a name already familiar to them. Whatever the name Yahweh may have meant originally (and this is still debated), its use in the narratives of Genesis 12—50 has given it all the connotations of the "God of the father" that I have summarized previously. Now God opens the way for this name to acquire new connotations, by playing on the verb at its root: *hawah / hayah*, "fall out, come to pass, become, be." So,

> God said to Moses,
>   "I will be who/what I will be." [*ehyeh asher ehyeh*]

> He said further, "Thus you shall say to the Isrealites,
>   'I will be [*ehyeh*] has sent me to you.'"

> God also said to Moses, "Thus you shall say to the Israelites,
>   '*Yahweh*, the God of your fathers, the God of Abraham, the God of Isaac,
>   and the God of Jacob, has sent me to you.' This is my name forever,
>   and this is my title for all generations."

Many interpreters take the statement "I will be who/what I will be" as a way of withholding the divine name, to protect the divine mystery from human manipulation and control. In my view, this first statement names and discloses God fully and without reservation and at the same time fully preserves God's freedom and mystery. Any other name for God or title descriptive of this or that typical function would limit God by defining God and making God finite. This name, however, identifies God as that ultimate mystery who is free to be whoever and whatever God chooses to be, in whatever situation or circumstance. It is this divine mystery, named then more briefly as "I will be," that sends Moses to the people. This God is not limited to their experience of "the God of the father" but is free to act in new ways in view of the crisis in Egypt.

This shortened name, "I will be" [*ehyeh*], is now equated with "Yahweh [*yhwh*] the God of your ancestors." By this means, the divine mystery is intensified. Even deeper than the mystery of absolute freedom is the mystery in which such freedom binds itself (without losing itself) in faithfulness to a particular community to which it has made promises that it now undertakes to fulfill. Robert Frost puts the general issue this way in his essay "The Constant Symbol":

> Every single poem written regular [he means, written within the constraints of meter and rhyme] is a symbol small or great of the way the will has to pitch into commitments deeper and deeper to a rounded conclusion and then be

judged for whether any original intention it had has been strongly spent or weakly lost; be it in art, politics, school, church, business, love, or marriage—in a piece of work or in a career. Strongly spent is synonymous with kept. (Frost, *Collected Poems, Prose, and Plays*, 786)

Abraham embodies just such a pitch of the will into commitments, in Genesis 22. Jesus enunciates it in the one saying that is common to all four Gospels, about losing one's life by trying to save it and finding life in losing it; his own Passion is the measure of how strongly the divine love he embodies will spend itself to keep not only itself but those whom it loves.

At the burning bush, God embodies just such a pitch of the will into commitments, by redefining the familiar name Yahweh in terms of absolute divine freedom and then reasserting the unbreakable covenant bond with the ancestors. "This," says God to Moses, "is my name forever, and this is my title for all generations." The word NRSV here translates "title" is literally "memorial," as in KJV. The RSV paraphrase, "this is how I am to be remembered," identifies the activity that is implied, for one meaning of the verb "remember" in the Old Testament is "to mention or call upon by name." According to this passage, then, the two-sided mystery—of absolute divine freedom and of unbreakable covenant with a particular people—is given a name, and that name is given to be used by the people "for all generations." We shall see how the reluctance to use this name begins with Moses.

MOSES' COMMISSION IN GOD'S NAME
Exodus 3:16–22

3:16 **Go and assemble the elders of Israel, and say to them, "The LORD, the God of your ancestors, the God of Abraham, of Isaac, and of Jacob, has appeared to me, saying: I have given heed to you and to what has been done to you in Egypt. 17 I declare that I will bring you up out of the misery of Egypt, to the land of the Canaanites, the Hittites, the Amorites, the Perizzites, the Hivites, and the Jebusites, a land flowing with milk and honey." 18 They will listen to your voice; and you and the elders of Israel shall go to the king of Egypt and say to him, "The LORD, the God of the Hebrews, has met with us; let us now go a three days' journey into the wilderness, so that we may sacrifice to the LORD our God." 19 I know, however, that the king of Egypt will not let you go unless compelled by a mighty hand. 20 So I will stretch out my hand and strike Egypt with all my wonders that I will perform in it; after that he will let you go. 21 I will bring this people into such favor with [RSV: "in**

the sight of"] the Egyptians that, when you go, you will not go empty-handed; 22 each woman shall ask her neighbor and any woman living in the neighbor's house for jewelry of silver and of gold, and clothing, and you shall put them on your sons and on your daughters; and so you shall plunder the Egyptians."

In 3:14–15, God answered Moses' question, "What shall I say to them?" Now God instructs Moses to deliver God's message to them, assuring him that "they will listen to your voice." At least at the outset, then, this greatest of Old Testament prophets will be honored among his own people. But when he and the elders appeal to Pharaoh for the people's release, it will be a different story. Notice that the appeal to Pharaoh is not for social justice but for religious freedom. The two are not unrelated, but in the ancient world all human necessities and possibilities, all human rights and duties, all human responsibilities and privileges, are grounded in God or the gods. Therefore, any appeal for justice, any advocacy of what we might call "civil rights" or "human rights," ultimately is an appeal to recognize what one should be able to enjoy at the hands of one's God.

Generations earlier, at the death of Jacob, Joseph had requested of Pharaoh permission to return to Canaan to bury his father there as he had sworn he would do. Insofar as Joseph's oath would have been sworn in the name of their ancestral God and the burial itself would have had religious character, the permission Pharaoh granted was a recognition of Joseph's religious freedom (Gen. 50:1–14). Earlier, Joseph's wisdom and skill in interpreting dreams had moved Pharaoh to recognize the spirit of God in him (Gen. 41:38–39). If the Hebrews' oppression in Egypt came upon them because the new ruling dynasty "did not know Joseph" (Exod. 1:8), the denial of freedom to go and worship will be another indication of the same thing. If the claims of Israel's God are not voluntarily recognized, therefore, Pharaoh will be made to know this God by language he will understand: a mighty hand that will do "wonders." By this means, God will demonstrate the new meaning of the name Yahweh, by "making a name for himself" as a warrior against oppressive empires (15:1–3; and see 2 Sam. 7:23; Neh. 9:10; Isa. 63:12, 14; Jer. 32:20; Dan. 9:15).

But Yahweh's victory is not only through force. In part, it comes about through a change of heart within some of the Egyptians. Just as Pharaoh's daughter had pity on the infant whom she *saw* in the basket, so God will give the Israelites favor "in the *sight* of the Egyptians" (RSV, following the Hebrew). So when each departing Israelite woman asks her female neighbor for a parting gift, it will be freely given. In such a case, the "plunder" becomes a token that Yahweh's "might" is not simply a matter of "force."

DOUBTING MOSES
Exodus 4:1

> 4:1 **Then Moses answered, "But suppose they do not believe me or listen to me, but say, 'The LORD did not appear to you.'"**

I have proposed that one response Moses anticipates from the people— "What is his name?" (3:13)—may reflect a suspicion that the ancestral God is insufficient for this new crisis. Now Moses anticipates another kind of problem that may arise out of God's words to him in 3:16–22. The God who appeared to Moses at the bush and who will meet Pharaoh and defeat him in a head-on show of force will not sound to the people like the Yahweh they know.

This issue is explored in Walter R. L. Moberly's *The Old Testament of the Old Testament: Patriarchal Narratives and Mosaic Yahwism*. As the title suggests, Moberly argues that the relation of the ancestral traditions in Genesis 12—50 to the rest of the Old Testament is similar to the relation of the Old Testament as a whole to the New Testament. He argues that the move from ancestral religion to Mosaic religion involves both continuity and change and that this move within the Old Testament provides a helpful basis for our study of the continuities and the changes involved in the move from the Old Testament to the New Testament. The gravity of the issue in the latter move is illustrated in two ways: Jews historically have not recognized in the Christian message of Jesus the presence and activity of God as they know God from their scripture and tradition. Conversely, Christians have all too often thought of the relation between the gospel and the God of the Old Testament in terms of two contrasting or even incompatible portrayals of God, as between law-giving and graceful, or between wrathful and loving. I raise this issue of continuity and change not to solve it but to shed light on Moses' concern in 4:1: If he goes back with a message from Yahweh as a God who will defeat the imperial power of Pharaoh by sheer force, the people may not take such a message as a sign that it is their Yahweh whom Moses has encountered at the bush, but perhaps some other deity or even a spirit of delusion. How should he meet such a problem?

FURTHER SIGNS OF MOSES' CALL
Exodus 4:2–9

4:2 The LORD said to him, "What is that in your hand?" He said, "A staff."
³ And he said, "Throw it on the ground." So he threw the staff on the ground,
and it became a snake; and Moses drew back from it. ⁴ Then the LORD said
to Moses, "Reach out your hand, and seize it by the tail"—so he reached out
his hand and grasped it, and it became a staff in his hand—⁵ "so that they
may believe that the LORD, the God of their ancestors, the God of Abraham,
the God of Isaac, and the God of Jacob, has appeared to you."
　⁶ Again, the LORD said to him, "Put your hand inside your cloak." He put
his hand into his cloak; and when he took it out, his hand was leprous, as
white as snow. ⁷ Then God said, "Put your hand back into your cloak"—so
he put his hand back into his cloak, and when he took it out, it was restored
like the rest of his body—⁸ "If they will not believe you or heed the first sign,
they may believe the second sign. ⁹ If they will not believe even these two
signs or heed you, you shall take some water from the Nile and pour it on
the dry ground; and the water that you shall take from the Nile will become
blood on the dry ground."

God now gives Moses three signs, to convince the people that it is indeed
Yahweh who has sent him. How will these signs achieve this? How will
they be credentials of the Yahweh the people have known and at the same
time give hope that this Yahweh can act in new ways in this crisis?

The first sign involves Moses' shepherd staff, which turns into a snake
and then, when he takes hold of it again, becomes a staff. These Israelites
would be familiar with the staff as an instrument and sign of the skill they
and their ancestors enjoyed as shepherds. That skill, that wisdom, would
be a gift of their family God, who could also be called a shepherd (Gen.
49:24). In the ancient world (as for Jesus in Matt. 10:16), the snake was a
symbol of wisdom. When the staff, thrown down, becomes a snake, it is as
though the wisdom and skill implicit in the shepherd's staff becomes manifest and available to take another form for other purposes. When Moses
seizes the snake and it becomes a staff again, it is as though the staff itself,
without ceasing to be a shepherd's staff, now can be used for those other
purposes. (We shall see later how Moses uses that staff in Egypt.) Just as
the root meaning of the name Yahweh became manifest as *ehyeh asher
ehyeh*, "I will be who I will be," and that new meaning then became woven
back into the familiar name, "Yahweh, the God of your fathers," so now
Moses' shepherding skill becomes manifest as possessing new potential,
and that new skill remains intimately connected to who he has been. This

sign is offered to assure the people that it is indeed Yahweh, the God of their shepherd ancestors (Gen. 47:3) and a shepherding God (Gen. 49:24), who has appeared to Moses, and that this Yahweh is capable of equipping Moses with new skills for a new situation.

If the first sign signifies the power to sustain life through shepherding skill, the second sign signifies the power of life and death. According to Numbers 12:10–12, a leprous person could resemble a child who had died in the womb. The ancestral traditions show the God of the ancestors as giving the power to conceive and to bear or withholding that power and signaling death (Gen. 20:3, 17–18). The third sign is in some respects similar to the second, for the Nile waters are the source and support of economic life in Egypt, and by Moses' action that life-giving water will turn into the sign of death. The specifically Egyptian locale of this sign now completes the transition from what is familiar to the people (the shepherd's staff) to Yahweh's promise of victory over Pharaoh.

In the face of this crisis, then, which calls into question the adequacy of both Moses and his ancestral God, the two questions, "Who am I?" (3:11) and (in effect) "Who are you?" (3:13), are answered. These two questions are particularly pressing in our own day, when we seem to be confronted by unprecedented new forms of challenge and crisis. Are we adequate to the challenge? Is the God of our ancestors, the God we have grown up believing in, adequate to the challenge? Exodus 3:1–4:9 encourages us to believe in a dynamic God who in freedom and loyalty, continuity and change, is more than adequate, a God who will take the skills and wisdoms we have become adept at using and show us how those skills and wisdoms can take new forms.

FINAL DOUBTS AND
GOD'S PREVAILING CALL
Exodus 4:10–17

4:10 But Moses said to the LORD, "O my Lord, I have never been eloquent, neither in the past nor even now that you have spoken to your servant; but I am slow of speech and slow of tongue." [11] Then the LORD said to him, "Who gives speech to mortals? Who makes them mute or deaf, seeing or blind? Is it not I, the LORD? [12] Now go, and I will be with your mouth and teach you what you are to speak." [13] But he said, "O my Lord, please send someone else." [14] Then the anger of the LORD was kindled against Moses and he said, "What of your brother Aaron, the Levite? I know that he can speak fluently; even now he is coming out to meet you, and when he sees you his heart will be glad. ¹⁵ You shall speak to him and put the words in his mouth; and I will be with your mouth and with his mouth, and will teach you what you shall do. ¹⁶ He indeed shall speak for you to the people; he shall serve as a mouth for you, and you shall serve as God for him. ¹⁷ Take in your hand this staff, with which you shall perform the signs."

Moses continues to shrink back from what God is calling him to do. First, he had raised the general objection, "Who am I?" (3:11). Then he had raised the question of who God is (3:13). Then he had questioned whether the people would believe him and listen to him (4:1). Now he returns to himself with the demurral that he has never been any good with words. Though Moses appears to speak with the greatest deference, his "my lord" (*adonay*, not "Yahweh") shows that, in spite of God's "this is how I am to be remembered" (3:15, RSV), he is unwilling to take on his lips the divine name as newly defined.

Yahweh responds in two ways. First, he reminds Moses who he is: the giver of speech to all people and the one who is ultimately accountable for everyone's condition, whether mute or deaf, seeing or blind. Then God makes a specific promise: "Go, and 'I will be' with your mouth and teach you what you are to speak." I have put "I will be" in quotes, because by now the verb should reverberate in Moses' ears with the overtones of 3:14, "I am who I am" or, as it may also be translated, "I will be who I will be." Given how Moses has addressed God only with the general term "my lord," God's reply is a hint that Yahweh will be with Moses' mouth as he takes the newly redefined divine name Yahweh on his lips.

In the book of Deuteronomy and in associated biblical literature, God is understood to be present wherever the divine name dwells. (Christians celebrate how the very hearing or saying aloud of the sacred name can bring comfort and strength, when they sing, "How sweet the name of Jesus sounds / In a believer's ear"; and "Take the name of Jesus with you, / Child of sorrow and of woe. / It will joy and comfort give you; / Take it then where'er you go.") But Moses refuses to risk such an act. Not only does he say again, *adonay*, "my lord," but also he rejects the potentiality implicit in God's "I will be who I will be" by saying (as the Hebrew literally has it), "send by the hand of whom you will send." At this, God becomes exasperated, for Moses shows that he is unwilling to venture in faith past his current understanding of himself and of God, even when he is assured that God as here newly revealed is the God of the ancestors and is about to do a new thing in faithfulness to the long-standing promises to them. Like a parent who has patiently responded to all a child's questions and objections, God finally has to say, "Do it because I say so." As we shall see, Moses will take the divine name on his lips, and he will become capable of speech and of action that will surpass what he could have dreamed possible.

If God finally says, "Do it!" God nevertheless makes a concession, providing Moses' brother Aaron as a mouthpiece for him. The language in 4:15 is telling. When Moses speaks to Aaron and puts the words in his mouth, God will be with Moses' mouth and then with Aaron's mouth, so that in this way "I . . . will teach you (plural) what you (plural) shall do." Here in miniature we have a high doctrine of tradition. As Robert Frost puts it in his poem "Sitting by a Bush in Broad Sunlight," the revelation at the burning bush occurred "one time and only the one." Yet whenever Moses speaks in and with the divine name, the God who appeared to him at the bush will be with his mouth. And when he teaches Aaron, God will also be with Aaron's mouth to teach yet others. A similar promise is given to the disciples, in the Great Commission at the end of the Gospel of Matthew (28:19–20), where the risen Jesus says to them, "Go . . . teaching. . . . And remember, I am with you always. . . ."

On the most ordinary level of experience, we can imagine a parent proposing to send a child on an errand and then, when the child hesitates out of a sense of inadequacy, saying, "How about if I go with you?" Of course, in this case we would not speak of the parent sending the child. But take a situation where the parent sends the child with these words: "If you get afraid, just say under your breath, 'my daddy says I can do it, and he's right behind me.'" The child who will do this is not simply alone but has a sense of inner presence and strength. Here is a profound two-sided mystery: On the one hand, each individual is profoundly alone and must finally "go," or act, by his or her own willingness to do so; on the other hand, in that very willingness to act, one can know the deepest community and support. At the burning bush, as at the end of the Gospel of Matthew, there is a sending and a promise of presence that both calls us into an individual responsibility grounded in a new self-understanding and, at the same time, calls us into a fellowship with God that cannot be broken.

BLESSED DEPARTURE
FROM A HOME AWAY FROM HOME
Exodus 4:18–20

> 4:18 Moses went back to his father-in-law Jethro and said to him, "Please let me go back to my kindred in Egypt and see whether they are still living." And Jethro said to Moses, "Go in peace." 19 The LORD said to Moses in

Midian, "Go back to Egypt; for all those who were seeking your life are dead." [20] **So Moses took his wife and his sons, put them on a donkey and went back to the land of Egypt; and Moses carried the staff of God in his hand.**

In his book *After Virtue*, Alasdair MacIntyre makes the point that, as much as we like to think we can shape our lives simply by our own decisions and according to our own values and goals, that is not so. "We are never more (and sometimes less) than the co-authors of our own narratives. Only in fantasy do we live what story we please. . . . Each of us being a main character in his own drama plays subordinate parts in the dramas of others, and each drama constrains the others." The different life stories of Moses and Jethro intersected unexpectedly at the well. For a time, they were woven together in a bond of mutual benefit, but God's call threatens to unravel that bond. As a man with seven daughters, Jethro would be loathe to lose Moses from his household. So we would not be surprised to see him repeat the behavior of Laban, the father-in-law of Jacob. After Jacob had met Rachel at a well, married into Laban's family, and worked for him for twenty years, Jacob sought to return to his own country (Gen. 30:26). But Laban could not see his son-in-law as anything other than a subordinate family member and contributor to its economic strength. When it came time for Jacob to follow what God called on him to do (Gen. 31:3), Laban could only see his own impoverishment (Gen. 31:43). Jacob's departure involved a rupture in family relations that was not so much healed as ended in the form of a mutual nonaggression settlement (Gen. 31: 44–55).

Jethro is a different kind of father-in-law. When Moses asks permission to visit his own people, Jethro says simply, "Go in peace [*shalom*]." He displays a generous character that we will see more fully displayed as the exodus narrative unfolds, a character all the more important for the fact that nothing identifies him at this point as a worshiper of Yahweh.

How many of life's tangled relationships, hostilities, and conflicts arise because we insist on being the central character in any drama that we find ourselves in? Jethro's action models a different understanding of dramatic integrity in his willingness to release Moses to follow a path that must move out of Jethro's immediate orbit, perhaps to his loss. But such a loss is only apparent. If one lesson from the burning bush is that the God who sends us can, in sending, still be with us, one lesson from Jethro's example is that when we are willing to let others go in the direction their lives must take and when we send with them our blessing in *shalom*, in a strange way at the deepest level they remain with us. *Shalom* means wholeness, and the relationship remains intact across the miles. Such a parting lays the groundwork for the kind of reunion we shall see later between these two.

PROBLEMATIC DEPARTURE
FROM A HOME AWAY FROM HOME
Exodus 4:21–23

> 4:21 **And the** LORD **said to Moses, "When you go back to Egypt, see that you perform before Pharaoh all the wonders that I have put in your power; but I will harden his heart, so that he will not let the people go.** 22 **Then you shall say to Pharaoh, 'Thus says the** LORD**: Israel is my firstborn son.** 23 **I said to you, "Let my son go that he may worship me." But you refused to let him go; now I will kill your firstborn son.'"**

This passage introduces a theme that will occupy us at greater length later: the hardening of Pharaoh's heart. It has been said that the warmth of the sun melts ice but hardens liquid wax. That is too simple a resolution of the issue, but it does underscore the fact that the very wonders designed to evoke belief among Moses' own people (4:1–9) apparently will have the opposite effect on Pharaoh. The theme resurfaces again in Isaiah 6 and in Mark 4:10–12, reminding us that we are in the presence of a mystery deeper than we can fathom. Meanwhile, we should note the language in verses 22–23 about firstborn sons.

In the ancient world and in our own tradition until recent times, the firstborn son was heir to his father's possessions and family authority. Politically, the firstborn son was heir to the throne and its authority. As king of Egypt and its imperial domains, Pharaoh would think of himself and his heirs as embodying the gods' rule in the world. As such, he felt that commanding the death of the male children of his Hebrew slaves was within his authority. Here his authority is challenged head-on. It is through Israel, not Egypt, that God's kingdom is present in the world. Acknowledging God's rule, therefore, will entail the release of Israel to worship God. Otherwise, Egypt will inherit its own actions, coming under the very policy it has imposed on Israel. This illustrates a common biblical understanding of the relation between sin and judgment: God will return their actions upon their own heads.

MORTAL DANGER AT A REST STOP
Exodus 4:24–26

4:24 **On the way, at a place where they spent the night, the LORD met him and tried to kill him.** 25 **But Zipporah took a flint and cut off her son's foreskin, and touched Moses' feet with it, and said, "Truly you are a bridegroom of blood to me!"** 26 **So he let him alone. It was then she said, "A bridegroom of blood by circumcision."**

This passage is one of the strangest in the Bible. It remains puzzling despite scholars' attempts to explain it on the basis of ritual practices of initiation in other traditional cultures. My own tentative attempt to enter into its meaning owes the most to philosopher-theologian Martin Buber. In his book *Moses: The Revelation and the Covenant,* he compares the incident (1) to Enoch, who was walking with God and then suddenly disappeared "because God took him" (Gen. 5:22–24); (2) to Abraham, who finally was enabled to father the son God had promised him and then was asked to give him back to God in sacrifice (Gen. 22:1–19); and (3) to Jacob, who was promised God's presence and help throughout his exile and return and yet had to wrestle for his life all night with a strange figure before being able to reenter his country (Gen. 32:22–32). Buber summarizes: "It is part of the basic character of this God that he claims the entirety of the one he has chosen; he takes complete possession of the one to whom he addresses himself."

This theme continues into the New Testament, in Jesus' saying about taking up one's own cross and losing one's life to find it, and in his own prayer in Gethsemane and his self-offering on Calvary; it resurfaces in Paul's words in Galatians 2:19–20 (where I adopt NRSV footnote "l" in place of NRSV text at that point) : "I have been crucified with Christ; and it is no longer I who live, but Christ who lives in me. And the life I now live in the flesh I live by the faith of the Son of God, who loved me and gave himself for me."

Misunderstanding of this theme has led some to acts of self-abnegation and self-denial that have have caused great harm. Yet the theme appears so often in the Bible, in one form or another, that it is doubtful that a faith that simply rejects it as primitive and unworthy of enlightened religion can claim to remain connected with biblical roots. The cost of discipleship is not negotiable. The story of the world is not just the interweaving and unraveling of the stories of individuals and groups and nations; finally, it is the story of God and of the world and all its creatures as they choose to be or not to be part of God's story. From time to time, the crucial issue in this story is posed as starkly as it is with Moses at this wayside place. That he survives the encounter is owing to a resourceful action (whatever it may mean) of his wife, Zipporah, who joins the women of Exodus 1—2 as pivotal members of God's supporting cast.

FAMILY REUNION
AND REBIRTH OF HOPE
Exodus 4:27–31

4:27 **The LORD said to Aaron, "Go into the wilderness to meet Moses." So he went; and he met him at the mountain of God and kissed him. 28 Moses told Aaron all the words of the LORD with which he had sent him, and all the signs with which he had charged him. 29 Then Moses and Aaron went and assembled all the elders of the Israelites. 30 Aaron spoke all the words that the LORD had spoken to Moses, and performed the signs in the sight of the people. 31 The people believed; and when they heard that the LORD had given heed to the Israelites and that he had seen their misery, they bowed down and worshiped.**

I have proposed that the similarity between 2:23–25 and 3:7–8 suggests that God's call to Moses to lead the people out of Egypt occurs simultaneously with God's attentiveness to the people's cry in Egypt. This passage, by the way it shows Aaron meeting Moses at the mountain of God (that is, before Moses had gone very far on his return) implies that God's instruction to Aaron takes place while or before God instructs Moses to return (4:19). The point of this observation is to draw attention to an aspect of divine providence that offers us reassurance and calls for our trust. In our own times of need, our knowledge of the total situation is limited largely to what is near at hand. Passages like this reassure us and invite us to trust that God is at work in places and through people beyond the horizon of our awareness and to trust that, as we offer ourselves to God in trust and obedience, the lines along which God is working will in time converge and weave together into a redemptive outcome.

The similarity between verses 28 and 30 gives a first picture of the accommodation God has made to Moses' oral timidity (4:10–17). While the text does not clearly say so, we may assume that by now Moses has found the courage to say the divine name. The result is that the people believe and bow their heads in worship. One may wonder: Does God's provision of Aaron as a mouthpiece for Moses function as a two-way accommodation? That is, does it serve not only to accommodate Moses' hesitations but also to overcome any hesitation the people might have about believing this virtual stranger? The fact that they hear Moses' message from Aaron, whom they know well and who himself obviously believes what Moses has said to him, may help them to believe. In a sense, they join Aaron in his belief in Moses. Thus God continues to work in the world. David Tracy, a Roman Catholic theologian, likes to say, "I believe in Jesus Christ with the Apostles." It is the people's belief through Aaron's words and signs that demonstrates the truth of 4:15, "I will be with your mouth and with his mouth," words that should give great encouragement to anyone who would speak a hopeful word in God's name.

For all the heartening character of this passage, a sobering observation may not be amiss. The people's hopeful response will shortly give way to despair under increased affliction. The reader of Jesus' parable of the word, in Mark 4:3–20, may hear in the reference to "rocky ground" (Mark 4:5–6, 16–17) an echo of Exodus 6:9. Fortunately, the "fertile ground" of Moses and Aaron will provide further seed to resow the hopeful word in their hearts.

A FIRST SKIRMISH WITH PHARAOH
Exodus 5:1–3

> 5:1 **Afterward Moses and Aaron went to Pharaoh and said, "Thus says the LORD, the God of Israel, 'Let my people go, so that they may celebrate a festival to me in the wilderness.'"** [2] **But Pharaoh said, "Who is the LORD, that I should heed him and let Israel go? I do not know the LORD, and I will not let Israel go."** [3] **Then they said, "The God of the Hebrews has revealed himself to us; let us go a three days' journey into the wilderness to sacrifice to the LORD our God, or he will fall upon us with pestilence or sword."**

Moses and Aaron now give Pharaoh the same message from God that had moved the Israelites to belief and worship. But as the Egyptian king of 1:8 did not know Joseph, this king does not know Yahweh. What would it mean to know Yahweh? To begin with, it would be to recognize Yahweh as having authority to command him in this way. But in the light of the redefinition of the name in 3:13–15 and of the implications of that redefinition, perhaps it would mean something further. The Pharaoh of 1:8 had reacted to the new situation with a policy that reflected the wisdom of long-standing imperial statecraft: Take measures that will guarantee national security; if necessary, take action against those resident aliens who might be thought to threaten that security. This new Pharaoh is addressed by a God who, out of the divine freedom to be who and what any new situation calls for, opens up for the people on earth the room to envision new responses to their new situations. In responding as he does, this Pharaoh (not unlike Moses at first) resists that opening, standing firm in who he knows himself to be and in what he understands the situation to call for.

Since a direct authoritative word of command from Yahweh does not work, Moses and Aaron try a different tack. In the Old Testament, the term *Hebrews* is never used by the descendants of Abraham and Sarah to identify themselves to themselves. It is one way foreigners refer to them, and Israelites use it only in adopting a name that others use for them. Likewise, when they speak of "the God of the Hebrews," they distinguish their God from the gods of other peoples and narrow the sphere of authority of their God to focus it on themselves. They make what we might call an appeal to human religious rights in a pluralistic world.

After centuries during which many Christians assumed it was appropriate to address all peoples and public issues in the name of "the God and Father of our Lord Jesus Christ," we are now becoming aware of the need to consider how we enter our religious convictions into an increasingly pluralistic public arena, both domestically and internationally. In this respect, we are perhaps recovering something of the pluralistic context within which the people of Yahweh in both testaments found themselves.

MOSES AND AARON
AS "OUTSIDE AGITATORS"
Exodus 5:4–9

5:4 But the king of Egypt said to them, "Moses and Aaron, why are you taking the people away from their work? Get to your labors!" 5 Pharaoh continued, "Now they are more numerous than the people of the land and yet you want them to stop working!" 6 That same day Pharaoh commanded the taskmasters of the people, as well as their supervisors, 7 "You shall no longer give the people straw to make bricks, as before; let them go and gather straw for themselves. 8 But you shall require of them the same quantity of bricks as they have made previously; do not diminish it, for they are lazy; that is why they cry, "Let us go and offer sacrifice to our God." 9 Let heavier work be laid on them; then they will labor at it and pay no attention to deceptive words."

Moses and Aaron's second approach works no better than their first. Rather than hearing their words as an appeal to be allowed to respond to the claims of their God upon them, all he can hear is the words of two agitators and troublemakers. His words are doubly ironic. He charges first that "you cause the people to slacken off [para'] from their work." The verb para' means to undo or untie (as when people "let their hair down"; Num. 5:18) and then to cast off restraint. In having Pharaoh accuse Moses and Aaron of "undoing" his orders concerning the Hebrew slaves, the narrator plays on the sound of Pharaoh's name (something that will happen again in chapter 32), for, of course, it is Pharaoh who in resisting their words is "undoing" God's orders.

Second, Pharaoh charges Moses and Aaron with wanting the people to stop working, literally to rest (šabat) from their burdens. The reader familiar with the Sabbath theme in Genesis 1:1–2:3 and Exodus 16 and 20:8–11 will appreciate the irony. What Pharaoh sees only in negative terms as a work stoppage would, in fact, be true to how God works and rests and would have us work and rest. But Pharaoh can see reality only as he defines it, so for him the words of Moses and Aaron are "lying words" (RSV).

In Jeremiah's time, there were those who, claiming to speak for Yahweh, spoke lying words (Jer. 14:14; 23:25; 27:10; 29:21). But Jeremiah, too, could come under the same charge (Jer. 43:2). Just as the prophetic movement has its first great figure in Moses, who confronts the Egyptian king in the name of Yahweh and on behalf of the oppressed Hebrews, so the history of prophecy in the Bible is often a story of rejection of the true prophetic word by those in power. The word is rejected because it appears to those in power as a lie. It appears to be a lie because it calls into question and threatens to undo how they have organized society, and they believe they have organized society in accordance with how reality truly works. Therefore, they can see the prophetic call for liberation only as a pretext for a rest that arises out of the workers' laziness.

For such powers, the counterclaims of liberating prophecy are what Freud called all religion: an illusion. The book of Exodus can be said to trace the future of such an "illusion." As Robert Frost puts it in his essay "Education by Poetry" and in his poems "The Black Cottage" and "The Gift Outright," the future of such an illusion is not something to *believe* in so much as something to believe *in*, by acting on its truth. The sort of religion Moses and Aaron confront Pharaoh with is the religion of a possible future that Yahweh opens up for the oppressed and which comes about as it is embraced and believed into reality. What appears to Pharaoh as a lie is thus to become the truth "on earth as it is in heaven."

MAKING BRICKS WITHOUT STRAW
Exodus 5:10–21

5:10 So the taskmasters and the supervisors of the people went out and said to the people, "Thus says Pharaoh, 'I will not give you straw. [11] Go and get straw yourselves, wherever you can find it; but your work will not be lessened in the least.'" [12] So the people scattered throughout the land of Egypt, to gather stubble for straw. [13] The taskmasters were urgent, saying, "Complete your work, the same daily assignment as when you were given straw." [14] And the supervisors of the Israelites, whom Pharaoh's taskmasters had set over them, were beaten, and were asked, "Why did you not finish the required quantity of bricks yesterday and today, as you did before?"
[15] Then the Israelite supervisors came to Pharaoh and cried, "Why do you treat your servants like this? [16] No straw is given to your servants, yet they say to us, 'Make bricks!' Look how your servants are beaten! You are unjust to your own people." [17] He said, "You are lazy, lazy; that is why you say, 'Let us go and sacrifice to the LORD.' [18] Go now, and work; for no straw shall be given you, but you shall still deliver the same number of bricks." [19] The Israelite supervisors saw that they were in trouble when they were told, "You shall not lessen your daily number of bricks." [20] As they left Pharaoh, they came upon Moses and Aaron who were waiting to meet them. [21] They said to them, "The LORD look upon you and judge! You have brought us into bad odor with Pharaoh and his officials, and have put a sword in their hand to kill us."

This passage has embedded a vivid figure of speech in our language: being asked to "make bricks without straw." It illustrates how those in power use their imaginations not to find solutions that would embrace the welfare of all parties but to preserve and enforce the arrangements already in place to their own benefit. Moreover, they do so in a top-down fashion, working with what some have termed a "dominance hierarchy." They put pressure on those immediately beneath them to put pressure on those at the bottom to produce. In this way, the middle managers are made to do the dirty work to avoid being punished from above.

But what is the "straw" without which the oppressed of this world are asked to make "bricks"? The "straw" can be any material resources that were formerly given to meet certain production quotas but that now are scaled back or withheld. For example, local retail managers may be asked to maintain previous sales levels with a significantly reduced budget for staff salaries. If sales levels are maintained, of course, top management is buffered from this crunch.

But "straw" does not refer only to material resources. It functions also as a figure of speech for something else. The clue lies in the preceding passage. In 5:1–10, Moses and Aaron ask for time off to worship the God of the Hebrews. Pharaoh views this request as an attempt to serve the people's laziness or "idleness" (RSV). In the eyes of some so-called efficiency experts, an idle machine or worker is an expense and a liability. Only when work is being done is a return realized on investment. This is the "wisdom" that informs Pharaoh here. To grant the people time off would be like giving them the straw with which to make their bricks. Depriving them of straw forces them to scatter over the fields and take more time to make their quota of bricks, leaving them even less time than before to rest at the end of the day.

The God of the exodus, opposed to such Pharaonic wisdom, builds rest time—Sabbath time—into the very structure of human society. If God calls us to work, God provides the straw with which to work by providing the rest that makes and keeps our work something creative and not simply a burden. Our work within our own sphere falls within God's work, which embraces the whole of creation. If there is a hierarchical relation here between us and God, it is a "nested hierarchy," in which greater authority and power are used to undergird those with smaller spheres of responsibility. When our work, in or out of the home, within or outside the church, becomes so heavy and demanding that we have no time for worship, rest, and re-creation, we are under the dominance of Pharaoh.

MOSES RECALLED AND RENEWED
Exodus 5:22–6:9

5:22 **Then Moses turned again to the LORD and said, "O LORD, why have you mistreated this people? Why did you ever send me?** 23 **Since I first came to Pharaoh to speak in your name, he has mistreated this people, and you have done nothing at all to deliver your people."**

6:1 **Then the LORD said to Moses, "Now you shall see what I will do to Pharaoh: Indeed, by a mighty hand he will let them go; by a mighty hand he will drive them out of his land."**

2 **God also spoke to Moses and said to him: "I am the LORD [Yahweh].** 3 **I appeared to Abraham, Isaac, and Jacob as God Almighty [El Shaddai], but by my name 'the LORD' [Yahweh] I did not make myself known to them.** 4 **I also established my covenant with them, to give them the land of Canaan, the land in which they resided as aliens.** 5 **I have also heard the groaning of the Israelites whom the Egyptians are holding as slaves, and I have remembered my covenant.** 6 **Say therefore to the Israelites, 'I am the LORD [Yahweh], and I will free you from the burdens of the Egyptians and deliver you**

from slavery to them. I will redeem you with an outstretched arm and with mighty acts of judgment. [7] I will take you as my people, and I will be your God. You shall know that I am the LORD [Yahweh] your God, who has freed you from the burdens of the Egyptians. [8] I will bring you into the land that I swore to give to Abraham, Isaac, and Jacob; I will give it to you for a possession. I am the LORD [Yahweh].'" [9] Moses told this to the Israelites; but they would not listen to Moses, because of their broken spirit and their cruel slavery.

Here for the first time Moses is shown addressing God by the name Yahweh. It is as though he is challenging God by holding up the newly redefined name and accusing God of not living up to it. His speaking to Pharaoh "in your name" has not resulted in the people's freedom, for "you have done nothing at all to deliver your people." The result is rather their greater suffering, a suffering for which, though it comes immediately from Pharaoh's hand, he holds God ultimately responsible. If Moses opposes God's apparent inaction, he does so "in the name of God." This attitude is a far cry from the Moses who tried to fight off his vocation at the burning bush and who at first refused to take the divine name on his lips. But this evidence of the beginning of a transformation in Moses is a sign of God's presence to deliver, in being "with his mouth" (compare 4:12).

As with Abraham in Genesis 15:1–6, so now with Moses, God meets delay, doubt, and discouragement by reiterating God's earlier promise. That reiteration comes first in a succinct declaration (6:1) and then in a lengthy affirmation (6:3–8) that brings into sharper focus the issues raised at the burning bush. These issues have to do with the relation between God as known since ancestral times and God as revealed in a new way for a new kind of crisis. Moses apparently is reassured, for he returns to the people with this message (6:9). The lengthy affirmation in 6:3–8 is so carefully shaped and worded—almost like a formal argument—that it calls for careful, unhurried reflection.

The first thing to notice is the use of the expression "I am Yahweh." Its repetition and its position focus the whole passage on the name. The expression frames God's entire speech to Moses (6:2, 8), and at the same time it frames what Moses is to say to the people (6:6, 8). Within the frame provided by verses 6 and 8, the expression also occurs at the very core of the passage (6:7), to identify the purpose and result of God's action. God will act as promised, so that the people will know that God is indeed Yahweh as newly redefined.

I will explore further the shape and significance of the message Moses is to give to the people (6:6–8), but first we must ponder the meaning of

6:3. For over a century and a half, most scholars have taken this verse to mean that, in the mind of the biblical writer of this passage (generally identified as the Priestly writer, or "P"), the name Yahweh was not known or used for God in the ancestral period but was introduced only at the burning bush. Where this name appears in Genesis, it is to be attributed to the biblical writer whom we refer to as "the Yahwist," abbreviated "J".

But the Priestly narrator in Exodus 6:3 need not be taken to assert that the name Yahweh was not in use in the ancestral period. When this narrator has God say, with reference to the ancestors, that "by my name 'Yahweh' I did not make myself known to them," the narrator means, "by my name *as redefined at the bush*." A study of all the occurrences in the Old Testament of the verb "make oneself known," with Yahweh as subject, shows that the verb does not refer to the announcing of a divine name previously unknown but, rather, refers to God acting in such a way as to be *consistent with the meaning* of the divine name Yahweh. In all of these passages, the action in question is either explicitly or implicitly one in which God overcomes the enemy to deliver the people or acts in judgment on the people of God for their unfaithfulness to the Mount Sinai covenant.

Exodus 6:3, therefore, means: Given how the divine name has been redefined at the bush, God is now emphasizing to Moses that, whether or not God was actually named Yahweh in the ancestral period, God's characteristic actions in behalf of the ancestors could best be identified in terms of the specific meaning of the name El Shaddai. That name signified God as giver of "blessings of heaven above, blessings of the deep that lies beneath, blessings of the breasts [šedayim] and of the womb [reḥem]" (Gen. 49:25). The word-play in this latter passage, involving the sound similarity between Shaddai and šedayim, underscores the mode of God's presence and activity in the ancestral period as a God of cosmic and human fertility, in a period when barrenness and drought-caused famine were the two greatest threats to ancestral survival. In such a context, there was no need for God to "make myself known" as a divine warrior delivering the people from state oppression.

The explicit statement in 6:3, on the one hand, distinguishes two different aspects of God's self-revelation and action in two different periods and, on the other hand, emphasizes that God in both periods is one and the same God. Moreover, it suggests that giving life by enabling barrenness to become fertile (i.e., "blessing") and rescuing and preserving life by deliverance from deadly enemies ("salvation") are two different forms of one fundamental divine disposition and intention toward humankind. Blessing and salvation may be contrasted in a number of ways. For example, blessing often works gradually and secretly, like yeast within the ordinary processes of the world as created by God to work. (Compare Jesus' parables of ripening grain and mustard seed in Mark 4:26–32.) Salvation more often is portrayed as a dramatic intervention. (Compare Jesus' parables of the lost sheep, the lost coin, and the good Samaritan in Luke 15:3–10; 10:30–37.) But blessing and salvation have their unity in two ways: They both issue from God's fundamental intention for creation, and they both issue in the achievement of that intention, which is, as Jesus says, "that they may have life, and have it abundantly" (John 10:10).

In the ancestral period, God promised children to a barren couple, Abraham and Sarah. But since life needs a place within which its roots can draw nourishment from the earth, God also promised land to this wandering couple. In Genesis 12—50, God was active primarily in fulfilling the first promise, while the second remained as yet unfulfilled. Now, in response to the groaning of people whose place (Egypt) no longer nourishes them, God reiterates the second promise. It is in the fulfillment of this second promise that the redefined name, Yahweh, will be made good.

Let us now focus on the message Moses is to take to the Israelites (6:6–8). It is helpful here to consider a point of Hebrew grammar. Most often the common conjunction "and" simply links two consecutive statements. Sometimes, however, this conjunction functions to introduce a second statement that explains or spells out the first one. When God says, in 6:6–8, "I am Yahweh, *and* I will free you," I take it that the seven following verbs of divine action serve to spell out the significance God's name: "I am Yahweh. This means I will free you . . . and I will deliver you . . . and I will redeem you . . . and I will take you to me . . . and I will be to you . . . and I will bring you in . . . and I will give to you. . . ."

These seven verbs with God as subject fall into three groups. The first group—"free you from," "deliver you from," and "redeem you with"—refers to the exodus from Egypt. The second group, in verse 7 (literally translated "I will take you to me for a people" and "I will be to you for a God") refers to the bonding between Yahweh and this redeemed people that is to occur through the covenant ceremony at Mount Sinai (compare 19:3–6). The third group—"I will bring you into" and "I will give it to you"—refers to the entry into the land, fulfilling the second promise to the ancestors.

The use of seven verbs in three groups (the first of which contains three verbs) is a stylistic device for signaling the completeness of the divine action and thereby the complete integrity of the divine character. But why is the one verb with a human subject ("you shall know") positioned between the second and third group? If what the people will know from all this is that "I am Yahweh who has freed you," why is this knowing not placed right after the first group of three verbs? Why is the knowing delayed until mention of the Mount Sinai covenant? And if knowing God as liberator from bondage is delayed at all, why does it not come after the seventh verb, when God's redemption is fully complete? What is the importance of Mount Sinai, in knowing that Yahweh is a liberator?

The book of Exodus, indeed the Bible as a whole, connects freedom and law in the deepest way. So deeply are they connected that one does not "know" freedom fully nor "know" the God who frees until one has entered into covenant with this God and accepted the claims of that covenant as defining what freedom is *for*. The purpose of covenant law is to give freedom ethical shape. It is to educate the covenant community into a freedom that images God in how the members of that community relate to God and to one another. Without covenant law, freedom allows the powerful to rule unbridled by justice and leaves the powerless at their mercy.

But if God's action as "Yahweh" is complete only with the entry into the land, how is it that "knowing Yahweh" can have occurred at Mount Sinai? Here we get into the paradox of what biblical scholars and theologians call *eschatology*. *Eschatology*, or the doctrine of "the last things," has to do with God's end-time redemption of all things. Biblical scholars apply the terms "unrealized" or "not yet realized" eschatology to biblical passages in which the redemptive process is not yet complete (1 John 3:2–3; Rom. 8:24–25). Yet other passages seem to present the end as already here, already "realized" (John 11:25–26). An analogous tension between "unrealized" and "realized" eschatology is created in Exodus 6:6–8, by positioning "you shall know that I am the LORD your God" between the second and third groups of the verbs of divine action. While the redemptive process will not be complete until the entry into the land, already with Mount Sinai the people will be able to know Yahweh for who Yahweh truly is. How is this?

The prepositions in our passage may help us. Earlier, in Exodus 3:8, the prepositions "from" and "to" identified Egypt as the beginning and Canaan as the destination and end of God's redemptive action. But here, where God spells out matters more fully to Moses, while the "from" still refers to Egypt, the "to" in "I will take you *to me* for a people" (so, literally, the Hebrew in v. 7) identifies God as the people's ultimate goal. This is underscored again later, in 19:4: "You have seen what I did to the Egyptians, and how I bore you on eagles' wings and brought you *to myself*." God's aim and desire are not simply to bring us into a land but to bring us into intimate relation to God. Psalm 16 puts this another way. Affirming that "The LORD is my chosen portion and my cup; you hold my lot," the psalmist, as James L. Mays puts it, "is using the vocabulary and concepts that are employed in the book of Joshua to describe Israel's occupation of the promised land as the outcome of God's salvation of Israel" (*Psalms*, p. 87). Therefore, whether or not the powers that control the earth leave room for the psalmist, that psalmist is safe "in" God. Do we have any human analogy for being safe "in" another person? There is at least one literal instance: when we dwelt in our mothers' nourishing and protecting bodies. It is fitting that the Yahweh who is continuous with El Shaddai, giver of the blessings of breasts and womb, seeks to give us room to live and, where others do not afford us that room, becomes our portion and our lot. Though our final dwelling in God is as yet unrealized, those who have experienced God's liberation from oppression and are drawn into God's covenant may already know that "I am Yahweh."

For all God's elaborate reassurance of the coming redemption in faithfulness to the ancestral covenant, the people do not listen to Moses. Their suffering has entered so deeply into them that they have lost the capacity to hope (compare Job 6:11–13). "While there's life, there's hope," we may say, but to the despairing, such a saying sounds like mockery; for them, it is truer to say, "Only while there's hope is there life." The "seed of the word" that sprang up into the Israelites' belief when it first fell on their ears (Exod. 4:31) threatens now to wither and die (compare Mark 4:16–17). That these people will live to believe again is because Moses and Aaron refuse to give up.

GENEALOGY AND COMMUNITY MORALE
Exodus 6:10–27

6:10 **Then the LORD spoke to Moses, ¹¹ "Go and tell Pharaoh king of Egypt to let the Israelites go out of his land." ¹² But Moses spoke to the LORD, "The Israelites have not listened to me; how then shall Pharaoh listen to me, poor speaker that I am?" ¹³ Thus the LORD spoke to Moses and Aaron, and gave them orders regarding the Israelites and Pharaoh king of Egypt, charging them to free the Israelites from the land of Egypt.**

¹⁴ The following are the heads of their ancestral houses: the sons of Reuben, the firstborn of Israel: Hanoch, Pallu, Hezron, and Carmi; these are the families of Reuben. ¹⁵ The sons of Simeon: Jemuel, Jamin, Ohad, Jachin, Zohar, and Shaul, the son of a Canaanite woman; these are the families of Simeon. ¹⁶ The following are the names of the sons of Levi according to their

genealogies: Gershon, Kohath, and Merari, and the length of Levi's life was one hundred thirty-seven years. [17] The sons of Gershon: Libni and Shimei, by their families. [18] The sons of Kohath: Amram, Izhar, Hebron, and Uzziel, and the length of Kohath's life was one hundred thirty-three years. [19] The sons of Merari: Mahli and Mushi. These are the families of the Levites according to their genealogies. [20] Amram married Jochebed his father's sister and she bore him Aaron and Moses, and the length of Amram's life was one hundred thirty-seven years. [21] The sons of Izhar: Korah, Nepheg, and Zichri. [22] The sons of Uzziel: Mishael, Elzaphan, and Sithri. [23] Aaron married Elisheba, daughter of Amminadab and sister of Nahshon, and she bore him Nadab, Abihu, Eleazar, and Ithamar. [24] The sons of Korah: Assir, Elkanah, and Abiasaph; these are the families of the Korahites. [25] Aaron's son Eleazar married one of the daughters of Putiel, and she bore him Phinehas. These are the heads of the ancestral houses of the Levites by their families.

[26] It was this same Aaron and Moses to whom the LORD said, "Bring the Israelites out of the land of Egypt, company by company." [27] It was they who spoke to Pharaoh king of Egypt to bring the Israelites out of Egypt, the same Moses and Aaron.

The genealogy that appears suddenly in the middle of this passage may strike a note dissident to modern ears for the way it serves as "an unwanted interruption" (Childs, *The Book of Exodus*, p. 116). One way to account for its presence is to take it as a means by which a later priestly party in Israel sought to provide credentials or legitimation for Moses and Aaron's activities in relation to Israel's institutions of worship. But when one of my American students accounted for the genealogy in this way, his report evoked a different interpretation from Chirevo Kwenda, a student from Zimbabwe. His proposal, informed by his own cultural experience, was based on two factors in the text: the precise point in the story where the genealogy is introduced and the function of a recitation of ancestors and descendants in such a setting.

The setting is that the Israelites in their despair have rejected Moses' message in God's name. How then will a foreign king listen to him? Moses here falls back into his earlier sense of inadequacy: "poor speaker that I am" (6:12). Yet, when God charges him and Aaron nevertheless to confront Pharaoh again, they do so. What enables them to overcome their discouragement and to act?

Kwenda appealed to the tradition among his people, whose recollection of their ancestors in time of crisis does not simply serve to legitimize leadership (though it may do that). More important, it is a means of empowerment, for the ancestors, though dead, are not without efficacy for the present situation. To the living, they are a vital part of the community, which embraces the living and the dead. In times of crisis, then, the community not only calls upon God but also draws encouragement and strength from the recollection of its dead ancestors.

Conviction of the efficacy of the dead ancestors is not unknown in Christian tradition, though in such specific forms as "the merits of the saints" it is typically rejected among Protestants. However one may view such a conviction, any one of us may test for ourselves how in times of crisis, when we feel isolated or in a distinct minority, the recitation of the names of our revered ancestors can have the effect of filling us with new energy and hope. If nothing else, there can arise in the midst of despondency a resolution to follow in our predecessors' footsteps and keep the faith as they did. Indeed, Hebrews 11:1–12:11, following after Hebrews 10:36–39, may be said to encourage such a practice.

Among those with a strong sense of intergenerational community, such an ancestral recollection need involve nothing more than the recitation of names to be efficacious. In accounting for the fact that Moses and Aaron overcame their discouragement to carry out God's reiterated commission, the narrator says it was "this same Aaron and Moses"—that is, the Aaron and Moses who stemmed from such a lineage—who despite their discouragement carried through on their calling. It is perhaps not by coincidence that the tradition elsewhere remembers Levi, the son of Jacob, as capable of a hot-tempered zeal that could move him to action (however ill-advised) while most of his brothers did nothing (Gen. 34:25–31; 49:5–7) and that, among the later descendants of Levi, Aaron's grandson Phinehas (with whom the genealogy closes in Exod. 6:25) became legendary for his aggressive zeal on behalf of God (Num. 25:6–13; Psalm 106:28–31; 4 Macc. 18:12). Kwenda argued that in times of crisis the community survives through the gracious intervention of God *and* through the energies of response that arise in the community through recollecting its ancestral roots. The point is worth pondering, in an age when dead ancestors are considered as merely "history" in the idiomatic sense that they are no longer relevant to the present.

A further point may also be offered here. In a time when the rest of the community falls into despair, Moses and Aaron are enabled to remain hopeful, however conflicted that hope may be. However, they are not simply to be contrasted with their despairing brothers and sisters. They are the keepers of the community hope on behalf of all. They are like the friends who lowered the paralyzed man through the roof on a stretcher to bring him to Jesus. As Luke tells us (Luke 5:20), it was *their* faith that Jesus saw in this action and that moved him to act.

SENDING MOSES AGAIN TO PHARAOH
Exodus 6:28–7:7

6:28 **On the day when the** LORD **spoke to Moses in the land of Egypt,** 29 **he said to him, "I am the** LORD**; tell Pharaoh king of Egypt all that I am speaking to you."** 30 **But Moses said in the** LORD**'s presence, "Since I am a poor speaker, why would Pharaoh listen to me?"**

7:1 **The** LORD **said to Moses, "See, I have made you like God to Pharaoh, and your brother Aaron shall be your prophet.** 2 **You shall speak all that I command you, and your brother Aaron shall tell Pharaoh to let the Israelites go out of his land.** 3 **But I will harden Pharaoh's heart, and I will multiply my signs and wonders in the land of Egypt.** 4 **When Pharaoh does not listen to you, I will lay my hand upon Egypt and bring my people the Israelites, company by company, out of the land of Egypt by great acts of judgment.** 5 **The Egyptians shall know that I am the** LORD**, when I stretch out my hand against Egypt and bring the Israelites out from among them."** 6 **Moses and Aaron did so; they did just as the** LORD **commanded them.** 7 **Moses was eighty years old and Aaron eighty-three when they spoke to Pharaoh.**

Like a story that returns to the main plot line after digressing briefly, 6:28–29 basically repeats 6:10–13. When Moses raises again the problem of his poor speaking ability (see 4:10), God reminds him of the earlier provision for this problem: Aaron will be his mouthpiece. As for the question of Pharaoh's willingness to listen, that, too, is in God's hands. When Pharaoh does not listen, it will be because God has hardened his heart.

Here we come upon one of the thorniest problems in the Bible, one that threatens to make a mockery of language about human freedom and dignity and to reduce humankind to puppets hanging from divinely manipulated strings. My attempt to grapple with this issue will come at the end of our reflection on the plagues narrative (7:8–11:9; 12:29–36). Here I will just observe that the word "harden," which occurs repeatedly in the next several chapters, translates several different Hebrew verbs that amount to the same general idea but carry somewhat different nuances. So we shall track their occurrence carefully. In the present instance, the basic form of the verb is *qashah*, "be hard, severe, fierce." The related adjective can describe a fierce battle, a strong wind, a stubborn (i.e., "stiff"-necked) people, or a passionate love that is strong as death and "*fierce*" (or intense) as the grave (Song of Sol. 8:6). In our passage, the form of the verb means "to make hard, to intensify." In 5:2, we saw Pharaoh refuse Moses and Aaron's call to let the people go. Now God says that when Pharaoh reiterates this refusal in even stronger terms, it will be because God has caused him to intensify his opposition to their renewed plea.

This refusal gives God the opportunity to "multiply my signs and wonders in the land of Egypt." By this open display of God's power in bringing Israel out of bondage, the Egyptians "shall know that I am Yahweh." Thus one and the same divine act will make God known among the Egyptians as well as among the Israelites (6:7). Will that knowing, however, mean the same thing to the Egyptians as to the Israelites?

In 6:7b God says, "You shall know that I am the LORD *your God*," an emphasis that comes after the covenant making at Mount Sinai (6:7a). In 7:5, God says simply, "The Egyptians shall know that I am the LORD." The question raised is whether there is such a thing as a "nonsaving" knowledge of God.

The prophet of the exile whom we call Second Isaiah more than once portrays God's deliverance of Israel from Babylonian exile as occurring on the pattern of the original exodus from Egypt, trek through the wilderness, and entry into the promised land. In Isaiah 41:8–20, one purpose of this act of deliverance is "so that all may see and know, / all may consider and understand, / that the hand of the LORD has done this, / the Holy One of Israel has created it." This affirmation comes in the context of other statements that seem to include all nations eventually within the scope of God's coming redemptive acts (see Isa. 42:4; 53:12; 55:5). The emphasis in Isaiah 41:20 seems to play off earlier statements in the Old Testament like Exodus 7:5. One could suppose that Isaiah 41:20 gives Exodus 7:5 a new twist, so that what was once self-condemning knowledge now becomes saving knowledge. Then again, there may be another way to look at this.

In common human experience, it is possible to live in ignorance of the truth, then belatedly acknowledge the truth, and have that acknowledgment make a "saving" difference. A recent newscast reported one doctor's claim that people with heart trouble, even in old age, can improve their health or at least slow down further deterioration by shifting to a low-fat vegetarian diet. But some belated acknowledgments cannot effect such reversals. The baseball player Mickey Mantle's public statements of rue for his abuse of his body through alcohol and other forms of hard living came too late to slow down his decline, let alone reverse it. Yet the fact of his belated "knowing," though it made no difference to his physical fate, was a moral and spiritual reversal that moved many to admire his humility and candor, however late it came. The Old Testament says very little about any "saving" difference such belated knowing may make for one's ultimate standing and destiny. Yet, as in the case of Achan and his family (Joshua

7), even if acknowledgment of the truth is too late to make a difference for one's worldly future, at least such a "knowing" has the effect of drawing one out of the realm of falsehood and, in some sense, into the community of those who acknowledge the truth.

PHARAOH'S HARD HEART, GOD'S HARDER PLAGUES
Exodus 7:8–11:10; 12:29–36

In the space they take up in the text, as well as in their melodramatic character, the plagues dominate the early part of the book of Exodus the way the covenant laws and instructions for the tabernacle dominate the latter part set at Mount Sinai. In contrast to the space given over to the tabernacle, which to anyone but an architect must seem excessive (chapters 25—31; 35—40), the space given to the plagues is readily understandable. The contest between God and Pharaoh has all the excitement of a Star Wars battle between Darth Vader and the forces of good, and the narrator uses a variety of devices to draw us into the story.

But there is more here than dramatic excitement. The narrator draws out the story and organizes its dramatic development to explore the issues at stake in the conflict between Yahweh, the God of the ancestors, and the wisdom and power of Pharaoh and his oppressive regime.

In the New Testament Gospels, the narrative of Jesus' Passion dominates in importance and in length, which enables us to get a close-up view of how God in Jesus Christ engages the powers of this world in acting to redeem the world. To be sure, God's redemptive action through passion in the Gospels seems strikingly different than God's redemptive action in the Exodus. Yet, if there are pronounced differences between the two sorts of redemptive action, the New Testament in many places and in many ways presents God's redemption through the passion of Jesus as standing in unbreakable continuity with the redemption achieved in the exodus. The issues of continuity and change in the relation between these two kinds of redemptive action are similar to those same issues in the relation between God's presence and activity in the lives of the ancestors (Genesis 12—50) and God's presence and activity in the book of Exodus. Here I shall first comment on aspects of the narrative form of the contest between God and Pharaoh and then offer some comments on the meaning of this contest for our understanding of both God and human life.

In regard to the form of the plagues narrative, recollect what happens in becoming intimately familiar with a story. At first all is new, and one is so immersed in the main story line as to note many of the details only in peripheral vision if at all. As repeated exposure gives one a sense of the shape of the story and its themes and subthemes, certain details suddenly stand out as markers to guide our understanding. The movie *Kramer vs. Kramer*, for example, is a sensitive portrayal of the pain involved in the breakup of a marriage and the struggle to make provision for the parental care of the child. The plot moves from marital breakup, through an ugly court case over child custody, to a place where former husband and wife are able to come to a relatively amicable agreement over custody and visitation. Not until my second or third viewing, however, did I notice a detail that structures the plot and signals shifts in its emotional atmosphere: three elevator scenes. At the beginning, the wife-mother walks out of the apartment and the marriage, and the husband-father, following her to beg her to stay, meets only the door of the "down" elevator slamming in his face. After the custody trial, in which the wife-mother's lawyer has to wash some of the husband-father's dirty linen before the judge to win the case, the wife tries to apologize to the husband, but he storms into the "down" elevator, the door of which slams in her face. At the end of the movie, when the two have come to an amicable resolution concerning the child, they part amicably in front of the door of an "up" elevator. A movie filled with downbeat moments ends on a modest upbeat.

In the following paragraphs, I first consider the preliminary engagement or "skirmish" that precedes the plagues story proper. After the presentation of the text of that story (keyed by letters I explain), I sketch a few large-scale features of the dramatic pattern of the plagues and then focus on developments in certain details that will help us gain at least some insight into the mystery of the hardening of Pharaoh's heart.

Preliminary Engagement
(7:8–13)

> 7:8 The LORD said to Moses and Aaron, ⁹ "When Pharaoh says to you, 'Perform a wonder,' then you shall say to Aaron, 'Take your staff and throw it down before Pharaoh, and it will become a snake.'" ¹⁰ So Moses and Aaron went to Pharaoh and did as the LORD had commanded; Aaron threw down his staff before Pharaoh and his officials, and it became a snake. ¹¹ Then Pharaoh summoned the wise men and the sorcerers; and they also, the magicians of Egypt, did the same by their secret arts. ¹² Each one threw down his staff, and they became snakes; but Aaron's staff swallowed up theirs. ¹³ Still Pharaoh's heart was hardened, and he would not listen to them, as the LORD had said.

This introductory scene involves the performance of the first sign God gave to Moses at the burning bush, turning the staff into a snake (4:2–4). At that earlier passage, I suggested that the snake symbolizes wisdom, and the first sign means that the wisdom (or skill) he possessed as a shepherd is now transformed into a wisdom by which he will be enabled to bring his people out of Egypt. The fact that his sign is duplicated by Pharaoh's *wise men* (7:11) underscores the wisdom theme. That his snake swallows theirs shows that the plagues are a matter not just of superior power but also of superior wisdom. God does, indeed, deliver Israel by a mighty hand, but it is through the forces of nature that embody God's wisdom (compare Job 38—40; Isa. 40:12–31; and, interpreting the exodus, Wisd. of Sol. 5:17–23). Thus God's wisdom defeats Pharaoh, who thinks he is acting wisely (see 1:10 and my comments).

The Plagues

1(a). Water into Blood (7:14–25)

7:14 Then the LORD said to Moses, "Pharaoh's heart is hardened; he refuses to let the people go. ¹⁵ Go to Pharaoh in the morning, as he is going out to the water; stand by at the river bank to meet him, and take in your hand the staff that was turned into a snake. ¹⁶ Say to him, 'The LORD, the God of the Hebrews, sent me to you to say, "Let my people go, so that they may worship me in the wilderness." But until now you have not listened.'" ¹⁷ Thus says the LORD, "By this you shall know that I am the LORD." See, with the staff that is in my hand I will strike the water that is in the Nile, and it shall be turned to blood. ¹⁸ The fish in the river shall die, the river itself shall stink, and the Egyptians shall be unable to drink water from the Nile.'" ¹⁹ The LORD said to Moses, "Say to Aaron, 'Take your staff and stretch out your hand over the waters of Egypt—over its rivers, its canals, and its ponds, and all its pools of water—so that they may become blood; and there shall be blood throughout the whole land of Egypt, even in vessels of wood and in vessels of stone.'"

²⁰ Moses and Aaron did just as the LORD commanded. In the sight of Pharaoh and of his officials he lifted up the staff and struck the water in the river, and all the water in the river was turned into blood, ²¹ and the fish in the river died. The river stank so that the Egyptians could not drink its water, and there was blood throughout the whole land of Egypt. ²² But the magicians of Egypt did the same by their secret arts; so Pharaoh's heart remained hardened, and he would not listen to them; as the LORD had said. ²³ Pharaoh turned and went into his house, and he did not take even this to

heart. 24 And all the Egyptians had to dig along the Nile for water to drink, for they could not drink the water of the river.

25 Seven days passed after the LORD had struck the Nile.

2(b). Frogs (8:1–15)

8:1 Then the LORD said to Moses, "Go to Pharaoh and say to him, 'Thus says the LORD: Let my people go, so that they may worship me. 2 If you refuse to let them go, I will plague your whole country with frogs. 3 The river shall swarm with frogs; they shall come up into your palace, into your bedchamber and your bed, and into the houses of your officials and of your people, and into your ovens and your kneading bowls. 4 The frogs shall come up on you and on your people and on all your officials.'" 5 And the LORD said to Moses, "Say to Aaron, 'Stretch out your hand with your staff over the rivers, the canals, and the pools, and make frogs come up on the land of Egypt.'" 6 So Aaron stretched out his hand over the waters of Egypt; and the frogs came up and covered the land of Egypt. 7 But the magicians did the same by their secret arts, and brought frogs up on the land of Egypt.

8 Then Pharaoh called Moses and Aaron, and said, "Pray to the LORD to take away the frogs from me and my people, and I will let the people go to sacrifice to the LORD." 9 Moses said to Pharaoh, "Kindly tell me when I am to pray for you and for your officials and for your people, that the frogs may be removed from you and your houses and be left only in the Nile." 10 And he said, "Tomorrow." Moses said, "As you say! So that you may know that there is no one like the LORD our God, 11 the frogs shall leave you and your houses and your officials and your people; they shall be left only in the Nile." 12 Then Moses and Aaron went out from Pharaoh; and Moses cried out to the LORD concerning the frogs that he had brought upon Pharaoh. 13 And the LORD did as Moses requested: the frogs died in the houses, the courtyards, and the fields. 14 And they gathered them together in heaps, and the land stank. 15 But when Pharaoh saw that there was a respite, he hardened his heart, and would not listen to them, just as the LORD had said.

3(c). Gnats (8:16–19)

8:16 Then the LORD said to Moses, "Say to Aaron, 'Stretch out your staff and strike the dust of the earth, so that it may become gnats throughout the whole land of Egypt.'" 17 And they did so; Aaron stretched out his hand with his staff and struck the dust of the earth, and gnats came on humans and animals alike; all the dust of the earth turned into gnats throughout the whole land of Egypt. 18 The magicians tried to produce gnats by their secret arts, but they could not. There were gnats on both humans and animals. 19 And

the magicians said to Pharaoh, "This is the finger of God!" But Pharaoh's
heart was hardened, and he would not listen to them, just as the LORD had
said.

4(a). Flies (8:20–32)

8:20 Then the LORD said to Moses, "Rise early in the morning and present
yourself before Pharaoh, as he goes out to the water, and say to him, 'Thus
says the LORD: Let my people go, so that they may worship me. 21 For if you
will not let my people go, I will send swarms of flies on you, your officials,
and your people, and into your houses; and the houses of the Egyptians shall
be filled with swarms of flies; so also the land where they live. 22 But on that
day I will set apart the land of Goshen, where my people live, so that no
swarms of flies shall be there, that you may know that I the LORD am in this
land. 23 Thus I will make a distinction between my people and your people.
This sign shall appear tomorrow.' " 24 The LORD did so, and great swarms of
flies came into the house of Pharaoh and into his officials' houses; in all of
Egypt the land was ruined because of the flies.

25 Then Pharaoh summoned Moses and Aaron, and said, "Go, sacrifice to
your God within the land." 26 But Moses said, "It would not be right to do
so; for the sacrifices that we offer to the LORD our God are offensive to the
Egyptians. If we offer in the sight of the Egyptians sacrifices that are offensive to them, will they not stone us? 27 We must go a three days' journey into
the wilderness and sacrifice to the LORD our God as he commands us." 28 So
Pharaoh said, "I will let you go to sacrifice to the LORD your God in the
wilderness, provided you do not go very far away. Pray for me." 29 Then
Moses said, "As soon as I leave you, I will pray to the LORD that the swarms
of flies may depart tomorrow from Pharaoh, from his officials, and from his
people; only do not let Pharaoh again deal falsely by not letting the people
go to sacrifice to the LORD."

30 So Moses went out from Pharaoh and prayed to the LORD. 31 And the
LORD did as Moses asked: he removed the swarms of flies from Pharaoh, from
his officials, and from his people; not one remained. 32 But Pharaoh hardened his heart this time also, and would not let the people go.

5(b). Diseased Livestock (9:1–7)

9:1 Then the LORD said to Moses, "Go to Pharaoh, and say to him, 'Thus says
the LORD, the God of the Hebrews: Let my people go, so that they may worship me. 2 For if you refuse to let them go and still hold them, 3 the hand of
the LORD will strike with a deadly pestilence your livestock in the field: the
horses, the donkeys, the camels, the herds, and the flocks. 4 But the LORD will

make a distinction between the livestock of Israel and the livestock of Egypt, so that nothing shall die of all that belongs to the Israelites.'" [5] The LORD set a time, saying, "Tomorrow the LORD will do this thing in the land." [6] And on the next day the LORD did so; all the livestock of the Egyptians died, but of the livestock of the Israelites not one died. [7] Pharaoh inquired and found that not one of the livestock of the Israelites was dead. But the heart of Pharaoh was hardened, and he would not let the people go.

6(c). Boils (9:8–12)

9:8 Then the LORD said to Moses and Aaron, "Take handfuls of soot from the kiln, and let Moses throw it in the air in the sight of Pharaoh. [9] It shall become fine dust all over the land of Egypt, and shall cause festering boils on humans and animals throughout the whole land of Egypt." [10] So they took soot from the kiln, and stood before Pharaoh, and Moses threw it in the air, and it caused festering boils on humans and animals. [11] The magicians could not stand before Moses because of the boils, for the boils afflicted the magicians as well as all the Egyptians. [12] But the LORD hardened the heart of Pharaoh, and he would not listen to them, just as the LORD had spoken to Moses.

7(a). Thunder and Hail (9:13–35)

9:13 Then the LORD said to Moses, "Rise up early in the morning and present yourself before Pharaoh, and say to him, 'Thus says the LORD, the God of the Hebrews: Let my people go, so that they may worship me. [14] For this time I will send all my plagues upon you yourself, and upon your officials, and upon your people, so that you may know that there is no one like me in all the earth. [15] For by now I could have stretched out my hand and struck you and your people with pestilence, and you would have been cut off from the earth. [16] But this is why I have let you live: to show you my power, and to make my name resound through all the earth. [17] You are still exalting yourself against my people, and will not let them go. [18] Tomorrow at this time I will cause the heaviest hail to fall that has ever fallen in Egypt from the day it was founded until now. [19] Send, therefore, and have your livestock and everything that you have in the open field brought to a secure place; every human or animal that is in the open field and is not brought under shelter will die when the hail comes down upon them.'" [20] Those officials of Pharaoh who feared the word of the LORD hurried their slaves and livestock off to a secure place. [21] Those who did not regard the word of the LORD left their slaves and livestock in the open field.

[22] The LORD said to Moses, "Stretch out your hand toward heaven so that hail may fall on the whole land of Egypt, on humans and animals and all the

plants of the field in the land of Egypt." 23 Then Moses stretched out his staff toward heaven, and the LORD sent thunder and hail, and fire came down on the earth. And the LORD rained hail on the land of Egypt; 24 there was hail with fire flashing continually in the midst of it, such heavy hail as had never fallen in all the land of Egypt since it became a nation. 25 The hail struck down everything that was in the open field throughout all the land of Egypt, both human and animal; the hail also struck down all the plants of the field, and shattered every tree in the field. 26 Only in the land of Goshen, where the Israelites were, there was no hail. 27 Then Pharaoh summoned Moses and Aaron, and said to them, "This time I have sinned; the LORD is in the right, and I and my people are in the wrong. 28 Pray to the LORD! Enough of God's thunder and hail! I will let you go; you need stay no longer." 29 Moses said to him, "As soon as I have gone out of the city, I will stretch out my hands to the LORD; the thunder will cease, and there will be no more hail, so that you may know that the earth is the LORD's. 30 But as for you and your officials, I know that you do not yet fear the LORD God." 31 (Now the flax and the barley were ruined, for the barley was in the ear and the flax was in bud. 32 But the wheat and the spelt were not ruined, for they are late in coming up.) 33 So Moses left Pharaoh, went out of the city, and stretched out his hands to the LORD; then the thunder and the hail ceased, and the rain no longer poured down on the earth. 34 But when Pharaoh saw that the rain and the hail and the thunder had ceased, he sinned once more and hardened his heart, he and his officials. 35 So the heart of Pharaoh was hardened, and he would not let the Israelites go, just as the LORD had spoken through Moses.

8(b). Locusts (10:1–20)

10:1 Then the LORD said to Moses, "Go to Pharaoh; for I have hardened his heart and the heart of his officials, in order that I may show these signs of mine among them, 2 and that you may tell your children and grandchildren how I have made fools of the Egyptians and what signs I have done among them—so that you may know that I am the LORD."

3 So Moses and Aaron went to Pharaoh, and said to him, "Thus says the LORD, the God of the Hebrews, 'How long will you refuse to humble yourself before me? Let my people go, so that they may worship me. 4 For if you refuse to let my people go, tomorrow I will bring locusts into your country. 5 They shall cover the surface of the land, so that no one will be able to see the land. They shall devour the last remnant left you after the hail, and they shall devour every tree of yours that grows in the field. 6 They shall fill your houses, and the houses of all your officials and of all the Egyptians—something that neither your parents nor your grandparents have seen, from the day they came on earth to this day.'" Then he turned and went out from Pharaoh.

[7] Pharaoh's officials said to him, "How long shall this fellow be a snare to us? Let the people go, so that they may worship the LORD their God; do you not yet understand that Egypt is ruined?" [8] So Moses and Aaron were brought back to Pharaoh, and he said to them, "Go, worship the LORD your God! But which ones are to go?" [9] Moses said, "We will go with our young and our old; we will go with our sons and daughters and with our flocks and herds, because we have the LORD's festival to celebrate." [10] He said to them, "The LORD indeed will be with you, if ever I let your little ones go with you! Plainly, you have some evil purpose in mind. [11] No, never! Your men may go and worship the LORD, for that is what you are asking." And they were driven out from Pharaoh's presence.

[12] Then the LORD said to Moses, "Stretch out your hand over the land of Egypt, so that the locusts may come upon it and eat every plant in the land, all that the hail has left." [13] So Moses stretched out his staff over the land of Egypt, and the LORD brought an east wind upon the land all that day and all that night; when morning came, the east wind had brought the locusts. [14] The locusts came upon all the land of Egypt and settled on the whole country of Egypt, such a dense swarm of locusts as had never been before, nor ever shall be again. [15] They covered the surface of the whole land, so that the land was black; and they ate all the plants in the land and all the fruit of the trees that the hail had left; nothing green was left, no tree, no plant in the field, in all the land of Egypt. [16] Pharaoh hurriedly summoned Moses and Aaron and said, "I have sinned against the LORD your God, and against you. [17] Do forgive my sin just this once, and pray to the LORD your God that at the least he remove this deadly thing from me." [18] So he went out from Pharaoh and prayed to the LORD. [19] The LORD changed the wind into a very strong west wind, which lifted the locusts and drove them into the Red Sea; not a single locust was left in all the country of Egypt. [20] But the LORD hardened Pharaoh's heart, and he would not let the Israelites go.

9(c). Darkness (10:21–29)

10:21 Then the LORD said to Moses, "Stretch out your hand toward heaven so that there may be darkness over the land of Egypt, a darkness that can be felt." [22] So Moses stretched out his hand toward heaven, and there was dense darkness in all the land of Egypt for three days. [23] People could not see one another, and for three days they could not move from where they were; but all the Israelites had light where they lived. [24] Then Pharaoh summoned Moses, and said, "Go, worship the LORD. Only your flocks and your herds shall remain behind. Even your children may go with you." [25] But Moses said, "You must also let us have sacrifices and burnt offerings to sacrifice to the LORD our God. [26] Our livestock also must go with us; not a hoof shall be left behind, for we must choose some of them for the worship of the LORD our

God, and we will not know what to use to worship the LORD until we arrive there." 27 But the LORD hardened Pharaoh's heart, and he was unwilling to let them go. 28 Then Pharaoh said to him, "Get away from me! Take care that you do not see my face again, for on the day you see my face you shall die." 29 Moses said, "Just as you say! I will never see your face again."

10. The Firstborn:
Warning, and Death (11:1–10; 12:29–36)

11:1 The LORD said to Moses, "I will bring one more plague upon Pharaoh and upon Egypt; afterwards he will let you go from here; indeed, when he lets you go, he will drive you away. 2 Tell the people that every man is to ask his neighbor and every woman is to ask her neighbor for objects of silver and gold." 3 The LORD gave the people favor in the sight of the Egyptians. Moreover, Moses himself was a man of great importance in the land of Egypt, in the sight of Pharaoh's officials and in the sight of the people.

4 Moses said, "Thus says the LORD: About midnight I will go out through Egypt. 5 Every firstborn in the land of Egypt shall die, from the firstborn of Pharaoh who sits on his throne to the firstborn of the female slave who is behind the handmill, and all the firstborn of the livestock. 6 Then there will be a loud cry throughout the whole land of Egypt, such as has never been or will ever be again. 7 But not a dog shall growl at any of the Israelites—not at people, not at animals—so that you may know that the LORD makes a distinction between Egypt and Israel. 8 Then all these officials of yours shall come down to me, and bow low to me, saying, 'Leave us, you and all the people who follow you.' After that I will leave." And in hot anger he left Pharaoh.

9 The LORD said to Moses, "Pharaoh will not listen to you, in order that my wonders may be multiplied in the land of Egypt." 10 Moses and Aaron performed all these wonders before Pharaoh; but the LORD hardened Pharaoh's heart, and he did not let the people of Israel go out of his land.

12:29 At midnight the LORD struck down all the firstborn in the land of Egypt, from the firstborn of Pharaoh who sat on his throne to the firstborn of the prisoner who was in the dungeon, and all the firstborn of the livestock. 30 Pharaoh arose in the night, he and all his officials and all the Egyptians; and there was a loud cry in Egypt, for there was not a house without someone dead. 31 Then he summoned Moses and Aaron in the night, and said, "Rise up, go away from my people, both you and the Israelites! Go, worship the LORD, as you said. 32 Take your flocks and your herds, as you said, and be gone. And bring a blessing on me too!"

33 The Egyptians urged the people to hasten their departure from the land, for they said, "We shall all be dead." 34 So the people took their dough before it was leavened, with their kneading bowls wrapped up in their cloaks

**on their shoulders. ³⁵ The Israelites had done as Moses told them; they had
asked the Egyptians for jewelry of silver and gold, and for clothing, ³⁶ and the
LORD had given the people favor in the sight of the Egyptians, so that they
let them have what they asked. And so they plundered the Egyptians.**

As I indicated earlier, the ten plagues are preceded by a preliminary contest (*A*). Certain recurring patterns of details (such as the introductions to
the various plagues) indicate that the plagues occur in three groups of
three, followed by the climactic tenth. The letters *a*, *b*, and *c* indicate the
first, second, and third plague in a given group. The tenth plague is introduced in 11:1–10 and, after a shift in scene for the institution of the
Passover, takes place in 12:29–36. In the following outline, the bottom row
indicates verses that refer to Pharaoh's hard heart.

A	1a	2b	3c	4a	5b	6c	7a	8b	9c	10
7:8–13	7:14–25	8:1–15	8:16–19	8:20–32	9:1–7	9:8–12	9:13–35	10:1–20	10:21–29	11:1–10/12:29–36
v. 13	v. 22	v.15	v.19	v.32	v.7	v.12	vv. 34, 35	vv.1, 20	v.27	v.10

Let us begin by noting the pattern of development in some of the details of the plagues themselves. The first two plagues (*a* and *b*) in each
group show Moses confronting Pharaoh with "Thus says the LORD," introducing God's command to Pharaoh that he release the people "so that
they may worship me." This repetition of the "worship" theme sets the
stage for Pharaoh's final word in 12:31–32, "Go, worship the LORD." But
while the first and second plagues in each group have this command, in
each group the second plague (2, 5, 8) has Pharaoh "refusing" to let the
people go. In plagues two and five, it is simply "if you refuse" (8:2; 9:2); in
plague eight, it becomes "*How long* will you refuse?" (10:3). This shift to
"how long?" dovetails with another repeated detail that in plague eight
ends in "how long?" So let us back up and track that detail, which has to
do with Pharaoh's magicians and officials.

Moses and Aaron's staff-into-snake "wonder" is duplicated by the
Egyptian magicians (7:8–13). Likewise, they are able to duplicate the first
two plagues. But they cannot duplicate the third; when they cannot, they
confess to Pharaoh, "This is the finger of God!" (8:19). This confession
implies that they are beginning to see something that Pharaoh does not yet
see, which opens up a "distinction" between him and them. (One feature
of the plagues from here on is that they "distinguish" between Pharaoh's
side and God's side of the conflict.) This distinction appears again in
plague seven, between those Egyptians who begin to fear the word of the

LORD and those who do not pay any regard to it (9:20–21). It appears again in plague eight, where Pharaoh's officials say to him, "How long shall this fellow be a snare to us? Let the people go, that they may worship the LORD their God; do you not yet understand [Hebrew "know"] that Egypt is ruined?" (10:7). Their "how long?" echoing God's own "how long?" in this same plague (10:3) shows them (whether they know it or not) joining Moses and Aaron in speaking for God to Pharaoh. Like his daughter in chapter 2, they here become the servants not of Pharaoh but of Yahweh.

The most complex progression through the various plagues appears in Pharaoh's response. At first, his hard heart simply has him not listen (7:13; 7:22). With the second plague, he asks Moses and Aaron to pray for him and he will let the people go (8:8), but when the plague lifts he reneges. With the fourth plague, he for the first time commands, "Go!" limits them to sacrificing somewhere nearby, and again asks to be prayed for; then, when the plague lifts, he reneges. After the seventh plague, he for the first time acknowledges that he has sinned, that Yahweh is right and he has been wrong. Asking again for prayer, he promises to release the people. Yet again, when the plague lifts, he reneges. After the eighth plague, for the second time he commands the Israelites to "Go!" but limits this permission to the men. Again, he acknowledges that he has sinned and asks for prayer, this time adding the request that he be forgiven. Once again, when the plague lifts, he reneges. With the ninth plague, he for the third time says, "Go!" widening the permission only to the children so as to keep Israel's livestock. When Moses protests that they cannot worship God without livestock for sacrifice, Pharaoh again reneges and orders them out of his sight, saying, "on the day you see my face you shall die." To this, Moses replies, "Just as you say! I will never see your face again." The finality of this exchange underscores the sense we gain from the formal pattern (three groups of three plagues) that the conflict between God and Pharaoh is verging on its climax. With the tenth plague in the form of death-dealing darkness, Pharaoh is forced to eat his own words about it being death to see his face again. Summoning Moses and Aaron in the night, he capitulates totally: "Go, worship the LORD, *as you said*. Take your flocks and your herds, *as you said*, and be gone." (12:31–32). And in an acknowledgment of Yahweh, he adds the forlorn request, "bring a blessing on me too!" (12:32).

In 6:7, God had announced to Moses that the purpose of the exodus and of the covenanting at Mount Sinai was that the people would come to "know that I am the LORD." In 7:5, God had announced to Moses that the purpose of God's hardening Pharaoh's heart, so that God might multiply signs and wonders, was so that the Egyptians might "know that I am the

LORD." This theme runs through the plagues narrative. With the very first plague, God says, "By this you shall know that I am the LORD" (7:17). This is repeated with the second plague, where Moses assures Pharaoh that God will *lift* the plague at Moses' prayer "so that you may know that there is no one like the LORD our God" (8:10). With the fourth plague, God "separates" Israel from Egypt so that no flies will settle on their houses, "that you may know that I the LORD am in this land" (8:22). In this way the "separated" Israelites become part of the sign of God's presence and activity in Egypt. With the seventh plague, this theme is elaborated. God says not only "so that you may know that there is no one like me in all the earth" (9:14) but also

For by now I could have stretched out my hand and struck you and your people with pestilence, and you would have been cut off from the earth. But this is why I have let you live [literally, "enabled you to stand fast"]: to *show you my power*, and to *make my name resound through all the earth*. (9:15–16)

Here we meet again the theme initiated in 3:13–15 and restated in 6:3–8, that the name Yahweh stands for divine power sufficient to overcome the greatest political power in the world. If here the emphasis is on the fame of this name "through all the earth," in 9:29 it is "so that you may know that the earth is the LORD's." If in Genesis 1 the earth belongs to God by right of the act of creation, here it belongs to God by right of the act of redeeming its oppressed people.

In 10:2 the focus shifts from Egypt's knowing to Israel's. God says to Israel that God is making fools of the Egyptians so that Israel may "know that I am the LORD" and pass this knowledge on to their children and grandchildren. Then God says to Pharaoh, "How long will you refuse to humble yourself before me?" (10:3), and God's "how long?" is reiterated in the "how long?" of Pharaoh's own officials, as they marvel that he still does not "know" (so the Hebrew; NRSV "understand") that the land is ruined by his policies (10:7). Only with the death of all Egypt's firstborn (but not Israel's) in the dead of night will Pharaoh finally "know that the LORD makes a distinction between Israel and Egypt" (11:7).

This theme of knowing and not knowing brings us to the knottiest issue in the book of Exodus and perhaps in the whole Bible: the hardening of Pharaoh's heart. If we cannot untie this knot, let us at least trace a few of its strands in order to move a little way into its mystery. The first thing to note is that in Hebrew psychology the "heart" is not only (as in much of our popular speech) the location of feeling but more inclusively the location of the person's feeling, perception, understanding, and intention or will. One way of bringing our current views on these matters into some kind of connection with ancient views is to note how we are beginning to rediscover and speak about how our strong feelings can color and even determine not only how but what we perceive. Likewise, how we feel about things is significantly shaped by the nature and direction of our will and intentions. So the scientific enterprise, as an "objective" search for truth, proceeds by trying to set aside our own feelings, desires, and intentions for fear that they may distort our perception and lead to false "understandings." By contrast, a recent book explores what the author calls "feeling intelligence." By this the author means the kind of common sense and even wisdom of those who, while perhaps not scoring high on standard IQ tests, are "put together" on the feeling level. This deep anchorage in happily schooled feelings (often through early nurture in affectionate, reliable, loyal relationships) seems to provide a lens through which such a person is able to size up situations fairly. And it provides a context of moral freedom within which such a person is able to identify appropriate objectives and act to achieve them.

All of these internal dynamics that we distinguish by such terms as "feeling," "will" or "intention," and "knowing" or "understanding," the Hebrews (like others in their times) can refer to by the term *heart*. A person after God's own heart (1 Sam. 13:14), then, is one who perceives as God perceives, feels as God feels, knows as God knows, intends as God intends. In 1 Kings 3:9, the Hebrew text has Solomon the young king ask God for "a hearing heart" (NRSV: "an understanding mind"). Anyone who has slept with an ear open for a baby's hungry cry or responded spontaneously to any cry of distress knows what this means. (A useful way to remember this aspect of Hebrew psychology is to think of our word "heart" as containing at its core the word "ear.")

In respect to the perceiving, knowing, and acting heart, the book of Exodus presents a study in contrasts. It contrasts God's heart and Moses' heart with Pharaoh's heart in the face of the cry of the Israelites under their oppression. What God hears connects with what God remembers; hearing and memory bring into focus what God sees; hearing, memory, and seeing issue in what God knows (2:23–25); and all of this leads God to act, in coming down to Moses at the bush (3:7–10). Likewise, the call of Moses solicits his awareness of God and of God's concern for the Israelites, it encounters his initial resistance to that call, and it results finally in what we might call a "change of heart" in Moses' acceptance of God's call. Pharaoh does not even hear that cry. For his heart, as a perceptual organ, is already shaped by a "wisdom" that sees the Israelites only as a threat. Their numbers evoke in him the response of fear and stir him to action aimed to enhance national security (1:8–10). Thus feeling and intention shape his understanding. It is no wonder that when Moses and Aaron address him in God's name, he responds by saying, "Who is the LORD [Yahweh], that I should hear [so the Hebrew] his voice and let the people go? I do not know the LORD [Yahweh]" (Exod. 5:2). Pharaoh's heart is so shaped by long-standing perception, understanding, and intention (what we may call his mind-set) that he cannot hear and know Yahweh. Therefore, he cannot truly read the situation in which he now finds himself. The contest between Yahweh and Pharaoh plays itself out most visibly on the public stage, where everyone can see the plagues and see or hear about Pharaoh's decisions and actions in interaction with Moses and Aaron. But it is on the hidden level of Pharaoh's heart that the ultimate battle is waged.

Before commenting further on these issues, it is helpful simply to notice certain patterns by which the plagues narrative develops the theme of the hardening of Pharaoh's heart. To identify these patterns, keep in mind how different forms of verbs characterize actions or processes. A brief review of relevant grammar will help to clarify this. When we say that a verb is in the *active* voice, we mean that the grammatical subject of the verb is the doer of the action. The subject of the verb acts on the direct object of the verb. (Mary *gave birth* to Jesus.) When we say that a verb is in the *passive* voice, we mean that the grammatical subject of the verb is the recipient or result of the action. (Jesus *was birthed* by Mary.) The difference between the active and passive voices lies in the direction in which each throws the focus of the reader's attention: The active voice focuses attention on the doer of the action; the passive voice focuses attention on the one who receives or undergoes the action. In addition, there is a kind of verb that describes a process or a state without indicating its cause. Thus, to say, "Jim's face *became* beet red" or "Boy, *was* my face red!" is to describe a process or a state without identifying the cause of that process or state.

In the material that follows concerning the hardening of Pharaoh's heart, I present all the texts in the book of Exodus, including the passages before 7:8 and after 12:36. Though all the verbs can be translated "harden," as English translations customarily do, I try to convey the variety of verbs and verb forms that actually occur in the Hebrew text. Correspondingly, I suggest the specific nuance of the Hebrew word *heart* by translating it in a variety of ways. Further, each occurrence is coded with the following symbols: *O* identifies a verb that says Pharaoh's heart becomes or remains hard, where there is no indication of whose activity caused it to be or remain hard; *P* identifies a verb that says Pharaoh hardened his own heart; and *Y* identifies a verb that says Yahweh hardened Pharaoh's heart.

	4:21	Y	"I will strengthen Pharaoh's resolve"
	7:3	Y	"I will intensify Pharaoh's feelings"
	7:13	O	Pharaoh's resolve grew strong
	7:14	O	"Pharaoh's heart is hard"
1(a)	7:22	O	Pharaoh's resolve remained strong
2(b)	8:15	P	Pharaoh hardened his heart
3(c)	8:19	O	Pharaoh's resolve remained strong
4(a)	8:32	P	Pharaoh hardened his heart
5(b)	9:7	O	Pharaoh's heart remained hard
6(c)	9:12	Y	Yahweh strengthened Pharaoh's resolve
7(a)	9:34	P	Pharaoh sinned yet again and hardened his heart
7(a)	9:35	O	So Pharaoh's resolve remained strong
8(b)	10:1	Y	"I have hardened Pharaoh's heart"
8(b)	10:20	Y	Yahweh strengthened Pharaoh's resolve
9(c)	10:27	Y	Yahweh strengthened Pharaoh's resolve
10	11:10	Y	Yahweh strengthened Pharaoh's resolve
	14:4	Y	"I will strengthen Pharaoh's resolve"
	[14:5	?	Pharaoh . . . had a change of heart toward the people]
	14:8	Y	Yahweh strengthened Pharaoh's resolve
	14:17	Y	"I will strengthen their resolve"

Notice first that, inside the plague narrative of 7:8–12:36, the succession of verbs for hardening displays a discernible pattern: In the preliminary engagement (7:13, 14) and in the first plague (7:22), the narrator simply notes that Pharaoh's heart (or resolve) grew or remained strong or hard. The cause is not indicated. In plagues two and four, the narrator indicates that Pharaoh hardened his heart (8:15, 32), and in each following instance (plagues three and five) the narrator notes simply that his resolve remained strong or his heart remained hard (8:19; 9:7). So far, there is no hint that the state of Pharaoh's heart is attributable to anything except his own mind-set and his own capacity for reaffirming or changing his mind in the face of changing circumstances. Of course, one may appeal to God's two statements to Moses in 4:21 and 7:3 and explain matters on that basis.

But I suggest that for now we bracket those two passages and stay within the plagues narrative. It will be helpful at this point to reflect on the dynamics of human feeling, attitude, understanding, and intention, in ourselves and in those around us.

Especially since the French Revolution, with its battle cry, "liberty, equality, fraternity," personal freedom has become an all-consuming passion and a defining term for what it means to be a human being. Yet, as the philosopher Alfred North Whitehead has said, we are never very free. We live within the constraints of our genetic heritage, our biological rhythms and needs, our social values and customs, our personal habits, and the "mind-set" associated with all of these. On any given day, our feelings, thoughts, intentions, words, and actions function largely in a routine and predictable way.

This situation is not at all a bad thing. It is the basis for the possibility of the development of a skill and the formation of dependable character. As I write this, I am listening to a recording of Glenn Gould performing J. S. Bach's *Goldberg Variations*. Why does this music so lift and at the same time quiet my spirit? Is it because somehow Bach has captured within the terms of Western music (the tonic sol-fa system, key signatures, rules of counterpoint, and so on) that elusive thing compounded of grace, beauty, and freedom? Is it not also because in this music I hear a performer in near-perfect command of his instrument? Yet how many hours has Gould practiced so that he does not need to make a decision of absolute freedom each time he wishes to press a key? The grace of his music is a mysterious combination of skilled habit and freedom. One measure of the freedom is that even though this was his first major recording at the beginning of his career, he recorded this piece several more times, each one distinctive in its own way. Here habit and convention adding up to skill did not stifle freedom and novelty but laid the basis for them.

It is the same with any skill. But sometimes habits of body and mind can blind us to what is new in new situations or to what might become new in ourselves in response to new situations. In that case, what was a positive asset can become a negative liability. In the biblical understanding, God is creator of the world both as providing and undergirding the laws, conventions, and habits by which life is sustained and may flourish, and as providing the elbow room or freedom by which life may develop in new ways. ("Where the Spirit of the Lord is, there is freedom" [2 Cor. 3:17]). But in that freedom or elbow room, we may act and develop in ways that are not in accordance with God's intention or persist in once-useful habits and patterns of activity that we are now called to move beyond. The mystery of God's providence includes God's provision of room for us to assume responsibility for our own actions. The irony is that, apart from God (that is, when God simply stands back and leaves us to ourselves), our own actions may lay down a pattern of behavior that can become a straitjacket, confining and constraining us in subsequent occasions.

In the passages we have considered so far (7:13 through 9:7), all we need "read into" the narrative is the supposition that Pharaoh responded to Moses and Aaron's various actions from within the mind-set that he had long since acquired from his royal predecessors and his own style of rule. That the Hebrew verb for "grow strong" or "strengthen" can refer to one's morale and resolve is illustrated by the pair of idioms in Job 4:3–4, "you have strengthened the weak hands. . . . you have made firm the feeble knees." That the Hebrew verb for "harden" indicates one's becoming insensitive or dull of perception is illustrated in Isaiah 6:10, where God's words through the prophet will "make the mind [Hebrew "heart"] of this people dull, and stop [that is, "harden"] their ears, and shut their eyes." Pharaoh's initial resolve to stay with his policies (7:13, 22) leads him to "turn off his hearing aid," so to speak (8:15, 32). This enables him to remain resolved (8:19) but also renders him less sensible of what is being said to him (9:7). To this point, I suggest, God has simply left Pharaoh to his own so-called freedom, that is, to such freedom as his mind-set affords him. With the sixth plague, the narrator tells us that God steps in to strengthen Pharaoh's resolve (9:12). How may we understand this?

The English philosopher George Berkeley coined a famous saying that captures what we all may test by reflecting on our own experience. He said, *esse est percipi*, "to be is to be perceived." Students and researchers of human development tell us that infants gain their first sense of themselves in significant measure through their dawning awareness of how their primary caregivers view them. Nursing infants who gaze up at their mothers' smiling faces from within their mothers' warm embraces gain a fundamental sense of themselves as loved beings. The struggling pupil who enjoys a teacher's reassuring and encouraging "You can do it! Let's try it again, a little slower this time" will come to a different sense of self than the pupil who labors under a teacher's unfeeling criticism and ridicule. We can be reinforced in our settled views (for good or ill) by others who see us as we see ourselves, or encouraged to move to new views (for good or ill) by others who see us in ways that lead us beyond our present selves. As I have tried to suggest, it is from Yahweh, the fountain of all freedom and, at the same time, of all faithful continuity with the past (3:13–15), that Moses discovers the capacity to become something he had not been before, and thereby, the capacity to recover his ancestral heritage and identity as a descendant of Abraham and Sarah.

When God confronts Pharaoh through Moses and Aaron with the command to "let my people go," this word presents Pharaoh with the opportunity to move beyond his own settled mind-set and to adopt a new policy. But he will not "listen" (or "hear"), for he does not know Yahweh. God's repeated offer of such a new opening is met only with Pharaoh's entrenched resolve to "stand firm." Now, with the sixth plague, God actively strengthens Pharaoh's resolve. How does God do that? Does God interfere in Pharaoh's deepest and most private interior self? No, just the opposite. All God has to do to strengthen Pharaoh's resolve is to accept Pharaoh's intentions at face value and mirror them back to Pharaoh—to see Pharaoh as he sees himself. If Pharaoh now has even less elbow room to change than before, this is only because Yahweh ceases to view Pharaoh as possibly changing and views Pharaoh as he views himself.

With the seventh plague, the narrator again shows us Pharaoh hardening his own heart, so that his resolve remains strong (9:34–35). This suggests that, while God's action in 9:12 decreases Pharaoh's inner freedom to imagine and enact a new response, his response in 9:34–35, insofar as it is shaped by his own previous actions and settled character, remains his own responsibility. But the last three plagues show a Pharaoh who is acting under God's now consistent action of hardening his heart and strengthening his resolve (10:1, 20, 27; 11:10). In a nutshell, "would not change" becomes "could not change." As the Bible puts it elsewhere (Psalm 81:12; Rom. 1:24, 26, 28), God simply "hands Pharaoh over" to his own mind-set and the acts it moves him to.

Interestingly, now, when Pharaoh finally capitulates and grants all Moses' demands, God does not at this point "strengthen his resolve," even though he ends by asking a blessing on himself for his conformity to God's word (12:31–32). The only "strengthening" that occurs is when "The Egyptians urged ["strongly encouraged"] the people to hasten their departure from the land" (12:33). Is it because God sees Pharaoh's capitulation to be only momentary, under the extremity of the tenth plague, to be soon followed by a "change of heart" (14:5)?

But wouldn't God's reinforcement of Pharaoh's penitent resolve forestall that change of heart? I shall come back to this question in a moment. First, I note that the idiom in 14:5 that NRSV translates "their minds were changed " and KJV translates "their heart was turned" occurs in Hosea 11:8 (NRSV, "my heart recoils within me"; KJV, "my heart is turned within me"), where it shows God having a change of heart in favor of compassion rather than judgment on sinful Israel. Is Pharaoh's change of heart a free act? Or is it an act that is in bondage to a mind-set for which he is responsible because of his earlier decisions but that now holds him in its grip?

But why does God reinforce only Pharaoh's negative actions? Why not reinforce his momentary, partial turns in a positive direction, in plagues two, four, seven, eight, and nine, and his complete positive turn in plague ten? The short biblical answer is that by this means God will make a spectacle of Pharaoh and his supposed sovereignty (10:1–2) and at the same time give a demonstration of who is finally sovereign in the affairs of the world (8:10; 9:15–16; 14:17). Yet this does not reduce us to puppets on a string; all it does is remind us that we are not God. The first mentions of the hardening theme in Exodus, in 4:21 and 7:3, need not, then, mean that Pharaoh is totally without freedom and responsibility for his actions. All we need suppose, in these two early passages, is that God knows Pharaoh's character well enough from his past royal actions to know how Pharaoh will use his freedom.

If, as Whitehead says, "we are never very free," we do usually have a margin of freedom within which we can reflect on our situation, with all its constraints, and respond to it in ways that promise to make our continued life possible and perhaps even better. But from time to time we wonder whether we have enough freedom to enable us to get out of the dead-end streets our exercise of freedom has gotten us into. If human freedom arises in what we call our will and finds its direction in what we call our imagination, the question is, Do we have the imagination to modify a social arrangement or course of action that our imagination once devised for what seemed good reasons but that now threatens to become a straitjacket on ourselves or others? In the biblical view, such freedom, such imagination, is the gift of God who, according to the word at the burning bush, is most deeply named in the words, "I will be who I will be." As I suggested earlier, such a name implies at least this much: However much we have known God in terms of our past typical experiences, needs, practices, and patterns of life, God is not limited to this past but remains free to respond to whatever new circumstances may arise in God's creation.

To say, then, that we are never *very* free, and that the freedom we enjoy comes by the gift of God whom we are created by and called to image, is to say that we are not God. Yet the temptation is to think that we are God. Rarely do we make that claim outright. But our claim for absolute freedom, uncurbed by any constraints, implies a self-idolatry that asserts, "I will be who I will be." We see this expressly in the time of Israel's exile under the yoke of Babylon, when Babylon is portrayed as saying, "I am, and there is no one besides me" (Isa. 47:8, 10). This is a claim that rightfully belongs only to the LORD (Isa. 43:10–11; 44:6–8; 45:5, 14, 21). Where human freedom takes such unbridled forms, the lesson of Pharaoh is that God judges it by "handing it over" to its own consequences. Such divine judgment comes only after Egypt has had ample opportunity to hear the cry of the Israelites in their suffering (Exod. 2:23–25) and to learn from the earlier plagues. Indeed, as we have observed, some in Egypt do wake up to what is demanded of them. But they are not in position to make a critical difference, and Pharaoh remains in control until he comes completely under the control of his own mind-set. If judgment is never the last word, that is because God remains free (as in Hos. 11:8 and 14:4) to enact a change of heart and lift the divine judgment. That such a divine change of heart may save us in ways known only to God—but may not involve a change in our historical fortunes—is the sobering lesson of Pharaoh, as well as of Israel in the time of Jeremiah, an Israel that fell before the might of Babylonia and went into exile.

THE FIRST PASSOVER
Exodus 12:1–28

12:1 The LORD said to Moses and Aaron in the land of Egypt: 2 This month shall mark for you the beginning of months; it shall be the first month of the year for you. 3 Tell the whole congregation of Israel that on the tenth of this month they are to take a lamb for each family, a lamb for each household. 4 If a household is too small for a whole lamb, it shall join its closest neighbor in obtaining one; the lamb shall be divided in proportion to the number of people who eat of it. 5 Your lamb shall be without blemish, a year-old male; you may take it from the sheep or from the goats. 6 You shall keep it until the fourteenth day of this month; then the whole assembled congregation of Israel shall slaughter it at twilight. 7 They shall take some of the blood and put it on the two doorposts and the lintel of the houses in which they eat it. 8 They shall eat the lamb that same night; they shall eat it roasted over the fire with unleavened bread and bitter herbs. 9 Do not eat any of it raw or boiled in water, but roasted over the fire, with its head, legs, and inner organs. 10 You shall let none of it remain until the morning; anything that remains until the morning you shall burn. 11 This is how you shall eat it: your loins girded, your sandals on your feet, and your staff in your hand; and you shall eat it hurriedly. It is the passover of the LORD. 12 For I will pass through the land of Egypt that night, and I will strike down every firstborn in the land of Egypt, both human beings and animals; on all the gods of Egypt I will execute judgments: I am the LORD. 13 The blood shall be a sign for you on the houses where you live: when I see the blood, I will pass over you, and no plague shall destroy you when I strike the land of Egypt.

[14] This day shall be a day of remembrance for you. You shall celebrate it as a festival to the LORD; throughout your generations you shall observe it as a perpetual ordinance. [15] Seven days you shall eat unleavened bread; on the first day you shall remove leaven from your houses, for whoever eats leavened bread from the first day until the seventh day shall be cut off from Israel. [16] On the first day you shall hold a solemn assembly, and on the seventh day a solemn assembly; no work shall be done on those days; only what everyone must eat, that alone may be prepared by you. [17] You shall observe the festival of unleavened bread, for on this very day I brought your companies out of the land of Egypt: you shall observe this day throughout your generations as a perpetual ordinance. [18] In the first month, from the evening of the fourteenth day until the evening of the twenty-first day, you shall eat unleavened bread. [19] For seven days no leaven shall be found in your houses; for whoever eats what is leavened shall be cut off from the congregation of Israel, whether an alien or a native of the land. [20] You shall eat nothing leavened; in all your settlements you shall eat unleavened bread.

[21] Then Moses called all the elders of Israel and said to them, "Go, select lambs for your families, and slaughter the passover lamb. [22] Take a bunch of hyssop, dip it in the blood that is in the basin, and touch the lintel and the two doorposts with the blood in the basin. None of you shall go outside the door of your house until morning. [23] For the LORD will pass through to strike down the Egyptians; when he sees the blood on the lintel and on the two doorposts, the LORD will pass over that door and will not allow the destroyer to enter your houses to strike you down. [24] You shall observe this rite as a perpetual ordinance for you and your children. [25] When you come to the land that the LORD will give you, as he has promised, you shall keep this observance. [26] And when your children ask you, 'What do you mean by this observance?' [27] you shall say, 'It is the passover sacrifice to the LORD, for he passed over the houses of the Israelites in Egypt, when he struck down the Egyptians but spared our houses.'" And the people bowed down and worshiped.

[28] The Israelites went and did just as the LORD had commanded Moses and Aaron.

The Passover, like the Lord's Supper, is a sacred meal. As a *meal*, it celebrates God's provision for the basic human need for nourishment and sustenance. As a *sacred* meal, the Passover, like the Lord's Supper, is inaugurated in the context of events through which God makes another basic provision: for safety and protection. If the Lord's Supper is inaugurated in the shadow of Jesus' crucifixion and resurrection—events through which God acts to save us from all that threatens our lives—the Passover is inaugurated in the shadow of God's triumph over "the gods of Egypt" (12:12), whose human servant, Pharaoh, threatens the Israelites. Thus, to eat this meal inside a home whose doorway is protected by the lamb's blood on the lintel is to be surrounded by God's protection and filled with God's nourishment.

Such provision for our needs, in the face of all that would threaten us, makes it understandable that, from now on in Israel, the month when Passover is celebrated is the first month of the year. What might this mean for those who celebrate Passover?

When Pharaoh is in charge of time, one's days become an endless repetition of wearisome toil that in time may seem to have been going on forever. Past and future are just limitless extensions of an intolerable present. Such a present spreads itself into the past and the future, with the result that memory and hope are turned into a growing mountain of pain and a lengthening shadow of despair. Passover celebrates Israel's experience of God's redemption, which turns the past into a fountain of celebration to which one can return annually in remembrance (12:14) and turns the future into an open prospect that one can anticipate in hope. Thus, by marking the redemption of the Israelites' experience of time, the Passover becomes "the beginning of months."

The fact that Jews and Christians observe religious calendars that differ from the secular calendar should be a sign that Jews and Christians, each in their own way, testify to a redemptive activity of God that has changed our ongoing experience of time. The fact that Jews and Christians observe different religious calendars is a sobering reminder of the differences in our experience and celebration of God's redemption to date. Yet the way that the New Testament associates the inauguration of the Lord's Supper with the Passover and the way that Jewish celebrations of Passover and Christian celebrations of Holy Week overlap on the calendar can become a source of hope that in time we may come together in our experience and understanding of time as shaped by God's redemptive activity.

If now Passover, as the beginning month, marks a new sense of time, it also marks a new sense of social relationships. Prior to the Passover and the exodus it celebrates, the Israelites are presented in familial terms, as descendants of "Abraham, Isaac, and Jacob" (2:24; 3:6, 15, 16; 4:5). As such, they understand God in terms of "family and clan religion." In the exodus, God acts in a new way, delivering these people by triumphing over Pharaoh and the gods of Egypt. Through this deliverance the people, while still knowing themselves as descendants of these ancestors, come to a new self-understanding: They become a "congregation." (The word occurs in the Bible first in 12:3.) In Genesis 17, circumcision is presented as the mark of those who may count themselves children of Abraham. Now, those who participate in the Passover feast make up this new social reality called a congregation. Each family eats the Passover in its own home, and what is eaten is a lamb, the central means of livelihood and source of food in ancestral times. Yet each family knows itself to be connected with all other families who eat the Passover, as making up one united congregation. In this way the Israelites become a "new people" while remaining deeply rooted in their social and religious past.

It is common to compare Old Testament and Jewish circumcision and Passover to Christian Baptism and the Lord's Supper. For Christians, these latter two rituals mark all those who make up the "new people" whom God has brought into being through the redemptive death and resurrection of Jesus Christ. For a long time, Christians have viewed these two sets of rituals as, so to speak, "parallel but separate." Perhaps if Christians reflect on how the exodus and the Passover bring about a new reality (the congregation) that yet remains deeply rooted and still connected with its past (ancestral religion), we may reflect more sensitively and more adequately on how the events of Holy Week and the rituals of Baptism and the Lord's Supper bring about a new reality (the church of Jesus Christ) that yet is called to remain deeply rooted and still connected with its past (Mosaic religion/Judaism). We may be more open to new ways of appreciating what God may be doing each year as Passover and Maundy Thursday occur in such close calendar connection.

In Genesis 17, God tells Abraham that circumcision will be a sign of the covenant between his descendants and God (17:11). But these descendants, as identified by circumcision, can include not only his own children but also his slaves, whether born in his household or bought with money (17:13). However, any one of these male children who remains uncircumcised "shall be cut off from his people." In other words, circumcision may celebrate God's free grace in calling Abraham and promising him many descendants with a land to live in, but circumcision also involves an element of voluntary response on the part of those who are or are not circumcised. Similarly, in the Passover there is a sign. It is the blood of the Passover lamb on the doorposts and the lintel (12:7, 13). It is "a sign for you," in the sense that God places in their hands a sign they are to use to signify their identity as members of the congregation. When God sees the sign, God will spare them from the judgment that is to fall on Egypt. A family is not persuading God of anything by this sign; rather, by this sign the family signifies its desire to be included within the circle of those God is acting to redeem from the power of Egypt.

The connections between these rituals in the Old Testament and Baptism and the Lord's Supper in the New Testament are complex and important. It would be too simple to say that what the one means the other means. There are striking differences. For example, the act of placing the blood on the lintel signals a family's desire to be included within that congregation that is spared God's death-dealing judgment on the firstborn sons of the Egyptians. But the act of participating in the Lord's Supper signals a Christian's desire to be included within a congregation for whom Jesus Christ, as God's "only son," died "for our salvation." And Baptism, as the rite of initiation into this congregation, signals the baptized person as dying and rising with Christ (Romans 6). Yet such differences are to be seen within the embracing context of God's ongoing work of redeeming the whole world, so that they should not become the basis for final divisions between Christians and Jews.

As part of the Passover observance, God now gives instructions for a seven-day festival of unleavened bread. If the Passover centers in a lamb, a product of the flock, this festival centers in flour and absence of yeast, products of the field. These two observances have their roots in religious festivals much older than the Hebrews. Such earlier festivals would have had their meaning in relation to general basic human needs and concerns. Just as Baptism is a specific form of general rituals of washing, and just as the Lord's Supper is a specific form of general rituals of eating, so Passover and unleavened bread are specific forms of general rituals celebrating the fruitfulness of flock and field. But just as Baptism and the Lord's Supper take on distinctive meanings that washing and eating do not have elsewhere, meanings connected with the death and resurrection of Jesus, so Passover and unleavened bread take on a distinctive meaning through their association with the exodus from Egypt.

What does it mean when members of the congregation for seven days following Passover eat bread made without yeast? According to 12:34, this observance memorializes the way in which Israel had to flee Egypt quickly (compare 12:11), before they had time to put yeast in their bread dough. What might this mean in the lives of later generations who eat unleavened bread? For one thing, it signifies that God's deliverance, which sometimes seems as though it will never come, can then come so quickly that there is no time to prepare for it. One just picks up what one has at hand and moves forward in haste.

Since the time of Paul, however (who would have celebrated many Passovers and many festivals of unleavened bread as a Pharisaic Jew before his encounter with the risen Christ), unleavened bread has taken on a new meaning. That meaning rests on what yeast is. Most simply, biblical yeast (properly, "leaven") is old, fermented dough, which, when a bit of it is mixed in with new ingredients, helps the new dough to rise and bake to a tasty lightness. Thus the new depends for its character in part on a "seed" element from the old. Throughout this book I have emphasized how the newness of the exodus does not simply render the old religion of the ancestors obsolete but also is based on it and in crucial ways carries it forward. Later, when we get to chapters 32—34, I will show how, without this continuing basis in the ancestral faith, the religion of the exodus and the Mount Sinai covenant would have come to grief before it really got off the ground.

Now the festival of unleavened bread makes just the opposite point: There are respects in which the new can become the new only if it brings forward no element of yeast from the old. Paul applies this analogy to such matters as "malice and evil" (1 Cor. 5:6–8), as a sort of yeast carried forward from old jealousies and animosities to contaminate new communications. The fact that Christ has been sacrificed as our Passover lamb should move us to deal with one another with the "unleavened bread" of sincerity and truth. Studies in human development and in the way societies reproduce themselves remind us how very difficult it is to get rid of old habits and patterns. Especially when we have lived for some time in our own version of "Egypt"—a social or political situation that has oppressed us and moved us to cry out for liberation—the danger is that in leaving Egypt we take with us the old yeast that will simply give rise to the same old habits and patterns. It is with a certain foreboding, therefore, that we should notice what is said in Exodus 12:33–36: While the people took with them only unleavened bread, leaving behind any leaven, they also took with them the silver, gold, and clothing they had been instructed to ask from the Egyptians. As we shall see later, their use of that silver and gold shows that the mind-set they brought from Egypt carried a sort of leaven hidden well within it.

In 12:1–20, God gives Moses the instructions for observing Passover and unleavened bread. In 12:21–27, Moses is shown passing these instructions on to the people, and the narrator says that "the people bowed down and worshiped." We first saw them do this in 4:31 after Moses and Aaron brought them the word of deliverance that God had given them at the bush. After that first act of belief and worship, their increased suffering under Pharaoh's increased demands (chapter 5) led them to greet Moses' further encouragement with disbelief and despair (6:9). That the people recover their initial response and greet the passover with worship is no doubt because of the signs given them in the plague. Thus we see in the exodus story the inner struggle between despair and hope expressed by the man who said to Jesus, "I believe; help my unbelief" (Mark 9:24). It is as though the hard sufferings in life can leave a residue of old yeast to contaminate our response to the message of hope. In the present instance, the Israelites are enabled by Moses' words to "cast out this old leaven" and meet his message with belief. So, the narrator says, "The Israelites went and did just as the LORD had commanded Moses and Aaron" (12:28).

At this point we may note in particular how God's instructions to Moses (12:1–20) are (with some differences) presented again in the text in the form of Moses' words to the people (12:21–27) and how it is then underscored (12:28, 50) that the people do as the LORD commanded Moses and Aaron. There is a narrative pattern here that we first see in Genesis 1 and then recognize again in such passages as Genesis 17 and, most prominently, Exodus 25—31 and 35—40. In Genesis 1, the pattern consists in God giving a command ("let there be . . .") and then going ahead and making what God had spoken of. In Genesis 17, the pattern consists in God giving Abraham detailed instructions and then Abraham carrying them out "as God had said to him" (17:23). In Exodus 25—31, God gives Moses exhaustively detailed instructions for building a sanctuary, and in Exodus 35—40 Moses is shown (with some differences) scrupulously carrying out those instructions. The pattern in these and other biblical manifestations is divine initiative through the spoken word and human response conforming to that word. That response takes the form of human ritual action or the shaping of human space. As we shall see, in the instance of Exodus 25—31 and 35—40 the space that is shaped according to God's instructions becomes a place where God can dwell in the people's midst (25:8). In these human actions and the space they shape, we can say that the Word of God is (already) becoming incarnate in Israel (compare John 1:14).

Moses' words to the people in 12:21–27 contain one item we must not pass over without comment. He says to them (12:25–27), "When you come to the land that the LORD will give you, as he has promised, you shall keep this observance. And when your children ask you, 'What do you mean by this observance?' you shall say, 'It is the passover sacrifice to the LORD, for he passed over the houses of the Israelites in Egypt, when he struck down the Egyptians but spared our houses.'"

(If the Passover, in the "beginning of months," marks God's redemption of time, its occurrence behind closed doors marked with blood on the lintel celebrates God's redemption of space. In a time of famine, Israel's ancestors enjoyed Egypt's hospitality and a space to become fruitful

[Gen. 47:27; Exod. 1:7]. Under a new king who knows not Joseph, Egypt becomes a place of oppression and death, so God promises to bring Israel into "a land flowing with milk and honey" [Exod. 3:8] where they will be safe from their enemies. In the Passover, while they are still in hostile Egypt, the safety of their own homes becomes a redeemed "home away from home.")

The scene, as we have observed, is the Israelite family celebrating Passover inside its own home. They are not in a sanctuary but within the home where the children have had their earliest experiences of parental nurture and care, including regular meals, solace when hurt, and protection from outside threats. Before they have come to the age of discretion or (at the very first) even of language, these children will have begun to absorb the annually repeated rhythms and images of Passover and unleavened bread, images textured and enlivened by distinctive sounds, smells, sights, tastes, and the feel of special festal vessels. With these images, they will have imbibed the atmosphere of special joy created by the adults in their family. Thus experience precedes knowledge.

Then they begin to wonder why such things are done and ask, not "why do *we* do this?" but "why do *you* do this?" It is as though they are enveloped in something they have not yet made their own—like the child Samuel dwelling within God's house when as yet he did not know the LORD (1 Samuel 3). The adult response ends, "he struck down the Egyptians but spared our houses." How will children hear the "our," followed by the word "houses"? Will they get a picture of that first exodus night as including ignorant, bewildered, questioning little children who are spared, along with knowledgeable adults who seem to know what is going on? Will children get a sense from "our houses" that, by being in the family home, they are wrapped in God's mercy along with those who seem to know what this observance means? And does the parental "our" implicitly invite a child's "you" to become a "we"?

In reflecting on 12:13, I suggested that the placing of the blood on the lintel was a way of signaling God that a family placed itself under the umbrella of God's saving intention. If 12:26–27 shows children coming to the point of "buying into" that umbrella for themselves, then we may have here a fine example of what I would call God's "preferential option" for our "yes" response to the divine goodness. There are those, of course, who do not hear of the God of the exodus, the God of Good Friday and Easter, until they have become adults. But, like the Israelite children of 12:26–27, many children have imbibed the ethos of Christian faith long before they could reflect on it and make what adults presume to call a reasoned response. Does this experience stack the deck in favor of a positive response to God?

Yes, it does, because God has a preferential option for life and against death. The Moses who says to Israel in Deuteronomy 30:19, "I have set before you life and death. . . . Choose life so that you and your descendants may live," has already instructed Israel to teach its children from an early age both the story of the exodus and the covenant laws of Mount Sinai (Deut. 6:4–9, 20–25). As Ezekiel will report God to say, "Have I any pleasure in the death of the wicked . . . ?" (Ezek. 18:23). Therefore, God provides in Israel, both through the everyday nurture and safety of the home and through the festivals that are rooted in the home and that extend to the sanctuary, a conditioning that will predispose growing children to say "Yes" and appropriate for themselves what at first they see as belonging to the world of their parents.

FUTURE PASSOVERS
Exodus 12:43–49

> 12:43 **The LORD said to Moses and Aaron: This is the ordinance for the passover: no foreigner shall eat of it, 44 but any slave who has been purchased may eat of it after he has been circumcised; 45 no bound or hired servant may eat of it. 46 It shall be eaten in one house; you shall not take any of the animal outside the house, and you shall not break any of its bones. 47 The whole congregation of Israel shall celebrate it. 48 If an alien who resides with you wants to celebrate the passover to the LORD, all his males shall be circumcised; then he may draw near to celebrate it; he shall be regarded as a native of the land. But no uncircumcised person shall eat of it; 49 there shall be one law for the native and for the alien who resides among you.**

The chapter opened by introducing the term *congregation*, signaling that the Passover celebration identifies the descendants of Abraham and Sarah as a new kind of community. It concludes by returning to two questions: How is the Passover to be eaten? Who is and is not included in this congregation?

First, the Passover is to be eaten within the household unit. All who make up the household share in it, and the lamb is not to be taken outside that sphere. However, all the households who observe the Passover are included in one congregation. In this way, something of the social and religious ethos of the old "family and clan" religion of ancestral times is continued, while the emergence of a new social and religious reality is affirmed: a community ranging as widely as the individual households that make it up. In Christian experience, every time an individual congregation celebrates the Lord's Supper, that observance identifies that congregation as a household gathered around one table under one roof and, at the same time, identifies it as a living member of the one church of Jesus Christ spread around the globe.

Second, the fundamental mark of inclusion in this congregation is circumcision. As Genesis 17 shows, one does not have to be a physical descendant of Abraham and Sarah to be circumcised. Any slaves born in the house or bought from foreigners are to be circumcised (Gen. 17:12, 23, 26–27) and, as such, are household members. Now the matter is spelled out more fully. In addition to those already mentioned, resident aliens who wish may also be circumcised and so included. But hired servants and those temporarily bound to a household are foreigners and may not share in the Passover meal.

The Passover congregation thus includes two of the three pairs of human groups Paul refers to in Galatians 3:28: There are males and females; there are slaves and slave owners. However, the congregation does not include foreigners. Like Paul, most of the early followers of Jesus were Jews; many, like him, had formerly been strict observers of the covenant requirements of circumcision and the kosher food laws. But one result of becoming disciples (Paul liked to say, "slaves") of Jesus as Messiah was their conviction that circumcision and the kosher food laws no longer should distinguish between those inside and those outside the covenant. From now on, in Paul's view, all who believe in Jesus are to be one, whether they are circumcised or not, and whether they personally keep kosher or not. For Paul, those who through faith belong to the community of Jesus Christ become a "new creation" (Gal. 6:15; 2 Cor. 5:16–17). This new community is to embrace Jew and Greek, slave and free, male and female (Gal. 3:28). Both the echo and the revision of Exodus 12:43–49 are unmistakable. What we should notice is Paul's conclusion: To enter into this new community is to become "Abraham's offspring, heirs according to the promise" (Gal. 3:29). But to become Abraham's offspring is to take on the vocation of becoming a means by which all the families of the earth shall be blessed and shall bless themselves (Gen. 12:3, NRSV text and margin).

If Paul and the early church revised the terms of inclusion and yet developed their own marks of inclusion (Baptism and the Lord's Supper), how does the church distinguish itself from those not in it, in such a way that it is a means of their blessing and not simply one more divisive agency in a divided world? The question is more easily asked than answered. Perhaps the first step toward answering it is for the question itself to become a burning issue for us.

One further matter invites discussion. The Passover celebrates God's liberation of Hebrew slaves from "the house of slavery" (Exod. 20:2). Yet, according to the Passover ordinance, Israelites may still own slaves. Is there not a contradiction between what is being celebrated and the master-slave distinctions between those celebrating it? At the very least, there is a tension here waiting to emerge into the consciousness of those who perhaps for years or even generations are oblivious to it. One thing is clear: According to covenant law, the experience of liberation from Egypt's "house of slavery" was to make a difference in how Israelites treated slaves and aliens (Exod. 22:21; 23:9; Deut. 15:12–18; 24:17–22). In our times, when outright human ownership of human beings has been abolished, Passover as a so-called festival of redemption may seem to have unfortunately and harmfully reinforced one of the very institutions it should have served to overturn. One may ask whether the "ordinance of the Passover" contains within it some of the very leaven that should have been left in Egypt.

That may be so. Yet, imagine a household within the congregation of Israel, year after year celebrating Passover. Every circumcised male, whether master, slave, or resident alien, and every wife and female child of such a person, may eat of the one lamb. What if, on a given Passover night, while the exodus story is being narrated with its language about slavery, harsh service, and oppressive overlordship, slave and household head look up, meet each other's gaze, and a slight shock of awareness passes between them? Might they share recognition of the discrepancy between the story they share in celebrating and the household status that separates them? Might there be defensive guilt on the one hand and mutinous resentment on the other? Perhaps. Would there be mutual agreement to dissolve the slave-owner relation? Perhaps. And perhaps, in some instances, there would be a "leavening" of their relationship by the new yeast of the Passover story, so that even while the institution of slavery remains in place, it becomes transformed in its practice. This much is clear: Both within Israel itself and later among the early Christians in the Roman Empire, the possibility emerged of a unity of spirit that joined people otherwise distinguished by the boundaries of Jew-Gentile, slave-free, and male-female (for example, Gal. 3:28). If that spirit eventually has provided impetus for the abolition of the institution of literal slavery, synagogue, church, and society continue to wrestle with the question of what distinctions may legitimately be drawn along social, economic, and gender lines, or whether unity awaits the obliteration in every respect of any such distinctions. For me, the lesson of the Passover ordinance is that God works through institutions that may contain "old leaven" within them yet also contain the "yeast" that, when allowed to do its quiet, time-consuming work, in a temperature neither too hot (the zealots for perfection) nor too cold (the sticklers for the status quo), will work until all is leavened with the kingdom of God (Matt. 13:33).

UNLEAVENED BREAD AND CONSECRATION OF FIRSTBORN
Exodus 13:1–16

13:1 The LORD said to Moses: 2 Consecrate to me all the firstborn; whatever is the first to open the womb among the Israelites, of human beings and animals, is mine.

3 Moses said to the people, "Remember this day on which you came out of Egypt, out of the house of slavery, because the LORD brought you out from there by strength of hand; no leavened bread shall be eaten. 4 Today, in the month of Abib, you are going out. 5 When the LORD brings you into the land of the Canaanites, the Hittites, the Amorites, the Hivites, and the Jebusites, which he swore to your ancestors to give you, a land flowing with milk and honey, you shall keep this observance in this month. 6 Seven days you shall eat unleavened bread, and on the seventh day there shall be a festival to the LORD. 7 Unleavened bread shall be eaten for seven days; no leavened bread shall be seen in your possession, and no leaven shall be seen among you in all your territory. 8 You shall tell your child on that day, 'It is because of what the LORD did for me when I came out of Egypt.' 9 It shall serve for you as a sign on your hand and as a reminder on your forehead, so that the teaching of the LORD may be on your lips; for with a strong hand the LORD brought you out of Egypt. 10 You shall keep this ordinance at its proper time from year to year.

11 "When the LORD has brought you into the land of the Canaanites, as he swore to you and your ancestors, and has given it to you, 12 you shall set apart to the LORD all that first opens the womb. All the firstborn of your livestock that are males shall be the LORD's. 13 But every firstborn donkey you shall redeem with a sheep; if you do not redeem it, you must break its neck. Every firstborn male among your children you shall redeem. 14 When in the future your child asks you, 'What does this mean?' you shall answer, 'By strength of hand the LORD brought us out of Egypt, from the house of slavery. 15 When Pharaoh stubbornly refused to let us go, the LORD killed all the firstborn in the land of Egypt, from human firstborn to the firstborn of animals. Therefore I sacrifice to the LORD every male that first opens the womb, but every

firstborn of my sons I redeem.' [16] It shall serve as a sign on your hand and as an emblem on your forehead that by strength of hand the LORD brought us out of Egypt."

The first thing to notice about this passage is that it contains a repetition of God's instruction to Moses (12:14–20) to have Israel observe the feast of unleavened bread. The second is that, as in chapter 12 this instruction came in the middle of the passage on Passover, so now this passage comes in the middle of God's instruction concerning the "redemption of the first-born." Why, in each instance, does unleavened bread intrude into the middle of a different instruction? Is this awkward editing, or is this a way of arranging the various materials so that the arrangement itself says something about the meaning of the exodus?

We have all experimented with the sort of picture that, if looked at one way, shows two faces looking at each other across a narrow space and, if looked at another way, becomes a single urn or vase. What is background in one view becomes the foreground picture in the other view, and vice versa. If we take unleavened bread as the "picture" in the two chapters, how do the two "frames" of Passover and the consecration of the firstborn give us two different ways of looking at unleavened bread? Or, if we take Passover and the consecration of the firstborn as the pictures, how does unleavened bread affect our understanding of each of them?

First, let us ponder this seemingly strange institution of the consecration of the firstborn. It is rooted in the fruitfulness of creation, human and animal. This fruitfulness is not of our doing (though our own activity enhances it). It comes from God. By an instinct as old as creation, the bounty we have received should move us to offer the first fruits to God in grateful recognition of God's provision (compare Cain and Abel in Gen. 4:1–7). Of course, we may not do so. In forgetfulness (like children who take their parents for granted), or in high-handed self-assertion (like those who attribute their well-being solely to their own efforts; Deut. 8:11–20), we may simply reap the fruits of field and flock as the reward for our own efforts. And our own firstborn children (in a patriarchal culture, firstborn males) will come to signify for us the continuation into the future of our own control of the earth and our position in it.

So God's claim on the first fruits of field (Exod. 23:16, 19; Deut. 26:1–15) and flock (Exod 13:1–2, 11–16) comes as our (re-)education into gratitude and humility. In the case of the firstborn son, however, this "first fruit" is not offered but redeemed. The son is spared through the substitution of a sacrificial animal, presumably a sheep (13:13). By these offerings, we acknowledge the one to whom we owe our bounty and in whose providential hands our future really lies. By these offerings, we relinquish the notion that we can control or secure that future ourselves.

Child sacrifice is a ritual that seems to have been practiced in ancient cultures in both hemispheres. It strikes contemporary readers as barbaric—all the more so insofar as it is viewed as a sacred act. Yet, as Jon Levenson shows (in *The Death and Resurrection of the Beloved Son: The Transformation of Child Sacrifice in Judaism and Christianity*), the offering to God of the firstborn or beloved son is one of the central themes in both the scriptures that Jews and Christians have in common and the scriptures that Christians call the New Testament. As Levenson argues, while we thankfully no longer should find ourselves called to practice this ritual, the moral and spiritual realities it embodied should remain central to anyone who seeks to live in accordance with the biblical understanding of our relation to God.

The practice of the consecration or redemption of the firstborn underlies the climactic episode in the Abraham story when, in Genesis 22, he is asked to offer Isaac as a sacrifice. (By this time in the story, Isaac has assumed the status of "firstborn son") Only because God intervenes at the very last moment, and because Abraham is able to offer a ram in place of Isaac, is his son spared. What significance does this episode have within the context of Abraham's story? We recall that at the outset Abraham and Sarah are wanderers and are barren (Gen. 11:30), that is, landless and childless. Into this doubly problematic situation comes God's double promise of land and children (Gen. 12:1–2). Furthermore, this family will become a means by which all the families of the earth shall be blessed, and shall bless themselves (Gen. 12:3).

But what is to prevent such a family, once it has achieved such status, from simply repeating the age-old pattern of domination of the weak by the strong? The pattern is broken in at least two ways: First, in conventional patriarchal society, the firstborn male inherits the father's wealth, power, and authority. In that case, Ishmael should have been Abraham's heir. But once it has been established that the problem of barrenness lies not with Abraham but with Sarah, God's agenda of choosing and working through the nobodies of this world to confound the somebodies (1 Cor. 1:18–31) focuses on Sarah. While Ishmael will enjoy all the benefits that God intends for the creation (compare Gen. 17:20 with 1:28 and 12:2), it is through Sarah's son Isaac that God will covenant to bless all the families of the earth. But, second, lest Abraham think he can control the future through his and his beloved son's specially covenanted relation with God, he is asked to place this future entirely in God's hands. He is asked to do so by an act so radical that that future is entirely out of his own hands. Only such a radical act will uproot what seems to be a deeply rooted tendency in the human heart to "become as God" and be the determiner of one's own destiny.

The ancestral narratives of Genesis 12—50 give further examples of God reeducating human tendencies to power by inculcating the need for trust, loyalty, and compassion. In Exodus, as we have seen, the critical issues shift from sterility of earth (famine) and hearth (childlessness) to political oppression. When the political establishment becomes oppressive, the continuation of that oppression is symbolized in the firstborn of Egypt. Therefore, when God undertakes to liberate Israel from that oppression, the issues are posed already in Exodus 4:22–23: "Then you shall say to Pharaoh, 'Thus says the LORD: Israel is my firstborn son. I said to you, "Let my son go that he may worship me." But you refused to let him go; now I will kill your firstborn son.'" The death of all Egypt's firstborn, human and animal (12:29), comes therefore as God's judgment on a society that has forgotten or misconstrued its proper relation both to God and to other human beings.

So the ritual of the consecration or redemption of the firstborn is to exercise a powerful educative force in Israel. In the midst of this ritual (13:14), as in the midst of the Passover (12:26), the son (so the Hebrew, in both places) is to ask, "What does this mean?" In a patriarchal society, the son will exercise great power in determining the character of that society. The response to this son's question is an unmistakable lesson in God's judgment on how such power can be misused to great evil effect: "When Pharaoh stubbornly refused [hiqshah] to let us go, the LORD killed all the firstborn in the land of Egypt, from human firstborn to the firstborn of animals. Therefore I sacrifice to the LORD every male that first opens the womb, but every firstborn of my sons I redeem." As the recurrence of the verb hiqshah in 7:3 shows, it is because Pharaoh "hardens [his heart]" that God brings to an end the kind of political power such a heart represents. Not only does God judge that understanding and practice of political power but also God judges the kind of theology that people appeal to in order to justify it (Exod. 12:12). The lesson for Israel is that, if it continues as a patriarchal society, it can do so only if patriarchy is transformed from within. And if Israel celebrates a God whose might overturns the might of Egypt, its understanding of divine might may also need to undergo a process of transformation. Such a transformation of our understanding of God may be traced through the Old Testament. One example of a later stage in that transformation appears in 1 Corinthians 1:17–2:8.

Another appears in John 3:16. Such passages show God exercising divine dominion in ways that confound conventional human wisdom and power. The son and heir of divine dominion sacrifices himself (Gal. 2:20) to enable all people to become heirs of that kingdom and share in its glory (Rom. 8:15–17, 29–30). Such passages find their roots in Old Testament passages such as those we have been discussing in this section.

What, now, may we gather from the way the feast of unleavened bread is presented in the midst of instructions for the Passover (chapter 12) and for the consecration and redemption of the firstborn? I proposed earlier that Paul's interpretation of unleavened bread in 1 Corinthians 5:6–8 points to its implicit significance already in chapter 12. To leave Egypt with dough that contains no yeast is to leave behind the bad residue of past experience that could contaminate Israel as a new society. To celebrate Passover with unleavened bread is to celebrate God's new beginning, to celebrate Israel as a "new creation" (compare 2 Cor. 5:16–17). Chapter 13 still includes a reference to the exodus *from Egypt* (13:8), but now the emphasis is on Israel's observance of unleavened bread in the new land *to which* they are going (13:5). The people in this land will exercise a strong influence on Israel to adopt their social and political and religious styles of life (compare 23:20–33). In such a context, unleavened bread is a powerful reminder of Israel's own identity, like markers of ownership on hand and forehead (13:9; see Gen. 4:15; Ezek. 9:3–6). Unleavened bread here becomes a symbol of "the teaching [*torah*] of the LORD" by which Israel is to become a new people.

That teaching will come in the form of the laws that are associated with the Mount Sinai covenant, but it is symbolized already in the three rituals of Passover, consecration and redemption of the firstborn, and unleavened bread. Those rituals provide the foundation for the Christian observances of Baptism and the Lord's Supper. In Baptism, according to Paul, we die with Christ and rise to new life (Romans 6). In dying with Christ, we enter into an understanding and practice of power in the service of redemptive love that leads God not to "withhold his own son" but to give him up for us all (Rom. 8:32, echoing Gen. 22:12). In the Lord's Supper, we are nourished and strengthened for such a style of life by "Christ our passover [who] is sacrificed for us"; and we are to celebrate this festival "not with the old yeast, the yeast of malice and evil, but with the unleavened bread of sincerity and truth" (1 Cor. 5:7–8). In this way, though Christians may not engage in the actual observance of these rituals set forth in Exodus 12—13, we are called to the transformation in understanding and practice that they called Israel to and still call our Jewish cousins to.

THE AMBIGUITY
OF THE OLD IN THE NEW
Exodus 12:33–36

[*Exod. 12:1–32 Institution and observances of the Passover (and unleavened bread)*.]

12:33 **The Egyptians urged the people to hasten their departure from the land, for they said, "We shall all be dead."** [34] **So the people took their dough before it was leavened, with their kneading bowls wrapped up in their cloaks on their shoulders.** [35] **The Israelites had done as Moses told them; they had asked the Egyptians for jewelery of silver and gold, and for clothing,** [36] **and the LORD had given the people favor in the sight of the Egyptians, so that they let them have what they asked. An so they plundered the Egyptians.**

This passage brings two themes together in a way that suggests a fateful ambiguity at the heart of the exodus and of any liberation for a new future. The two themes concern the Egyptian gifts of jewelery and clothing to the Israelites and the departure in haste with unleavened bread.

Commenting on Exodus 3:16–22, I interpreted God's announcement of the Egyptian gifts as a sign that the victory of Yahweh is not only through force. If Pharaoh let the Hebrews go reluctantly and only under the pressure of the death of all the firstborn of Egypt, the Egyptian women freely gave their Israelite neighbors gifts for the journey. In this perspective, the theme works positively as a sign of the positive relations between these groups of women amid the general conflict. Commenting on Exodus 12:1–28, I discussed the feast of unleavened bread as marking a new beginning and a complete break with the old habits and patterns of Israel's Egyptian past.

The juxtaposition of these two themes in 12:33–36 sounds a faint yet unmistakable note of foreboding. For while the Egyptian gifts will be used to make the tabernacle for God to dwell in (25:1–9), they will also be used to make the idolatrous golden calf (32:1–6). These gifts, then, are ambiguous, depending on how they are used: When used in obedience to God they serve the new beginning—the new creation—of which the tabernacle is the architectural symbol. When used in disregard of God they serve to perpetuate the old past with its idolatry and oppression.

Once again we confront questions concerning the relation between past and future, old and new: How shall we begin anew? Can we in fact make an absolute break with the past, or must we incorporate elements from the past even in radical new beginnings? And how shall we incorporate those elements so that they contribute to the building of a future in which God may truly dwell (25:8) while avoiding a repetition of the very problems from which we seek to be delivered (32:1–6)?

FLIGHT IN HASTE
AND HOT PURSUIT
Exodus 12:37–14:9

12:37 **The Israelites journeyed from Rameses to Succoth, about six hundred thousand men on foot, besides children.** 38 **A mixed crowd also went up with them, and livestock in great numbers, both flocks and herds.** 39 **They baked unleavened cakes of the dough that they had brought out of Egypt; it was not leavened, because they were driven out of Egypt and could not wait, nor had they prepared any provisions for themselves.**

40 **The time that the Israelites had lived in Egypt was four hundred thirty years.** 41 **At the end of four hundred thirty years, on that very day, all the companies of the LORD went out from the land of Egypt.** 42 **That was for the LORD a night of vigil, to bring them out of the land of Egypt. That same night is a vigil to be kept for the LORD by all the Israelites throughout their generations.**

[*Exod. 12:43–49 The Ordinance of the Passover.*]

12:50 **All the Israelites did just as the LORD had commanded Moses and Aaron.** 51 **That very day the LORD brought the Israelites out of the land of Egypt, company by company.**

[*Exod. 13:1–16 Institution of the Consecration and Redemption of the First-born (and further comments on unleavened bread)*]

13:17 **When Pharaoh let the people go, God did not lead them by way of the land of the Philistines, although that was nearer; for God thought, "If the people face war, they may change their minds and return to Egypt."** 18 **So God led the people by the roundabout way of the wilderness toward the Red Sea. The Israelites went up out of the land of Egypt prepared for battle.** 19 **And Moses took with him the bones of Joseph who had required a solemn oath of the Israelites, saying, "God will surely take notice of you, and then you must carry my bones with you from here."** 20 **They set out from Succoth, and camped at Etham, on the edge of the wilderness.** 21 **The LORD went in front of them in a pillar of cloud by day, to lead them along the way, and in a pillar of fire by night, to give them light, so that they might travel by day and by night.** 22 **Neither the pillar of cloud by day nor the pillar of fire by night left its place in front of the people.**

14:1 **Then the LORD said to Moses:** 2 **Tell the Israelites to turn back and camp in front of Pi-hahiroth, between Migdol and the sea, in front of Baal-**

zephon; you shall camp opposite it, by the sea. ³ Pharaoh will say of the Israelites, 'They are wandering aimlessly in the land; the wilderness has closed
in on them.' ⁴ I will harden Pharaoh's heart, and he will pursue them, so that
I will gain glory for myself over Pharaoh and all his army; and the Egyptians
shall know that I am the LORD. And they did so.

⁵ When the king of Egypt was told that the people had fled, the minds of
Pharaoh and his officials were changed toward the people, and they said,
"What have we done, letting Israel leave our service?" ⁶ So he had his chariot made ready, and took his army with him; ⁷ he took six hundred picked
chariots and all the other chariots of Egypt with officers over all of them.
⁸ The LORD hardened the heart of Pharaoh king of Egypt and he pursued the
Israelites, who were going out boldly. ⁹ The Egyptians pursued them, all
Pharaoh's horses and chariots, his chariot drivers and his army; they over-
took them camped by the sea, by Pi-hahiroth, in front of Baal-zephon.

As the text and summaries show, the biblical narrative interweaves the
events of the exodus with instructions for ritual observances that are to celebrate the exodus. Most biblical scholars nowadays believe the instructions
for the observances draw upon practices of a later time. Thus the events of
the exodus are portrayed by projecting backward from these later practices
and understandings. The situation here, then, resembles the situation in
the first three Gospels, each of which narrates how, on the night when he
was betrayed, Jesus instituted the Lord's Supper. New Testament scholars generally hold that the words and actions of Jesus on that night, as presented in these Gospels, probably reflect, in some measure, the practice of
the earliest church.

The way we commonly think about time, nowadays, leads us to want to
establish "what actually happened then" and to distinguish that clearly
from "what happens now," even when the latter event is a ritual celebration of the former event. In many ways, we have gained from our increased
ability to distinguish the present from the past by the various techniques
we have developed for investigating history. But we may also have lost a
good deal of our ancestors' ability to experience the interrelation between
our past and our present. One way to begin to recover this sense is to take
seriously the arrangement of the materials in Exodus 12:1–13:9, which
suggests that we who come so many generations after the exodus can yet
become one with those who that night left in such haste that they had to
carry their dough unleavened.

We do so by participating in the same ritual actions in which the narrative portrays them as immersed. To be sure, they are shown celebrating the
Passover *before* the exodus from Egypt; for them, the Passover has an *anticipatory* character. Later generations, for their part, celebrate the Passover

after the exodus from Egypt; for them, it has a *memorial* character. But later generations may well find themselves in circumstances that in some degree are their own "Egypt." In such circumstances, their entry into Passover through *remembrance* places them, like the first generation, in a position also to *hope* for God's liberation. This same mystery, by which the past and the present interpenetrate in ritual celebration, is reflected in the New Testament in the practice of the Lord's Supper. This is most clearly reflected in Paul's words in 1 Corinthians 11:23–26, ending with, "For as often as you eat this bread and drink the cup, you proclaim the Lord's death until he comes." This proclaiming of the death of Jesus may be understood in the terms Luke's Gospel uses, where Jesus, taking the loaf, giving thanks, breaking it, and giving it to his disciples, says, "This is my body, which is given for you. Do this in remembrance of me" (Luke 22:19). At the same time that it is done in remembrance, it is done in hope, for the consummation in which the reign of God becomes complete lies still in the future.

There is a mystery here deeper than we can fathom. But from time to time we may experience it with an immediacy that, however fleeting, can be so potent as to transform our sense of time. At one level, past, present, and future remain "in their places," and we experience the stretch of time between the present and any past or future time primarily as separating us. Yet, especially in the Lord's Supper, the "communion" we celebrate opens out for us to embrace all who have gone before and all who will come after, and we find ourselves at one with all of God's creation. At such times, we enter very deeply into the dynamic of redemption whose groundwork is laid out in these narratives in Exodus 12:1–14:9.

Let us now focus on the narrative in 13:17–14:9. We are given two reasons why God does not lead the Israelites directly into the promised land but, instead, has them wander around in the wilderness for a while. The first reason is that a direct entry will not give the Israelites time to digest the lessons of the exodus, in which God defeated the military power of Egypt. Presumably a time in the wilderness following God's cloud by day and pillar of fire by night will reinforce in a day-to-day fashion the more dramatic way in which God led them out before the Egyptians. The second reason (which dovetails with the first) is that God wants to lure Pharaoh into a change of mind, whereby he will set out after these confused and lost runaway slaves. By this means, God's victory over Pharaoh will reinforce the lesson of the tenth plague and so become doubly evident. God will accomplish this objective by strengthening Pharaoh's resolve (14:4, 8) which he arrived at through his own "change of heart" (14:5).

A WAY THROUGH THE WATERS
Exodus 14:10–31

14:10 As Pharaoh drew near, the Israelites looked back, and there were the Egyptians advancing on them. In great fear the Israelites cried out to the LORD. [11] They said to Moses, "Was it because there were no graves in Egypt that you have taken us away to die in the wilderness? What have you done to us, bringing us out of Egypt? [12] Is this not the very thing we told you in Egypt, 'Let us alone and let us serve the Egyptians'? For it would have been better for us to serve the Egyptians than to die in the wilderness." [13] But Moses said to the people, "Do not be afraid, stand firm, and see the deliverance that the LORD will accomplish for you today; for the Egyptians whom you see today you shall never see again. [14] The LORD will fight for you, and you have only to keep still."

[15] Then the LORD said to Moses, "Why do you cry out to me? Tell the Israelites to go forward. [16] But you lift up your staff, and stretch out your hand over the sea and divide it, that the Israelites may go into the sea on dry ground. [17] Then I will harden the hearts of the Egyptians so that they will go in after them; and so I will gain glory for myself over Pharaoh and all his army, his chariots, and his chariot drivers. [18] And the Egyptians shall know that I am the LORD, when I have gained glory for myself over Pharaoh, his chariots, and his chariot drivers."

[19] The angel of God who was going before the Israelite army moved and went behind them; and the pillar of cloud moved from in front of them and took its place behind them. [20] It came between the army of Egypt and the army of Israel. And so the cloud was there with the darkness, and it lit up the night; one did not come near the other all night.

[21] Then Moses stretched out his hand over the sea. The LORD drove the sea back by a strong east wind all night, and turned the sea into dry land; and the waters were divided. [22] The Israelites went into the sea on dry ground, the waters forming a wall for them on their right and on their left. [23] The Egyptians pursued, and went into the sea after them, all of Pharaoh's horses, chariots, and chariot drivers. [24] At the morning watch the LORD in the pillar of fire and cloud looked down upon the Egyptian army, and threw the Egyptian army into panic. [25] He clogged their chariot wheels so that they turned with difficulty. The Egyptians said, "Let us flee from the Israelites, for the LORD is fighting for them against Egypt."

[26] Then the LORD said to Moses, "Stretch out your hand over the sea, so that the water may come back upon the Egyptians, upon their chariots and chariot drivers." [27] So Moses stretched out his hand over the sea, and at dawn the sea returned to its normal depth. As the Egyptians fled before it, the LORD tossed the Egyptians into the sea. [28] The waters returned and covered the chariots and the chariot drivers, the entire army of Pharaoh that had followed

them into the sea; not one of them remained. ²⁹ But the Israelites walked on
dry ground through the sea, the waters forming a wall for them on their right
and on their left. ³⁰ Thus the LORD saved Israel that day from the Egyptians;
and Israel saw the Egyptians dead on the seashore. ³¹ Israel saw the great work
that the LORD did against the Egyptians. So the people feared the LORD and
believed in the LORD and in his servant Moses.

This climactic event moves from the Israelites' looking back and fearing
Pharaoh (14:10), through Moses' "do not be afraid, stand firm and see"
(v. 13) and God's instructions to Moses (vv. 15–18), to the conclusion,
when they see what God has done, fear the LORD, and believe in the
LORD and in his servant Moses (vv. 30–31). It is thus a movement from
fear amid their circumstances through experience of God in those circumstances to another kind of fear that takes the form of belief, trust, or
faith.

Traditionally, "God-fearing" was a positive term. Nowadays "the fear
of the LORD" is often heard negatively, as expressing a servile, anxious
piety before a temperamental God one must "get on the right side of."
This shift in understanding fear is not entirely a gain. For one thing, it
overlooks fear's primarily positive function. Fear serves life by alerting us
to danger and helping to energize us into life-preserving action. As such,
our spontaneous fear response is part of the built-in equipment God provides as our creator and sustainer.

But fear sometimes works overtime, like a hypersensitive smoke alarm
that goes off at the lighting of a match. Sometimes the danger seems so
overwhelming that fear can paralyze us into inactivity and plunge us into
despair. In such situations, it can obscure the deeper attitude and orienta-
tion of basic trust that is our birthright as God's creatures. Where experience has given repeated cause for fear and little cause to trust (as in the case
of the Israelites in Egypt), our deeply grooved fear response can lead us to
prefer the life we have known, however miserable, to the great danger that
we have brought down on us by reaching for the hope that has been offered us. So the Israelites in their fear cry out in a babble of voices, not for
the last time wishing they were back in Egypt rather than in this exposed,
vulnerable place (vv. 11–12).

Moses responds in words that occur some eighty times in the Bible,
from Genesis 15:1 to Revelation 1:17: "do not be afraid" or "fear not."
Twelve times this phrase in the Old Testament is translated into Greek
with a verb that means "take heart," "be of good cheer," or "courage!" Of
the seven occurrences of this expression in the New Testament, especially

noteworthy are Mark 6:50 and John 16:33. So this expression goes to the heart of the biblical message. Where our spontaneous response is fear, and we cry out in that fear, God's reassuring response is "don't be afraid."

The earliest context for such fear and answering reassurance is the family setting, especially the relation between parent and anxious or upset child. For example, we find our expression in Genesis 15:1 (father); 21:17 (mother); 26:24 (father); 35:17 (mother); 43:23 (brother); 46:3 (father); and 50:19, 21 (brother). Answering their concern for the family's continuance, God promises Abraham, Isaac, and Jacob numerous descendants. In their dire circumstances, God similarly reassures Hagar and Rachel. And Joseph reassures his brothers in the face of their guilt toward him. We recall that in the ancestral religion individuals and families relate to God as to a divine parent; typically, their fears would relate to survival of the family through children and family cohesion in the face of family strife.

In Exodus, the danger is a new kind: overwhelming political force on the heels of long-standing political oppression. Will the old reassurances work? Moses' "do not be afraid," calls on Israel not to do something but simply to "stand firm" and "keep still." Yet there is something they are to do, and that is to redirect their looking (v. 10). As long as they focus on the Egyptians, fear will paralyze them. Now they are called to see what the LORD is going to do to the Egyptians. This "seeing" will turn their paralysis into quiet trust, as the Egyptians they now see they shall never see again.

Does Moses encourage the people because he himself is free from fear and filled with confidence? Apparently not. For God asks Moses, "Why do you cry out to me?" ("Cry out" here is the verb form of the noun "cry" in 3:7.) The picture is of someone who inwardly is as anxious as the people yet is able to muster a word of reassurance. He is like the parent who, not knowing how the family crisis is going to be resolved, nevertheless soothes an upset child with words like "don't worry; everything is going to be all right." (For a picture of Moses as a concerned foster mother, see Num. 11:10–15.) In such a picture, faith is not the absence of fear. Faith is fear that takes itself to God and there finds the freedom and the voice both to call for God to act and to give reassurance to others whose own fear leads them only backward.

Now God has Moses tell the people to "go forward." They are to take in hand their desire to return to Egypt and, instead, go the other way. In this respect, too, faith is not the absence of fear. Faith is the willingness to pick up and carry one's fear in one's bosom like a weaned child (compare Psalm 131) and go forward in the direction that trust calls for.

The image of the angel and the pillar that move from in front of the Israelites to the rear is vivid. It has become even more powerful for me since a backpacking experience with three friends several years ago. I had known the older brother since college days, but the younger brother more recently and primarily as "my friend's younger brother." Our plan was to trek over the dauntingly rugged Bruce Trail in single file, taking turns leading and then dropping to the rear. Midway through the day, after my turn to lead, I dropped to the rear. Then I discovered that I was not in the same physical condition as my friends. I began to lag and stumble. What should I do? Then I noticed: The younger brother, Rudy, had dropped behind me. He stayed there for the rest of the day while the other two traded leads. That day Rudy became a cherished friend, and he remains so to this day. Leadership, human or divine, is a fine thing. True pastoral leadership knows not only how to go ahead (Psalm 77:20; Gen. 33:12–14), but also how to act as a rear guard (Isa. 40:9–11; 52:12).

The picture the narrator paints for us in verses 21–29 makes for a great action movie. Did it happen that way? Most biblical scholars would say that this scene, like the plagues narrative, has been "heightened" for dramatic effect. But is the heightening only something added by the narrator, or is it part of the experience itself—what I would call the objective reality of subjective states of mind?

Suppose the body of water in question was, as many scholars have proposed, not the Red Sea, but the Sea of Reeds, one of the shallow lakes that lie between the Nile delta and the Sinai peninsula. Suppose that escaping Hebrew slaves found their progress blocked by such a shallow lake and the pursuing Egyptian forces hot on their trail. In such a plight, fear magnifies all things. Suppose (as many have suggested) that a providential wind blew back the waters, the light-traveling Hebrews slipped across to safety, and when the heavily armed Egyptians bogged down in the soft lake bed, the wind eased, and the enemy was drowned. That may be how a nonparticipant observer might "see" the event from a distant lookout. To a fearful people involved in the event, however, the shallow lake would become a towering obstacle. And given that fear itself can become an objective force, threatening to engulf and overwhelm us, the sort of narrative we have in this chapter may be the only adequate way of giving a realistic "insider" account of the experience of deliverance.

With verses 30–31 we come to the climax of the whole drama that began in chapter 1. The drama turns on a "great work" that is unprecedented in the experience of the children of Abraham, and so it introduces a new term into their vocabulary. The verb is *hoshia*ʿ (associated with the proper name, *yehoshua'*, "Joshua," in Aramaic, *yeshua'*, "Jesus"), meaning "deliver, save." The noun is *yesha'*, or *yeshu'ah*, "deliverance, salvation." The verb does not occur in Genesis, and the noun occurs there only in 49:18 where (like 49:10) it probably is to be understood as part of the experience of Jacob's descendants "in days to come" (49:1). The verb occurs first in Exodus 2:17. There, when shepherds harass the daughters of Jethro at a watering well, Moses "delivers" the women (NRSV "came to their defense") and waters their flock. In retrospect, we may view this action as foreshadowing his role in delivering God's flock from the Egyptians. The first time the verb and the noun are applied directly to a current action of God is in Exodus 14:13 and 14:30. It is no wonder that, in the song that follows (15:1–18), Moses and the Israelites sing, "The LORD . . . *has become* my salvation." Thus we see how new religious experiences may call for new forms of language, if we are to remain faithful to the continuing work in our time of the God of our ancestors.

The climax now moves quickly (14:30–31), with a tightly packed sequence of key words that will repay careful reflection. What turns the *sight* of the Egyptians dead on the seashore into the *sight* of a great work that the LORD did against the Egyptians? The first seeing is something that anybody with physical eyesight could and would see. But the second seeing is different. It is a recognition of the hand of God in this event. In the present instance, we are told that all Israel came to this recognition. In some places in the Bible, all see the physical event, but only some believe. What makes the difference? I have a suggestion, but it must await our study of 15:19–21.

Meanwhile, we may note that when Israel "saw" in both senses, they "*feared* the LORD and *believed* in the LORD and in his servant Moses." In Genesis 15:6, Abraham believed in the LORD's promise despite everything in his circumstance that would cast doubt on the possibility of its fulfillment. Here Israel believes in the LORD not on the basis of a promise that God holds out but on the basis of an action that makes good on an earlier promise. That earlier promise was given to the oppressed slaves through Moses, who had feared that they would not believe him (4:1). When they first heard the promise from him, they had believed (4:31); then, when Pharaoh tightened the screws on them, they lost their capacity to believe (6:9). The slow regaining of their initial belief now comes into flower, as they put their trust not only in God but also in Moses. They are saved in a double sense. Not only are they delivered from the power of Egypt but they are also delivered from the power of their fear and their doubt. Already, before they have entered into the land promised to Abraham, a land from which they have long been exiled, they have begun to reenter a relation with their God that has the character of fundamental trust.

That this relation can be spoken of in the same breath as one of "fear" and one of "belief" or trust should not be dismissed too quickly as reflecting an unworthy form of piety. To be sure, in any relationship, especially our relationship to God, fear without trust leads to anxiety and servility. But conversely, trust without fear can lead to presumption and arrogance. Where fear and trust exist together, each can deepen the other to open the possibility of great intimacy grounded in respect.

THE SINGING SOUND OF DELIVERANCE
Exodus 15:1–18

15:1 Then Moses and the Israelites sang this song to the LORD:
"I will sing to the LORD, for he has triumphed gloriously;
horse and rider he has thrown into the sea.
  2 The LORD is my strength and my song [RSV: might],
and he has become my salvation;
this is my God, and I will praise him,
my father's God, and I will exalt him.
  3 The LORD is a warrior;
the LORD is his name.

  4 "Pharaoh's chariots and his army he cast into the sea;
his picked officers were sunk in the Red Sea.
  5 The floods covered them;
they went down into the depths like a stone.
  6 Your right hand, O LORD, glorious in power—
your right hand, O LORD, shattered the enemy.
  7 In the greatness of your majesty you overthrew your adversaries;
you sent out your fury, it consumed them like stubble.
  8 At the blast of your nostrils the waters piled up,
the floods stood up in a heap;
the deeps congealed in the heart of the sea.
  9 The enemy said, 'I will pursue, I will overtake,
I will divide the spoil, my desire shall have its fill of them.
I will draw my sword, my hand shall destroy them.'
  10 You blew with your wind, the sea covered them;
they sank like lead in the mighty waters.
  11 Who is like you, O LORD, among the gods?
Who is like you, majestic in holiness,
awesome in splendor, doing wonders?

^{12} **You stretched out your right hand,**
the earth swallowed them.

^{13} **"In your steadfast love you led the people whom you redeemed;**
you guided them by your strength to your holy abode.
^{14} **The peoples heard, they trembled;**
pangs seized the inhabitants of Philistia.
^{15} **Then the chiefs of Edom were dismayed;**
trembling seized the leaders of Moab;
all the inhabitants of Canaan melted away.
^{16} **Terror and dread fell upon them;**
by the might of your arm, they became still as a stone
until your people, O LORD, passed by,
until the people whom you acquired passed by.
^{17} **You brought them in and planted them on the mountain of your**
     own possession,
the place, O LORD, that you made your abode,
the sanctuary, O LORD, that your hands have established.
^{18} **The LORD will reign forever and ever."**

Before getting into the content of this song, let us reflect on the significance of poetry and song. In a nutshell, poetry and song are to prose speech what dancing is to walking. Walking gets you there, but dancing expresses vivacity of spirit and style of soul. So, too, with poetry and song: They are the freedom and overflowing liveliness of the soul expressing the joy of life—unless, of course, we are singing the blues, in which case prose speech cannot take us down deep enough into our pain or despair, and again we must resort to poetry and song. So it is that the psalms take two basic forms that encompass all other more specific types: the psalms of weeping and the psalms of laughter (Psalm 126). Laughter rises in our throats; our tears fall heavily to the ground. The terms "levity" and "gravity" identify where we are. If in the book of Psalms these two types bear us up to the heights and accompany us to the depths, in Exodus the same two types mark the forward movement of the plot, from 2:23–25 to 15:1–18.

Just as weeping can leave us exhausted, laughter and joy can furnish new resources of morale, energy, and strength. So Robert Frost's poem identifies the spring song of birds as "Our Singing Strength." The fertility of spring that he attributes in part to their singing appears in a similar connection in Isaiah 40—55, which interweaves the themes of new exodus (from exile), singing, and the blossoming of the earth. For this reason, I follow the NRSV note in verse 2: "The LORD is my strength and my song, and he has become my salvation." An illustration that comes to mind is the little girl who fell down an abandoned well. During the days that it took rescuers to tunnel down to her, they lowered a microphone to her so that they could reassure her with their words. To their surprise, they heard her singing songs her mother had taught her. As with her, with Paul and Silas in prison (Acts 16:25), and countless others, songs convey strength; when people sing in praise of God, they convey God's strength, a strength through which God becomes one's salvation.

With these comments, let us examine briefly the song's contents. While Moses and all the Israelites join in the song, each one says, "I will sing to the LORD." The song of praise thus becomes a vehicle for communal solidarity and at the same time a vehicle for each individual to buy into that solidarity personally. Verses 2–3 play on the theme of the relation of ancestral religion to the religion that arises with Moses and the exodus. For they celebrate the way in which, through defeat of Pharaoh's forces (v. 1), Yahweh as "my father's God" becomes "a warrior," and that warrior's name is Yahweh. Thus, the interconnection between these two religious eras that was made known to Moses (3:1–15; 6:3–8) now is affirmed by all Israelites.

The affirmation of God's victory in verse 1 receives ample elaboration in verses 4–12. In this battle, the lines are drawn between Pharaoh and his forces and all his gods, on the one side, and on the other side Yahweh and the forces of nature, sea, fiery fury, wind, and earth (like the Greeks' four basic elements: air, earth, fire, water). In this way, the song gathers up the basic theme of the plagues narrative, where God's signs and wonders are all occurrences in nature. This portrayal of the forces of nature as God's allies in the war against oppression and injustice can be seen also in Judges 5:20–21, where "the stars . . . from their courses" fight for God against Sisera. It appears again in Isaiah 40:25–26, where the "host" of heaven is presented as an army mustered and ready to battle for God on behalf of the demoralized exiles. (The term "host" most often in the Bible refers to a military force, as in "LORD of hosts.") The most dramatic instance appears in Joshua 10:12–14. The Wisdom of Solomon, written perhaps in the late first century before Christ, offers an extended interpretation of the exodus from Egypt: "The Lord will take his zeal as his whole armor, and will arm all creation to repel his enemies; . . . and creation will join with him to fight against the madmen" (5:15–23). One wonders whether such a line of interpretation may not lie behind Paul's affirmation in Romans 8:28 that "all things work together for good for those who love God." In that case, "all things" need not mean "whatever happens," as though "whatever happens is for the best." Rather, "all things" here would refer to "the whole creation," which up to now groans in pain and travail, looking for God's redemption (8:18–27). The point, then—whether in Romans 8, Wisdom of Solomon 5, Isaiah 40, Judges 5, or Joshua 10—is that God's forces for redemption are the very forces God has created and that form the natural order. If these forces sometimes behave in ways that make it difficult for us to see God's redemptive activity in them, it is, says Paul, because they, too, have been brought in subjection to powers of anticreation. But when God acts in redemption, as in the exodus, we may confidently celebrate and affirm that redemption as being of a piece with God's activity in creation (compare Psalm 148).

There is another aspect to all this. In Mesopotamian and Canaanite mythology, the sea frequently appears as the symbolic embodiment of forces of chaos and disruption that threaten the realm of the gods and the world as the gods have ordered it. In such a scenario, the conquest of the sea reestablishes cosmic order and the royal rule of the high god. Israel could employ this language in the same way (Psalm 29:10; 74:12–17; Isa. 27:1; 51:9). Jesus' rebuke of the sea in Mark 4:39 has also been interpreted in this context. Yet in the book of Job, where this imagery also appears several times (7:12; 9:8; 26:13), when Yahweh speaks the sea is presented not as an enemy but as a vigorous infant at whose birth God is present as midwife to coddle and to discipline (Job 38:8–11). Likewise, when the Babylonian exiles cry out for God to deliver them according to this model (Isa. 51:9–11), God responds with a different picture of cosmic creation (Isa. 51:12–13). In this picture it is God, the LORD of hosts, who stirs up the sea so that its waves roar (Isa. 51:15).

To go back to Exodus 15:1–18, then, in Egypt the Pharaoh would experience Moses and Aaron as "outside agitators" come to disrupt the "order" created by his royal rule. They would have, for him and his gods, the chaotic character that in Babylonia and Canaan would be symbolized by the sea. But Yahweh is not like those gods (v. 11). Yahweh can work "disorder," through the sea (and through fire, wind, and earth). Yet it is disorder only for a false and oppressive order, a disorder whose God the exodus and its song celebrates.

No wonder the established political powers tremble at this (vv. 14–16)! But the God who threatens their established orders does so to establish a new order, a new creation, at God's "holy abode" in God's holy mountain (vv. 13, 17). These terms may look forward to the holy land and to Mount Zion with its royal temple. But some would argue that this abode is in the desert and this mountain is Sinai. Even when God does come to dwell on Zion, after David, the Bible can still speak of God dwelling in the desert (Hab. 3:3; Teman and Mount Paran are in the desert). This means that, while God may be associated with forms of social order such as Jerusalem represents, God may never simply be identified and equated with them. As "I will be who I will be," God continues to live in the desert. Where Israel's social order itself becomes oppressive, and the religious order infected with idolatry, an Elijah will trek to Horeb to meet this God (1 Kings 19) and to be renewed in the faith of Moses and the exodus traditions.

The song concludes in celebration of the royal rule of God, a rule governed by God's "steadfast love" (v. 13), God's *hesed* or "loyalty." This quality of divine loyalty has its roots in the family-kinship religion of the ancestors. That such a God is loyal across so many generations and under so many different circumstances should be enough to move anyone to break out in praise and, in such praise, to experience how song becomes strength and salvation.

MIRIAM AS ISRAEL'S SONG LEADER
Exodus 15:19–21

> 15:19 **When the horses of Pharaoh with his chariots and his chariot drivers went into the sea, the LORD brought back the waters of the sea upon them; but the Israelites walked through the sea on dry ground.**
>
> [20] **Then the prophet Miriam, Aaron's sister, took a tambourine in her hand; and all the women went out after her with tambourines and with dancing.** [21] **And Miriam sang to them:**
>
> > **"Sing to the LORD, for he has triumphed gloriously;**
> > **horse and rider he has thrown into the sea."**

From NRSV, the impression could be gained that verse 19 simply recapitulates 14:23–29 and that, after Moses and Israel sang the song in verses 1–18, Miriam and the women sang the song, or part of it, again (vv. 20–21). But three features in the text suggest a significantly different sequence of events.

First of all, 15:19, in fact, begins with "for" (as in RSV, "For when the horses of Pharaoh"). This word suggests that the singing in verses 1–18 is explained by what follows. Is the singing explained simply by 14:23–29 as summarized in verse 19, or is it explained by all that happens in verses 19–21? The RSV and NRSV put a period at the end of verse 19, but the Hebrew allows a translation with a comma at the end of verse 19, so that we may also include verses 20–21 as part of the explanation for the singing in verses 1–18.

This leads to the second feature of the text. In Hebrew, third-person plural pronouns ("they, them," and so forth) are distinguished as masculine or feminine. Normally, if women are referred to, the feminine plural form is used, while the masculine plural form is used to refer to men or to men and women. The Hebrew text of verse 21 reads, "And Miriam sang to them [masculine]." The most natural reading is that, while the women accompanied her with instruments and dancing, Miriam called on Moses and Israel to "Sing to the LORD." This fits one typical form of a "call to worship" in Israel (compare, e.g., Psalm 96:1–3, 7–9; 98:1, 4–6; 100:1–2; 105:1–2). But when did they call on Israel to do so? After the initial song, as a sort of "let's sing it again"?

Here, third, is the significance of the recapitulation of 14:23–29 in verse 19. It places the actions and words of 15:20–21 back behind 15:1–18, back to the point reached in 14:29. The words in 15:1, "I will sing to the LORD," come, then, as each Israelite's response to Miriam's call to worship.

But if Miriam's song comes after 14:29, it provides the lens through which Israel is able, in seeing the Egyptians dead on the seashore (14:30), to see this as the great work that the LORD does against the Egyptians (14:31). It is *God's action as celebrated in Miriam's song* that moves them to fear the LORD and believe in the LORD and in his servant Moses. Like Mary Magdalene in respect to the resurrection of Jesus, Miriam is the first witness to God's saving action, and her testimony forms the basis for the others' perception and experience of it. Miriam's song is not simply her response to God's salvation but part of the total saving event. The mystery of "inspiration" is that the song is Miriam's and yet is part of God's action. This is beautifully put in Psalm 40:1–3, which could be taken as a celebration in more general terms of the specific process of salvation in Exodus 2:23–15:21:

I waited patiently for the LORD; he inclined to me and heard my cry.	[compare Exod. 2:23–25]

He drew me up from the desolate pit,
    out of the miry bog,
and set my feet upon a rock,
    making my steps secure.
	[compare Exod.3:1–14:29]

He put a new song in my mouth, a song of praise to our God.	[compare Exod. 15:19–21]
Many will see and fear, and put their trust in the LORD.	[compare Exod. 14:30–31]

If Aaron became the mouthpiece for Moses who was as God to him (4:14–17), Miriam here becomes the mouthpiece for God.

There are texts in the Bible and in other literature of this period that speak of the worship of God by heavenly beings (e.g., Psalm 29:1–2; 148:1–2; Job 38:7; see also the hymn by Richard Baxter beginning, "Ye holy angels bright," also the verse beginning, "Angels help us to adore him," in Henry Francis Lyte's hymn, "Praise, My soul, the King of Heaven"). In this tradition, the praise that arises from earth to God participates in a praise that is already occurring in God's immediate presence. In such a setting, "inspiration" for our singing and witness comes as we become open to that praise and let it form our own words and music. If Moses at the burning bush was drawn into what God saw, heard, remembered, knew, and resolved to do (2:23–25; 3:7–10), so that he became part of God's saving action, Miriam also becomes part of it in her singing celebration of it. No wonder God reminds Israel:

> For I brought you up from the land of Egypt,
>   and redeemed you from the house of slavery;
> and I sent before you Moses,
>   Aaron, and Miriam.
>
> (Micah 6:4)

But why does the narrator delay telling us of Miriam's action until after 15:1–18? Why not tell us after 14:29?

There is a structuring device that occurs frequently in biblical prose and poetry, which is called "envelope" or "chiastic" structure. This device ties the end and the beginning together, or even organizes details in concentric fashion. (Exodus 14:13–14 gives a good example: "[a] Do not be afraid, stand firm, and [b] see the deliverance that the LORD will accomplish for you today; [c] for the Egyptians whom you see today you shall never see again. [b'] The LORD will fight for you, and [a'] you have only to keep still.") This kind of structure can mark very short passages, but it also can be used to organize long passages or even whole books.

By having the first long section of the book of Exodus end with Miriam and her call to worship, the narrator ends on a theme prominently displayed in chapters 1—2. That theme is the role of women in God's saving actions. The work of the Hebrew midwives, Moses' mother, his sister, Pharaoh's daughter, and Zipporah (4:24–26) comes to a fitting climax in Miriam's action at the sea.

If she is called a prophetess, what does she prophesy? It is common nowadays to speak of biblical prophets as not only foretelling but also forth-telling. They speak God's word concerning the future and concerning their own time as seen from God's point of view. The preceding remarks suggest how as a prophetess Miriam "forth-tells" God's presence and activity in the deliverance from the Egyptians. How might we hear her today as a foreteller of the role of women in God's redemption of the world through our Lord Jesus Christ?

BITTER WATER MADE SWEET
Exodus 15:22–27

15:22 **Then Moses ordered Israel to set out from the Red Sea, and they went into the wilderness of Shur. They went three days in the wilderness and found no water.** 23 **When they came to Marah, they could not drink the water of Marah because it was bitter. That is why it was called Marah.** 24 **And the people complained against Moses, saying, "What shall we drink?"** 25 **He cried out to the LORD; and the LORD showed him a piece of wood; he threw it into the water, and the water became sweet.**

There the LORD made for them a statute and an ordinance and there he put them to the test. 26 **He said, "If you will listen carefully to the voice of the LORD your God, and do what is right in his sight, and give heed to his commandments and keep all his statutes, I will not bring upon you any of the diseases that I brought upon the Egyptians; for I am the LORD who heals you."**

27 **Then they came to Elim, where there were twelve springs of water and seventy palm trees; and they camped there by the water.**

This passage revolves around two concerns: the need for water in the wilderness (15:22–25a) and the need for laws in Israelite society (15:25b–26). These concerns are interwoven to establish a metaphorical relation between bitter water and bad laws and between sweet water and good laws.

In Genesis 1—2, the earth is a lush garden providing abundantly for human and animal life. In addition to this abundance is a tree of life and a strange tree whose fruit promises wisdom (Gen. 3:6) but delivers death. When humans eat of this last tree, the garden is replaced by a wilderness (Gen. 3:17). This implies that the earth as we know it is not the earth as God made it and intends it to be because of human reaching after a certain kind of wisdom. Such is the biblical background to the present passage.

After the euphoria of Exodus 15:1–21, Israel travels three days in the wilderness without water. When they find some, it is bitter. As Naomi and Job know (Ruth 1:19–21; Job 3:20; 6:4–7; 27:2), bitter disappointment can leave us bitter in soul. Israel had been led to expect that three days' journey in the wilderness would bring them to worship at God's mountain (5:3; see 3:12). Instead, they find themselves by a pool of undrinkable water. Just as the first flush of their belief in God's promised deliverance (4:31) gave way after further hardships to disbelief (6:9), so now the initial sweetness of the song in their mouths (15:1–21) gives way to bitterness. According to NRSV, they "complained." That is not an adequate translation. In Job, the Psalms, and elsewhere, the Bible is full of entirely appropriate complaints. Here they do something the Bible always criticizes, for which it reserves the word *lun*. This is not a loud outcry *to* God, but a rebellious muttering *about* God, "under their breath" plotting to pull out of the enterprise and head back to Egypt (16:2–3; 17:1–3; see already 14:11–12).

Jewish author Elie Wiesel, in *Souls on Fire*, tells of the Hasidic Rabbi Yitzhak of Berditchaev. Every year in the synagogue on Yom Kippur he would try God and find God guilty of crimes against the people of God. Then he would forgive God. How, asks Wiesel, was this not blasphemy? His answer: Because it took place within the synagogue, within the covenant relation. Inside that relation, nothing is out of bounds. But step outside the covenant relation—break it off—and such language becomes blasphemy. This, I suggest, is the difference between the most extreme complaint inside the God-human relation and *lun*, the murmuring that wants to break off the relation and return to Egypt.

Moses does not join in the "murmuring," but cries out to the LORD. He may, like the murmurers, ask, "What shall we drink?" But if he does, he stands within the covenant relation and directs his cry to God. In response, God directs him to a piece of wood, or a tree. This wood, or tree, when thrown into the bitter water, makes it sweet. The verb for "direct" in verse 25 is cognate with the noun, *torah*, "direction, instruction, teaching, law," setting up a metaphorical relation between the tree and sweetened water, and the statutes and ordinances.

The laws Pharaoh adopted in his wisdom have meant bitter suffering for Israel (see the "bitter herbs" symbolism in 12:8). In 1:10, NRSV follows RSV in translating the verb, "let us deal shrewdly." The Hebrew verb is the standard verb for indicating wise actions or dealings. "Let us deal shrewdly" reflects the translators' wry suspicion at Pharaoh's actions, as though he were intent on "pulling a fast one" on the Hebrews. Such an inference obscures the possibility that Pharaoh was acting in all sincerity as measured by the best theologically informed wisdom available to him. Such sincerity, needless to say, did not prevent him from adopting laws that were unjust. Under God's judgment, these same laws have eventually brought "diseases" upon Egypt in the form of the plagues. Just as the "wood/tree" sweetened the bitter water in the wilderness, so the *torah* of Sinai will heal Israel of the "diseases" that otherwise will plague its social relations. For the *torah* is God's wisdom for human society (Deut. 4:5–8), and this wisdom will be "a tree of life to those who lay hold of her" (Prov. 3:18). If our sufferings, amid bad human relations and under unjust laws, can enter into our soul and produce pathologies of the spirit, God's *torah* is here presented as God's sweet remedy (Psalm 19:10) by which we may be revived and restored to health (Psalm 19:7). In this way, the covenant community is to avoid Egypt's choice of bad wisdom and its bad results.

By the interweaving of the two panels in 15:22–25a and 25b–26, water and laws become metaphors for each other. Here in the wilderness, the experience of thirst, bitterness, transformation by a tree, and sweetness foreshadows Mount Sinai and its laws. In this way, the people are partly prepared ahead of time to understand what Mount Sinai is all about. After Mount Sinai, as Israel shapes its life in accordance with God's *torah*, it will find *torah* sweet and nourishing in whatever future lies ahead.

The passage ends with yet a third panel (v. 27), as Israel arrives at an oasis with twelve springs of water and seventy palm trees. The number of the springs and trees gives assurance of God's faithfulness to those who are reminded of how their ancestors came down to Egypt as twelve families numbering seventy persons in all (1:1–5). Like the small inner-city congregation that named its storefront church Gershom, after Moses' naming of his son in the wilderness (2:22 and my comments there), a Pentecostal congregation in Saskatoon, Saskatchewan, named its place of worship "Elim Tabernacle." Like an oasis, such a place offers rest and refreshment to people in the midst of their journey.

BREAD FROM HEAVEN
AND THE SABBATH
Exodus 16:1–36

16:1 **The whole congregation of the Israelites set out from Elim; and Israel came to the wilderness of Sin, which is between Elim and Sinai, on the fifteenth day of the second month after they had departed from the land of Egypt.** 2 **The whole congregation of the Israelites complained against Moses** and Aaron in the wilderness. ³ The Israelites said to them, "If only we had died by the hand of the LORD in the land of Egypt, when we sat by the flesh-pots and ate our fill of bread; for you have brought us out into this wilderness to kill this whole assembly with hunger."

⁴ Then the LORD said to Moses, "I am going to rain bread from heaven for you, and each day the people shall go out and gather enough for that day. In that way I will test them, whether they will follow my instruction [*torah*] or not. ⁵ On the sixth day, when they prepare what they bring in, it will be twice as much as they gather on other days." ⁶ So Moses and Aaron said to all the Israelites, "In the evening you shall know that it was the LORD who brought you out of the land of Egypt, ⁷ and in the morning you shall see the glory of the LORD, because he has heard your complaining against the LORD. For what are we, that you complain against us?" ⁸ And Moses said, "When the LORD gives you meat to eat in the evening and your fill of bread in the morning, because the LORD has heard the complaining that you utter [literally: "complain"] against him—what are we? Your complaining is not against us but against the LORD."

⁹ Then Moses said to Aaron, "Say to the whole congregation of the Israelites, 'Draw near to the LORD, for he has heard your complaining.'" ¹⁰ And as Aaron spoke to the whole congregation of the Israelites, they looked toward the wilderness, and the glory of the LORD appeared in the cloud. ¹¹ The LORD spoke to Moses and said, ¹² "I have heard the complaining of the Israelites; say to them, 'At twilight you shall eat meat, and in the morning you shall have your fill of bread; then you shall know that I am the LORD your God.'"

¹³ In the evening quails came up and covered the camp; and in the morning there was a layer of dew around the camp. ¹⁴ When the layer of dew lifted, there on the surface of the wilderness was a fine flaky substance, as fine as frost on the ground. ¹⁵ When the Israelites saw it, they said to one another, "What is it?" For they did not know what it was. Moses said to them, "It is the bread that the LORD has given you to eat. ¹⁶ This is what the LORD has commanded: 'Gather as much of it as each of you needs, an omer to a person according to the number of persons, all providing for those in their own tents.'" ¹⁷ The Israelites did so, some gathering more, some less. ¹⁸ But when they measured it with an omer, those who gathered much had nothing over, and those who gathered little had no shortage; they gathered as much as each of them needed. ¹⁹ And Moses said to them, "Let no one leave any of it over until morning." ²⁰ But they did not listen to Moses; some left part of it until morning, and it bred worms and became foul. And Moses was angry with them. ²¹ Morning by morning they gathered it, as much as each needed; but when the sun grew hot, it melted.

²² On the sixth day they gathered twice as much food, two omers apiece. When all the leaders of the congregation came and told Moses, ²³ he said to

them, "This is what the LORD has commanded: 'Tomorrow is a day of solemn rest, a holy sabbath to the LORD; bake what you want to bake and boil what you want to boil, and all that is left over put aside to be kept until morning.'" 24 So they put it aside until morning, as Moses commanded them; and it did not become foul, and there were no worms in it. 25 Moses said, "Eat it today, for today is a sabbath to the LORD; today you will not find it in the field. 26 Six days you shall gather it; but on the seventh day, which is a sabbath, there will be none."

27 On the seventh day some of the people went out to gather, and they found none. 28 The LORD said to Moses, "How long will you refuse to keep my commandments and instructions [torot]? 29 See! The LORD has given you the sabbath [shabbat], therefore on the sixth day he gives you food for two days; each of you stay where you are; do not leave your place on the seventh day." 30 So the people rested [shabat] on the seventh day.

31 The house of Israel called it manna; it was like coriander seed, white, and the taste of it was like wafers made with honey. 32 Moses said, "This is what the LORD has commanded: 'Let an omer of it be kept throughout your generations, in order that they may see the food with which I fed you in the wilderness, when I brought you out of the land of Egypt.'" 33 And Moses said to Aaron, "Take a jar, and put an omer of manna in it, and place it before the LORD, to be kept throughout your generations." 34 As the LORD commanded Moses, so Aaron placed it before the covenant, for safekeeping. 35 The Israelites ate manna forty years, until they came to a habitable land; they ate manna, until they came to the border of the land of Canaan. 36 An omer is a tenth of an ephah.

Ancestral religion in Genesis 12—50 revolved around concerns for the bearing and nurture of children and for land in which to find pasture for flocks and fields for crops. At such a time, God was worshiped as El Shaddai, giver of the fertile blessings of heaven and earth and of the blessings of breast and womb (Gen. 49:25). Mosaic religion has its foundation in the experience of Yahweh as divine warrior who delivers the oppressed from political bondage. The wilderness experiences in chapters 15, 16, and 17 reintroduce the concern for food and drink in a land that seems ill equipped to furnish either. In such a setting, a warrior God seems of little relevance, and Yahweh ("I will be who/what I will be") needs to be present and active in the old character of El Shaddai, even if that old name is not used.

As in chapter 15, so in chapter 16, the need for food moves Israel to "murmur" (NRSV, "complain"). Again they hanker to be back in Egypt, where supposedly they ate their fill.

God promises to provide meat from the sky every evening and a strange victual on the ground every morning—as if to dramatize that, as Yahweh, God will continue to furnish the blessings of heaven and earth formerly associated with the name El Shaddai. (Commentators have often associated these provisions with two unusual but observed happenings in this part of the world: Migrating birds sometimes fall to the ground exhausted from strong head winds, and at certain seasons certain desert plants exude a sweet, sticky, edible substance overnight.)

As important as the provision of food is, the emphasis of this passage is on the timetable on which food is provided and is to be sought. God will provide food daily, except for a double portion on the sixth day. Israel is to gather it daily, except for the sixth day, when they are to lay up a double portion. We have, then, a story emphasizing the rhythm of six days' labor and a seventh of rest or sabbath (vv. 29–30). Some commentators take this reference to the sabbath as anachronistic, presupposing the sabbath law or *torah* of Exodus 20:8–11. No doubt this chapter is actually written after the giving of that law, but this timing does not mean that mention of the sabbath here is anachronistic. Rather, it is anticipatory. As in 15:22–26 (see my comments there), an experience occurs on the way to Mount Sinai that provides God with the opportunity to introduce the theme of a sabbath *torah* (16:4, 28) in an ad hoc way, as preparation for the more formal covenant laws to be given at Mount Sinai. The laws of Mount Sinai do not then come as a complete surprise, for they already have a preliminary basis in experience.

As is often observed, the sabbath as instituted in the Decalogue is given two different rationales. In the "Priestly" version of the Decalogue (Exod. 20:1–17), Israelites are enjoined to "remember" the sabbath, refraining from work on it because God created the world in six days and rested on the seventh (20:8–11; so also 31:12–17). (It is called the Priestly version because scholars attribute it to the stream of literary tradition in the Bible that flows from Priestly circles in Israel.) In the "Deuteronomic" version (Deut. 5:6–21), Israelites are enjoined to "observe" the sabbath in celebration of God's deliverance of their ancestors from servitude in Egypt. Thus, the Priestly version grounds the sabbath in God as creator while the Deuteronomic version grounds the sabbath in God as redeemer. The present chapter (which is largely Priestly) shows that for the Priestly writers creation and redemption are intimately related, for the sabbath instruction in it contrasts the temporal pattern of life in Israel with the temporal pattern formerly imposed on them by Pharaoh.

In chapter 5, the people as slaves of Pharaoh must scatter day by day to look for straw with which to make their daily quota of bricks. In chapter

16, the people of God scatter day by day to look for the daily quota of food that God promises to provide. The common emphasis on "daily quota" is signaled by the use of the same Hebrew idiom in both chapters (5:13, 19; 16:4). Also, both chapters refer to rest (*shabat*) from work. Here is where the contrast comes in: For Pharaoh, the slaves are not to rest; to ensure this, he forces them to scour the land for their own straw while keeping to their daily production quota. For Yahweh, six days of work is enough, and on the seventh they may rest from gathering.

The Israelites, unaccustomed to this shift in the rhythm of their days, disregard God's instruction in two ways. On days when food is to be gathered only for that day, they try to keep some over; on the sabbath, when food is not to be gathered, they go out anyway to gather it. In terms of 15:26 ("I am the LORD who heals you"), part of what God has to heal the people of is a deeply ingrained but flawed sense of the relation between food and time.

During the the wilderness wanderings, God teaches the rhythm of six days' work and one day of rest by providing daily food on five days and a double supply on the sixth, with none on the seventh. With the entry into the land, the manna stops (16:35; see Josh. 5:10–12), and Israel's food comes by the more normal processes of fieldwork and animal husbandry. Yet, even though these processes do not by themselves operate on a 6 + 1 (or 5 + 2 + 0) rhythm, by then the wilderness practice is reinforced by the Decalogue's sabbath law, to give the same rhythm to all aspects of Israel's work. To perpetuate the learning experience of the wilderness, a memorial is to be kept in the sanctuary (vv. 33–34).

Observance of the sabbath is a "defining practice" identifying observant Jews as Jews. It has long continued as a "defining practice" among Christians, though transferred to Sunday to celebrate Christ's resurrection as the basis of our redemption and new creation. Indeed, North Americans of sufficient age or historical memory will recollect the so-called blue laws that used to restrict activities on Sunday for religious and nonreligious people alike. The question of the nature and meaning of sabbath observance arises at several points in the New Testament, in such a way as eventually to distinguish between Jews and Christians (Mark 2:23–38; John 5; Rom. 14:5–12). There is no space here to go into all these issues. But, as I suggested at chapter 5, the question in principle for Christians is whether we have ceased to serve God as the Lord of time and have begun to serve Pharaoh instead. What would it be like to be assured of one day a week when no demands could be made on our time, and we would have leisure for nothing but worship, refreshment of soul, and enjoyment of the earth as God's good creation? So far as food is concerned, the issue of "daily portion" appears in the prayer of Proverbs 30:7–9; in the Lord's Prayer ("give us this day our daily bread"); and in the Sermon on the Mount (Matt. 6:25–26). It may be that natural calamities like drought and famine lie beyond our power to modify significantly. But if we learned to pray the prayer in Proverbs 30:7–9 (not too little and not too much) and to conform our economic activities to the spirit of that prayer, we would be more open to the rhythms of work and rest into which chapter 16 would educate us. We might even learn to break the vicious cycle of instant and incessant gratification that defines us as a society of "consumers."

WATER FROM HOREB/SINAI
Exodus 17:1–7

17:1 **From the wilderness of Sin the whole congregation of the Israelites journeyed by stages, as the LORD commanded. They camped at Rephidim, but there was no water for the people to drink.** 2 **The people quarreled with Moses, and said, "Give us water to drink." Moses said to them, "Why do you quarrel with me? Why do you test the LORD?"** 3 **But the people thirsted there for water; and the people complained against Moses and said, "Why did you bring us out of Egypt, to kill us and our children and livestock with thirst?"** 4 **So Moses cried out to the LORD, "What shall I do with this people? They are almost ready to stone me."** 5 **The LORD said to Moses, "Go on ahead of the people, and take some of the elders of Israel with you; take in your hand the staff with which you struck the Nile, and go.** 6 **I will be standing there in front of you on the rock at Horeb. Strike the rock, and water will come out of it, so that the people may drink." Moses did so, in the sight of the elders of Israel.** 7 **He called the place Massah and Meribah, because the Israelites quarreled and tested the LORD, saying, "Is the LORD among us or not?"**

The congregation moves on "by stages," camping each night, traveling and stopping, as the Hebrew puts it, "according to the mouth of Yahweh." At one stopping place, they find no water. So they "quarrel" with Moses. The verb for "quarrel" can indicate a simple disagreement, but it can also indicate a formal legal proceeding. Here it amounts to the latter, for they seek to put God to the test. This testing has the same significance as their murmuring (v. 3). Just as murmuring is an attitude and behavior that begin to step outside the covenant relation and move back toward Egypt (v. 3; compare 14:11–12; 16:2–3), so, too, "testing" God is more than simply crying out to God in bewildered questioning. To test God is to pose an ultimatum, in which we decide what shall count as evidence of God's presence in our midst (17:7), and then decide on God's presence or absence on the basis of whether God has met the test we have posed. But if we are the ones to decide what shall count as evidence of God's good presence and activity among us, does this not make us like God in respect to "knowing good and evil"? If absence of water in this instance counts against God, what of all the "stages" along the way where water has been provided? Do they not count positively for God? Which experiences, the negative or the positive, shall we take as the most reliable evidence concerning God in the world and in our lives? Here, faith and trust vie with fear and doubt.

We can readily identify with the congregation at Rephidim, recalling how fear and doubt have gripped us at certain "stages" along our own way. At such times, what is it that keeps us going? In part, it is surely the memory of oasis points in our past, where provision of our needs has carried with it a strong sense of God's presence. In part, it can also be something that reaches back to us from the future, to give us a foretaste of what lies ahead. This is the significance of the water that flows to the people from the rock at Horeb.

When the people quarrel with Moses and God, he asks God, "What am I to do with them?" God instructs him to take some of the elders and go on ahead to Mount Sinai (here called Horeb, which in Hebrew means "waste, desert"). There, Moses is to take the staff and strike the "rock," presumably the mountain itself. When he does so, water issues from the mountain and flows through the desert to where the people are encamped at Rephidim.

For the most part, the people are sustained along the way by food and water found at each point. But in cases like Rephidim, sustaining water comes not from where they are but from where they are headed *for*. Mount Sinai/Horeb is thus brought near to them, both to sustain them where they are and to encourage them to keep on pressing forward, for at Rephidim they are given a foretaste of the "water" they are to find at the holy mountain.

In 15:22–26, we saw the themes of water and *torah* (law) woven together in such a way that each could become a metaphor for the other. Like water, *torah* is essential to life and health. In the present passage, we see water coming from the mountain where Israel will later receive the *torah* and will eat and drink in God's presence (24:9–11). When Martin Luther King, Jr., said that he might not get to the promised land but that he had been to the mountain, and when Jesse Jackson punctuates his speeches with the refrain "keep hope alive," they walk in the steps of Moses at Rephidim. When they call for social justice for their own kin, in a society that has yet fully to realize the vision enshrined in its Declaration of Independence, they show their understanding of Mount Sinai/Horeb as the source, at one and the same time, of the life-giving water of hope and of the claims and promise of justice in God's *torah*.

This passage presents the last instance of "murmuring" in Exodus. In the Old Testament it occurs only in Exodus 15, 16, and 17; then again (after the sojourn at Mount Sinai) in Numbers 14, 16, and 17; and finally in Joshua 9:18. The word used by the translators of the Old Testament into Greek is used several times in its Old Testament sense by the writers of the New Testament (Matt. 20:11; Luke 5:30; John 7:12, 32; Acts 6:1; Phil. 2:14; 1 Peter 4:9; Jude 16). The two most striking places are in John 6:41, 43, 61 and in 1 Corinthians 10:10 (twice).

In the latter instance, Paul warns the Corinthian followers of Jesus against "complaining" (that is, against "murmuring"). He compares the grumblers' situation to Israel's experiences in the wilderness as reread in the light of Christ (1 Cor. 10:1–13). In this rereading, Paul identifies Christ as the "spiritual rock" from which the Israelites drank—that is, the rock Moses struck with his staff. Paul here sees the stricken rock as an analogy (or "type," as a longstanding tradition of interpretation calls it) of Christ's crucifixion as the source of Christian sustenance. When he goes on to speak of God meeting every trial we must undergo by providing "the way out so that you may be able to endure it" (1 Cor. 10:13), we wonder if he doesn't have in mind how Moses and the elders went ahead to Mount Sinai/Horeb to draw water from the rock. In such a case, Paul might be intimating that under our own severe desert trials, where we are tempted to murmur and put God to the test, we may draw strength and encouragement from Christ, our stricken rock; for from Christ, whom God raised from the dead, we learn that "God is faithful" (10:13; compare 2 Cor. 1:18–22).

The occurrences of murmuring in John 6 relate to a strikingly similar theme. Here, drawing on the manna theme initiated in Exodus 16 (and see Psalm 78:23–25), Jesus is presented as identifying the true manna, given for the life of the world as "my flesh" (6:51). When his fellow Jews "dispute" (or grumble) among themselves, he reiterates the claim even more vividly: "unless you eat the flesh of the Son of Man and drink his blood, you have no life in you" (v. 53). This causes many of his own disciples to "complain" or murmur (6:60–61). When he responds to their murmuring (6:62–65), some of them "turn back" (6:66), reminiscent of the Israelites in the wilderness who repeatedly want to return to Egypt. When Jesus says to the Twelve, "Do you also wish to go away?" Peter answers, "Lord, to whom can we go? You have the words of eternal life" (6:67–68).

Many interpreters associate the words "flesh" and "blood" in John 6:53–58 with the Christian Eucharist or Holy Communion. What is of particular interest is that Jesus goes on to say, "It is the spirit that gives life; the flesh is useless. The words that I have spoken to you are spirit and life" (v. 63). The connection here between "my flesh" and "my blood" and "the words that I have spoken to you" is like the connection between water and *torah* at Mount Sinai/Horeb. The purpose of the water in the wilderness is to lead to the life-giving "water" of *torah*. The "life" in the Eucharist is conveyed in the words of Jesus that his flesh and blood "speak" to our souls. That is to say, the "flesh and blood" in the Eucharist proclaim the mystery that our life is renewed and sustained for "eternal life" (v. 54) through the death of God's incarnate word. As often as the dry patches in our wilderness journey tempt us to put God to the test, the Lord's Supper offers us refreshment and renewal; for the barrenness of the crucifixion issues in resurrection and eternal life, a life of which we are already given a foretaste in the way it renews us for the journey toward the final feast.

THE SECRET
OF VICTORY AGAINST AMALEK
Exodus 17:8–16

17:8 Then Amalek came and fought with Israel at Rephidim. [9] Moses said to Joshua, "Choose some men for us and go out, fight with Amalek. Tomorrow I will stand on the top of the hill with the staff of God in my hand." [10] So Joshua did as Moses told him, and fought with Amalek, while Moses, Aaron, and Hur went up to the top of the hill. [11] Whenever Moses held up his hand, Israel prevailed; and whenever he lowered his hand, Amalek prevailed. [12] But Moses' hands grew weary; so they took a stone and put it under him, and he sat on it. Aaron and Hur held up his hands, one on one side, and the other on the other side; so his hands were steady until the sun set. [13] And Joshua defeated Amalek and his people with the sword.
[14] Then the LORD said to Moses, "Write this as a reminder in a book and recite it in the hearing of Joshua: I will utterly blot out the remembrance of Amalek from under heaven." [15] And Moses built an altar and called it, The LORD is my banner. [16] He said, "A hand upon the banner of the LORD! The LORD will have war with Amalek from generation to generation."

Since their deliverance from Pharaoh's chariots, the Israelites have undergone a series of crises in the wilderness involving lack of water, food, and, again, water. These crises have called for God to act in ways characteristic of divine presence in the ancestral period—nourishment from the earth and from the heavens (Gen. 49:25). Now, still at Rephidim, the people face a crisis more like Pharaoh and yet not identical. At the sea, the threat came from the military arm of a political state whose laws and policies had become oppressive. Here in the wilderness, the threat comes from a lawless band.

Whereas at the sea God acted through the elements of nature at the movement of Moses' staff (14:16, 21, 26–27), here God acts through Joshua and his fighting men, again at the movement of Moses' staff. Thus Joshua is drawn into a role that will grow in prominence until its climax in the book of Joshua. In this way, thematic continuities are established between the exodus and the entry into the land.

Now, up to this point Moses' use of the staff has been a simple matter of raising it and accomplishing the result, whether sign, plague, parting of the waters, or water from the rock. But this time the struggle is drawn out, to the point where Moses becomes so tired that from time to time he has to lower his arms; whenever this happens, the fortunes of Joshua and his men are reversed. Taken as an object lesson, we may suppose the point of this to be that, when Israel fights under the leadership of Joshua or anyone else, it is not their might or skill that determines the outcome but the might and wisdom of God as signified by Moses' staff. Interestingly, though, when Moses gets tired, the help does not come directly from God, but through Aaron and Hur, as each one supports one of Moses' arms after seating him on a stone. What is this symbolism, of Moses seated on a stone, holding up his and God's staff, and supported on both sides by Aaron and Hur?

This scene foreshadows the ark with its cherubim, which will serve as Yahweh's throne-seat and which, when carried into battle by priests, will achieve God's victory against Israel's enemies (see Num. 10:35–36; 1 Sam. 4:1b–4). To put it the other way around, when the ark is later so used, it recalls this earlier scene and encourages Israel to believe that the God who delivered Israel from Egypt and from Amalek through Moses and his staff will deliver them still, though Moses is long dead. Certainly, verse 14 suggests that the scene as written in a book and read to Joshua will encourage him in his later battles. (After Numbers 10:35–36, we may supppose that he went into battle behind the ark, for example, Joshua 3.). Thus, by two means—this battle story and the material symbol of the ark—later generations will be encouraged in the face of all who oppose them.

Our passage goes on to show Moses building an altar and naming it "Yahweh is my banner." Such an act is reminiscent of Abraham, Isaac, and

Jacob, who built altars after God appeared to them. Just as their altars celebrated the promises God made to them, so Moses' altar celebrates God's deliverance in battle. To say, "Yahweh is my banner" is to pledge by the sacredness of the altar that it will be under Yahweh, and no other god, that Moses will seek protection from his and the people's enemies.

But what does Moses mean by the first half of verse 16? The meaning of the Hebrew is uncertain (see NRSV margin). The Hebrew word translated "banner" is not the word commonly translated this way, but a different, rare word that may also be translated "throne." If we follow some of the ancient versions of the Old Testament, the words of the text are, literally, "hand-upon-throne-Yah." The question then is whether we understand this to mean "a hand upon the throne of Yah(weh)" or "a hand upon the throne is Yah(weh)." What attracts me to the latter possibility is that (1) a throne is a royal seat, (2) the cherubim are the royal seat of Yahweh on the ark, (3) the ark is, among other things, emblematic of Yahweh as divine warrior, (4) as a "hand upon the throne," Yahweh would be celebrated for royal might and victory in battle, (5) hand and throne in this case would correspond to Moses' upraised hand and staff as he was seated on the stone, and (6) like Moses' arms held up by Aaron and Hur, the ark was to be carried into battle by Israel's priests beginning with Aaron (e.g., 1 Sam. 4:4).

But what about Amalek? Whether this people is to be annihilated (genocide?) or fought against interminably, does this passage not dehumanize and demonize them and perpetuate the very sort of undying conflict that still plagues our own world? The Jewish biblical scholar and theologian Jon Levenson finds in this passage an Old Testament equivalent of what he terms the strain of anti-Semitism or anti-Judaism in the New Testament. He does so in order to reject any claim that fellow Jews might make against their enemies on the basis of such a passage. Needless to say, he does so also in order to challenge Christians to reject New Testament texts as a basis for unrelenting opposition against and physical attack on their enemies.

Levenson's point in both respects is well taken. Yet do we simply draw a red line around such passages and hereafter read around them when we read the Bible? What then shall we do with the book of Joshua and the whole tradition of God's gift of the land to Israel in the face of those who formerly lived there? These parts of the Bible raise all sorts of questions for us, but simply to ignore them and read the rest of the Bible as if they were not part of it is to create a Bible out of our own wishes.

The fact is that human history is a drama moved not only by love but by hate, not only by cooperation but also by conflict. It is a drama whose plot is a thick weave of people's loves and their wars. The passages of the Bible that portray war at least make contact with the dark strands in our emotions and motivations. The way to deal with them, I suggest, is to stay with the story, and see what happens to the themes, motifs, images, and scenarios that relate to Yahweh as warrior (Exod. 15:3) as we move through the biblical narrative from Exodus through to Revelation. What we find is a progressive transformation of these images, in such a way that the very theme of Yahweh as warrior who vanquishes the enemy becomes the theme of God who in Christ conquers the world (John 16:33), not with the sword, but simply by bearing witness to the truth as he is crucified by this world's political and military powers (John 18:33–38). One stage along the path of this transformation is marked in Isaiah 51—53, where the exiles invoke the old "arm of the LORD" to overcome their enemies with the sword (Isa. 51:9–11), and where the arm of Yahweh that is raised in response to this invocation is the suffering servant (Isa. 53:1–9) whose victory leads him to share the spoils of victory with the very "great" and "many" who were responsible for his death (Isa. 53:10–12). One fine study of this transformation is a book by Paul Valliere, *Holy War and Pentecostal Peace*. Among other things, Valliere shows how the very traditions of holy war in the Old Testament become the basis for what he calls "prophetic pacifism."

But if the themes of war are eventually transformed in this way, already in the Old Testament and unmistakably in the New Testament, why bother any longer with these earlier texts, especially when their misuse can provide religious motivation and sanction for so much human conflict and suffering? We need to keep wrestling with them until they force us to identify within ourselves the very animosities and oaths of undying hostility that repel us when we see them in the text. Then, if we stay with the story and follow it in its transformations, perhaps our own tangled motivations, emotions, and resolves can undergo a steady transformation until we find ourselves in the place where the New Testament would leave us: Jesus' warfare against untruth and evil, a warfare he conducts simply by his witness to the truth. In such a struggle, says Paul at the end of his long passage in Romans 8, "we are more than conquerors through him who loved us" (8:37; the "him who loved us" is Christ, if Galatians 2:20 is any guide.)

Mention of Romans 8 brings us back to another motif in our passage. It has to do with Aaron and Hur's support of Moses' uplifted arms. As we shall see, a chief function of the high priest is to bear the children of Israel up before God in intercession, by carrying their names on his shoulders and on his breast (28:15–30). Further, in any holy war it is the function of the priests to seek God's intervention on the side of Israel. This motif, of

Aaron and Hur holding up Moses' arms and of his staff empowering Joshua and his men, will find its transformation in that form of prayer we hear on the lips of Jesus on the cross ("Father, forgive them; for they do not know what they are doing," Luke 23:34) and of Stephen as he is being stoned ("Lord, do not hold this sin against them," Acts 7:60). In the light of such a transformation, no one who wishes to live in accordance with the biblical narrative should find it possible to take the present passage, or any so-called anti-Judaic text in the New Testament, as a mandate for hate and aggression. The struggle against evil will continue to be real and may at times arise to the pitch of conflict, but the conflict is to be engaged in prayer and nonviolent struggle. When we grow weary of such prayer and such engagement, we may find support in the dual intercession of the Spirit of God who dwells within us (Rom. 8:26–27) and Christ Jesus who intercedes for us at God's right hand (Rom. 8:34).

JETHRO'S FEAST
Exodus 18:1–12

18:1 Jethro, the priest of Midian, Moses' father-in-law, heard of all that God had done for Moses and for his people Israel, how the LORD had brought Israel out of Egypt. ² After Moses had sent away his wife Zipporah, his father-in-law Jethro took her back, ³ along with her two sons. The name of the one was Gershom (for he said, "I have been an alien in a foreign land"), ⁴ and the name of the other, Eliezer (for he said, "The God of my father was my help, and delivered me from the sword of Pharaoh"). ⁵ Jethro, Moses' father-in-law, came into the wilderness where Moses was encamped at the mountain of God, bringing Moses' sons and wife to him. ⁶ He sent word to Moses, "I, your father-in-law Jethro, am coming to you, with your wife and her two sons." ⁷ Moses went out to meet his father-in-law; he bowed down and kissed him; each asked after the other's welfare, and they went into the tent. ⁸ Then Moses told his father-in-law all that the LORD had done to Pharaoh and to the Egyptians for Israel's sake, all the hardship that had beset them on the way, and how the LORD had delivered them. ⁹ Jethro rejoiced for all the good that the LORD had done to Israel, in delivering them from the Egyptians.

¹⁰ Jethro said, "Blessed be the LORD, who has delivered you from the Egyptians and from Pharaoh. ¹¹ Now I know that the LORD is greater than all gods, because he delivered the people from the Egyptians, when they dealt arrogantly with them." ¹² And Jethro, Moses' father-in-law, brought a burnt offering and sacrifices to God; and Aaron came with all the elders of Israel to eat bread with Moses' father-in-law in the presence of God.

In two important connections (ritual, vv. 1–12; law, vv. 13–27) the spotlight in this chapter shifts from Moses to Jethro. Of stylistic interest is the fact that this man is mentioned seven times by name (vv. 1, 2, 5, 6, 9, 10, 12), and is identified fourteen times by title, once as "the priest of Midian" (v. 1, as in 2:16; 3:1), and thirteen times as "Moses' father-in-law" (vv. 1, 2, 5, 6, 7, 8, 12, 12, 14, 15, 17, 24, 27). In Exodus 3:1, the two titles occurred in the order "his father-in-law, Jethro, the priest of Midian." The emphasis there was appropriate to the focus on Moses as a son-in-law tending sheep. Now (18:1) the order is reversed: "Jethro, the priest of Midian, Moses' father-in-law." The emphasis on Jethro as priest befits the chapter's first climax (v. 12), where Jethro carries out a priestly duty. Yet, oddly enough, there he is not called a priest but twice is identified as Moses' father-in-law. What are we to make of these different titles?

To begin with, who are the Midianites? In a culture and literature where genealogy is important both for identity and for how one relates to others as "insiders" or "outsiders," it cannot be insignificant that the Midianites are identified as descendants of Abraham through his third wife, Keturah (Gen. 25:1–2). So Jethro is a distant kin of Moses. Might that account in some measure for the amicable relations between these two and for the positive picture painted of him? Yet like Ishmael, son of Abraham by Hagar the Egyptian maidservant, Midian was sent away from Abraham's household, apparently not a member of the community of promise traced through Isaac (Gen. 17:15–22; 21:8–21; 25:5–6). Their exclusion did not banish them from the sphere of God's blessing and providence, but God's redemptive work through Abraham for the sake of "all the families of the earth" (Gen. 12:3) would continue through Isaac (Gen. 17:19, 21; 26:1–5) and Jacob (Gen. 28:1–4, 13–15). So biologically Jethro is an insider, but covenantally he is an outsider. This "liminal" status is the key to understanding Jethro's significance in Israel's story of redemption, as that story fulfills the promise to Abraham in Genesis 12:3. A "limen" is a threshold. A subliminal awareness, for example, is an awareness of something that does not stand entirely within the clear "interior" light of consciousness or entirely in darkness "outside" that light. The something is just outside the threshold, with one foot sufficiently inside the door for us to see it. So, as a liminal figure, Jethro is neither simply "inside" nor simply "outside" the covenant community. He is a figure who by his position holds the door ajar.

Now, the Midianites are desert dwellers, and as such Jethro is a shepherd (Exod. 2:16–22; 3:1). As a priest, he may tend a desert wayside shrine at which passers-by may worship. We are never told the identity of his god. As a desert shepherd, we may assume that he worships a family or kinship god like the ancestors in Genesis 12—50. In such a setting, the family or clan head is also priest, officiating in the relatively informal (that is, custom-shaped rather than regulation-ordered) rites relevant to family concerns. (I am reminded of an Episcopal bishop who, in the days when only men were ordained, would decline his lay host's request that he say grace, with the words, "every man a priest in his own house." That nicely catches the distinction between family piety and piety as regulated in terms of sanctuary worship and its ordained leadership.)

To come, then, to 18:1–12, the scenes described are affectingly familial. Hearing from others what God has done for Moses and his people Israel (compare 4:18), Jethro goes out to meet Moses, bringing with him the wife and two children that Moses apparently left behind. So eager is he that he sends word ahead announcing his approach.

For his part, Moses, too, goes out to meet his father-in-law. When they meet, the man who had stood before Pharaoh and spoken commandingly in Yahweh's name (5:1) now prostrates himself (so the Hebrew) before his father-in-law, acknowledging their relative status within the family into which he has married, and he kisses him. Having satisfied themselves as to each other's welfare (shalom, as in 4:18 when they had parted), they go into the tent. This may be Jethro's desert home, or it may be his desert shrine. We cannot be sure.

The exchange in verses 8–11 is noteworthy. Jethro has heard from others what God has done for Moses and his people, how Yahweh has brought Israel out of Egypt. In a polytheistic culture, it would not be problematic for Jethro, worshiping a different god, to recognize what Moses' god had done for him. Now he hears it from Moses himself. As an insider to those experiences, Moses tells also of "all the hardship that had beset them on the way" (v. 8), something the outsider reporters (v. 1) and Jethro himself (v. 9) seem unaware of. Moses' addition emphasizes that for him Yahweh's deliverance encompasses not only the exodus from Egypt but also the crises of survival in the wilderness. Is Jethro's obliviousness because for him the wilderness is not such a difficult place to live?

Jethro rejoices at Moses' story—the mark of a soul free from envy, capable of sympathetic identification with others in their good fortune (Rom. 12:15). Then he blesses Yahweh and makes a confession that contrasts with Pharaoh's refusal to "know" Yahweh (5:2) and harmonizes with the people's own knowing, for his, "Now I know that the LORD is greater than all gods" joins their acclamation in Exodus 15:11.

Does this confession signal Jethro's conversion to Yahweh? Commentators differ. In my view, a clear yes or a clear no obscures Jethro's status as an important liminal figure. All the more should we resist the "insider *or* outsider" alternatives when we come to the climax of this scene, when Jethro is involved in an act of sacrificial worship and communal fellowship. How is he involved? Much turns on the meaning of the first verb in verse 12, which NRSV translates "brought" but is literally "took." What does it mean to "take a burnt offering and sacrifices to God"? In the Hebrew of passages like Leviticus 12:8; 15:14, 29; Numbers 19:2, a layperson "takes" an offering to a priest, who then presents it to God. If that is what the verb means here, then Jethro is simply a worshiper along with others at a sacrifice over which Moses presides. But since "to eat bread . . . in the presence of God" is also a ritual act, and it occurs under Jethro's leadership, this may suggest that at the sacrifice, too, Jethro acts as priest. That this is possible, is shown by those passages in which the Hebrew text says that a priest "takes" a sacrifice or offering from others (Lev. 9:2, 3, 5, 15; Num. 5:25; especially Num. 16:5–7) and presents it to God.

For later institutional religion, where outsiders are clearly distinguished from insiders and laity from priesthood, the scene here is unsettling. (It is important to ordained insiders like myself to note that the first two celebrations of the exodus are led by a woman [Miriam in chapter 15] and an outsider [Jethro], while the officially designated high priest, Aaron, soon leads the people into idolatry [chapter 32].) No wonder some wish to see Jethro converted, or the sacrifice offered by someone else! Yet Jethro is not a member of the covenanted descendants of Abraham and Sarah, he never went through the exodus, he will not enter the covenant at Mount Sinai (v. 27), and he will not enter the promised land; for all this, he confesses and ritually celebrates the supremacy of Israel's god. As such, I take him to be a liminal figure, one who stands neither clearly inside the community of Israel nor obscurely outside it, but on the threshhold, where, by standing there, he holds the door open. In doing so, he prevents both insiders and outsiders from drawing the boundary too neatly and sealing it too tightly. As such, he helps to preserve the freedom of Yahweh as "I will be who I will be." As such, he should remind the covenant community that its experience, confession, and tradition are a generous gift it receives and not an exclusive possession, something to be offered to any who would enter and not something with which to beat those who choose to stay outside.

Jethro is a liminal figure in another respect. In celebrating Yahweh's deliverance of Israel from Egypt, he stands in solidarity with the community that comes into existence with that deliverance, and he acknowledges the new meaning of the name Yahweh as a deliverer from political oppression.

Yet, as a desert-dwelling clan leader and priestly figure, he is like Israel's ancestors in their social ethos and religious practices. So in this chapter he appears twice as a transitional figure, between older and newer forms of worship (vv. 10–12) and between older and newer arrangements for adjudication of interpersonal dispute (vv. 13–33). As such a transitional or liminal figure, he holds old and new together so that they may not simply be sharply distinguished from one another. Rather, he is one of those figures within the Bible who encourage us to pass back and forth between old and new through the door he holds open.

JETHRO'S ADVICE
Exodus 18:13–27

18:13 The next day Moses sat as judge for the people, while the people stood around him from morning until evening. [14] When Moses' father-in-law saw all that he was doing for the people, he said, "What is this that you are doing for the people? Why do you sit alone, while all the people stand around you from morning until evening?" [15] Moses said to his father-in-law, "Because the people come to me to inquire of God. [16] When they have a dispute, they come to me and I decide between one person and another, and I make known to them the statutes and instructions of God." [17] Moses' father-in-law said to him, "What you are doing is not good. [18] You will surely wear yourself out, both you and these people with you. For the task is too heavy for you; you cannot do it alone. [19] Now listen to me. I will give you counsel, and God be with you! You should represent the people before God, and you should bring their cases before God; [20] teach them the statutes and instructions and make known to them the way they are to go and the things they are to do. [21] You should also look for able men among all the people, men who fear God, are trustworthy, and hate dishonest gain; set such men over them as officers over thousands, hundreds, fifties and tens. [22] Let them sit as judges for the people at all times; let them bring every important case to you, but decide every minor case themselves. So it will be easier for you, and they will bear the burden with you. [23] If you do this, and God so commands you, then you will be able to endure, and all these people will go to their home in peace."
[24] So Moses listened to his father-in-law and did all that he had said. [25] Moses chose able men from all Israel and appointed them as heads over the people, as officers over thousands, hundreds, fifties, and tens. [26] And they judged the people at all times; hard cases they brought to Moses, but any minor case they decided themselves. [27] Then Moses let his father-in-law depart, and he went off to his own country.

The scene opens with Moses sitting in the middle of the community, from morning to evening attempting to adjudicate the people's disputes. This, as we might say, blows Jethro's mind. He has seen nothing like it. He no doubt has heard and settled disputes within his own household (compare Gen. 13:8–9; 16:5–6; and, in its own way, 50:15–17). Such disputes no doubt involved the use of a human wisdom originating in his family or clan god (compare Gen. 21:8–14). But such disputes would occupy only a small part of a clan father's time, whereas the disputes of this large crowd occupy Moses all day long and will wear him out. So Jethro asks, in effect, "What makes you think you can do this *alone*? (v. 14). Moses' response implies that in the people's mind he has become so identified with God's presence and direction that they have no one else to go to. When they come to him with their disputes, he inquires of God, case by case, and then informs them of how God would have them settle matters. The statutes and the instructions here are not promulgated laws (as later, at Mount Sinai) but precedents arising out of specific situations with God's help in each instance.

Jethro's response to Moses is reminiscent of God's observation in Genesis 2:18: "It is not good that the man should be alone; I will make him a helper as his partner." He does not challenge Moses' status as mediator between God and the people, but he offers Moses wise counsel so that God may more effectively be with him. Moses should search out able men who are God-fearing, trustworthy, and scornful of dishonest gain. Such men are to be appointed to various spheres and levels of judicial responsibility, with the hardest cases referred to Moses. The benefit of this—God would have Moses do it (v. 23)—will be twofold: Moses himself will be able to endure, and the people will go home in *shalom*, that is, reconciled with one another.

So far in Exodus, we have been given a picture in which only Moses is unswervingly on God's side, while the people sometimes believe and sometimes are on the verge of mutiny. How can Moses take the risk, then, of delegating into other, perhaps less worthy hands the delicate task of judging and giving God's instructions? Jethro's response is that, in fact, there are those even within such a community who may be entrusted with this task. Their credentials are not primarily a law degree or prior experience, but a scorn of dishonest gain that is grounded in their trustworthiness, and a trustworthiness that, in turn, is grounded in their fear of God. Where there is no fear of God, desire for gain may have its sway. Where the judges know themselves to be under the judgment of God, a system of higher and lower courts may be entrusted with tasks that so far Moses has felt he alone can carry out.

Where does this desert-dwelling, family-situated Jethro get the idea for such a multilayered system? We are not told. One thing is clear: The figure whom the narrator presents to us repeatedly continues to be identified as Moses' father-in-law, as though even in this situation he is acting out of his own familial identity. As clan head, he has had to come up with solutions for other kinds of novel situations. May we assume that, as with Moses' staff, which began as an embodiment of shepherd skill and wisdom and ended as the instrument of God's deliverance of Israel from Egypt, so, too, Jethro's skill in handling clan disputes translates into a wisdom adequate to this new social situation?

The system of higher and lower courts may strike some today as liable to the shortcomings of all hierarchical arrangements. In that connection, it may be helpful to distinguish between dominant and nested hierarchies. While the first is a top-down model and lends itself to the imposition of the will and aims of those at the top, the second is a bottom-up model in which the smaller, more local units are undergirded and supported by larger units, which are themselves undergirded by a more encompassing unit. The key here lies in the notion of "bearing." While others help to bear the burdens Moses otherwise would have to bear alone, in the last analysis all burdens they cannot bear devolve onto him, and he must take them to God.

A second feature should protect this system from becoming simply machinery for the elite to have their way. If each judge is a God-fearer, no judge is closer to or farther from the seat of ultimate justice than anyone else. Every judge who is truly God-fearing is a God-given bulwark against the corruption of the system. That corruption, moreover, is envisaged as arising, not from within, but from outside, as parties to disputes try to bribe the judge in their own direction. (Where the judicial process no longer delivers justice, the implication is that parties inside and outside the judicial system have lost their interest in justice as such and are merely working the system for their own ends.)

Earlier, we saw that while God speaks to Moses, Moses speaks "as God" to and through Aaron. Later, in the building of the tabernacle (chapters 35—40), we shall see Moses repeatedly described as doing all that God has commanded him to do. Here, Moses is shown listening to his father-in-law and doing all he has said. Both of the scenes in this chapter are presented to us by biblical writers who write after Mount Sinai with its provisions for legitimate priesthood and its laws for governing justice. It is remarkable that these writers should be willing to paint Jethro in such positive terms. When he departs and goes off to his own country, we are sorry to see him go. Yet the stories about him remain in our Bible, as a reminder that God's presence and activity in our midst may come from unexpected quarters, and the matter is not something that even our own most sacred traditions and arrangements can enable us to control.

EAGLES' WINGS
AND A PRIESTLY KINGDOM
Exodus 19:1–9a

> 19:1 On the third new moon after the Israelites had gone out of the land of Egypt, on that very day, they came into the wilderness of Sinai. 2 They had journeyed from Rephidim, entered the wilderness of Sinai, and camped in the wilderness; Israel camped there in front of the mountain. 3 Then Moses went up to God; the LORD called to him from the mountain, saying, "Thus you shall say to the house of Jacob, and tell the Israelites: 4 You have seen what I did to the Egyptians, and how I bore you on eagles' wings and brought you to myself. 5 Now therefore, if you obey my voice and keep my covenant, you shall be my treasured possession out of all the peoples. Indeed, the whole earth is mine, 6 but you shall be for me a priestly kingdom and a holy nation. These are the words that you shall speak to the Israelites." 7 So Moses came, summoned the elders of the people, and set before them all these words that the LORD had commanded him. 8 The people all answered as one: "Everything that the LORD has spoken we will do." Moses reported the words of the people to the LORD. 9a Then the LORD said to Moses, "I am going to come to you in a dense cloud, in order that the people may hear when I speak with you and so trust you ever after."

In Exodus 6:6–8, God instructed Moses to announce three new divine acts by which the Israelites would know the new meaning and significance of the divine name. Those divine acts involved liberating Israel from oppression in Egypt, taking this people to God's own self in covenant, and bringing them into the land promised to the ancestors. Now, with the arrival at Mount Sinai, we enter on the second act, which occupies the biblical narrative until Numbers 10:11.

But whereas in Exodus 6:6–8 the Mount Sinai covenant was spoken of purely in terms of God's action ("I will take you as my people, and I will be your God"), here at Mount Sinai this covenant is presented as calling for the action of both God and people. That is, both parties are to enter into the covenant freely and willingly, without hesitation or coercion on either side. How then shall we reconcile the apparently unilateral action of 6:7 with the bilateral action at Mount Sinai itself?

Here we enter into one of the deepest mysteries of our experience and knowledge of God: how our acts can be freely our own and yet the gift of God. Like all true mysteries, this one can never be fully explained, but it can be experienced and recognized and, in that sense, known. One way it comes is when we find ourselves unable to do what we know we should do or wish we could do. I once overheard my sister-in-law urge her kindergarten daughter to eat something that would be good for her, to which my niece responded in a mixture of stubborn resistance and plaintive appeal, "But I can't want to!" I remember, too, a July Fourth outing that almost came to grief because a little boy refused to get into the station wagon, since his older sister had already chosen the place he wanted to sit. The father, knowing that the boy really did want to go on the picnic but was caught in a point of honor, was inclined to just pick him up, dump him unceremoniously in the back, and drive off. But what kind of outing would that have been? The mother, with a wiser combination of patience, sympathy, and humor, in a few minutes had the little fellow perched happily in his own place, and the outing came off as originally planned. How do parents enable children to want to do something they "can't want to"? How are we enabled to do something we "can't want to"? When it happens, we can't fully explain it, but we can recognize it and rejoice in it.

In the present instance, the enabling act on God's part is set forth in 19:4. We may recall that part of God's enabling act was Miriam's song (her own composition and, at the same time, God's gift), a song that enabled Israel to "see" their escape at the sea as God's act. Just as the Israelites were liberated from their fear so that they could see not just the Egyptians but also God's act, now they are liberated for a free response to God's invitation to enter into covenant: "If you obey my voice and keep my covenant." The "if" is part of what conveys the freedom. It shows that in God's eyes Israel is free to respond one way or another: not "You *will* obey my voice," but "*if* you obey my voice"; that is, "will you?" In some forms of marriage, the binding vows are preceded by the question asked of each party, "N., will you take N. to be . . . ?" and the service can proceed only if each party says, "I will." The intentional "I will" (not merely a descriptive "I do") signifies that the marriage is being entered into out of each party's own free will.

In the case of the Mount Sinai covenant, the free will is a free decision to obey God's voice. The Hebrew here is, literally, "if you will hear my voice." When we say, "Listen to your mother," we use a word for hearing in the sense of obeying. Our word "obey" itself contains this idea, coming from Latin *ab* + *audire*, which means to act "on the basis of hearing." What we should note here is that Israel is being called into a covenant relation of *mutual hearing*. As 2:23–25, and 3:7–9 show, God acts to deliver Israel from Egypt because God has heard their cry. In view of this, we may take 19:4–5 as saying, in effect, "You have seen how I heard your voice. . . . Now, therefore, if you will hear my voice . . ."

If Israel will hear God and act out of what Israel hears, then Israel will be God's treasured possession. The Hebrew word here apparently refers literally (as in 1 Chron. 29:3; Eccles. 2:8) to a king's personal treasury, in distinction from what we might call the public purse. In some ancient texts, it is used figuratively when an imperial king wishes to single out one or other of his subject states for "favored nation status." What is to distinguish Israel from all other peoples is, on the one hand, its experience of God in deliverance from Egypt (compare Deut. 4:7, 32–34) and, on the other hand, its character as a holy priesthood through its observance of God's covenant teaching and laws (compare Deut. 4:8).

Here, priesthood and holiness are characterized in terms of the justice and harmony that should mark the quality of life within the covenant community. It is such a quality of life that will be Israel's true "sacrificial worship" (compare Rom. 12:1–2). But just as, within Israel, the priests are set apart from the people in order to represent them to God and in order to bless them in God's name, so here Israel as a priestly kingdom is set apart from the nations in order to represent them to God and in order to be a means whereby God may bless all nations. Thus the promise given to Abraham in Genesis 12:3 begins to take on flesh in a wider communal form. It has been proposed that the common distinction between "the holy, and the common or not-holy" be restated as a distinction between "the holy, and the not-yet holy." If Israel is a special treasure, it is to serve God's aim that all nations may become such.

When Moses lays these words of God before the elders, the people "as one" respond, "Everything that the LORD has spoken we will do" (19:8). When Moses reports their response to God, the preliminaries to the covenant are over, and preparations to enter into it may now begin. First, God informs Moses of a means by which God will elicit the people's unending trust in his leadership (19:9). The Hebrew verb translated in NRSV "and so *trust* you" is the same as in Exodus 14:31: "the people . . . *believed in* the LORD and *in* his servant Moses." This similarity between 19:9 and 14:31 underscores the dual significance of Moses in Israel's life and memory: He is associated with the liberation from Egypt and with the teaching and laws of the Mount Sinai covenant. He stands for a human freedom that is willing to discipline itself to live in accordance with those claims of God that will ensure that all within the covenant shall remain free.

Like the words in 6:6–8, the words in 19:4–6 are tightly packed, containing all that will be elaborated at Mount Sinai and beyond. In verse 4, God says, "I bore you on eagles' wings and brought you to myself." As the development of this image in Deuteronomy 32:10–14 shows, the picture is of a parent bird tenderly caring for its young, especially in time of danger. This image occurs again in Isaiah 40:31 (where the Hebrew may be translated "with wings like eagles" [NRSV] or "on wings like eagles," leaving the reader to decide whether the wings are their own or God's). This image may be associated with other related images for God, such as the wings on the cherubim, from which God may be called upon to save Israel in distress (Psalm 80:1–2). Psalm 91 begins by speaking of those who live in "the shelter of the Most High" and who "abide in the shadow of El Shaddai [the Almighty]" and goes on to develop that "shadow" in terms of God's covering pinions and wings under which one may find refuge. In this last instance, the parental connotations of El Shaddai and the parental connotations of the sheltering wings reinforce each other. It is striking, then, that when Jesus is tempted in the wilderness over what it means to be "Son of God," one form the temptation takes is to appropriate the assurances of Psalm 91 in an inappropriate way (Matt. 4:5–7). Later, Jesus goes on to say how often he has desired to gather Jerusalem's children together as a hen gathers her chickens (Matt. 23:37). But apparently his way of "gathering" the children—through death and resurrection—meets with an "I can't want to." One example is Peter's rejection of his talk of the cross, "God forbid it, Lord!" (Matt. 16:21–22), a response in which Jesus hears the same mind-set as he heard in his own temptations (Matt. 16:23).

The image of God's care in the form of an eagle or parent bird does not begin even at Exodus 19:4. Its redemptive use begins here, but the image itself begins at the very beginning, in creation. In Genesis 1:2, "a wind from God *swept* over the face of the waters," the verb for "swept" is the same as in Deuteronomy 32:11: "As an eagle . . . *hovers* over its young." Like the raven and the dove after the flood, which hovered over the waters until they could find a place to build a nest for their young, God in Genesis 1:2 is portrayed as hovering over the waters of chaos in preparation for creating a world filled with all kinds of life. So we see how the image of the caring parent bird can portray God both in creation and in redemption.

In commenting on Exodus 6:7, I noted that the Hebrew text reads, literally, "I will take you to me for a people" and that this language is echoed in 19:4, "I bore you on eagles' wings and brought you to myself." I suggested that the meaning of the phrase "to me/to myself" may be taken at several levels. Geographically, it refers to God bringing Israel to the holy mountain and later to the holy land. Morally, it refers to the covenant relation into which God draws Israel as they receive and commit themselves to the covenant laws. I referred also to James Luther Mays's comment on Psalm 16, which, using language associated with Israel's inheritance of the holy land, speaks of God as the psalmist's "portion" and "lot." In the New Testament, Psalm 16 is used to speak of Christ's resurrection (Acts 2:25–28; 13:35). Within Judaism also, there is a tradition according to which Israel became immortal when they received God's covenant *torah* at Mount Sinai (but became mortal again through the sin of the golden calf [Exodus 32]). Thus at different levels the text may refer to Mount Sinai and later the holy land, to the covenant relation and its laws, and to God as our final inheritance.

This third level of reading "to me/to myself" has fallen out of favor in many circles, as "reading back into the text" views that arose only later than the Old Testament. Instead, scholars have concentrated on the plain historical meaning of the text, in this instance, on the geographical and covenantal meanings of "to me/to myself." Yet even among rigorously "historical" scholars, under certain circumstances this phrase can be heard to speak a word at the third level. In graduate school I sat in a seminar discussion led by the Old Testament scholar G. Ernest Wright and colleagues in New Testament and systematic theology. I remember the passion with which Wright spoke of God's redemptive grace as the basis of God's claim on us for social justice, and I remember being puzzled by his apparent indifference to someone's proposal that God's redemptive grace finds ultimate expression in the defeat of death and the gift of eternal life. Years later, when he died, it was a great comfort to read the memorial eulogy in the alumni magazine. His colleague, Frank Moore Cross, opened the eulogy by quoting Exodus 19:4–6 as one of Wright's favorite biblical texts celebrating the God of liberation and social justice. He closed the eulogy by saying,

> The God who bore Israel on eagles' wings, the sovereign God to whom belongs the future, was a sufficient ground of hope to Ernest Wright in the days of his life. With his work done, and his vocation fulfilled, he waits upon the God who lifts up the weak and the dying, and bears them on eagles' wings, to Himself.

PREPARING TO MEET GOD
Exodus 19:9b–25

19:9b When Moses had told the words of the people to the LORD, [10] the LORD said to Moses: "Go to the people and consecrate them today and tomorrow. Have them wash their clothes [11] and prepare for the third day, because on the third day the LORD will come down upon Mount Sinai in the sight of all the people. [12] You shall set limits for the people all around, saying, 'Be careful not to go up the mountain or to touch the edge of it. Any who touch the mountain shall be put to death. [13] No hand shall touch them, but they shall be stoned or shot with arrows; whether animal or human being, they shall not live.' When the trumpet sounds a long blast, they may go up on the mountain." [14] So Moses went down from the mountain to the people. He consecrated the people, and they washed their clothes. [15] And he said to the people, "Prepare for the third day; do not go near a woman."

[16] On the morning of the third day there was thunder and lightning, as well as a thick cloud on the mountain, and a blast of a trumpet so loud that all the people who were in the camp trembled. [17] Moses brought the people out of the camp to meet God. They took their stand at the foot of the mountain. [18] Now Mount Sinai was wrapped in smoke, because the LORD had descended upon it in fire; the smoke went up like the smoke of a kiln, while the whole mountain shook violently. [19] As the blast of the trumpet grew louder and louder, Moses would speak and God would answer him in thunder. [20] When the LORD descended upon Mount Sinai, to the top of the mountain, the LORD summoned Moses to the top of the mountain, and Moses went up. [21] Then the LORD said to Moses, "Go down and warn the people not to break through to the LORD to look; otherwise many of them will perish. [22] Even the priests who approach the LORD must consecrate themselves or the LORD will break out against them." [23] Moses said to the LORD, "The people are not permitted to come up to Mount Sinai; for you yourself warned us, saying, 'Set limits around the mountain and keep it holy.'" [24] The LORD said to him, "Go down, and come up bringing Aaron with you; but do not let either the priests or the people break through to come up to the LORD; otherwise he will break out against them." [25] So Moses went down to the people and told them.

The covenant ceremony begins with an act of consecration or "making holy." In 19:4–5, the whole community is marked by priestly holiness through obedience to the teachings and laws of the covenant. If the covenant contains ceremonial laws about how to worship God acceptably, it also contains moral and social laws governing people's behavior toward one another. In this passage, the consecration is purely ceremonial. In view of what is said elsewhere in the Bible about the emptiness of ceremonial holiness divorced from moral uprightness and social justice (for example, Psalm 50; Isa. 1:10–17), it is easy to skip over ceremonial passages as so much "mere ritual." Moreover, we tend to resist the division of areas of life into holy and common, or ritually clean and unclean. When we do so, we miss the wisdom reflected in such ceremonial practices.

For one thing, the division between holy and common or clean and unclean symbolically expresses our awareness that our life and our world do not fully display the character and quality that they should or could. (Even 19:4–5, which marks the whole community as priestly and holy, thereby marks it off from "all the earth.") So the ancient distinction between the holy and the common may be viewed as marking the gap between what is and what might be or, as Martin Buber put it, between "the holy" and "the not-yet holy."

Further, the expression of such a division through the symbolic enactments of rituals gives us a bodily feel of the life to which we are called and to which we would aspire. To wash one's clothes of their marks of daily toil and to spend the remainder of that day, and the whole of the following day, in a readiness for a third day in which even the most intimate and covenanted of human relationships are suspended, helps to make a space deep within oneself for a relationship whose claims supersede all others. It is not, for example, that human sexual relations are unclean (19:15) but that all normal human activities are suspended in favor of the concern that is to take absolute precedence over everything else. If, as earlier proposed, the distinction is between the holy and the not-yet holy, the return from such special ceremonial celebrations to one's normal activities should bring with it a deepened or renewed sense of the holiness to which all life is called.

So at Mount Sinai. On the morning of the third day, God appears on the mountain, in sounds and sights so awesome as to cause all who witness them to tremble. (Compare Moses' initial reaction to God's voice in the burning bush.) Such a scene conveys the awareness that to be in the presence of God is to be caught up in the one and only truly life-and-death relationship. To be rightly related to God is to be utterly safe and "at home"; to be wrongly related to God is to be utterly at risk. Moreover, it is not we who say what it is to be rightly related to God. That is God's to say. The Bible has much to say about the intimate love and grace of God, in the Old Testament as well as in the New. But if we are to appreciate fully what is meant by "the breadth and length and height and depth" of the love of God (Eph. 3:18), we should allow passages such as the present one to register fully on us. As the writer to the Ephesians reminds us, this love has chosen us "to be holy and blameless before him" (Eph. 1:4).

If the distinction between the holy and the common is made through the symbolism of time (the three days of preparation), it is also made through the symbolism of space. The passage divides space into different areas, one that the people may occupy, one into which Aaron and his fellow priests may enter, and one—the top of the mountain—that only Moses can approach. This threefold division will be repeated in the design of the tabernacle, with its space for the congregation, its holy place where only the priests may enter to minister, and its Holy of Holies behind the veil or curtain, where God dwells and where the high priest can enter only at certain times and under certain conditions. As a transportable tent, the sanctuary will function as an ever-present symbol of the spatial character of the holiness of Mount Sinai. In this way, the people who worship within it are enabled to understand themselves (wherever they and the tent are) as once again standing at Mount Sinai to enter into covenant with God.

THE TEN COMMANDMENTS
Exodus 20:1–17

20:1 **Then God spoke all these words:**

2 I am the LORD your God, who brought you out of the land of Egypt, out of the house of slavery; 3 you shall have no other gods before me.

4 You shall not make for yourself an idol, whether in the form of anything that is in heaven above, or that is on the earth beneath, or that is in the water under the earth. 5 You shall not bow down to them or worship them; for I the LORD your God am a jealous God, punishing children for the iniquity of parents, to the third and the fourth generation of those who reject me, 6 but showing steadfast love to the thousandth generation of those who love me and keep my commandments.

7 You shall not make wrongful use of the name of the LORD your God, for the LORD will not acquit anyone who misuses his name.

8 Remember the sabbath day, and keep it holy. 9 Six days you shall labor and do all your work. 10 But the seventh day is a sabbath to the LORD your God; you shall not do any work—you, your son or your daughter, your male or female slave, your livestock, or the alien resident in your towns. 11 For in six days the LORD made heaven and earth, the sea, and all that is in them, but rested the seventh day; therefore the LORD blessed the sabbath day and consecrated it.

12 Honor your father and your mother, so that your days may be long in the land that the LORD your God is giving you.

13 You shall not murder.

14 You shall not commit adultery.

[15] **You shall not steal.**

[16] **You shall not bear false witness against your neighbor.**

[17] **You shall not covet your neighbor's house; you shall not covet your neighbor's wife, or male or female slave, or ox, or donkey, or anything that belongs to your neighbor.**

One can hardly overstate the importance of the Ten Commandments (or "Decalogue") in the Bible and in communities shaped by the Bible. It is the cornerstone of biblical law, in relation to which all other biblical laws may be said to be aligned. It is exceeded in its dense brevity only by the Shema (Deut. 6:4–5). So important is the Decalogue that it is presented again in the book of Deuteronomy. In this series, the volume on Deuteronomy by Thomas W. Mann offers a full discussion of each commandment and a superb discussion of how Deuteronomy as a whole draws out the theology of the Decalogue. My discussion will be briefer, and at some points will offer a somewhat different angle of approach.

The first question is, Whom does God address in verse 1? The second person pronoun throughout the Decalogue is masculine singular. Does this mean the Decalogue is addressed to Israel as a single corporate body (as God's "firstborn son," 4:22–23; see also Hos. 11:1), or does it mean each Israelite is addressed individually? (In Hebrew, groups of mixed gender are referenced with masculine pronouns.) Or is each Israelite male family head addressed (as in the Passover instruction of 12:2–3)? Let us suppose that in a patriarchal society the latter is the case, which would not mean that women and children were exempt from the prohibitions against murder, adultery, stealing, false witness, and covetousness, let alone the first four commandments. It would mean, rather, that the male heads would be addressed both as individuals and as representatives of their families as a unit, representatives responsible for that family's practice of the Decalogue's claims. This already would be a clue to how the Bible portrays the relation between the individual and the community. The community is not simply a collection of individuals but has an organic unity, identity, and character. Yet individuals within that community bear responsibility for their own actions, represent the community in their own actions, and so bear individual responsibility for the identity and character of that community. We ourselves know how this works when one of our own number acts courageously and honorably (or shamefully) in a foreign country. And we know how this works when, alone in a foreign country, we are moved to defend or apologize for something our country has done. Perhaps we should hear the Decalogue as spoken to us through a set of stereo speakers: The woofer addresses all of us as an organically united community, while the tweeter addresses each of us individually; the two give us the full range of God's address. Sometimes we will want to turn one speaker down so as to concentrate on the other, but the concerns for individual and corporate response to God should never be played off against each other.

How, then, is the Decalogue shaped? (We may compare 6:3–8 and 19:3–6 as examples of how such pithy divine addresses can be carefully shaped.) It is set forth as (1) an announcement and reminder of who God is (v. 2), followed by (2) a statement of Israel's proper response to such a God. Let us assume the vision of humanity presented in Genesis 1:27, according to which humankind is made in God's image. (Since the fourth commandment will recall Genesis 1:1–3, it is clear that the framers of the Decalogue are familiar with the understanding of humankind as *imago dei,* "God's image.") If working for six days and resting on the seventh images the God who in six days created heaven and earth and rested on the seventh, can we say more generally that as we respond to God through lives shaped by the Ten Commandments, we image God?

Israel's response to God is presented through Ten Commandments. Why ten? Is it that one learns to recite them on one's ten fingers and that the association of the ten in this way with one's hands is a reminder that one's hands, as the instruments of all one's actions, are to be guided by God's claims on us? (Idols, too, are called "the work of human hands" [Deut. 4:28; Psalm 115:4; Isa. 2:8; Hos. 14:3]). Such an explanation for there being ten must remain speculative, but as a practical device for learning and remembering, it would fit with the direction to bind the Shema on one's hand, fix it as an emblem on one's forehead, and write it on one's doorpost and gate (Deut. 6:8–9).

The ten are usually grouped into two tables (or "tablets"; see Exod. 31:18). The first four focus "vertically" on our relation to God, while the last six focus "horizontally" on our relation to one another. (Jesus' version of the Shema [Mark 12:33] summarizes these two dimensions as love of God and love of neighbor as oneself.) The two tablets may be viewed as bearing on one another in this way: The first four are presented as the religious foundation of our relation to one another, and the last six image our relation to God.

In the first table, we see that the first two commandments (vv. 3–5) conclude in a "for" clause (v. 5) and that the third and fourth also each conclude in a "for" clause (vv. 7, 11). Thus, three times the "vertical" commandments are grounded in a reason.

In the second table, we do not see any reasons given for the commandments, and only once a motivation (the fifth, v. 12). As Thomas Mann has noted (in *Deuteronomy*), the fifth commandment is not addressed to minors but to adults and mandates how the heads of families are to relate to their elderly parents. If that is the case (as commentators now generally agree), we may discern a shape within the second table: The first horizontal commandment (the fifth of ten) mandates relations to one's retired "superiors," the last one (the tenth) mandates relations to one's dependent "inferiors," and the four in between (the sixth through ninth) mandate relations to one's peers.

Now let us examine in more detail these ten "words" of God. (In 34:28 and Deuteronomy 4:13; 10:4, what we call the Ten Commandments are called, literally, "ten words.") The first thing to notice is that these ten words are preceded by a word concerning who the LORD is (v. 2). The God who makes these ten claims on Israel is the God who has brought them out of the land of Egypt, out of the house of slavery. Claim is based in faithful, gracious action. Law arises out of gospel, as its extension. The importance of getting this right may be illustrated in two ways, from my own Christian tradition:

1. For hundreds of years the Anglican Book of Common Prayer included the Decalogue at the beginning of the service of Holy Communion, in this form: "I am the LORD thy God; Thou shalt have none other gods but me." Generation after generation whose understanding was shaped by their worship were allowed to suppose that the commandments may have come out of the blue, imposed as a naked assertion of dominating and demanding power.
2. One wonders to what degree such liturgical practice shaped the religious sensibilities of the early-nineteenth-century Anglican poet and theologian John Keble. In 1827, he wrote a hymn that begins, "When God of old came down from heaven, / In power and wrath he came," and in the next verse continues, "But, when he came a second time, He came in power and love." Five more verses contrast the "coming down" of God in the Old Testament and the New Testament, concluding with the prayer, "Save, LORD, by love or fear." What Keble's hymn abysmally overlooks is that "When God of old came down from heaven," it was to deliver Israel from Egypt as promised to Moses at the burning bush (3:8).

A proper use of the Decalogue in worship, together with a faithful interpretation of the divine self-identification in Exodus 20:2, would go far to prevent such a gross parody of the God of the Old Testament. The book of Exodus nowhere uses the word "love" to identify God's motivation on Israel's behalf, but the book of Deuteronomy, in referring to God's love (Deut. 7:7, 13; 10:15), makes explicit the motivation implicit in Exodus.

The point may be appreciated from another angle. In Deuteronomy 6:20–25, the Israelite child is shown asking, "What is the meaning of the decrees and the statutes and the ordinances that the LORD our God has commanded you?" From the parent's response, we gather that the child is not asking to have the laws spelled out, but, rather, why God has given Israel such laws. The parent answers by describing Israel's slavery in Egypt and God's deliverance from that slavery, bringing Israel into the land to fulfill the promise to the ancestors. As for the laws, says the parent, "The LORD commanded us to observe all these statutes, to fear the LORD our God, *for our lasting good, so as to keep us alive, as is now the case.*" These last words echo in a wonderful way the words Joseph speaks to his brothers in Genesis 50:20: "God intended it for good, in order to preserve a numerous people, as he is doing today." They indicate that God's laws are another means by which God's gracious providence seems to sustain us in life for our lasting good.

First Commandment (v. 3)

Only now, after God's gracious action has been recollected, do we begin to hear God's claims on the people delivered from bondage. The first claim is for complete loyalty to Yahweh alone. The claim is understandable at a time when many other peoples and nations worshiped other gods and when Israelites themselves felt strongly attracted to worship those gods. Does the claim have any relevance today? According to NRSV's introductory "To the Reader," "The use of any proper name for the one and only God, as though there were other gods from whom the true God had to be distinguished, . . . is inappropriate for the universal faith of the Christian Church." This view is doubly problematical. It overlooks other current religious traditions (see the concerns of Nancy Cardoso Pereira, referred to on p. 182). Further, it suggests that idolatry no longer exists as a temptation within biblically based communities. For a fuller discussion of the forms idolatry may take today, see Thomas W. Mann's discussion of the Decalogue in his book *Deuteronomy.* Here I just underscore his point that worship in the ancient world was given to that ultimate mystery or those ultimate mysteries whose wisdom and power were experienced as making an effective difference in their day-to-day lives. In worship, they paid deepest attention to those powers to understand them, conform to their demands, and benefit from them. The reality of a god was experienced through the effective reality of the life processes with which that god was associated. When we understand the gods in this way and then reflect on what today claims people's ultimate allegiance and shapes their lives, we may recover a healthy appreciation for the relevance of the first commandment in our time. The gods are alive and well, and they are many. Some are ideological (Marxist or Capitalist), some are political (national security), some are economic (the bottom line), some are social-mathematical ("statistics show that the majority of . . ."), some are strictly personal ("I Did It My Way" and "I Gotta Be Me"), and many are increasingly tribal ("our" group versus "them"). The words of William Cowper's hymn "O for a Closer Walk with God" are still integral to contemporary worship: "The dearest idol I have known, / Whate'er that idol be, / Help me to tear it from thy throne, / And worship only thee."

Second Commandment (vv. 4–6)

This commandment comes in two parts (the double "you shall not"), which for the moment we may put this way: "You shall not make for yourself, bow down to, or worship an idol." This commandment is distinguishable from the first and yet intimately connected with it, for the idol is not the god, but a physical representation of the god. Yet the physical representation points to the reality—the effective wisdom and power—of the god to which it points. Insofar as the idol brings the god into the awareness of the worshiper and so fills the worshiper with a sense of the reality, presence, and activity of the god, the worshiper's experience of the idol is inseparable from the worshiper's experience of the god. The idol "communicates" the god to the worshiper.

We have a good deal of personal experience of how images and symbols convey what they represent. Try removing the wedding ring from your finger, smashing it with a hammer or flushing it down the toilet, and then saying to your spouse, "My action didn't mean anything. The ring was only a material object that I can easily replace. My love for you is constant and unbroken." Try tearing up a child's offering of a colored picture and then hugging and kissing the child, without totally confusing the child as to which "symbol" of relationship to believe and trust. When it comes to religious realities, however, we (especially Protestants) tend to think that idols and images are empty and that anyone who uses them is superstitious or primitive in understanding. The second commandment is necessary and continues to be relevant today, precisely because the religious use of images is rooted in how we relate to our world. Whether our images are physical, verbal, or imaginative (whether metal or mental), they are the means, the coinage, by which we interact with the realities of the life in which we are immersed.

In the ancient world, then, it was most natural to relate to the life-giving light and heat of the sun by making an image of the sun and worshiping its power. The moon and the stars were worshiped and imaged for the way their seasons were understood to shape the economic calendar and to give signs of military success. Likewise, it was most natural to worship the various powers underlying fertility in field, flock, and family and the powers manifest in the various skills and activities in human society. In addition to these powers "in heaven above and on the earth beneath," there were powers below, "in the water under the earth," powers experienced in their own peculiar ways. In any given ancient society, the list of the gods is a reliable clue to how that society identified the effective realities on which its well-being was understood to rest. The ranking of the gods is a reliable clue to the relative importance of these effective realities.

When we start with our experience of the holy, we find ourselves starting with this or that particular experience, at this or that particular time and place, and relating to this or that specific concern. Generally, the experience has a physical dimension, which can become the symbol for our experience of the divine. Because human experience takes many forms, the divine will be imaged in various ways, and we may well image the divine as in itself being plural: many gods. Also, different people have experiences that in part differ, and different people will have different gods. The problem with polytheism is that human experience taken as a whole often sends a conflicting message. Not all experiences are life-sustaining or life-enhancing, and so the gods may in part be for us and in part against us or indifferent to us. Further, the different gods of different groups will only legitimate and intensify the struggles and conflicts that from time to time spring up between them. The problem with images is that they connect the gods so closely to a particular type of event, process, or power in the world that the gods can become just another name for "whatever happens to us and in and through us."

The God to whom the Bible bears witness—the God who comes to bear and redefine the name, Yahweh—is the divine mystery fully disclosed and at the same time fully veiled in the self-naming, "I will be who/what I will be." This God cannot be adequately symbolized by any of the processes in the cosmos. Therefore, to make an image in the form of anything in heaven or earth or under the earth—even if one intends it to be an image of Yahweh—is to reduce Yahweh to an idol. If there is an "image" by which God can be known and related to, it is the narrative of the exodus from Egypt, the covenanting at Mount Sinai, and the giving of the land in faithfulness to the ancestors. And perhaps there is another image. If humankind is created and called to image God (Gen. 1:27), then God is imaged as communities and individuals worship the God who liberates and covenants with the liberated, and as they relate to one another in faithful justice.

Now we come to the first "for" clause (vv. 5–6). The reason we are to have no other gods nor make any idol or image of the divine is because "I the LORD your God, am a jealous God." The notion of divine "jealousy" sticks in our craw, yet it is central to the Old Testament (see also 34:14; Deut. 4:24; 6:15; Josh. 24:19). It is helpful to remind ourselves that our words "jealous" and "jealousy" come from the same root as our words "zealous" and "zeal." That the same range of meaning reflected in the Hebrew word here translated "jealous" is clear from its use in noun, adjective, and verb forms elsewhere in the Bible. For example, in the Song of Solomon (8:6) it refers to "ardent love" (NRSV, "passion"). In a number of places (Isa. 9:7; 37:32; 42:13; 63:15; Zech. 1:14; 8:2), it refers to divine zeal for God's people, especially in battle. From these contexts, we see that God's zeal/jealousy is God's passionate love for Israel as expressed both in the exodus from Egypt and in the provision of good laws by which this people may continue to live and flourish (Deut. 6:20–25). But such zeal/jealousy cannot be indifferent to behavior that works against the well-being of the objects of God's love—even, or rather especially, when it is the behavior of the objects of God's love. The issue is put vividly in Hosea 13:8: "I will fall upon them like a bear robbed of her cubs, / and will tear open the covering of their heart." These lines are framed by the imagery of attacking and devouring animals—lion and leopard on one side (v. 7), lion and wild animal on the other (v. 8). In between these framing images, the image of the bear is tellingly complex, as befits the nature of zeal/jealousy. Yet the central two lines introduce a strange two-sidedness. It expresses the maternal anger of a God who alone brought Israel out of Egypt (v. 4) and fed them in the wilderness and beyond (vv. 5–6), a people who, once satisfied, forgot the one true source of their well-being (v. 6; compare Deut. 8; 32:10–18; Isa. 1:2–4). The cubs have robbed their mother of themselves. Therefore, her rage against the robbers is the measure of her love for what she has been robbed of. This perfectly catches the meaning of zeal/jealousy.

When the second commandment goes on, however, to say, "punishing children for the iniquity of parents," this seems to us a flagrant miscarriage of justice. Why should God take out on the innocent the iniquity of their parents? Surely it would make more sense that people themselves should bear the consequences of their own actions. As a matter of fact, this is how the book of Deuteronomy re-presents the issues in this commandment, in Deuteronomy 7:7–11: "Know therefore that the LORD your God is God, the faithful God who maintains covenant loyalty [*hesed*] with those who love him and keep his commandments, to a thousand generations, and who repays *in their own person* those who reject him. He does not delay but repays *in their own person* those who reject him" (vv. 9–10). In the same vein, Ezekiel several times announces to the discouraged exiles that God is not willing that any should die, but that people will die for their own sins, and not for the sins of their forebears. In chapter 18 (vv. 2–4), Ezekiel reproduces the complaint that the exiles utter in Jeremiah's hearing (Jer. 31:29), about the parents having eaten sour grapes and the children's teeth being set on edge, and Ezekiel gives the same response as Jeremiah (Jer. 31:30).

But the shocking character of Exodus 20:5–6 should not blind us to the sobering fact that human life is interwoven in a web of interaction and mutual influence, for good and for ill. None of us lives solely to ourselves, and none of us dies solely to ourselves. Much of who we are is the result of the lives and actions of others; each of us, by the very fact that we are alive, has a bearing on the lives of others. The way in which we bear on the lives of others will turn in significant measure on how we choose to live, even where we may think those choices concern only us and affect only us. The world is such an interrelated web of action and consequence as created and sustained by God, who apparently will not change this dynamic design simply because of the way we choose to live within it. As I see it, then, the point of the "for" clause in the first two commandments is to bring home vividly the impact our worship and the actions it inspires will have on those nearest and dearest to us (those most likely to be influenced by us).

The gravity of such a description of the consequences of our freedom is enough to paralyze us into inactivity. So now comes the up side. If God has created the world as a web of interrelations and reciprocal influences, that can also work to everyone's enrichment. The tilt that we are encouraged to see in God's sustaining providence is that, although iniquity has negative consequences on the innocent for three or four generations, covenant loyalty has positive consequences for a thousand generations. This is one measure of the positive versus the negative (or gracious versus judging) dimensions in God's zeal/jealousy. The well-being of the world at any given time is owing in part to the covenant loyalty of people long since departed.

Third Commandment (v. 7)

The close connection of this commandment and the first two becomes clear when we consider the relation between those first two and the divine name itself. One reason why no physical image can adequately represent Israel's God is that Yahweh is free to be who Yahweh wills to be. In the book of Exodus, that freedom is governed by God's compassion for Israel and God's faithfulness to the ancestors (Exod. 2:23–25), so that through them all families of the earth may be blessed (Gen. 12:3). Therefore, we may say, the name Yahweh takes up the role in Israel that names and physical images of the gods took up among Israel's neighbors. This, however, opens up the possibility that, instead of worshiping God as God and letting God be God, Israel might be inclined to put Yahweh's name to a self-serving purpose. In such a case, Israel would not be worshiping Yahweh, but its own purposes as invested in its use of the divine name. A good example is given in Proverbs 30:7–9. In this prayer for daily food, the petitioner fears two possibilities: That, having too much to eat, he or she will forget and deny God (compare Deut. 32:10–18; Hos. 13:5–6); or that, having not enough to eat, he or she will resort to robbery and justify the robbery by misusing the name of Yahweh. The NRSV "profane" here translates a Hebrew verb that means "lay hold of, wield, use." In Jeremiah 2:8 this verb is used critically of priests as those who "handle" the law in teaching it to others and applying it in priestly judgments.

If the name Yahweh is given to Israel as the means by which to invoke God's presence (Jer. 2:6), ask or pronounce God's blessing (Num. 6:22–27), and assure oneself of God's protection (Prov. 18:10), it must remain a name through which, if we say, "Abba, Father, for you all things are possible," we must add, "yet, not what I want, but what you want" (Mark 14:36). If we seek only the infinite possibilities hidden in the divine name and are not willing to add what Jesus added in the Garden of Gethsemane, then we have turned even the divine name into an idol that enthrones our own wishes. God will not absolve us of responsibility in such a case. This is a warning of particular relevance in a time when individuals and groups have become caught up in the heady wine of "possibility thinking."

Fourth Commandment (vv. 8–11)

If the first three commandments are about idolatry in one form or another, so is the fourth. Here we are told how to image God in the shape that the rhythm of our daily activity gives to time. The dignity of daily work is that it images God who worked for six days to bring the world into existence. Put another way, in and through our work we participate in God's work in shaping a viable world. But to work seven days a week is to pattern our activity on something else than God, and in so doing to worship an idol who looks more like the Pharaoh of Exodus 5. That in doing so we shall become like Pharaoh is implied in verse 10. If we ourselves insist on working all seven days, the likelihood is that we will impose such a work schedule (hardly a rhythm!) on son and daughter, male and female slave, livestock and alien resident.

Now we move into the second tablet, which governs our "horizontal" relations, that is, those with other human beings. These relations will provide opportunity for us to image God as we honor God's image in one another, or they will misrepresent God and so will be not only unjust but idolatrous.

Fifth Commandment (v. 12)

This commandment has to do with how adults relate to their parents. For the necessity of such a commandment, we may go to Sigmund Freud, whose Oedipus complex is a staple of modern psychological understanding. As he saw it, the son comes to an age when he finds himself in competition with his father over his mother and over more general issues of power and authority. Though at this young age the father prevails, the time will come when the son overcomes the father to become an adult in his own right. Such attempts to take over are illustrated in the Bible by Reuben, who sleeps with Bilhah, the concubine of his father, Jacob (Gen. 35:22; 49:3–4) and by David's various sons who try to displace him on the throne. (Perhaps the earliest example is in a text from ancient Babylonia, describing relations of descent and power through seven generations of the gods. For six generations, the young male god kills his father and marries his mother; in the seventh generation, the son merely chains his father.)

The commandment says, simply, "honor your father and your mother." Having begun by receiving life freely from them, one is now not to wrest anything from them, whether authority, property, or respect and esteem. But what is the connection between one's relation to one's parents and one's relation to the land that God gives each family? In Israelite society, one receives one's land from one's parents—in some rare instances through the mother, but usually through the father. To wrest the inheritance from one's parents is not only to dishonor them but to break the sacred familial relation to the land and so to forfeit one's right to it. At a much deeper level, we may discern also another awareness. At a number of points in the Bible, we are spoken of as being made of dust or clods of earth, so that under God we are "from the earth" (e.g., Job 4:19; 10:9; Eccles. 12:7). This is especially vivid in Genesis 2:7, where the sequel shows the first human pair, for disobedience to their creator, expelled from the land where they have been placed. From these considerations, we may appreciate that there is a deep connection between one's parents and the land within which one lives and hopes to live. It is as though those who do not know how to live within the horizon of their parents' honor and authority are unreliable stewards of their inheritance.

Sixth Commandment (v. 13)

Now we come to a group of four commandments—six through nine—that are primarily about relations with neighbors or peers (see v. 16). First comes the prohibition against murder. Older translations of verse 13 read "Thou shalt not kill," but the Hebrew verb is more specific than that. The verb is generally not used to refer to accidental death or manslaughter, to death in battle, or to execution of a criminal as the result of due legal process. Rather, as biblical scholar Brevard Childs says, "The verb came to designate those acts of violence against a person which arose from personal feelings of hatred and malice. The command in its present form forbids such an act of violence and rejects the right of a person to take the law into his own hands out of a feeling of personal injury" (*The Book of Exodus*, p. 421). Such acts are wrong in at least two respects: They are an ultimate injustice against the victim, and they contribute to a progressive tearing of the social fabric, as murderous violence begets murderous violence. Each individual has a stake in this commandment because it gives divine protection to him or her from the murderous intent of one's neighbors, and society as a whole has a stake in it as well.

Reflect for a moment on the first murderer, Cain. For our purposes, it is not necessary to know why God regards Abel's sacrifice and disregards Cain's. Whatever the reason, it is clear that Cain is crestfallen and angry, to the point of a murderous jealous rage against his younger brother. God says to Cain, "you must master it." Rage does not justify murderous actions; we are responsible for managing such feelings and not simply acting them out. Interestingly, as a murderer Cain becomes aware that he is now a target of feuding blood vengeance. God, however, puts a mark on Cain so that no one who comes upon him will kill him. What is that mark? Presumably, a sign that Cain belongs to God. We may take the sixth commandment, together with the *imago dei* doctrine of Genesis 1:27 and Paul's later injunction in Romans 12:19–21, as God's triple protective sign on our neighbor's forehead. The alternative is a society caught in a vicious cycle of blood vengeance under the sign of Lamech (Gen. 4:23–24).

Seventh Commandment (v. 14)

If the sixth commandment relates to violence, the seventh may be thought to relate to sex, both of them arising out of deep and strong emotion that either will not or cannot master itself. The sin in murder is self-evident: It is a crime against the victim, and it is a crime against the social fabric. What is the sin in adultery?

To begin with, we must recognize a difference between what the Old Testament means by adultery and what most people today mean by it. In our day, adultery is an act of physical sexual intercourse between two people, at least one of whom is married. In the Old Testament, adultery is an act of physical sexual intercourse between two people where the woman is married. A married man's sexual intercourse with a woman who is not married is not termed adultery, though it may come under other forms of condemnation and legal consequence. It is hard to imagine how anyone today would defend the perpetuation of this double standard, apart from male vested interest or a literal-mindedness about scripture unrelieved by moral imagination.

What was at stake in such a one-sided view of adultery in Israel? We may view this commandment as simply one more evidence that the Old Testament is the product of a patriarchal society that wrote the rules in men's favor and that therefore it has no moral force for us today, or we may view a commandment such as this one in terms of "progressive revelation." Let us return for a moment to the previous commandment. It addressed a social custom according to which a certain type of slaying called forth blood vengeance. A victim's next of kin was honor-bound by the code of vengeance to slay the victim's killer, and so the cycle of feuding would go on. The sixth commandment aims at breaking that cycle. Murder is not to occur; where it does, it is to be dealt with through society's legal processes. Neither the desire for blood vengeance, nor malice or hatred generally, is a justification for taking another individual's life. Thus, this commandment does not address all aspects of the question of human life and death at the hands of other humans, but one specific aspect in which society as a whole has a vital interest.

The seventh commandment addresses a situation in which an adult male enjoys preeminent power and authority in the family or house of which he is the head. As such, he also represents his family or house in the affairs of the wider community. In such a situation, for any man to invade another family through his sexual relations with the wife and mother in that family is to usurp the structure of authority in that family and to sow the seed of violence within the community. Out of jealousy and wounded honor, the cuckolded husband will seek revenge, most likely through personal violence. Thus adultery, like murder, threatens the social fabric and the structure of the family.

From our vantage point, we may posit a more basic and fateful kind of damage inflicted by adultery. The family relation, which depends for its character and quality upon the parents, is the matrix for the nurture of children in humane virtues and ideals. It also controls biological fatherhood, and secures the social and economic responsibilities that go with it. Those virtues and ideals, of course, have their ultimate matrix in a family's religious understandings and practices. Among the virtues that establish and maintain that matrix, the most basic are compassion and loyalty—in Hebrew, *rahamim* and *hesed*. The first word (as we shall explore more fully at 34:6–7) is developed from *rehem*, the Hebrew word for womb. (In this sense, compassion is the matrix of all other virtues.) The second word names the quality of loyalty or steadfast love that kin owe to one another as kin. (Our noun "kindness," like our adjective "kind" and our verb "be kind," is from the same English root as our noun "kind," meaning type or sort. So "kindness" means how one ought to treat one's own kind.) Adultery betrays these matrixal virtues by alienating the affection and compassion of the wife and mother from those to whom she owes her first and deepest loyalty.

The prophet Hosea proclaims the implications of this for Israelite society and apparently acts them out in his own life (Hosea 1 and 4). When the wife and mother breaches the circle of family affection and loyalty through adultery, the result is likely to show up in "children of adultery," that is, children whose own affections will not remain constant to vowed relations but lead them also into adulterous relations. By adulterous relations, Hosea here refers both to interhuman relations and to human relations to the divine, as Israelites forsake Yahweh and go after other gods. Thus adultery attacks the very matrix of all relationships, human and divine.

Yet the picture as so far painted remains one-sided, which continues to stick in the craw of many in our own day. I suggest that we follow the ancient picture as far as we can, "from within," before we distance ourselves from it on the basis of distaste for or revulsion against the double standard. If we allow ourselves to work with an understanding of revelation as progressive, we may appreciate the social, moral, and religious concerns that are expressed in the prohibition of adultery and then embody those concerns in new understandings of how they apply to us. Two points could help us here.

First, when we seek to understand the seventh commandment in its own historical context, we tend to interpret it rather strictly in terms of the other laws and practices relating to marriage in the rest of the Old Testament. We do this with the implicit assumption that the range of meaning and application of the seventh commandment is to be understood in terms of those other laws and practices. What if we commit a mistake here? Consider how, within the Old Testament itself, there is abundant evidence of changing laws that adapt fundamental principles to changing times. This process becomes clear when we compare such bodies of laws as Exodus 21:1–23:19 and Deuteronomy 12—26. It is often proposed that the Ten Commandments have a fundamental character that is then, in the bodies of laws that follow, applied in specific and detailed ways to specific and varied situations. What if we understand the various laws within these collections as applying, but not exhausting, the meaning of one or another of the Ten Commandments? In that case, the fundamental concerns in the seventh commandment can be seen to remain essential even when other aspects of family life undergo change under the influence of later revelation.

Second, what now becomes highly relevant is the way prophets like Hosea, Jeremiah, Ezekiel, and Second Isaiah interpret Yahweh's relation to Israel as a relation of husband to wife. This analogy often enables the prophets to bring home to Israelites in a vivid way what their worship of other gods actually means: It is adultery. In a male-centered society, the import is clear. It is these *males* who (as political and religious leaders) are presented as committing adultery with other gods like Baal. Now the males know, "from the inside," what it is like to be accused of being the adulterous wife! At the same time, their anger and wounded affection over their wives' adultery and their sympathy for their cuckolded male friends' anger and hurt will bring home to them vividly God's own wrath. Suddenly, in a male-oriented society, the shoe is on the other foot!

But how far does the analogy apply? If Israelite society, as led by Israelite men, is held responsible for being adulterous, what about God's side of the picture? Let us recall: In Israelite society as represented in its laws and practices, adultery is sexual relations with a married woman. A married man does not commit adultery (though it may otherwise be wrong) in sexual relations outside of marriage. Is Yahweh free to divorce Israel? Various prophets speak of such a threat and even of such an action.

But even when they do, Yahweh is never portrayed as "marrying" another people and continuing with them the covenanted relation originally made with Israel. Instead, the prophetic tradition speaks of a remarriage of Yahweh and Israel. I want to suggest that Israel's experience of God as "loyal husband" lays a theological basis for our reinterpretation of the seventh commandment. In such a reinterpretation, we are not limited by the situation-specific marriage laws in the various collections of the Old Testament. We are free—I would say we are driven—to understand the seventh commandment in such a way as to claim loyalty and fidelity from both parties to the marriage covenant.

Eighth Commandment (v. 15)

Like our English verb "steal," the Hebrew verb in this commandment refers to an action undertaken "by stealth." On occasion, this verb can be used positively. Africans stolen from their homeland for slavery in America came to sing, "Steal away to Jesus." In the Bible, a princess can "steal away" a young prince and hide him from the murderous intent of Queen Athaliah (2 Kings 11:1–3); a word of revelation can "steal" into a person's ear, in the middle of the night (Job 4:12–16). But most often, stealth is invading someone else's space unobserved to take what does not rightfully belong to one, most often goods or property. In 2 Samuel 15:1–6, it refers to Absalom, who "steals" the loyalty of the people from David and attaches it to himself. How he does so is very instructive. He stands in a place where people pass by when they have a petition to bring to the king. After he has ascertained which tribe they come from, he informs them that there is no one deputed by the king to hear the king. Is this true, or is he making it up? As the king's son, he could help them get their case before the king, but instead he destroys their confidence in the king's concern for their need. Then he campaigns for their confidence by advertising how he would look after their cases if he were judge. Responding to their "obeisance" with a handshake and a kiss, he steals the hearts of the people of Israel.

Again, Jeremiah, who is immersed in a struggle with "false" prophets, has his troubles increased by the way these prophets steal his own words and pass them off as their own (Jer. 23:30). From Jeremiah's point of view, the words in question are truly God's (and therefore not Jeremiah's own possession), so why should he object to this assisted spread of his message? But the credibility of a prophet's word at any given time arises in part out of how reliable that prophet's previous words turned out to be. By passing

Jeremiah's words off as their own, the prophets are stealing his reputation to give added weight to their own word when it disagrees with Jeremiah's.

These examples illustrate the point that "stealing" involves complex issues. It is not simply a matter of robbing a bank or snitching a candy bar from the store shelf, though training in observance of the commandment may start there. To live under this commandment is to be involved in a lifelong "continuing education" course in learning what it means not to take from people what belongs to them or withhold from them what they are entitled to receive.

Ninth Commandment (v. 16)

"You shall not bear false witness against your neighbor" is positioned significantly. The tenth commandment is unlike the first eight in that it moves from prohibited acts to the inner appetite and tendency from which those acts arise. As an inner appetite and tendency, coveting is unobservable to a second human party. It is known only to the one who covets and to the God who says, "You shall not covet." Thus the tenth commandment is an education of one's interior conscience, for only one's conscience can "bear witness" as to whether one is coveting. (On conscience as a witness, see Job 27:6, following the oath formulas "As God lives" and "Far be it from me" [vv. 1, 5]; also, see Rom. 2:15–16.)

The difference between the tenth and the ninth commandment is that the tenth has to do with an inner state and tendency before it has erupted into action and, therefore, before any second human party can testify to its presence. The ninth has to do with testimony concerning actions carried out in violation of the commandments. If those actions are carried out flagrantly, so that the whole community knows, the testimony of a single individual is not so crucial. If the witnesses are few in number, then the act (like coveting) is hidden from public knowledge, and the formal witness (like conscience) is crucial to establishing whether the alleged act has occurred. To bear true witness concerning this act is to help to maintain the moral fabric of a society based on truth, loyalty, and justice. To bear false witness is to collude in the wrongful act and to contribute to the decay of society's moral fabric. It is, ultimately, to commit idolatry, for it serves a "god" other than Yahweh. Thus the ninth and tenth commandments bring the ten to a fitting conclusion, for together they address public life and the interactions of individuals at the point where they disappear into inner depths, where only God knows the truth and conscience is our only guide to the truth God knows.

Tenth Commandment (v. 17)

As already noted, this commandment introduces a new dimension to the Decalogue, focusing on the inner urge that leads to overt actions. That urge is to "covet." "Covetousness" carries a negative connotation, similar to "greed." Similarly, in the Old Testament the Hebrew word for "covet" or "desire," whether as a verb, noun, or adjective, often carries a negative overtone. But the word can also be used positively, in reference to something desirable, attractive, or delightful. One use of the Hebrew word in particular will help us to appreciate more fully what the tenth commandment is aimed at.

In Genesis 2, God creates the first human being of dust from the ground and places that individual in a garden filled with all manner of trees. These trees are said to be "pleasant to the sight and good for food." The word translated, "pleasant," means "desirable/to be desired." In 3:6, after the snake has spoken to the woman, she views the tree of the knowledge of good and evil as "to be desired to make one wise." This passage and others like it have given desire a bad name. As one result, Christian morality has often tended to paint desire as something suspect, to the point where virtue lies in the direction of duty, and sin in the direction of desire. It is not surprising then that a controversial writer like Mary Daly can seek to rehabilitate the place of desire in human life through her book, *Pure Lust*. Her choice of the term, *lust*, turns on its frequent connotation of sexual appetite. Its Latin root and even its earlier English usage, however, shows that it means, more generally, "vigorous appetite, desire" (as when, for example, we speak of a luscious apple). The picture in Genesis 2:9 is of God providing for human beings a garden filled with goodies, luscious in appearance and good in the eating. (In Genesis 2:9, NRSV "pleasant" translates Hebrew *nehmad*, a word cognate with the verb *hamad* [NRSV "covet"] in Exodus 20:17.) The very sight of these trees makes one's mouth water, so the only question is, Which one shall I eat today? In the first instance, then, desire is part of the world God has created. It is the organic means by which we are drawn to enjoy the world in which God has placed us. Indeed, as the Song of Solomon celebrates with its unblushingly lush and lusty imagery, desire can be the happy servant of the most intimate communion.

But desire is created to be a servant, not a master. As with murderous rage, we are responsible for what we do with our desire. Moreover, not all that looks luscious is good in the eating. In the Genesis story, we are alerted to this fact by God, who first gives a resoundingly positive permission to "enjoy!" and then places just one of the trees off limits: "Don't eat this one; it will kill you." What has happened here? Prior to this commandment, to be a human being is to exist in a garden where desire is the trigger to action, and action leads to physical enjoyment of what was first enjoyed in anticipation through shape, color, texture, and smell. With this commandment, to be a human being is to exist in a garden whose owner provides all manner of means to fulfill our appetites but declares one possible means off limits. In this situation, if we are to exist in a positive relation to our host, we recognize the limits set on the range of our desires and appetites. If we are led to desire what is off limits, we are (like Cain) to "master" that desire so that it does not lead to inappropriate action. In summary, desire is neither simply good nor simply bad; it is, to begin with, a matter of how desire serves the relationships into which we are called by God.

But the tenth commandment does not simply say, "You shall not act on your desire for your neighbor's house," and so on. It says, "You shall not covet" that is, we are not even to have the desire and appetite for what is off-limits to us. Is this possible? The question is whether appetite and desire are purely and simply biological, organic, "natural" impulses, or whether they are also subject to education, training, and even "reprogramming" by our moral sense of what God calls us to be and do. A long tradition in Western culture, stemming both from the Bible and from Aristotle, holds that our desires can be trained. Moral and spiritual training (what the Bible calls "growth in grace" or "sanctification") consists at least in part in a reeducation of our desires.

In our time, it is dangerous to suggest this. In reaction to a tradition that suspected and repressed desire, we as a society have arrived at a point where desire increasingly becomes its own justification, no matter what the nature of that desire or the identity of the objects on which it seeks to satisfy itself. To tamper with desire is felt to be unnatural, unhealthy, repressive, oppressive, and wrong. What we overlook is that through modern advertising, and the entertainment media which have learned well the lessons of advertising, all of us go to school every day to what one sociologist has called "the taste-makers." The function of a good ad is not simply to inform us of a product's existence but also to create in us an appetite for it, even if it is junk food. As the story in Genesis 3 illustrates, desire has ceased to be simply natural (or "God-given") and has already been reeducated so as to attach itself to what, in the end, can kill us.

If desire and appetite can be slowly cultivated, however, they can also (though it is much harder) be abruptly redirected or deactivated. To begin with, we can choose not to entertain desires for what is off-limits. If and as such desires stir within us, we have the choice of allowing those desires to enter the spacious room of our thoughts and play themselves out in delectable fantasies, or we can politely but firmly ask them to leave and redirect our thoughts.

In other words, if the previous commandments have to do with our actions, the tenth commandment has to do with the springs of our actions in our felt desires and appetites. Our willingness to engage our appetites and to reeducate them in conformity with God's covenant claims on us is one measure of our willingness to participate as co-workers in the redemption of the world.

THE PEOPLE'S RESPONSE
TO GOD'S VOICE
Exodus 20:18–21

> 20:18 **When all the people witnessed the thunder and lightning, the sound of the trumpet, and the mountain smoking, they were afraid and trembled and stood at a distance,** [19] **and said to Moses, "You speak to us, and we will listen; but do not let God speak to us, or we will die."** [20] **Moses said to the people, "Do not be afraid; for God has come only to test you and to put the fear of him upon you so that you do not sin."** [21] **Then the people stood at a distance, while Moses drew near to the thick darkness where God was.**

The most obvious basis of the people's fear is the awesome physical manifestation of God's presence. Yet even more fearful is what God has said to them. Such moral and spiritual claims on them, backed up by such an awesome display of power, are more than they can bear. Indeed God's words are so powerful that the people cannot hear them and live. So they beg Moses to stand between them and God to mediate God's words to them. As once before, he says to them, "Do not be afraid." When they had trembled in fear before Pharaoh's advancing chariots (14:13), his "do not be afraid" conveyed the promise of God's deliverance. Now his "do not be afraid" assures them that the fear God's presence has aroused in them is meant only to convey the gravity of the issues involved in covenant obedience and covenant betrayal.

In the letter to the Hebrews, the writer contrasts Mount Sinai with Mount Zion and Jesus, "the mediator of a new covenant, and . . . the sprinkled blood that speaks a better word than the word of Abel" (Heb. 12:24). The impression is that the new covenant is more gracious, less threatening and terrifying, than the old. Yet if anything just the reverse is true!

See that you do not refuse the one who is speaking; for if they did not escape when they refused the one who warned them on earth, how much less will we escape if we reject the one who warns from heaven! At that time his voice shook the earth; but now he has promised, "Yet once more I will shake not only the earth but also the heaven." This phrase, "Yet once more," indicates the removal of what is shaken—that is, created things—so that what cannot be shaken may remain. Therefore, since we are receiving a kingdom that cannot be shaken, let us give thanks, by which we offer to God an acceptable worship with reverence and awe; for indeed our God is a consuming fire. (Heb. 12:25–29)

We may compare this with Jesus' reinterpretation of the Decalogue, in his Sermon on the Mount. In Exodus 20, the turn to inner attitude and motivation marks only the last of the commandments. Jesus radicalizes this turn, extends it through them all, and states the judgment for their violation in the most severe terms. The God of the New Testament is no less a "consuming fire" than the God of the burning bush and Mount Sinai, when it comes to the claim for moral and spiritual response worthy of the God who has created us and acted to save us and who now calls us into a community of justice and fellowship.

THE BOOK OF THE COVENANT
Exodus 20:22–22:17

In this discussion, I follow closely the analysis and interpretation of Joe Sprinkle. In *The Book of the Covenant*, Sprinkle pays particularly close attention to the form in which the covenant laws are arranged. A prominent feature of this form is what is variously called "envelope" or "concentric" or "chiastic" arrangement of material. A good example of this chiastic or envelope arrangement appears in Exodus 20:22–26, as I now demonstrate.

On Images and Altars (20:22–26)

20:22 **The LORD said to Moses: Thus you shall say to the Israelites: "You have seen for yourselves that I spoke with you from heaven.**

A¹   23 **You shall not make gods of silver alongside me, nor shall you make for yourselves gods of gold.**

B¹   24 *You need make for me* **only an altar of earth and sacrifice on it your burnt offerings and your offerings of well-being, your sheep and your oxen;**

C   **in every place where I cause my name to be remembered
I will come to you and bless you.**

B[2]   **25 But *if you make for me* an altar of stone,**

A[2]   **do not build it of hewn stones; for if you use a chisel upon it you profane it.**

      26 You shall not go up by steps to my altar, so that your nakedness may not be exposed on it."

Chapters 25—31 provide elaborate provision for worship in a sanctuary, including an altar highly crafted by artisans inspired by God (27:1–8). This passage stands in stark contrast to those chapters.

Since Genesis 9:1–7, all animal food must be ritually prepared before it can be eaten. This preparation is done by first pouring the animal's blood on the altar. In pre-Mosaic times (Genesis 12—50), the ancestors are often shown building altars. Once a single official sanctuary is built, there will not be room for everyone to prepare their animal food ritually at its altars. Moreover, many will be too distant to have access to it. So 20:22–26 enables the ordinary Israelite to continue to prepare animal food ritually, without violating the new laws against idolatry. To this end, three things are prohibited:

1. There must be no images of the LORD at these altars. (Among Israel's neighbors, god and goddess figurines were a staple of household piety.)
2. A stone altar may not be shaped. This emphasizes the difference between the permitted local worship and the mandated central worship. In polytheistic religion, the local cults of a given god often became so distinctive from one another as to suggest different gods. Permitting local altars but prohibiting shaped stone altars may have served to inculcate and sustain the "oneness" of Yahweh.
3. Among Israel's neighbors, worship sometimes included sexual rituals to enhance fertility. The Old Testament excludes such rituals from Israel's worship. Since the ordinary Israelite does not wear a loincloth undergarment, even a raised altar with approaching steps is also prohibited. (A raised altar is permitted in the central sanctuary, where the priests are to wear a loincloth; Exodus 28:42).

The chiastic structure of the passage moves from what is prohibited (A[1]/A[2]) through what is permitted (B[1]/B[2]) to what is promised (C). Though elaborate provision will be made for Israel's public worship in a central sanctuary, God will still be present for blessing at every local altar built for daily needs, for God's blessing does not depend on the material structure but comes through the divine name that God provides for use.

The blessing comes as God is invoked as Yahweh. This way of understanding the relation between 20:22–26 and chapters 25—31 enables us to
appreciate that, while even the most elaborate provisions for our worship
do not adequately celebrate God's glory (1 Kings 8:27), God will meet to
bless us in the simplicity of our own individual, everyday, bread-and-butter
piety, when that piety is shaped in accordance with God's will and connected in its own way with the stated worship of God's people.

The Question of Servitude and Freedom (21:1–11)

21:1 **These are the ordinances that you shall set before them:**

**² When you buy a male Hebrew slave, he shall serve six years, but in the
seventh he shall go out a free person, without debt. ³ If he comes in single,
he shall go out single; if he comes in married, then his wife shall go out with
him. ⁴ If his master gives him a wife and she bears him sons or daughters, the
wife and her children shall be her master's and he shall go out alone. ⁵ But
if the slave declares, "I love my master, my wife, and my children; I will not
go out a free person," ⁶ then his master shall bring him before God. He shall
be brought to the door or the doorpost; and his master shall pierce his ear
with an awl; and he shall serve him for life.**

**⁷ When a man sells his daughter as a slave, she shall not go out as the male
slaves do. ⁸ If she does not please her master, who designated her for himself, then he shall let her be redeemed; he shall have no right to sell her to a
foreign people, since he has dealt unfairly with her. ⁹ If he designates her for
his son, he shall deal with her as with a daughter. ¹⁰ If he takes another wife
to himself, he shall not diminish the food, clothing, or marital rights of the
first wife. ¹¹ And if he does not do these three things for her, she shall go out
without debt, without payment of money.**

In our contemporary passion for freedom, our first reaction to a biblical
law that assumes the existence of slavery may well be aversion or dismis-
sive protest. Yet people are still bound to one another by all sorts of economic and contractual ties that limit their freedom. The question is
whether those ties are informed by humanitarian concerns or allowed to
become opportunities for unbridled exploitation.

The law concerning servitude and freedom contains interesting echoes of
the theme of liberation from slavery in Exodus 20:2. For example, the verb
"bring out" in 20:2 is a form of the verb "go out" in 21:2, 11. Again, "house
of slavery" in 20:2 is echoed in 21:6 by the "door or doorpost" of the slave-
master's house. These associations should alert us to the possibility that

these slave-related *laws* go some way toward embodying what we might call the *gospel* of the exodus.

In the ancient world, one could become a slave through poverty, debt, capture in war, abandonment as a child, kidnap, or punishment for a crime. The question then would be, What assurances of fair treatment might a slave hope for? This passage takes up two types of slave: a Hebrew male sold into slavery (perhaps for debt), and a Hebrew female sold by her father to be a slave-wife (perhaps because he was too poor to provide a dowry). The NRSV "slave" translates *amah*, which some take to mean not simply a female slave but a slave-wife or concubine. Presumably, a female slave would enjoy the same opportunity for release as a male (Deut. 15:12–18). It is only the slave-wife who does not.

The humanitarian character of these laws becomes more evident when we consider the vulnerability of powerless individuals to starvation and abuse and their relative security when attached to an economically viable household. In the case of the male slave, the ritual of the ear pierced against the door(post) may be doubly significant. First, the ear is the organ of hearing and obedience. As bored into the door(post), it attaches the slave's obedience to the master's house at the point through which he will daily go out to work and return to rest. Second, the word *elohim* in verse 6 may refer not to God or "the judges" (NRSV note) but to household figures of deceased ancestors. Such symbolism suggests that the slave is being incorporated into the larger family. In the case of the female slave, she cannot be deprived of conjugal rights to proper care and respect. Otherwise, she is to be given her freedom, presumably to seek a more secure domestic arrangement.

We have tended to understand freedom increasingly in terms of individual "freedom from" attachments and obligations and "freedom for" doing our own thing. Perhaps an initially unpromising law concerning slavery can still witness to concerns that should inform the relationships we are driven into out of economic need or other social forces. While such principles may be called "humanitarian," more deeply they are religious, in that they seek to embody in social relations God's redemption of Israel from Egypt.

Offenses by Humans against Other Humans (21:12–27)

> 21:12 **Whoever strikes a person mortally shall be put to death.** [13] **If it was not premeditated, but came about by an act of God, then I will appoint for you a place to which the killer may flee.** [14] **But if someone willfully attacks and kills another by treachery, you shall take the killer from my altar for execution.**

¹⁵ Whoever strikes father or mother shall be put to death.

¹⁶ Whoever kidnaps a person, whether that person has been sold or is still held in possession, shall be put to death.

¹⁷ Whoever curses father or mother shall be put to death.

¹⁸ When individuals quarrel and one strikes the other with a stone or fist so that the injured party, though not dead, is confined to bed, ¹⁹ but recovers and walks around outside with the help of a staff, then the assailant shall be free of liability, except to pay for the loss of time, and to arrange for full recovery.

²⁰ When a slaveowner strikes a male or female slave with a rod and the slave dies immediately, the owner shall be punished. ²¹ But if the slave survives a day or two, there is no punishment; for the slave is the owner's property.

²² When people who are fighting injure a pregnant woman so that there is a miscarriage, and yet no further harm follows, the one responsible shall be fined what the woman's husband demands, paying as much as the judges determine. ²³ If any harm follows, then you shall give life for life, ²⁴ eye for eye, tooth for tooth, hand for hand, foot for foot, ²⁵ burn for burn, wound for wound, stripe for stripe.

²⁶ When a slaveowner strikes the eye of a male or female slave, destroying it, the owner shall let the slave go, a free person, to compensate for the eye. ²⁷ If the owner knocks out a tooth of a male or female slave, the slave shall be let go, a free person, to compensate for the tooth.

These laws fall into two groups of four. In Group A (vv. 12–17), the offense is so grave as to merit death; in Group B (vv. 18–27), the offense is viewed as less grievous.

Group A begins with homicide (vv. 12–13). Such is the sanctity of life, that to kill another intentionally is to forfeit one's own life. In the case of unpremeditated homicide, a refuge is provided to protect the guilty party from blood vengeance by an outraged relative of the victim. The next three cases all have to do with violations against parents. The first involves physical abuse short of homicide (v. 15). The second (which most naturally refers to the kidnapping of children) involves depriving parents of their source of economic support in old age (v. 16). The third involves neglect of filial duties, including but not limited to verbal respect (v. 17). (The verb is not the standard verb for pronouncing curse but means "to treat with disregard, abuse, denigrate, repudiate" (as in Gen. 16:4, "looked with contempt").

Strikingly, the three actions against parents are considered so grave as to be comparable to homicide. In a culture where food supplies were heavily dependent on annual weather and grain storage and survival in old age was most immediately dependent on caring children, these offenses could bode ill for the parents' survival. Sprinkle asks whether we should view these four laws as binding legal provisions or as moral directives (*The Book of the Covenant*, pp. 84–88). For example, he and others doubt whether the second and fourth laws were often if ever invoked to execute a miscreant son or daughter. For this reason, he proposes that the Hebrew "shall be put to death" may best be translated "deserves to be put to death." (This sentence is closely related in form to "you shall die" in Genesis 2:17, and that sentence is not carried out literally even though the first couple do act in high-handed disregard of God's explicit command.) Such an approach means that these laws, and others like them in the Book of the Covenant, are not strictly legal statutes, in every case to be followed to the letter. Though they undeniably have a legal aspect, their force is largely that of moral directive as a context for human relations and a guide to those who adjudicate specific cases.

Group B shifts the focus to cases of lesser gravity. In the first law (vv. 18–19), the blow that sends its victim to bed (unable to work) is clearly intentional if delivered with stone or fist. In that case, the aggressor is to compensate the victim for lost work time and medical expenses. The next three cases similarly are concerned for economic consequences. The law in verses 20–21 applies the disciplinary rod (compare Prov. 10:13; 13:24) to a slave who will not work or will not work with any will and energy. Such disciplinary force is allowable because the slave's owner has an economic investment in the slave's work and is entitled to a return, but it is limited in its severity. A slave who dies immediately is evidence of overwhelmingly excessive force; in such a case, the slave is (as the Hebrew text says) "to be avenged." A slave who survives for a few days is evidence of less (though still excessive) force. In this case, the owner's loss of monetary value is sufficient punishment.

The law in verses 22–25 seems to interrupt the connection between the laws that precede and follow it concerning slave abuse. But when social and economic assumptions are kept in mind, its placement may become more meaningful. In ancient societies, individual rights were much more closely intertwined with family and communal needs than is the case in contemporary North America. So, for example, ancient Israelites would be puzzled by the view that a woman's treatment of her fetus is purely a matter of individual rights over her own body, for their communal well-being depended on their capacity to beget, bear, and raise children who could contribute to the group's economic support. The law in verses 22–25 may address the concern of the family over the loss of a potential "breadwinner." Since the miscarriage was caused unintentionally, by a blow intended for a third party, the penalty is compensation for the loss of the future breadwinner. In case of further "harm" (a rare Hebrew word perhaps indicating an injury requiring medical attention), there is a further penalty. The notorious "eye for an eye" calls for further comment.

The sanctions fall into a series of three groups. The first is the most serious, "life for life" (v. 23). The second comprises injuries to various parts of the body, from "head to foot" (v. 24). The third comprises various types of injuries (v. 25). The poetic-proverbial character of this series suggests that a general principle of tit for tat is being brought to bear on this particular case. The reason for its introduction and application to this case will become apparent shortly. For now, we may note two points. First, the principle is that the liability should match the damage. (This principle also underlies the compensation for damages mentioned in v. 19; and will underlie the compensation in v. 26.) Second, the principle is that the liability should not exceed the damage. This restrains vengeful overkill of the sort reflected in Genesis 4:23. This so-called *lex talionis*, or "law of retaliation," is often cited as an example of the vengeful spirit of Old Testament law in contrast to the grace-filled ethos of the New Testament To be sure, Jesus in Matthew 5:38 cites it as a foil for his injunction to turn the other cheek and go the second mile and by such responses to evil, to "be perfect . . . as your heavenly Father is perfect" (5:48). But in a world where not everyone emulates nor even aspires to such a vision of perfection, the principle of fair but not excessive compensation helps to inculcate a vision of viable justice.

The law in verses 26–27, finally, returns to the question of a slaveowner striking a slave. What if the blow results in a lost eye or tooth? How is the law of retaliation to be applied here? In this case, the male or female slave is to be compensated by being "let go, a free person." Significantly, the verb "let go" here is the same as in 4:23, 5:1. Thus, this overall section of laws concerning offenses by humans against other humans ends on the same note with which the previous section began and ended (vv. 2, 11): the conditions for the going out (or exodus) of slaves in Israel. These laws in their specific details may not embody all that the community eventually will come to believe God calls for (e.g., Matt. 5:38–48). But they show how the new leaven of the gospel of the exodus (20:2) is beginning to transform the actual structures and practices of Israelite society.

Goring Oxen and Dangerous Pits
(21:28–36)

21:28 **When an ox gores a man or a woman to death, the ox shall be stoned, and its flesh shall not be eaten; but the owner of the ox shall not be liable.** [29] **If the ox has been accustomed to gore in the past, and its owner has been warned** but has not restrained it, and it kills a man or a woman, the ox shall be stoned, and its owner also shall be put to death. [30] If a ransom is imposed on the owner, then the owner shall pay whatever is imposed for the redemption of the victim's life. [31] If it gores a boy or a girl, the owner shall be dealt with according to this same rule. [32] If the ox gores a male or female slave, the owner shall pay to the slaveowner thirty shekels of silver, and the ox shall be stoned.

[33] If someone leaves a pit open, or digs a pit and does not cover it, and an ox or a donkey falls into it, [34] the owner of the pit shall make restitution, giving money to its owner, but keeping the dead animal.

[35] If someone's ox hurts the ox of another, so that it dies, then they shall sell the live ox and divide the price of it; and the dead animal they shall also divide. [36] But if it was known that the ox was accustomed to gore in the past, and its owner has not restrained it, the owner shall restore ox for ox, but keep the dead animal.

These laws "have to do with injuries or damages caused by someone's property (ox or pit) to a human being or to another person's (live) property, and the question of the degree of the owner's liability" (Sprinkle, *The Book of the Covenant*, p. 104). Differentiation is made between the value of lost human life (vv. 28–32) and the value of lost property (vv. 33–36). Further, a distinction is made between first-time liability (vv. 28, 35) and liability due to negligence in spite of prior knowledge (vv. 29, 36).

Where live property is lost (v. 33–36), some form of fair compensation is made. This may be "a primitive form of 'shared risk' accident insurance" (Sprinkle, *The Book of the Covenant*, p. 120). Where human life is lost (vv. 28–32) matters are more complicated, for more than economic value is involved. Why is the ox stoned? Why is it not slaughtered and its valuable meat eaten? A theological principle may be involved. The ox has violated the order of existence established in creation and redefined after the flood. In Genesis 1, humankind is made in God's image and given rule over the beasts (Gen. 1:27–28). In Genesis 9:1–7 that rule is extended to allow humans to kill and eat animals. Killing of humans, however, whether by humans or animals, renders the killer liable to death, so an ox that kills a human is not slaughtered and eaten but executed. Where human negligence is involved, the owner, too, becomes liable to death, though since the liability did not involve intention, provision is made for ransom.

Human death involves another distinction in regard to the status of the victim. Sprinkle argues that "son or daughter" (so the Hebrew) does not refer to the person's age (NRSV, "boy or girl") but to the person's status as a freeborn member of the household regardless of age. In contrast to such a victim (where the owner is to be dealt with as stated previously), in the case of a slave its owner is to be compensated at "top dollar" market value, but the owner of the ox is not liable to death. Yet the slave is a human being whose status as God's image vis-à-vis the animal realm has been violated; therefore, the ox is to be stoned.

Are these laws legally binding, or do they function as moral norms to guide human affairs, with variable applicability to specific cases? Several scholars argue, both on the basis of these biblical laws and on the basis of Mesopotamian parallels, that such laws "serve an admonitory function" (J. J. Finkelstein, quoted in Sprinkle, *The Book of the Covenant*, p. 116). In such laws, the specific cases are cited primarily to exemplify a principle, so that they may guide moral and legal reasoning in related cases. When we approach these laws in this fashion, we can appreciate how, though very few of us nowadays own oxen or have uncovered pits in our backyards, careful study of these laws in their biblical contexts may help to hone our sense of what covenant justice and fairness should look like in our day.

Theft and Damage of Property
(22:1–17)

22:1 **When someone steals an ox or a sheep, and slaughters it or sells it, the thief shall pay five oxen for an ox, and four sheep for a sheep. The thief shall make restitution, but if unable to do so, shall be sold for the theft.** [4] **When the animal, whether ox or donkey or sheep, is found alive in the thief's possession, the thief shall pay double.**

[2] **If a thief is found breaking in, and is beaten to death, no bloodguilt is incurred;** [3] **but if it happens after sunrise, bloodguilt is incurred.**

[5] **When someone causes a field or vineyard to be grazed over, or lets livestock loose to graze in someone else's field, restitution shall be made from the best in the owner's field or vineyard.**

[6] **When fire breaks out and catches in thorns so that the stacked grain or the standing grain or the field is consumed, the one who started the fire shall make full restitution.**

[7] **When someone delivers to a neighbor money or goods for safekeeping, and they are stolen from the neighbor's house, then the thief, if caught, shall pay double.** [8] **If the thief is not caught, the owner of the house shall be brought before God, to determine whether or not the owner had laid hands on the neighbor's goods.**

[9] **In any case of disputed ownership involving ox, donkey, sheep, clothing, or any other loss, of which one party says, "This is mine," the case of both parties shall come before God; the one whom God condemns shall pay double to the other.**

[10] When someone delivers to another a donkey, ox, sheep, or any other animal for safekeeping, and it dies or is injured or is carried off, without anyone seeing it, [11] an oath before the LORD shall decide between the two of them that the one has not laid hands on the property of the other; the owner shall accept the oath, and no restitution shall be made. [12] But if it was stolen, restitution shall be made to its owner. [13] If it was mangled by beasts, let it be brought as evidence; restitution shall not be made for the mangled remains.

[14] When someone borrows an animal from another and it is injured or dies, the owner not being present, full restitution shall be made. [15] If the owner was present, there shall be no restitution; if it was hired, only the hiring fee is due.

[16] When a man seduces a virgin who is not engaged to be married, and lies with her, he shall give the bride-price for her and make her his wife. [17] But if her father refuses to give her to him, he shall pay an amount equal to the bride-price for virgins.

Penalties for Theft, Especially of Animals

These laws begin in verses 1–4 with theft of the most valuable property—livestock, which is demonstrated by the greater restitution. The RSV and NRSV reorder the text to clarify its logic. Sprinkle offers attractive arguments for the Hebrew order (see KJV), which for convenience I will reproduce.

A[1] 1. When someone steals an ox or a sheep, and slaughters it or sells it, the thief shall pay five oxen for an ox, and four sheep for a sheep.

B[1] 2. If a thief is found breaking in, and is beaten to death, no bloodguilt is incurred;

   3. but if it happens after sunrise, bloodguilt is incurred.

B[2]   The thief shall make restitution, but if unable to do so, shall be sold for [the value of] the theft.

A[2] 4. When the animal, whether ox or donkey or sheep, is found alive in the thief's possession, the thief shall pay double.

Some Mesopotamian laws called for execution of any housebreaker and up to thirtyfold restitution for thievery or death if he could not pay. So the question might arise in Israel, "Is not death sometimes a legitimate punishment for a thief?" (Sprinkle, *The Book of the Covenant*, p. 123). This law says no. While the thief is to pay a high restitution, killing him is itself a capital offense, unless at night, when self-defense would be assumed. So B[1] "parenthetically" establishes the upper limit of the penalty. Then B^2 establishes its lower limit: If too poor to pay, the thief is sold into slavery for a duration equal to the value of the penalty. (Sprinkle takes "for" in "for the theft" to indicate "amount of price.") In this way, the law makes poor and rich alike accountable before the law but assesses their penalty in terms relevant to how they can discharge it. One may assume the motives for stealing to differ: the thief out of hunger (Prov. 30:8), and the rich out of greed (Job 20:12–29). In the penalties, at least the poor thief as a slave will eat, and moreover will serve a slave period only equal to what he stole, while the rich thief will pay by forfeiting fourfold or fivefold what was sought in the theft.

With these two parenthetical considerations, the law returns to the main issue, with a lesser restitution if the stolen animal is recoverable. Brevard S. Childs comments: "To my knowledge no other law code seems to have a similar concern for the life of the thief!" (*The Book of Exodus*, p. 474).

Two Cases of the Destruction of Crops

The verbs "graze" and "burn" are homonyms (like-sounding words) in Hebrew, *bi'er*. I shall return to this play on words shortly.

In the first case, someone turns out his livestock to graze. In either case, they stray into a neighbor's field and graze it. Since cattle head for the greenest part of a field, and the owner benefits from this free prime feeding, he must make good from the best of his own field. In the second case, someone has harvested and is burning the stubble. The fire moves to surrounding uncultivated land, and its thorns and thistles provide a bridge for the fire to burn a neighbor's unharvested crop. Since there was no question of the first farmer's gaining anything by this, the restitution is simply in kind.

What shall we make of the word-play? Grazing cattle and burning fire both "consume" what they "feed" on. (The verb "eat/consume" is often used of fire.) Further, grazing cattle and a field fire have in common that, unless carefully controlled, both will spread wider and wider to feed their appetites. This play on grazing or burning as consuming aptly fits the damage, for the crop is what the owner of the damaged field had hoped to consume or to sell to human consumers.

What we have, then, is one producer's cattle or fire consuming the potential produce of another producer because the first fails to control what is otherwise an activity legitimate to his own efforts to gain a livelihood. This law beautifully lends itself to contemporary application if we know how to play with it. For example, what is the liability of an industry for the damage caused downwind or downstream by discharged chemicals? Or of a farmer for similar damage by chemicals used in spraying crops? Or of householders who dispose of toxic wastes through the sewage system instead of following the special disposal instructions on the label? Or of smokers in a confined public space?

Cases of Suspected Theft Involving the Loss or Damage of Bailments

Once again, we have several laws in which the first (vv. 6–7) and the last (vv. 9–11) are closely connected, having to do with bailments (goods delivered in trust for a particular purpose), and the intervening law (v. 8) seems to interrupt that connection. However, the intervening law serves a threefold function in relation to the two that surround it (Sprinkle, *The Book of the Covenant*, p. 152). First, it makes clear "that the use of oath is applicable more generally to situations other than those involving bailments." Second, it casts a wider net than the other two by "including both animate and inanimate property under its scope." Third, it makes explicit what the other two leave implicit: That being "brought before God" (v. 7) and taking "an oath before the LORD" (v. 10) will result in ascertaining "the one whom God condemns" (v. 8).

What all three cases have in common is that they involve lack of direct evidence for guilt or innocence; given this lack, the result of the oath serves to guide the parties concerned. How is the result manifest? In a culture that believes implicitly that the ultimate fate of each individual lies in the hands of a righteous, all-seeing God, the individual conscience is powerfully informed by the awefulness of an oath. To lie under oath is to become liable to an ultimate judgment worse than physical death. Some ways in which guilt would become manifest would be refusal to take an oath; under the stress of the oath, telling an inconsistent story or breaking down and confessing; or confession later, when adverse circumstances are taken as evidence that God is punishing the oath taker. Contrariwise, an oath firmly taken with a steady eye and calm demeanor in the face of accusers must satisfy the accusers, and a potential cause for ongoing bickering and resentment is laid to rest. Perhaps we could draw from these three laws at least this moral: When society has done all it can to ascertain guilt or innocence, then regardless of what an individual may continue to suspect are the facts, the matter has to be let go of. As Robert Frost concludes in his poem "Goodbye and Keep Cold," "something has to be left to God."

Injury to a Borrowed or Rented Animal

This law makes two kinds of distinctions: between a borrowed or rented animal and between an animal used in the owner's absence or his presence. Why is the penalty lower for a hired beast than for a borrowed one? It may be that an owner who can rent out a beast is wealthy enough to work a profitable side business and that the hiring fee is set to cover the risks involved, whereas one who lends a beast (on a neighborly basis) has no other protection of property than full restitution for the loss. Once again, we see at work the concern to find what is fair and just.

The Seduction of a Man's Virgin Daughter

This law is connected with the preceding group insofar as monetary recompense for loss is involved. The law is relevant in a society in which the groom or groom's family pays a bride-price to the father of the bride and a virgin is able to bring a much higher bride-price than a nonvirgin. Coming at the very end of a series of laws on property, this law offends contemporary sensibilities for the way it reduces a marriageable daughter to the level of chattel.

If this law is indeed best connected with the preceding group, then it may be suggested that (typical of a chiastic structure) the passage ends as it begins, on matters of most important note. But it is doubtful that the daughter is mere property, for no mention is made of restitution or adequate compensation for her loss. The monetary value to her birth family can be ensured by insisting on the bride-price one way or another, but it is not called restitution. If the woman marries the man, the result is as though they had contracted to marry in the ordinary fashion. If the woman's father refuses to allow the marriage, the father has his monetary compensation and the woman remains unmarried. Such a refusal, we may hope, would be made if the father considers the seducer an unsuitable husband for his daughter. In such cases, the law protects her interests to this extent, but she would now suffer the social humiliation of her loss of virginity and lesser marriage prospects. Then again, she could still become a wife to someone in such economic circumstances that her lower bride-price outweighed her social disrepute.

This law is intended to cover cases of seduction, not rape. It views the woman, not as a passive victim, but as an enticed correspondent and thereby as a person socially and morally responsible for her own actions. Needless to say, the man is likewise responsible. Viewed in these terms, this law acts as a deterrent to both parties. A marriageable virgin yields to seduction at the risk that it does not lead to marriage and thereby at the risk of great loss to herself in several respects. A potential seducer runs the risk of paying a bride-price (a considerable investment, compared with the compensations mentioned in the previous laws) with no bride to show for it. All this is very foreign to many contemporary sensibilities, yet it raises the general question as to whether those who enter into consensual sexual relations outside of marriage are fully prepared to live with the possibly hard consequences to which the passionate tryst momentarily can blind them. One significance of marriage is that it enacts in the form of profound vows the intention of both parties to be responsible to one another for all consequences of their relationship. To suppose, as tendencies in our culture would have it, that sexual relations need have no "responsible" consequences and may be enjoyed simply for the momentary pleasure or meaning is at best naive and at worst corrosive of communal moral and spiritual fiber.

CULTIC REGULATIONS AND SOCIAL JUSTICE
Exodus 22:18–23:19

The order and arrangement of these cultic regulations and issues of social justice reflect the assumption "that there is no dichotomy between the secular and sacred, between 'church' and 'state,' between justice and religion in Israel, but that these are inextricably intertwined" (Sprinkle, *The Book of the Covenant*, p. 161).

Cultic Matters (22:18–20)

22:18 **You shall not permit a female sorcerer to live.**
    [19] **Whoever lies with an animal shall be put to death.**
    [20] **Whoever sacrifices to any god, other than the LORD alone, shall be devoted to destruction.**

The penalty for these offenses indicates their seriousness, which probably explains their position at the head of this group. Sorcery means to determine the future by appeal to principles to which even the divine realm is subject. To lie with an animal violates the created hierarchy within which humankind images God in ruling over the animal realm. Moreover, in emulating pagan stories of gods cohabiting with animals, it misrepresents Israel's God. These two laws thus imply an idolatry that in the third law becomes explicit.

Social Justice (22:21–28)

> 22:21 You shall not wrong or oppress a resident alien, for you were aliens in the land of Egypt. 22 You shall not abuse any widow or orphan. 23 If you do abuse them, when they cry out to me, I will surely heed their cry; 24 my wrath will burn, and I will kill you with the sword, and your wives shall become widows and your children orphans.
>
> 25 If you lend money to my people, to the poor among you, you shall not deal with them as a creditor; you shall not exact interest from them. 26 If you take your neighbor's cloak in pawn, you shall restore it before the sun goes down; 27 for it may be your neighbor's only clothing to use as cover; in what else shall that person sleep? And if your neighbor cries out to me, I will listen, for I am compassionate.
>
> 28 You shall not revile God, or curse a leader of your people.

This section protects social groups vulnerable to exploitation: resident aliens, widows, fatherless children, and poor debtors. The resident alien leads off the group because "though the worship of foreign gods is condemned [vv. 18–20], a foreigner must not be mistreated even if he had an idolatrous past" (Sprinkle, *The Book of the Covenant*, p. 166). The motive clause, "for you were aliens in the land of Egypt," suggests that by the way in which Israelites deal with foreigners, they image the God of the exodus. In the instance of widows and orphans, God will hear their cry (compare 2:23–25) and will visit affliction on the afflictors (as on the firstborn of Egypt). The instance of the poor is spelled out in greater detail and ends on a note that may refer to all four laws so far: "I am compassionate." The Hebrew word for "compassionate" occurs again in 34:6, where it is translated "gracious." In Christian usage, "grace" often is taken to signify unmerited favor. In the present context, the four types of exploited groups are in no way undeserving in God's eyes. Rather, their very condition should single them out for special sensitivity and care. (See the more extended treatment of this adjective at 34:6.) Verse 28 may sum up the preceding four laws by emphasizing that to violate them would mean to curse God and the civil authority (Sprinkle, *The Book of the Covenant*, p. 168; compare Jezebel's charge in 1 Kings 21:10, abetting Ahab's designs on Naboth's vineyard).

Cultic Matters (22:29–31)

> 22:29 You shall not delay to make offerings from the fullness of your harvest and from the outflow of your presses.
>
> The firstborn of your sons you shall give to me. 30 You shall do the same

with your oxen and with your sheep: seven days it shall remain with its mother; on the eighth day you shall give it to me.
      [31] You shall be people consecrated to me; therefore you shall not eat any meat that is mangled by beasts in the field; you shall throw it to the dogs.

The laws in this subsection variously underline how Israel is to dedicate itself to God ("to me," vv. 29, 30, 31). The preceding social justice subsection begins, and the following social justice subsection ends, with a reference to the exodus from Egypt (22:21; 23:9); while this intervening cultic subsection repeats "commands given during the exodus (13:2, 11–13, consecration of the firstborn; 19:6, Israel's call to holiness at Sinai)" (Sprinkle, *The Book of the Covenant*, p. 173).

Social Justice (23:1–9)

23:1 You shall not spread a false report. You shall not join hands with the wicked to act as a malicious witness. [2] You shall not follow a majority in wrongdoing; when you bear witness in a lawsuit, you shall not side with the majority so as to pervert justice; [3] nor shall you be partial to the poor in a lawsuit.
      [4] When you come upon your enemy's ox or donkey going astray, you shall bring it back.
      [5] When you see the donkey of one who hates you lying under its burden and you would hold back from setting it free, you must help to set it free.
      [6] You shall not pervert the justice due to your poor in their lawsuits. [7] Keep far from a false charge, and do not kill the innocent and those in the right, for I will not acquit the guilty. [8] You shall take no bribe, for a bribe blinds the officials, and subverts the cause of those who are in the right.
      [9] You shall not oppress a resident alien; you know the heart of an alien, for you were aliens in the land of Egypt.

This text concerns primarily upholding justice in the courts by giving reliable testimony and not slanting it to favor either rich or poor. This concern comes in the form of ten apodictic or unqualified commands, five in 22:29–23:3 and five in 23:6–9. These two sets of verses bracket or envelop 23:4–5, a passage that concerns the treatment of an enemy's strayed or over-burdened ox or ass, which seems oddly placed. Its placement, however, between two calls to reliable testimony in court, may be "designed to show the extent to which one is to be impartial as a witness in court" (Sprinkle, *The Book of the Covenant*, p. 180). In addition to its own force as an injunction to humane treatment of animals, it has a metaphorical force: Just as one should not allow enmity to prevent one from helping an enemy's beast of burden that is in trouble, so in giving testimony in court, "One should never act out of rancor towards the persons involved, but you should help the one in need . . . even if in doing so you help your enemy" (Sprinkle, p. 182).

In this section, the second set of social justice laws (23:1–9) ends as the first one (22:21–28) began: with reference to (1) oppression of a resident alien and (2) the exodus. To the casual eye, these two references seem like a casual repetition within a group of laws haphazardly jumbled together. If we allow that the moral-legal mind has an aesthetic eye in arranging its laws, we may appreciate how these two references contribute to the concentric structure of the whole section.

Cultic Matters (23:10–19)

23:10 **For six years you shall sow your land and gather in its yield; ¹¹ but the seventh year you shall let it rest and lie fallow, so that the poor of your people may eat; and what they leave the wild animals may eat. You shall do the same with your vineyard, and with your olive orchard.**

¹² Six days you shall do your work, but on the seventh day you shall rest, so that your ox and your donkey may have relief, and your homeborn slave and the resident alien may be refreshed. ¹³ Be attentive to all that I have said to you. Do not invoke the names of other gods; do not let them be heard on your lips.

¹⁴ Three times in the year you shall hold a festival for me. ¹⁵ You shall observe the festival of unleavened bread; as I commanded you, you shall eat unleavened bread for seven days at the appointed time in the month of Abib, for in it you came out of Egypt.

No one shall appear before me empty-handed.

¹⁶ You shall observe the festival of harvest, of the first fruits of your labor, of what you sow in the field. You shall observe the festival of ingathering at the end of the year, when you gather in from the field the fruit of your labor. ¹⁷ Three times in the year all your males shall appear before the Lord God.

¹⁸ You shall not offer the blood of my sacrifice with anything leavened, or let the fat of my festival remain until the morning.

¹⁹ The choicest of the first fruits of your ground you shall bring into the house of the Lord your God.

You shall not boil a kid in its mother's milk.

As already noted, the subsections on social justice are interspersed within those concerning faithful worship of Yahweh. Conversely, this final subsection concerning faithful worship begins with two sabbath provisions, one with special relevance for the poor and the wild animals (v. 11), the other for the ox and the donkey, the homeborn slave, and the resident alien (v. 12). Presumably, not all Israel was to let the land lie fallow in the same year, for fear of general starvation. If the fallow year rotated among various Israelites, the poor and the wild animals would annually have some place to enjoy this "movable feast." The sabbath is referenced by three different verbs, "rest," "have relief," and "be refreshed." The first means primarily to cease from work (like God in Genesis 2:1–3 and Israel in Exodus 5:5). The second means primarily to settle down and remain in a place (like Noah's ark in Genesis 8:4; God's ark in Psalm 132:8; and the sheep in Psalm 23:2 [NRSV note].) The third verb means, literally, be refreshed by catching one's breath. Taken as a group, they aptly describe the process appropriate to sabbath observance.

The first social justice subsection ended in 22:28 in such a way as to imply that failure to observe the preceding laws would be to revile God and curse the civic leader. The laws pertaining to the two sabbaths (with their social dimension) are followed by a call to "be attentive to all that I have said to you." The immediately following prohibition, "Do not invoke the names of other gods; do not let them be heard on your lips," implies that violation of the two types of sabbath goes hand in hand with idolatry.

This final cultic subsection now moves from two types of sabbath to three annual feasts. First they are specified and briefly described: unleavened bread (vv. 14–15), harvest (v. 16a), and ingathering (v. 16b). The comments in verse 18 and in verse 19a clearly relate to the first two festivals, and the comment in verse 19b may therefore relate to the third, for the feast of ingathering occurs in the fall, and flocks begin to conceive in June, so that some lambs could be born in time for this fall festival. The reason for the prohibition, however, is unclear.

EPILOGUE
FOREWARNED IS FOREARMED
Exodus 23:20–33

23:20 **I am going to send an angel in front of you, to guard ["keep"] you on the way and to bring you to the place that I have prepared. ²¹ Be attentive ["keep yourself"] to him and listen to his voice; do not rebel against him, for he will not pardon your transgression; for my name is in him.**

²² But if you listen attentively to his voice and do all that I say, then I will be an enemy to your enemies and a foe to your foes.

²³ When my angel goes in front of you, and brings you to the Amorites, the Hittites, the Perizzites, the Canaanites, the Hivites, and the Jebusites, and

I blot them out, 24 you shall not bow down to their gods, or worship them, or follow their practices, but you shall utterly demolish them and break their pillars in pieces. 25 You shall worship the LORD your God, and I will bless your bread and your water; and I will take sickness away from among you. 26 No one shall miscarry or be barren in your land; I will fulfill the number of your days. 27 I will send my terror in front of you, and will throw into confusion all the people against whom you shall come, and I will make all your enemies turn their backs to you. 28 And I will send the pestilence in front of you, which shall drive out the Hivites, the Canaanites, and the Hittites from before you. 29 I will not drive them out from before you in one year, or the land would become desolate and the wild animals would multiply against you. 30 Little by little I will drive them out from before you, until you have increased and possess the land. 31 I will set your borders from the Red Sea to the sea of the Philistines, and from the wilderness to the Euphrates; for I will hand over to you the inhabitants of the land, and you shall drive them out before you. 32 You shall make no covenant with them and their gods. 33 They shall not live in your land, or they will make you sin against me; for if you worship their gods, it will surely be a snare to you.

The book of Exodus is primarily a story of God delivering Israel from Egypt and covenanting with them at Mount Sinai. This story is part of a larger story that begins with the ancestors and reaches its goal with Israel's entry into the land of Canaan (2:23–25; 3:1–17; 6:3–8). But God's promise to the ancestors comes in the context of a yet larger story of God's concern for the whole world. Through Israel's story that begins with Abraham and Sarah, God seeks to bring blessing to "all the families of the earth" (Gen. 12:1–3). There is an integral connection, then, between God's work in and for Israel and God's universal concern for the well-being of all whom God has created. It is important to keep this connection in mind as we reflect on the passage before us.

Exodus 23:20–33 functions as an epilogue to the laws presented in 20:22–23:19. Let us pause to trace the emergence of the theme of laws in the exodus story:

1. The theme is introduced indirectly in 4:10–17. When Moses complains of his difficulty in speaking, God says, "I will be with your mouth." (I have suggested that it is God's name in Moses' mouth that will enable him to speak for God.) Then God says, I will "teach you what you are to speak." The verb "teach" is *horah*, (point out, direct, guide, teach, instruct), which gives rise to the noun *torah* (teaching, instruction, covenant law). The verb occurs again to reassure Moses

that, with Aaron as his "mouthpiece," "I will be with your mouth and with his mouth, and will teach you [plural] what you [plural] shall do."

2. The theme appears again in 15:22–27, where God "shows" [*horah*] Moses a piece of wood, or tree, that turns sweet the bitter wilderness water (15:25), which becomes a parable for how observing God's commandments and keeping God's statutes will keep Israel's life from the kind of societal diseases that God brought on the Egyptians.

3. The association between sweet water and covenant law is implicit also in 17:1–7, where the water that keeps the people alive in the wilderness flows to them from Horeb (another name for Sinai).

4. The theme of laws is central in 19:3–6, where Israel is called to obey God's voice and keep God's covenant as a priestly kingdom and holy nation amid all the nations.

The theme of laws finally comes into its own in 20:1–23:33. This long passage: (a) begins by recollecting the exodus from Egypt (20:2), (b) continues at length with God giving to Moses the Ten Commandments and the ordinances (20:22–23:19), and (c) concludes by looking forward to further travel through the wilderness and entry into the land (23:20–33). In this way, the short three-stage synopsis in 6:6–8 ([a] exodus, [b] covenant at Mount Sinai, [c] entry) is echoed again in the "a-b-c" sequence in 20:1–23:33. This sequence appears again and again in the Bible. It is as though Israel (and all who would become part of Israel's and the world's ongoing story) need to let this sequence, this movement, sink as deeply as possible into their hearts: "out-through-into, out-through-into, out-through-into."

Why is this so important? Because every person has begun life in the wider world by going out of a place that was for the longest time hospitable and nurturing, but at the very end was experienced as expulsive, sometimes painfully so. Once in the world, life is more uncertain and risky. Depending on factors that differ from person to person, this uncertainty can give rise to great anxiety and lead to defensive and aggressive strategies for survival. So there is great truth in the diagnostic image of "thrownness" coined by the philosopher Martin Heidegger. In his study of the riskiness of human existence called *Being and Time*, he says in effect that to be a human being is to experience oneself as "thrown" into the world and having to make one's way in the world, until time takes one into the unfathomable mystery of death. Because of this end, to be a "being in time" is to be a "being unto death." Such an end, coloring all our days, intensifies the uncertainties of everyday life.

However, the rhythm the Bible never tires of inculcating is an "out-through-in" where God is our beginning, our path, and our end. Even the land of Canaan is for Israel not an end in itself. Rather, it is the concrete symbol of 19:4, "and brought you *to myself.*" This rhythm and movement is to sustain us amid the deep uncertainties of our life in this world, uncertainties that otherwise would crown anxiety, fear, and calculating strategy as the ruling forces in our lives (compare Rom. 5:14; Heb. 2:14–15). It is no accident, then, that when Paul wrestles with the issue that troubles him most deeply (Rom. 9:1–5), he begins with the ancestors (9:6–13), moves to a text from the book of Exodus (9:15), and ends with a doxology (Rom. 11:36) that concludes, "For from him and through him and to him are all things. To him be the glory forever. Amen." As this conclusion shows, he has allowed his Bible to enter deeply into his soul and conform him to its narrative rhythm.

Let us now turn to Exodus 23:20–33 and see how it looks forward to Israel's post–Mount Sinai story. The passage falls into two subsections. First, verses 20–22 introduce an unidentified "angel," or "messenger," to go before them, keep them on the way, and bring them into the place prepared for them. Then verses 23–33 focus on what they are to beware of once they are there. In verses 20–22, the angel is referred to by noun or pronoun seven times; in verses 23–33 there is a threefold reference, in which the angel who brings the people to the land (v. 23) is succeeded by another even more mysterious agency called a "terror" (v. 27) and a "pestilence" (v. 28). I propose that the angel is Moses, who leads the people to the land, and the terror and pestilence are Joshua and his successors, who lead the people into the land and against their enemies. Let us now consider the two subsections in turn.

The angel is to go before the people and guard or keep them on the way. In Hebrew as in English, "keep" means more than "guard." It includes, for example, nurture, care, and cherishing, as the embracing concern that, when necessary, guards those cared for from danger. Thus, Moses has not only led Israel out of Egypt and against the Amalekites but also has seen to their food and water in the wilderness. When the priests bless Israel with words beginning, "Yahweh bless you and keep you," they invoke God's all-embracing care, which includes but is not exhausted in God's protection.

Israel is called to "be attentive [literally, "keep yourself"] to him and listen to his voice" (v. 21). This involves a self-keeping in loyal relation to another. (Compare the old Book of Common Prayer, where bride and groom were called upon to "keep thyself only unto her/him, as long as ye both shall live.") The angel's keeping, for all its importance, will not work without Israel's responsive self-keeping. This self-keeping consists in listening to the angel's voice.

Here is where the angel begins to look like Moses. Like the Moses of 4:10–16, the angel speaks; like that Moses, God's name is in this angel. Moreover, just as Moses' speaking is God speaking through him or putting the words in his mouth (4:12–15), so the angel's voice will convey all that God says (23:22). There is a further hint in 34:29–35 that the Moses who speaks God's commandments to the people is the angel who will go before them.

How are we to understand the clause, "for my name is in him"? One could connect this clause closely with the preceding one, as though "he will not pardon your transgression" because "my name is in him." But I take "for my name is in him" to be connected to "be attentive to him and listen to his voice," with the intervening words parenthetical, which brings us back to the point about the relation between the angel's "keeping" and Israel's "self-keeping" toward the angel. The angel simply will not keep apart from such self-keeping, for rebellion will betray the angel and the God whom the angel serves. Centuries later, Jeremiah will paint a picture of people who break every commandment, do all sorts of injustice to the poor and the powerless, go into the temple and say, "We are safe," and then go on doing all these abominations (Jer. 7:8–10). To think that the "angel" will pardon such transgression is not to worship the God of the exodus but an idol that is the projection of one's own desires. In such a case, the angel will turn against Israel! (compare Exod. 32:19–20, 25–29). But if the people will emulate the angel's keeping in their own self-keeping, the angel will indeed be an enemy to their enemies. The self-keeping, as the second subsection goes on to spell out, consists in keeping the covenant and its laws.

So we come to verses 23–33. Once Israel is in the land, victorious over their enemies, they are to take care not to "bow down to their gods, or worship them, or follow their practices." In these clauses, we may see an echo of the two tables of the Decalogue, the first having to do with the human-divine relation, the second having to do with relations within human society. To worship the gods of Canaan will be to adopt also the social practices of Canaan. Over against this, Israel is to be a priestly kingdom and a holy nation.

While the angel's keeping in verse 20 involves more than just guarding, the latter is the primary emphasis in verses 21–22. However, once the people are in the land and given rest from war against their enemies, another sort of danger arises. Especially as former enemies become bordering neighbors (and in some instances resident aliens), their way of worshiping the gods of productivity and fertility may prove very attractive to Israel. It will be especially true to the degree that Israel's understanding and worship of Yahweh focuses primarily on the theme that "The LORD is a warrior; the LORD is his name" (15:3). Given how this name is redefined at the burning bush expressly in relation to Israel's political and social oppression, and redefined therefore expressly in terms of God's mighty "hand" with its "wonders" (3:20), Israel may begin to think that new needs (butter, not guns) call for new gods. If Israel understands 6:3 as simple replacement or supersession rendering the old understanding obsolete (Yahweh the warrior in place of El Shaddai the provider), their turning to other gods is at least understandable. It will be a misunderstanding, though, for the El Shaddai who is the giver of the blessings of cosmic productivity and of the blessings of breast and womb (Gen. 49:25) has been still present in the Yahweh who in the wilderness provides bread, meat, and water, most especially the water that, like the laws, flows toward them, wherever they are, from Mount Sinai (17:1–7). So the people are not only forewarned against worshiping these gods of Canaan but also reassured that there will be no need. If they will keep themselves in God's covenant, God will keep them by blessing them in regard to all their needs.

With this reassurance, God returns to the more immediate concern. The "terror" God will send "in front of you" (like the angel of vv. 20, 23) is the "terror" spoken of already in 15:16. We will see an example in the words of Rahab in Jericho to Joshua's spies (Josh. 2:9, "dread"). The "confusion" is a common means by which God throws opposing armies into panic and disarray. The "pestilence" God will send "in front of you" reappears in the farewell speech of Joshua, where NRSV translates it "the hornet" (Josh. 24:12). But now comes a further forewarning that underscores the importance of the warnings in verses 23–26. The people are not to expect that victory against the people in the land will be sudden, for it will be long and drawn out. It will be some time before Israel is numerous enough to fill the land. Until then, the present inhabitants will serve to keep the land itself under cultivation so that it does not revert to wilderness and likewise to prevent the land from being overrun by wild animals who would endanger human habitation. Because, then, Israel and these people will live side by side in the land, it is all the more important to emphasize that "if you worship their gods, it will surely be a snare to you."

This passage raises profound issues about cultural imperialism with a religious base, about genocide and ethnic cleansing, and about religiously fueled intolerance. It is easy to read a passage like this as sponsoring such things and then either to act accordingly in one's own time and place or to repudiate the passage as well as a Bible that contains such passages. Such interpretations are too simple. The scriptural story, as it goes on, progressively transforms these themes until in Jesus Christ they become transformed radically. The nature of this transformation in Christ is such, in my view, that no Christian can simply take Exodus 23:20–33 as a scriptural basis for cultural imperialism and ethnic cleansing. But the complexity of the issues is ironically illustrated by the way certain contemporary movements that would repudiate the imperialism of this passage also vigorously pursue a policy of eradicating all traces of sexist or perceived sexist language from daily speech and even from historical documents like the Bible. I use this example, as one who strives to divest my own speech and writing of gender-exclusive language. But the vigor with which some people pounce on those who use gender-exclusive language is one sign that concerns for pluralism and tolerance can be limited by concerns for justice and truth. There is a difference between justice and injustice, between truth and untruth; given how both exist in our midst (and in our own hearts), there is a battle to be waged, and we need to decide whose side we are on. The transformation that Jesus Christ brings to these issues has to do with *how* the battle is waged (compare John 18:33–38; Phil. 2:5–11).

One illustration of the contemporary relevance of this passage may be found in a report in *The Christian Century* (March 22–29, 1995, pages 317–319) concerning the Third General Assembly of the Latin American Council of Churches, in Concepción, Chile, in January 1995. The report refers to religious movements in Latin America, noting a decline in Roman Catholic membership, "unbelievable growth" in Protestant adherents, and the appearance of new religious movements, "including Afro-Brazilian religious expressions as well as New Age and Oriental groups." In this context, theologian José Míguez-Bonino affirmed that "there is only one God, one Lord Jesus Christ, one Holy Spirit," and consequently "there can only be one people of God." Taking sharp issue with this affirmation, a Methodist pastor and professor, Nancy Cardoso Pereira, responded: "All reflection on this topic begins with a challenge: there is not just one God, there is not just one Lord, Jesus Christ, and there is not just one people of God." The article goes on to report, "She went on to urge greater openness to the many gods and goddesses worshiped in Latin America (such as Pachamama, Tuypa, Olorum, Zambi)."

On Cardoso Pereira's behalf, I would agree that too often the Christian church has acted in the world as though its final mandate were given in Exodus 23:20–33. I understand her to challenge the church to repudiate words and actions that imperialize and oppress. What Exodus 23:20–33 does continue to call us to, however, is to strip ourselves of our idols and to worship and serve the one true God. Those who do not find the presence and activity of the one true God supremely and definitively embodied in Jesus Christ must, of course, march to a different drummer. But the church today, no less than Israel at Mount Sinai, is called to resist those other drumbeats and to walk in the rhythm of the God who in Jesus Christ brings us out, carries us along, and will bring us in. That God, who calls us to a servant ministry in the world after the pattern of Jesus (Phil. 2:5–11), will, amid all that could make us anxious and drive us to our own survival strategies, "guard your hearts and your minds in Christ Jesus" (Phil. 4:7). As the "out-through-in" rhythm of Exodus 20:2–23:33 promises, "I am confident of this, that the one who began a good work among you will bring it to completion by the day of Jesus Christ" (Phil. 1:6). One way this is put is in the Gospel of John, where Jesus says (echoing Exod. 23:20?), "If it were not so, would I have told you that I go to prepare a place for you? And if I go and prepare a place for you, I will come again and will take you to myself, so that where I am, there you may be also" (John 14:2–3). This assurance rests, ultimately, in Jesus' intercession in which he prays that the father will "protect [or "keep"] them in your name that you have given me [Exod. 23:21?], so that they may be one, as we are one. While I was with them, I protected [or "kept"] them in your name that you have given me" (John 17:11–12). Similar to the sequence between the angel and the terror-pestilence, or the sequence between Moses and Joshua, Jesus' departure to be "with the Father" is followed by the gift of the Spirit, who among other things will "guide you into all the truth" (John 16:13). That this Spirit will not be without its own hornet sting of truth is suggested when Jesus says, "it is to your advantage that I go away, for if I do not go away, the Advocate will not come to you; but if I go, I will send him to you. And when he comes, he will prove the world wrong about sin and righteousness and judgment: about sin, because they do not believe in me; about righteousness, because I am going to the Father and you will see me no longer; about judgment, because the ruler of this world has been condemned" (John 16:7–11). These are just some examples of how themes and patterns of meaning laid down in Exodus reappear in the New Testament.

COVENANT AND CONSUMMATION
Exodus 24:1–11

24:1 Then he said to Moses, "Come up to the LORD, you and Aaron, Nadab, and Abihu, and seventy of the elders of Israel, and worship at a distance. ² Moses alone shall come near the LORD; but the others shall not come near, and the people shall not come up with him."

³ Moses came and told the people all the words of the LORD and all the ordinances; and all the people answered with one voice, and said, "All the words that the LORD has spoken we will do." ⁴ And Moses wrote down all the words of the LORD. He rose early in the morning, and built an altar at the foot of the mountain, and set up twelve pillars, corresponding to the twelve tribes of Israel. ⁵ He sent young men of the people of Israel, who offered burnt offerings and sacrificed oxen as offerings of well-being to the LORD. ⁶ Moses took half of the blood and put it in basins, and half of the blood he dashed against the altar. ⁷ Then he took the book of the covenant, and read it in the hearing of the people; and they said, "All that the LORD has spoken we will do, and we will be obedient [literally, we will hear]." ⁸ Moses took the blood and dashed it on the people, and said, "See the blood of the covenant that the LORD has made with you in accordance with all these words."

⁹ Then Moses and Aaron, Nadab, and Abihu, and seventy of the elders of Israel went up, ¹⁰ and they saw the God of Israel. Under his feet there was something like a pavement of sapphire stone, like the very heaven for clearness. ¹¹ God did not lay his hand on the chief men of the people of Israel; also they beheld God, and they ate and drank.

Before discussing this pasage, it is helpful to consider the shape of the larger narrative once the people arrive at Mount Sinai. I see the following two-phase movement, with four elements in each phase:

Phase A		Phase B	
1. 19:9b–25	the mountain	1. 24:1–2	the mountain
2. 20:1–17	the Ten "Words"	2. 24:3–8	the covenant
3. 20:18–21	fear/distance	3. 24:9–11	safety/nearness
4. 20:22–23:33	covenant laws	4. 25–31	the sanctuary

The eagle in 19:4 is a figure of parental nurture, guidance, and protection, climaxing in the statement "and brought you to myself." Yet the intimacy of that climax is immediately balanced by the following "if" that focuses on Israel's ability and willingness to hear God's voice and keep God's covenant. In 19:9b–25 (A1), the emphasis on God's awesome majesty obscures the eagle image and connects with the "if" language of covenant, underscoring the gravity of the people's responsibility. When God then addresses them in the Ten Words or Ten Commandments (A2), their response is filled with fear and a sense of God's distance, while Moses goes back up the mountain, disappearing into "the thick darkness where God was" (A3). There he receives laws that spell out in detail how the Ten Words should shape their relation to God and one another.

Now (B1) God instructs Moses to bring Aaron, his two sons, and seventy elders to worship at a distance (compare 19:22, 24) and then for Moses by himself to draw near. But first Moses leads the people in a covenant-making ceremony (B2). In this ceremony, Moses re-presents the Ten Words and the covenant laws to the people (24:3), and they agree to do them (24:3, 7; compare 19:8). The initial giving of the Decalogue filled the people with fear and a sense of God's distance. But this time, following the binding ceremony with its exchange of words and the action with the blood, we are shown a scene of overwhelming and completely unexpected intimacy and safe nearness to God (B3). As in 20:21, Moses goes up the mountain and disappears from the people's sight. This time, what follows is not detailed laws to govern the people's daily lives, but detailed instructions for building a sanctuary so that God may dwell in the people's midst (25:8). If the laws of 20:22–23:33 (like the Ten Words of 20:1–17) are associated with the majesty of God that inspires great fear and a sense of God's distance, the instructions for the sanctuary in chapters 25—31 are associated with the sense of the communing nearness of God in 24:9–11. In this scene and throughout chapters 25—31, I suggest, we have returned to the overtones of the eagle figure in 19:4. God as parent eagle has delivered the people from Egypt and "brought you to myself." The eagle imagery associated with the ark and its cherubim in the most holy part of the sanctuary (25:10–23) suggests the final meaning of "to myself": the communion of God's presence in the sanctuary.

If we compare the two phases of the Mount Sinai narrative in this way, we are struck with the contrast between the fear and distance that permeates the first phase (continuing from the fear in 3:6), and the intimacy and "at-homeness" that the second phase arrives at. What makes the difference? It is what happens in 24:3–8.

When Moses tells the people all the Words (20:1–17) and ordinances (21:1–23:33), they respond a second time as they had in 19:8. There they had used the more general "everything the LORD has spoken," for God had to that point spoken only in general terms of "my voice . . . my covenant" (19:5). Here they use the more specific "all the words that the

LORD has spoken." Even so, the response in 24:3 is still a preliminary assent and not yet a binding commitment.

The next morning, Moses builds an altar at the foot of the mountain and sets up twelve pillars. If the pillars represent the twelve tribes who will enter into the covenant, the altar represents God as the other covenant party. Then Moses has "young men of the people of Israel" offer two kinds of animal sacrifice: burnt offerings and "well-being" (or "peace") offerings. The first sort, in which the whole animal is consumed by fire on the altar, signifies the total self-offering of the worshiper to God. We may recall that in Genesis 22 Abraham was asked to offer Isaac to God as a burnt offering and that in Exodus 13:11–16 all firstborn male children are to be redeemed by a sacrifice, so that they may belong to God without themselves being sacrificially slain. Here, then, when the young men offer burnt offerings on behalf of the people of Israel, it is as though the people through the ritual actions of their young men are promising to love the LORD their God with all their heart, and with all their soul, and with all their might (Deut. 6:4–5). When they go on to sacrifice a "well-being" (or "peace") offering, this may be "designed to effect amicable relations with the deity" (T. H. Gaster, "Sacrifices and Offerings," p. 155). Or it may celebrate the *shalom* that follows from the whole burnt offering and point already toward the scene in verses 9–11.

Moses now takes the blood from these two types of sacrifice and dashes half of it against the altar. Then he reads God's words in the people's hearing. They respond by saying that they will *do* all these words, thereby showing that they have truly *heard* what God has said to them. Following their words, Moses dashes the other half of the blood on them and says, "See the blood of the covenant."

The covenant ceremony is rich in a meaning partly spoken and partly acted out. The words give the actions their focus and clarity of meaning; the actions give the words a depth and range of meaning that words can only hint at. For example, what do we see when we "see the blood of the covenant"? If we are there in person or in imagination, we will see first of all an altar and twelve pillars. Since we will identify the twelve pillars with ourselves, we will identify the altar with God. When we see the blood, we see the very life fluid that only moments before flowed whole through the veins of these living animals, which then was separated into two halves and now covers the altar on the one hand and ourselves on the other. Through the words that have been exchanged (v. 7) and through the actions with the blood that surround those words and ritually "embrace" them (vv. 6b, 8a), the two parties to the covenant have entered into a bond of unity that suggests one covenanted divine-human life.

Many recent scholars have proposed that the Mount Sinai covenant is like a treaty between an imperial "king of kings" and the petty king of a subordinate "vassal" state. There is much to support such an interpretation, in Exodus and elsewhere in the Old Testament. But the symmetrical character of the symbolic actions here in verses 6–8, the totally unexpected scene that immediately follows in verses 9–11, and the figure of the parent eagle in 19:4 combine to suggest that the Mount Sinai covenant, for all its royal-imperial features, at heart is a kinship covenant. If kinship is at base a matter of blood relations, then here Israel and God enter into, or reaffirm in a new way, the kind of kinship relation that existed between God and the ancestors of Genesis 12—50 and that was hinted at still in Exodus 4:21–23.

But if the blood dashed on the altar and the people signifies the one life that binds God and people in a relation of *shalom*, that blood also implies a life so committed to the covenant relation that it is prepared to lay itself down for the sake of that relation. Anything less than total commitment on either side would mean the loss of that party's moral and spiritual integrity and the death of the covenant relation. But within the mutual embrace of such a commitment, the relation that is now possible so beggars the imagination that it can only be hinted at, through the scene in verses 9–11.

This passage gives scholars and commentators no end of trouble, for it flies in the face of what everybody knows: that "no one shall see me and live" (33:20). Therefore, "seeing" in this passage is frequently explained in a way that conforms to the prohibition in 33:20, but this blunts the shocking simplicity of our passage. Moreover, it overlooks the narrative context of both passages. The prohibition is pronounced in a specific context: after the sin of the calf. The seeing in verses 9–11 comes in dramatic contrast to Moses' response at the burning bush (3:6) and the scenes in 19:9–25 and 20:18–21. This contrast serves to indicate the difference made by the mutual covenanting commitment in 24:3–8. It is only the betrayal of this commitment that leads to the prohibition in 33:20.

Anyone who has ever had a dream charged with the sense of the holiness of the presence of God, filling the dreamer with wonder, awe, and solemn joy, and at the same time a kind of simple awareness of the matter-of-fact rightness of being in that presence, will recognize the dreamlike quality of this passage (compare Psalm 126; Jer. 31:26): the sight of God; the clarity of the vision, as if looking through a pavement of infinitely precious sapphire stones. (The word translated "clearness" is a standard Priestly term for sacred purity.) Amazingly, the seeing is all right with God, for no harm comes to them! And again, they behold God. Not only so, but they eat and drink.

In his book *Insearch*, James Hillman advises his readers how to respond to their dreams: neither ignore them nor analyze them to death; befriend them, he says. Rehearse and review them in the mind's eye on waking. Perhaps tell them to a trusted family member or friend. Let them lodge in the memory, and then go your way, trusting what they speak of to carry on its work inside you.

That Israel "befriended" this dreamlike episode and experiences like it is suggested by passages like Psalm 27:4; 34:5. Such experiences arise momentarily like an artesian well from an underground stream—the underground stream being the obscure, haunting underground memory of Eden, before shame and guilt brought down a veil between us and God. This episode comes as the climax of the exodus–Mount Sinai narrative, the fulfillment of God's words in 3:12, 6:7 ("you shall know"), and 19:4 ("to myself"), suggesting the ultimate goal of God's redemptive activity: a communion in which God may be seen fully and unreservedly, and in which to see God is to eat and drink. Jesus' beatitude says that seeing God is a matter of being pure in heart. Perhaps that can guide our interpretation of the "purity" of the sapphire pavement through which these representatives of Israel momentarily see God, for the vision comes after total (or "pure in heart") commitment to the covenant sealed in the blood that binds people and God in kinship.

Meanwhile, 24:9–11 can be viewed as a context within which to hear the words of Aaron and his descendants when they pronounce the LORD's blessing according to Numbers 6:24–26 (my translation):

> The LORD bless you   and keep you;
> the LORD shine his face on you   and grace you;
> the LORD lift up his face to you   and give you peace.

The one repeated element—God's radiant, gracious, upraised face—suggests the intimacy into which God seeks to draw us, an intimacy of presence that is both the source and the goal of God's blessing and keeping.

WITH GOD IN GLORY
Exodus 24:12–18

24:12 **The LORD said to Moses, "Come up to me on the mountain, and wait there; and I will give you the tablets of stone, with the law and the commandment, which I have written for their instruction."** [13] **So Moses set out** with his assistant Joshua, and Moses went up into the mountain of God. [14] To the elders he had said, "Wait here for us, until we come to you again; for Aaron and Hur are with you; whoever has a dispute may go to them."

[15] Then Moses went up on the mountain, and the cloud covered the mountain. [16] The glory of the LORD settled on Mount Sinai, and the cloud covered it for six days; on the seventh day he called to Moses out of the cloud. [17] Now the appearance of the glory of the LORD was like a devouring fire on the top of the mountain in the sight of the people of Israel. [18] Moses entered the cloud, and went up on the mountain. Moses was on the mountain for forty days and forty nights.

This scene exceeds, if possible, the one in verses 9–11. In 3:6 Moses hid his face in fear before the God who appeared to him in a burning bush. Now he goes up the mountain, enveloped by a cloud in which the glory of the LORD is manifest "like a devouring fire"—yet he is not consumed! While he is inside this glory cloud, he is instructed to make God a sanctuary "in accordance with all that I show you concerning the pattern of the tabernacle and all of its furniture" (25:9).

The tabernacle of chapters 25—31 is an architectural representation of Moses' experience of God's glory on the mountain. The following features of the narrative support this:

1. Moses goes up the mountain. We may recall how commentators on chapter 19 see in its three levels of accessibility—the people, then the priests, then Moses only—a parallel to the three divisions of the tabernacle.
2. A cloud *covers* the mountain, and the glory of the LORD *settles* ("tents" or "tabernacles") on the mountain. Exodus 26:13 will describe the provision to *cover* the tabernacle or tent; 40:34 will narrate how "the cloud *covered* the tent of meeting, and the glory of the LORD filled the tabernacle."
3. We are told that the "appearance of the glory of the LORD" is like a devouring fire. The divine presence, earlier seen "in the heavens" as through a clear or pure sapphire pavement (vv. 9–11), now comes down and "settles" (literally, "tents") on the mountain itself. On the seventh day, God calls Moses, and he enters into this glory cloud, disappearing into its consuming fire.

Once inside that fire, he begins to receive God's instructions to build the tabernacle (25:9), as a sanctuary within which God may "dwell" or "tent" among the people (25:8). If such a tent sanctuary is a portable dwelling place for God wherever the people go, then in leaving Mount Sinai behind they do not really leave it behind. The God of Mount Sinai travels with them, tenting in the sanctuary that is an architectural replica of the sacred geography of the mountain. Whenever God "fills" the tabernacle (40:34), the way is open for the kind of communication and communion that after chapter 24 is forever connected with Mount Sinai.

The imagery of the tabernacle may be traced in many places in the New Testament. One instance is the Transfiguration (Matt. 17:1–8; Mark 9:2–8; Luke 9:28–36). The prologue to John's Gospel draws on themes from Exodus 25:8, 40:34, and (as we shall see) 34:6, in testifying that "the Word became flesh and lived [literally, "tented"] among us, and we have seen his glory, the glory as of a father's only son, full of grace and truth" (1:14). This theme of God's glory in the Word incarnate comes to a climax in Jesus' high priestly prayer in John 17. Indeed, the more deeply we immerse ourselves in the book of Exodus, the more fully we are equipped to recognize how often the Gospel of John applies the themes of Exodus to Jesus. Of course, the tabernacle itself, together with its priestly ministry and sacrificial offerings, is most elaborately interpreted in reference to Jesus in the letter to the Hebrews. I shall offer further comment along these lines in the next chapter.

2. Planning a Place for Presence
Exodus 25—31

THE TABERNACLE:
A HOME AWAY FROM HOME
Exodus 25:1–9

25:1 **The LORD said to Moses: ² Tell the Israelites to take for me an offering; from all whose hearts prompt them to give you shall receive the offering for me. ³ This is the offering that you shall receive from them: gold, silver, and bronze, ⁴ blue, purple, and crimson yarns and fine linen, goats' hair, ⁵ tanned rams' skins, fine leather, acacia wood, ⁶ oil for the lamps, spices for the anointing oil and for the fragrant incense, ⁷ onyx stones and gems to be set in the ephod and for the breastpiece. ⁸ And have them make me a sanctuary, so that I may dwell among them. ⁹ In accordance with all that I show you concerning the pattern of the tabernacle and of all its furniture, so you shall make it.**

This passage contains the keys to the detailed instructions that follow. The master key lies in verse 8, which gives God's motivation for the sanctuary: "so that I may dwell among them." A great theologian, St. Anselm, Archbishop of Canterbury, profoundly influenced the way Christians in the West have understood the incarnation. In *Cur Deus Homo?* (literally, "Why God Human?"), he proposed that God became human so that the sins of the world could adequately be atoned for.

Several years ago a colleague gave an informal talk in which, on the basis of his own experience as a married man, he questioned Anselm's proposal. Anyone who knows his wife knows her as a person of warm, gracious hospitality and exquisite taste, so that it is a pleasure to be in their home. But, said my colleague, she is a woman of variable taste: She likes to move the furniture and the pictures around from time to time, to bring out some new aspect of the home's potential beauty. When they arrive home from work, and he looks forward to a relaxing hour preparing supper or reading the newspaper when it is her turn, as often as not she says, "Could we first just move this couch over there?" or "Help me hang this painting in the other room." Only then can they settle into their suppertime routine. Now, he said, someone looking in the window only at moving time might suppose that the reason he goes home each day is to help his wife move the furniture. To be sure, that is often the first thing they do, and on those occasions supper will not take place until they have done it. But whether or not there is furniture to be moved, the reason he goes home is to be with his wife. *That*, said my colleague, is *Cur Deus Homo*. There may indeed be "stuff" to be lifted and moved, like a weight of guilt or a cloak of shame, or pangs of grief and jagged edges of pain to be bound up and healed. In such cases, the tabernacle is the place where that "stuff" is dealt with. But the reason for the tabernacle, and in time God's tenting in Jesus, is most deeply so that God may be with us. Just so, in the further course of time it will be said,

> "See, the home [or tabernacle] of God is among mortals.
> He will dwell [or tabernacle] with them as their God;
> they will be his peoples,
> and God himself will be with them;
> he will wipe every tear from their eyes.
> Death will be no more;
> mourning and crying and pain will be no more,
> for the first things have passed away."
>
> (Rev. 21:3–4)

The tabernacle is to be a sanctuary, a "holy place," like the bush and the ground in which it grows (3:5) and like Mount Sinai itself (19:10–25). As a tent, it is a movable sanctuary. Because its division into three areas parallels the threefold division of Mount Sinai, this movable tent means that Mount Sinai and the burning bush will travel with the people on their journey through the wilderness and dwell in their midst when they dwell in the land promised to their ancestors.

But the tent does not only signify God in their midst. As often as the Israelites or their priests enter the tent, they are in God's midst. The tabernacle, then, presents a picture of divine-human relations as a theology of mutual indwelling. In the New Testament, such a theology is presented in a number of different ways. In the Gospel of John, its first note is sounded in 1:14; "And the Word became flesh and lived ["tented"] among us, and we have seen his glory, the glory as of a father's only son, full of grace and truth." The mutual indwelling comes to fullest expression in Jesus' prayer in 17:20–26. A similar theology of mutual indwelling may be discerned in the way Paul speaks of a Christian as being "in Christ" (e.g., "If anyone is in Christ, there is a new creation," 2 Cor. 5:17) and in such texts as "I have been crucified with Christ; and it is no longer I who live, but it is Christ who lives in me" (Gal. 2:19–20; compare Col. 1:27).

There is also another dimension to the significance of the tabernacle. In the ancient Near East, the sanctuary could be viewed as the cosmos in microcosm. In Israel, the Solomonic temple at times is presented as such a cosmos in miniature, and the cosmos, in turn, can be presented as an all-inclusive building erected on foundations. But in Isaiah 40—55, the cosmos is several times portrayed as a tent pitched by God so that life may flourish in it, the flip side of the tabernacle as a minicosmos. Now, in the Bible, the tabernacle as a minicosmos is distinguished from the real world by the fact that it is a holy place and the real world is not; or perhaps we can say, the real world is no longer and not yet a holy place but has been profaned by what has been perpetrated in it. So the tabernacle functions as a kind of virtual reality that, when we are in it, presents us with the cosmos as God sees it and would have it become.

Let us follow this line of reflection a little further. The materials out of which the tabernacle is made are all drawn from the real world. Let us think of the tabernacle, then, as the real world at that point where the real world shapes itself in such a way as to give God appropriate place in it. (I think of the way a woman's body, already containing within it the potential for new life, receives into itself a complementary potential for new life, and then shapes itself to make room for the embryo that in time becomes a brand new person.) In and through the animal, vegetable, and mineral materials given for the tabernacle, the nonhuman creation representatively makes room for God to dwell in its midst. But what do humans offer from themselves for God to dwell in?

First, the materials are to be offered by "all whose hearts prompt them." The offerings are not assessed as a tribute or tax. The Hebrew expression is, literally, "all whose heart makes them willing." Earlier I referred to the niece who protested, "I can't want to." The tabernacle is to be built only out of materials offered by those whose hearts have been enabled to want to offer them. Every piece of material is to be clothed in an invisible garment of human freedom. God seeks to dwell in the midst of God's material creation and in the midst of the human heart that freely makes room for God through the material it offers God. (The contrast here is between the liberated heart and the heart of Pharaoh, who would not make room for God.) The depth of the mystery of the divine-human relation is that the God who is divine freedom ("I will be who I will be") seeks to dwell within our freedom, so that "deep calls to deep" (Psalm 42:7). The mystery of divine redemption lies in how God moves us to make free response, so that a heart that "can't want to" can want to enter into such a relation.

Second, the materials are to be shaped by those with "ability [Hebrew "wisdom"], intelligence, and knowledge in every kind of craft" (31:3). These gifts are the endowment of God's Spirit, suggesting that the same Spirit of wisdom that initiated the creation of the cosmos (Gen. 1:2; compare Isa. 40:12–14, 27–31) is at work in the building of the tabernacle as a microcosmos. So God dwells in the freedom with which everyone offers the materials and in the shape that gifted workers give to these materials. It seems most fitting that the chief artisan is named Bezalel (31:2, "In the shadow/protection of El [God]"; compare Psalm 91:1–2) and that his chief assistant is named Oholiab (31:6, "Father's tent").

A final note on the reference in 31:1–11 to artistic ability is that the mere listing of the materials for the tabernacle (vv. 3–7)—rich and varied in colors, textures, and aromas—already stimulates the imagination to anticipate the sanctuary as a feast for the senses. The psalmist cries out, "How lovely is your dwelling place, O LORD of hosts!" (Psalm 84:1). Built out of such materials, given in God-enabled human freedom and shaped through God-inspired human ingenuity, the tabernacle becomes a place where worship arises to God not just from the human heart and the human spirit but also from the human body as engaged through its various senses and the emotions connected to them. This is one way, I suggest, in which God works toward "the redemption of our bodies" (Rom. 8:23). Such is the ambiguity of the real world in which we live, and such is the ambiguity of the virtual realities offered to us by our various advertising and entertainment industries and our electioneering politicians, that unless God's sanctuary and the ceremonies in it engage us bodily as well as spiritually, the real world will remain unredeemed. But, as Paul says, "if anyone is in Christ, there is a new creation: everything old has passed away; see, everything has become new!" (2 Cor. 5:17).

THE ARK
Exodus 25:10–22

> 25:10 **They shall make an ark of acacia wood; it shall be two and a half cubits long, a cubit and a half wide, and a cubit and a half high. 11 You shall overlay it with pure gold, inside and outside you shall overlay it, and you**

shall make a molding of gold upon it all around. [12] You shall cast four rings of gold for it and put them on its four feet, two rings on the one side of it, and two rings on the other side. [13] You shall make poles of acacia wood, and overlay them with gold. [14] And you shall put the poles into the rings on the sides of the ark, by which to carry the ark. [15] The poles shall remain in the rings of the ark; they shall not be taken from it. [16] You shall put into the ark the covenant that I shall give you.

[17] Then you shall make a mercy seat of pure gold; two cubits and a half shall be its length, and a cubit and a half its width. [18] You shall make two cherubim of gold; you shall make them of hammered work, at the two ends of the mercy seat. [19] Make one cherub at the one end, and one cherub at the other; of one piece with the mercy seat you shall make the cherubim at its two ends. [20] The cherubim shall spread out their wings above, overshadowing the mercy seat with their wings. They shall face one to another; the faces of the cherubim shall be turned toward the mercy seat. [21] You shall put the mercy seat on the top of the ark; and in the ark you shall put the covenant that I shall give you. [22] There I will meet with you, and from above the mercy seat, from between the two cherubim that are on the ark of the covenant, I will deliver to you all my commands for the Israelites.

The ark is described from the bottom up. At the bottom is a rectangular chest for the covenant tablets, with poles to carry it. The lid of this chest is a solid gold plate, a "mercy seat," after the Greek translation of Hebrew *kapporet*. (The Hebrew term is from the verb *kipper*, which has to do with making atonement. See the phrase *yom kippur*, "Day of Atonement." A good picture of what is at issue here occurs in Genesis 32:20: Jacob, about to meet Esau whom he had long ago doubly wronged, thinks to himself, "I may appease [*kipper*] him with the present that goes ahead of me, and afterwards I shall see his face; perhaps he will accept me.") On the mercy seat rest two cherubim, creatures with animal bodies, human faces, and outstretched wings.

The cherubim resemble figures in Assyrian and Canaanite art that can flank a throne. In the tabernacle, they serve as the throne or throne-flank above which the LORD is invisibly seated. Their symbolism receives added dimension from the reference to cherubim in Genesis 3:24. There, the cherubim guard a sacred garden with its tree of life, intended for human habitation but now guarded from further profanation by those who have violated the life-serving law of that garden.

As a portable chest with the cherubim on top, the ark serves in time of danger as the emblem of God who fights for the people (Num. 10:35–36; compare Psalm 80:1–2; 91:1–2; and the eagle figure in Exod. 19:4). But it does not automatically guarantee success in battle. As 1 Samuel 4 shows, its presence on the field of battle can give added energy to Israel's enemies, so that Israel's defeat is only greater. Such a reverse effect may be attributed to the fact that the LORD is enthroned upon an ark that contains within it a covenant that calls for Israel to renounce all other gods and their idols and to practice justice within the community. If (as in 1 Samuel 1—3) Israel does not live up to the covenant, it cannot expect God to fight for it. Indeed, in the name of the truth and justice for which the covenant stands, God will act in judgment (at times amounting to "holy war") against Israel. This works to prevent the ark from becoming an idol that the people can manipulate to their own ends.

But if God's royal reign and parental presence in Israel's midst are founded on truth and justice, they rest also on God's provision of the "mercy seat," where the high priest makes atonement for the people's covenant violations. (Compare Psalm 89:14, where "righteousness and justice" as the foundation of God's throne are balanced by "steadfast love and faithfulness," agencies then appealed to in 89:49.) The concluding verse identifies the ark as the place where God will "meet" with Moses, to deliver to him all such commands as shall from time to time be called for in God's reign among the people. On this account, the tabernacle can also be referred to as the "tent of meeting" (27:21).

Thus the ark is a sacral symbol rich in meaning. It and the meanings it bears will radiate out through the rest of the Bible. If we confine ourselves to the themes of revelation and atonement, the following examples may be noted in the New Testament:

1. In Romans 3:25, Paul identifies Jesus as a "sacrifice [or place] of atonement" (*hilasterion*, the Greek word that translates *kapporet* in Exod. 25:18) in whom God deals with the problem of human sin.
2. The prologue to John's Gospel has already spoken of the Word becoming flesh and tenting among us, manifesting God's glory, and full of grace and truth. It concludes by affirming (1:18), "No one has ever seen God. It is God the only Son, who is close to the Father's heart, who has made him known." The "made him known" may be interpreted in relation to Exodus 25:22, as affirming that the continuing revelation by which God guides the people in the ways of the covenant is now to be found in "God the only Son."

Finally, we may ponder the ark as an emblem of God's providence. While the covenant community still basks in the afterglow of the amazing experience in 24:9–11, and before they have done anything to sully the intimacy that experience discloses, God makes provision for what may go wrong. (Compare Job's parental concern for his children, in Job 1:4–5.) Such a picture may help us appreciate what led New Testament writers to speak of Christ as the lamb of God, "destined before the foundation of the world, but . . . revealed at the end of the ages for your sake" (1 Peter 1:20; compare Rev. 13:8 in NRSV margin; also Eph. 1:4). The God who calls the covenant community to exacting forms of religious and ethical response as heralds of a "new creation," makes provision in advance to deal with responses that "fall short of the glory of God" (Rom. 3:23).

THE TABLE FOR THE
BREAD OF THE PRESENCE
Exodus 25:23–30

25:23 **You shall make a table of acacia wood, two cubits long, one cubit wide, and a cubit and a half high.** [24] **You shall overlay it with pure gold, and make a molding of gold around it.** [25] **You shall make around it a rim a hand-breadth wide, and a molding of gold around the rim.** [26] **You shall make for it four rings of gold, and fasten the rings to the four corners at its four legs.** [27] **The rings that hold the poles used for carrying the table shall be close to the rim.** [28] **You shall make the poles of acacia wood, and overlay them with gold, and the table shall be carried with these.** [29] **You shall make its plates and dishes for incense, and its flagons and bowls with which to pour drink offerings; you shall make them of pure gold.** [30] **And you shall set the bread of the Presence on the table before me always.**

The purpose of the table and its articles is hospitality. But who is hosting whom? In Psalm 23:5 God hosts the psalmist: "You prepare a table before me in the presence of my enemies." But Genesis 18:1–9 shows Abraham hosting three men, and in so doing hosting the LORD (18:9–33). Psalm 50:7–13 challenges the notion that God depends on human offerings of food. But there, the offerers have ignored the claims of the Decalogue and failed to offer thanksgiving for what God has done for Israel (50:16–23). In that situation, animal sacrifices serve to cover up the worshipers' covenant shortcomings, so the rejection of their sacrifices there is rejection of a bribe, not a universal rejection of the possibility of offering anything to God. If we take the table in Exodus 25:23–30 as our hospitality to God, a marvelous possibility is suggested: That it would please God, who provides for us in every way, to come as guest and dine at a table laid out with what we prepare from our own resources. (Anyone who has sat down to a meal prepared by a son or daughter may have some idea of what this could mean to God.) Jesus is notorious for eating in the homes of people whose hospitality others would spurn (e.g., Luke 5:27–32; 19:1–10). In a context filled with sanctuary imagery (Rev. 1:9–4:11; e.g., the candlesticks), compare also Revelation 3:20: "I am standing at the door, knocking; if you hear my voice and open the door, I will come in to you and eat with you, and you with me."

THE LAMPSTAND
Exodus 25:31–40

25:31 **You shall make a lampstand of pure gold. The base and the shaft of the lampstand shall be made of hammered work; its cups, its calyxes, and its petals shall be of one piece with it;** [32] **and there shall be six branches going out of its sides, three branches of the lampstand out of one side of it and three branches of the lampstand out of the other side of it;** [33] **three cups shaped like almond blossoms, each with calyx and petals, on one branch, and three cups shaped like almond blossoms, each with calyx and petals, on the other branch—so for the six branches going out of the lampstand.** [34] **On the lampstand itself there shall be four cups shaped like almond blossoms, each with its calyxes and petals.** [35] **There shall be a calyx of one piece with it under the first pair of branches, a calyx of one piece with it under the next pair of branches, and a calyx of one piece with it under the last pair of branches—so for the six branches that go out of the lampstand.** [36] **Their calyxes and their branches shall be of one piece with it, the whole of it one hammered piece of pure gold.** [37] **You shall make the seven lamps for it; and the lamps shall be set up so as to give light on the space in front of it.** [38] **Its snuffers and trays shall be of pure gold.** [39] **It, and all these utensils, shall be made from a talent of pure gold.** [40] **And see that you make them according to the pattern for them, which is being shown you on the mountain.**

Like food and drink, light is a basic necessity. Without a lamp, a dwelling would be dark just when its inhabitants are most in need of its shelter or would offer their guests the most intimate hospitality. A lighted dwelling is a welcome sign that someone is home (the most extreme contrast is Job 18:5–21). In the ancient world, light came from the sun or at night from moon, stars, and campfire. Indoors, people had to furnish their own light. Thus, light from the heavens became a symbol of divine illumination, and light indoors a symbol of both divine presence and illumination, and human consciousness and intelligence.

The lampstand in the tabernacle was spectacularly valuable (about ninety-six pounds of solid gold) and beautiful (a seven-branched flowering almond tree). An almond tree is the first to blossom in an Israelite spring, its white petals signaling new life following the dormant winter. As such, it becomes a symbol of God's "wakefulness" to perform what God has announced through the prophet (Jer. 1:11). The lampstand may be a representation of the tree of life. In Genesis 2—3 the tree of life is counterfeited by the tree of the knowledge of good and evil. The contrast may be between the life-giving light of God's instruction to us (Gen. 2:16–17) and that wisdom we would seize, the power to decide for ourselves what is right and what is wrong (Gen. 3:6–7). Isaiah 50:10–11 contrasts those who walk by a light they kindle for themselves, with the servant of God who walks in a darkness illumined only by the servant's trust in the name of the LORD. A proverb states that "The human spirit is the lamp of the LORD, searching every innermost part" (Prov. 20:27). The prophet Zechariah, contrasting human might and power with the spirit of God (Zech. 4:1–6), interprets the seven branches of the lampstand as "the eyes of the LORD, which range through the whole earth" (4:10). In the New Testament, seven lampstands stand for the seven churches in Asia, among whom the risen and glorious One walks to recall them to the light of the gospel (Rev. 1:9–3:22). He is the One whom the Gospel of John calls the Word made flesh to tabernacle among us (John 1:14) and who claims, "I am the light of the world" (John 8:12; 9:5). This light has come into the world, "not . . . to condemn the world, but in order that the world might be saved through him" (John 3:17).

We may, then, take the lamp as standing for light, life, and presence, and especially for the consciousness and conscience of the one in whom it burns or flickers. Its importance for Israel is underscored by the fact that only in connection with the lampstand is the general instruction of Exodus 25:9 explicitly repeated and underlined: "And see that you make them according to the pattern for them, which is being shown you on the mountain" (25:40). The light is to be fashioned according to God's design, not ours. Yet we are to fashion it. We are responsible for training our consciences (what the Bible calls our hearts, as, for example, in Job 27:6 and Proverbs 4:23) in the ways of God (Psalm 119:105). Those ways, the Fourth Gospel testifies, are now fully made known in Jesus, the light of the world (John 1:18; 3:16–21; 12:27–36, 44–50).

THE TABERNACLE
Exodus 26:1–27:21

26:1 Moreover you shall make the tabernacle with ten curtains of fine twisted linen, and blue, purple, and crimson yarns; you shall make them with cherubim skillfully worked into them. 2 The length of each curtain shall be twenty-eight cubits, and the width of each curtain four cubits; all the curtains shall be of the same size. 3 Five curtains shall be joined to one another; and the other five curtains shall be joined to one another. 4 You shall make loops of blue on the edge of the outermost curtain in the first set; and likewise you shall make loops on the edge of the outermost curtain in the second set. 5 You shall make fifty loops on the one curtain, and you shall make fifty loops on the edge of the curtain that is in the second set; the loops shall be opposite one another. 6 You shall make fifty clasps of gold, and join the curtains to one another with the clasps, so that the tabernacle may be one whole.

7 You shall also make curtains of goats' hair for a tent over the tabernacle; you shall make eleven curtains. 8 The length of each curtain shall be thirty cubits, and the width of each curtain four cubits; the eleven curtains shall be of the same size. 9 You shall join five curtains by themselves, and six curtains by themselves, and the sixth curtain you shall double over at the front of the tent. 10 You shall make fifty loops on the edge of the curtain that is outermost in one set, and fifty loops on the edge of the curtain that is outermost in the second set.

11 You shall make fifty clasps of bronze, and put the clasps into the loops, and join the tent together, so that it may be one whole. 12 The part that remains of the curtains of the tent, the half curtain that remains, shall hang over the back of the tabernacle. 13 The cubit on the one side, and the cubit on the other side, of what remains in the length of the curtains of the tent, shall hang over the sides of the tabernacle, on this side and that side, to cover it. 14 You shall make for the tent a covering of tanned rams' skins and an outer covering of fine leather.

15 You shall make upright frames of acacia wood for the tabernacle. 16 Ten cubits shall be the length of a frame, and a cubit and a half the width of each frame. 17 There shall be two pegs in each frame to fit the frames together; you shall make these for all the frames of the tabernacle. 18 You shall make the frames for the tabernacle: twenty frames for the south side; 19 and you shall make forty bases of silver under the twenty frames, two bases under the first frame for its two pegs, and two bases under the next frame for its two pegs; 20 and for the second side of the tabernacle, on the north side twenty frames, 21 and their forty bases of silver, two bases under the first frame, and two bases under the next frame; 22 and for the rear of the tabernacle westward you shall make six frames. 23 You shall make two frames for corners of

the tabernacle in the rear; ²⁴ they shall be separate beneath, but joined at the top, at the first ring; it shall be the same with both of them; they shall form the two corners. ²⁵ And so there shall be eight frames, with their bases of silver, sixteen bases; two bases under the first frame, and two bases under the next frame.

²⁶ You shall make bars of acacia wood, five for the frames of the one side of the tabernacle, ²⁷ and five bars for the frames of the other side of the tabernacle, and five bars for the frames of the side of the tabernacle at the rear westward. ²⁸ The middle bar, halfway up the frames, shall pass through from end to end. ²⁹ You shall overlay the frames with gold, and shall make their rings of gold to hold the bars; and you shall overlay the bars with gold. ³⁰ Then you shall erect the tabernacle according to the plan for it that you were shown on the mountain.

³¹ You shall make a curtain of blue, purple, and crimson yarns, and of fine twisted linen; it shall be made with cherubim skillfully worked into it. ³² You shall hang it on four pillars of acacia overlaid with gold, which have hooks of gold and rest on four bases of silver. ³³ You shall hang the curtain under the clasps, and bring the ark of the covenant in there, within the curtain; and the curtain shall separate for you the holy place from the most holy. ³⁴ You shall put the mercy seat on the ark of the covenant in the most holy place. ³⁵ You shall set the table outside the curtain, and the lampstand on the south side of the tabernacle opposite the table; and you shall put the table on the north side.

³⁶ You shall make a screen for the entrance of the tent, of blue, purple, and crimson yarns, and of fine twisted linen, embroidered with needlework. ³⁷ You shall make for the screen five pillars of acacia, and overlay them with gold; their hooks shall be of gold, and you shall cast five bases of bronze for them.

27:1 You shall make the altar of acacia wood, five cubits long and five cubits wide; the altar shall be square, and it shall be three cubits high. ² You shall make horns for it on its four corners; its horns shall be of one piece with it, and you shall overlay it with bronze. ³ You shall make pots for it to receive its ashes, and shovels and basins and forks and firepans; you shall make all its utensils of bronze. ⁴ You shall also make for it a grating, a network of bronze; and on the net you shall make four bronze rings at its four corners. ⁵ You shall set it under the ledge of the altar so that the net shall extend halfway down the altar. ⁶ You shall make poles for the altar, poles of acacia wood, and overlay them with bronze; ⁷ the poles shall be put through the rings, so that the poles shall be on the two sides of the altar when it is carried. ⁸ You shall make it hollow, with boards. They shall be made just as you were shown on the mountain.

⁹ You shall make the court of the tabernacle. On the south side the court shall have hangings of fine twisted linen one hundred cubits long for that

side; [10] its twenty pillars and their twenty bases shall be of bronze, but the hooks of the pillars and their bands shall be of silver. [11] Likewise for its length on the north side there shall be hangings one hundred cubits long, their pillars twenty and their bases twenty, of bronze, but the hooks of the pillars and their bands shall be of silver. [12] For the width of the court on the west side there shall be fifty cubits of hangings, with ten pillars and ten bases. [13] The width of the court on the front to the east shall be fifty cubits. [14] There shall be fifteen cubits of hangings on the one side, with three pillars and three bases. [15] There shall be fifteen cubits of hangings on the other side, with three pillars and three bases. [16] For the gate of the court there shall be a screen twenty cubits long, of blue, purple, and crimson yarns, and of fine twisted linen, embroidered with needlework; it shall have four pillars and with them four bases. [17] All the pillars around the court shall be banded with silver; their hooks shall be of silver, and their bases of bronze. [18] The length of the court shall be one hundred cubits, the width fifty, and the height five cubits, with hangings of fine twisted linen and bases of bronze. [19] All the utensils of the tabernacle for every use, and all its pegs and all the pegs of the court, shall be of bronze.

[20] You shall further command the Israelites to bring you pure oil of beaten olives for the light, so that a lamp may be set up to burn regularly. [21] In the tent of meeting, outside the curtain that is before the covenant, Aaron and his sons shall tend it from evening to morning before the LORD. It shall be a perpetual ordinance to be observed throughout their generations by the Israelites.

The sanctuary is made up of the tabernacle proper (26:1), sheltered within a larger tent (26:7). The tabernacle is divided by a curtain into a "holy place" and a "most holy" place (or "holy of holies") (26:31–37). Thus, the sanctuary comprises three spaces:

1. Within the outer tent, space surrounds the tabernacle proper on four sides. In the forecourt, before the entrance to the tabernacle, stands an altar of burnt offering (27:1–8) and a laver, or bronze basin (30:17–21).
2. Within the tabernacle, the "holy place" holds the lampstand and the bread of the presence, as well as the incense altar (30:1–10).
3. The "most holy" place holds the ark with the mercy seat and the cherubim and marks the invisible indwelling of God—invisible because it is unilluminated by any light.

Earlier, I noted interpretations that draw a parallel between this threefold division of the tabernacle and the boundaries that mark off Mount

Sinai in Exodus 19. Now I propose another aspect of the symbolism of the tabernacle. This aspect turns on the ease with which any dwelling and its interior spaces can become a figure for the human self. A dwelling, like the clothes we wear, shelters our bodies like another skin. As such, it already has an implicit symbolic significance and lends itself to explicit use as an image of the embodied self. I have already referred to the "darkened tent" image in Job 18 for the wicked person driven out of life and out of the world. In 2 Corinthians 5:1–5 Paul describes our present existence as dwelling in an "earthly tent," and in 1 Corinthians 6:19 he refers to the Christian's body as a sanctuary of the Holy Spirit. Earlier I proposed that the tabernacle embodies a theology of divine-human relations understood as mutual indwelling. The structure, beauty, and divisions of the sanctuary give further elaboration of those relations.

The stuff out of which the sanctuary is made (vegetable and animal materials for coverings; wood frames overlaid with precious metals and based in sockets) is reminiscent of the human body held erect by its skeletal structure. The colors, the textures, and the designs woven into the coverings give it a variegated beauty. The structure is not just functional, it is "lovely" (Psalm 84:1). As such, it is suggestive of "the beauty of the LORD" (Psalm 27:4; compare 26:8). But the theology of the sanctuary is of a piece with the theology of creation in Genesis 1. If to be a human being is to be created in God's image (Gen. 1:27), then the sanctuary is a picture also of human beings as intended and created by God. In a culture where so much turns on image and the possible grounds for one's own realistic self-image, it may be salutary to take the Israelite sanctuary in all its glorious detail and its successive interior spaces as a clue to how God sees us.

What, then, of these successive interior spaces? We may think of the space outside the tabernacle as the public world where one works and interacts with others. Relations here largely take the form of civility and general courtesy, as between members of the same community. Altar and bronze basin make provision for one's negotiation of public relations in this area, as well as for one's readiness to enter into the greater intimacy of the tabernacle itself. We may think, then, of the "holy place" inside the tabernacle as one's "inner space," into which one invites those with whom one would have a relation of special intimacy. With these persons we share our hopes and dreams, joys and sorrows, and feel safe in disclosing our foibles. This space is like our own home, where we live and know ourselves.

But, whether we know it or not, there is a "space" so interior that we rarely if ever enter it, and then only under certain conditions. This is the space where God alone dwells or, rather, where God dwells alone with the individual. It is that inner freedom out of which the materials have been offered to make the sanctuary (25:2). It is that depth of spirit in which our true identity is veiled and out of which our actions arise, a depth to which our conscious intelligence cannot penetrate but only the Spirit of God (1 Cor. 2:11–12), so that we remain a mystery to ourselves and finally rest our well-being in the fact that we are known by God (Gal. 4:8–9). It is at this depth, I suggest, that the blessing of the LORD pronounced by the priests (Num. 6:24–26) does its deepest work. Here the only light is the light of God's face, shining in grace on the face of the soul turned up to receive this blessing. Where this mystery is entrusted to God, and we resist the temptation to dispel it with idols and images of our own making, we have an anchor against all the forces that would distort God's image in us. This may be the secret of the Servant of the LORD in the face of his adversaries in Isaiah 50:4–11: The darkness in which he walks is the darkness of his inner holy of holies, where his trust in God images God's face shining graciously on him.

VESTMENTS FOR THE PRIESTHOOD
Exodus 28:1–43

Priestly Garments (28:1–5)

> 28:1 **Then bring near to you your brother Aaron, and his sons with him, from among the Israelites, to serve me as priests—Aaron and Aaron's sons, Nadab and Abihu, Eleazar and Ithamar. ² You shall make sacred vestments for the glorious adornment of your brother Aaron. ³ And you shall speak to all who have ability, whom I have endowed with skill, that they make Aaron's vestments to consecrate him for my priesthood. ⁴ These are the vestments that they shall make: a breastpiece, an ephod, a robe, a checkered tunic, a turban, and a sash. When they make these sacred vestments for your brother Aaron and his sons to serve me as priests, ⁵ they shall use gold, blue, purple, and crimson yarns, and fine linen.**

Except for the altar of incense and the bronze basin (30:1–10, 17–21), instructions for the tabernacle and its furnishings are now complete. Now God provides for its priestly ministry. Whereas the fashioners of the tabernacle are selected on the basis of their direct spiritual endowments from God, the priestly ministry is selected on the basis of its lineage: Aaron, brother of Moses, and thereafter his descendants. Is this connected with the fact that the sanctuary priesthood is largely a representative ministry of carefully orchestrated symbolic actions? (By representative, I mean that these priests do not function on the basis of their own personal charisma or spiritual endowments but fill an office that represents the whole people of Israel before God. Therefore, perhaps, their own personal qualities are less prominently singled out.)

As if to emphasize this, two things are immediately said about those selected for priestly service: First, they are to wear vestments that symbolize their ministry; second, these vestments are to be fashioned (like the tabernacle) by those "wise in heart" (Hebrew; NRSV "have ability"), whom God has "filled with a spirit of wisdom" (NRSV, "endowed with skill"). Let us reflect further on these two things.

Aaron and his sons are to wear "sacred vestments" for "glorious adornment" (literally, "garments of holiness . . . for glory and for beauty"). Our word "vestments" has a formality associated with robes of office. The Hebrew word, *beged*, is a garment (as the Hebrew lexicon says) "of any kind, from the filthy clothing of the leper to the holy robes of the high priest, the simplest covering of the poor as well as the costly raiment of the rich and noble." So the priests are to appear before God clothed like any human being "to cover their naked flesh" (28:42; see 20:26 and my comments there). In the Garden of Eden, the human community originally was naked and not ashamed. The first sign that something had gone wrong was the couple's attempt to cover their nakedness by making loincloths (Gen. 3:7). The second sign was that, when they heard God walking in the garden, they hid among the trees (3:8). Thus the wronging of relationships issues in a sense of guilt and shame that manifests itself in the desire to cover oneself from another's gaze. Today, much is written and said concerning false guilt and shame imposed on the innocent and the oppressed to control their inner spirit and their public behavior. In the Bible, such false guilt and shame is identified as the work of the "false accuser," Satan or the devil. But there is a true guilt and shame, signaling that we have wronged the relations in which we stand. This guilt and shame are good servants—servants of God and of ourselves. As a philosopher has said, "Guilt is the call of being for itself in silence." It is God calling out and saying, "Where are you?" (3:9).

The couple's attempts in the garden to cover themselves and hide from God are unavailing, as God "finds them out" (Gen. 3:10–19). But God does not leave them in the unbearable self-consciousness of being naked before accusing eyes. Instead, "the LORD God made garments of skins for the man and for his wife, and clothed them" (3:21). If their lost innocence is manifest in the difference between their original (2:25) and their subsequent (3:7–8) sense of their nakedness, God's provision of clothing is a gracious means by which they can be present to one another and to God without being overwhelmed by their sense of their own wrongdoing.

Now, in Hebrew, *beged* ("vestments" in Exod. 28:2) comes from the verb *bagad*, which invariably has a negative meaning! It means (as the lexicon says) "to act or deal treacherously, faithlessly, deceitfully, in the marriage relation, in matters of property or right, in covenants, in word and in general conduct." This does not mean that clothing is always deceitful or a prelude to treachery. But it does get at something that is profoundly important, both about our ordinary relations and about our appearance before God. This is the two-sided need, in any complex and problematic relation, to save face and to allow the other to save face. Confession and repentance are a coming clean with the wronged party, and the mending of any ruptured relation will sooner or later involve such a coming to terms with the truth of what went wrong. But the path to that point is not easily trod. Often those who most need to walk it "can't want to," for among other things we fear a condemnation (including a self-condemnation) that will consume and annihilate us. The gift of clothing is God's face-saving provision whereby the human community can come before God in all the ambiguity (and at times terrible failures) of its humanity and find acceptance in God's grace.

For if the priests' garments stand in continuity with the garments any and every person wears, yet they have a special, threefold character: "garments of holiness . . . for glory and for beauty." The first term, "holiness," identifies the attracting and terrifying mystery of God in distinction to all that is not God. When the term is applied to anything or anyone other than God, it identifies that thing or person as set apart for God's service. The second term, "glory," carries connotations of brightness and heaviness (as in our admiring description of something as "heavy!"). While it can be used to describe anything, its "heaviest" use comes in reference to God. The third term, "beauty," can be applied to jewels, a flock of sheep, a city, a nation, a monarch, or garments. Often it is an attribute of God, the sanctuary, or the ark. When the priests are to be clothed in garments of holiness, for glory and for beauty, provision is made for them, as representing the whole people, to appear before God as God originally intended and redemptively seeks for them to appear—that is, as made in God's image. This is underscored by the fact that the garments are to be fashioned by those whom God directly inspires with the spirit of divine wisdom and skill.

The discrepancy between the priests' actual condition and what their priestly garments represent may be called hypocrisy. But it should not be surprising (though it is lamentable) that hypocrisy is the besetting sin of religious people, and perhaps especially of religious leaders. Hypocrisy is the negative side of the positive potential in the "deceit" involved in the cloak God provides for us. The positive potential lies in the way the garments become a call to grow into what they represent. The habit we wear over our bodies is to become the habit of our thoughts, words, and actions. In the New Testament, this is spoken of as putting on Christ and being clothed in his righteousness (Rom. 13:11–14; Gal. 3:27), so that we may grow into increasing conformity to the image of God (Eph. 4:24; Col. 3:10; Rom. 8:29). It is in this sense that the New Testament speaks of those who are in Christ as "saints" (e.g., Rom. 8:27).

The Ephod (28:6–14)

28:6 **They shall make the ephod of gold, of blue, purple, and crimson yarns, and of fine twisted linen, skillfully worked. 7 It shall have two shoulder-pieces attached to its two edges, so that it may be joined together. 8 The decorated band on it shall be of the same workmanship and materials, of gold, of blue, purple, and crimson yarns, and of fine twisted linen. 9 You shall take two onyx stones, and engrave on them the names of the sons of Israel, 10 six of their names on the one stone, and the names of the remaining six on the other stone, in the order of their birth. 11 As a gem-cutter engraves signets, so you shall engrave the two stones with the names of the sons of Israel; you shall mount them in settings of gold filigree. 12 You shall set the two stones on the shoulder-pieces of the ephod, as stones of remembrance for the sons of Israel; and Aaron shall bear their names before the LORD on his two shoulders for remembrance. 13 You shall make settings of gold filigree, 14 and two chains of pure gold, twisted like cords; and you shall attach the corded chains to the settings.**

The description of the tabernacle begins with the most important items in the most holy place, and from there moves outward (25:10–26:37). Likewise, the description of the priestly garments begins with the most important item, the ephod. Made of richly beautiful materials, it features two onyx stones set on the shoulder-pieces, each stone bearing the names of six of the Israelite tribes who claim descent from Jacob (also known as Israel). In this way, "Aaron shall bear their names before the LORD on his two shoulders for remembrance." An intercessory prayer in the Anglican tradition ends with the words, "those whom we have forgotten, do thou, O LORD, remember." The fact that God instructs that these tribal names be placed on the ephod shows that God intends to remember. But the fact that God instructs the priests to bear these names on their shoulders shows that God calls the priests (and through them the whole people of God) to participate with God in the act of intercessory remembrance. Thus already, in the symbolism of the ephod, we see the two-sided character of intercession as something we do and something God does in and through us (Rom. 8:26–27).

Breastpiece (28:15–30)

28:15 You shall make a breastpiece of judgment, in skilled work; you shall make it in the style of the ephod; of gold, of blue and purple and crimson yarns, and of fine twisted linen you shall make it. [16] It shall be square and doubled, a span in length and a span in width. [17] You shall set in it four rows of stones. A row of carnelian, chrysolite, and emerald shall be the first row; [18] and the second row a turquoise, a sapphire and a moonstone; [19] and the third row a jacinth, an agate, and an amethyst; [20] and the fourth row a beryl, an onyx, and a jasper; they shall be set in gold filigree. [21] There shall be twelve stones with names corresponding to the names of the sons of Israel; they shall be like signets, each engraved with its name, for the twelve tribes. [22] You shall make for the breastpiece chains of pure gold, twisted like cords; [23] and you shall make for the breastpiece two rings of gold, and put the two rings on the two edges of the breastpiece. [24] You shall put the two cords of gold in the two rings at the edges of the breastpiece; [25] the two ends of the two cords you shall attach to the two settings, and so attach it in front to the shoulder-pieces of the ephod. [26] You shall make two rings of gold, and put them at the two ends of the breastpiece, on its inside edge next to the ephod. [27] You shall make two rings of gold, and attach them in front to the lower part of the two shoulder-pieces of the ephod, at its joining above the decorated band of the ephod. [28] The breastpiece shall be bound by its rings to the rings of the ephod with a blue cord, so that it may lie on the decorated band of the ephod, and so that the breastpiece shall not come loose from the ephod. [29] So Aaron shall bear the names of the sons of Israel in the breastpiece of judgment on his heart when he goes into the holy place, for a continual remembrance before the LORD. [30] In the breastpiece of judgment you shall put the Urim and the Thummim, and they shall be on Aaron's heart when he goes in before the LORD; thus Aaron shall bear the judgment of the Israelites on his heart before the LORD continually.

The breastpiece also bears the names of the twelve tribes, this time each name on a separate and unique stone. It is called the "breastpiece of judgment" and, fashioned like a pouch, contains within it the Urim and the Thummim. These are sacred dice, by which the priest is to seek the decision of God in a difficult situation. (A question whose answer could be a simple yes or no would be laid before God, and the dice would be marked to provide such a clear answer. See, for example, 1 Samuel 23:9–12; 30:7–8.) But the priest who places the question before God at the same time bears the names of the twelve tribes before God, as though the search for divine guidance is placed in the context of intercession. Thus the names are borne not only on the shoulders (28:12) but also on the heart (28:29). (One is reminded of Robert Frost's poem, "The Armful." The speaker, carrying a load that contains "Extremes too hard to comprehend at once, / Yet nothing I should care to leave behind" resolves that "With all I have to hold with, hand and mind / And heart, if need be, I will do my best / To keep their building balanced at my breast.") Insofar as the search for divine guidance through the Urim and Thummim is placed in the context of intercessory remembrance through the inscribed names, and insofar as all this is to be done by God's instruction, we are again reminded of Romans 8:26–27, this time especially the phrases, "we do not know how to pray as we ought" and "God, who searches the heart."

Other Vestments (28:31–43)

28:31 **You shall make the robe of the ephod all of blue. 32 It shall have an opening for the head in the middle of it, with a woven binding around the opening, like the opening in a coat of mail, so that it may not be torn. 33 On its lower hem you shall make pomegranates of blue, purple, and crimson yarns, all around the lower hem, with bells of gold between them all around—34 a golden bell and a pomegranate alternating all around the lower hem of the robe. 35 Aaron shall wear it when he ministers, and its sound shall be heard when he goes into the holy place before the LORD, and when he comes out, so that he may not die.**

36 You shall make a rosette of pure gold, and engrave on it, like the engraving of a signet, "Holy to the LORD." 37 You shall fasten it on the turban with a blue cord; it shall be on the front of the turban. 38 It shall be on Aaron's forehead, and Aaron shall take on himself any guilt incurred in the holy offering that the Israelites consecrate as their sacred donations; it shall always be on his forehead, in order that they may find favor before the LORD.

39 You shall make the checkered tunic of fine linen, and you shall make a turban of fine linen, and you shall make a sash embroidered with needlework.

40 For Aaron's sons you shall make tunics and sashes and headdresses; you shall make them for their glorious adornment. 41 You shall put them on your brother Aaron, and on his sons with him, and shall anoint them and ordain them and consecrate them, so that they may serve me as priests. 42 You shall make for them linen undergarments to cover their naked flesh; they shall

reach from the hips to the thighs; [43] **Aaron and his sons shall wear them when they go into the tent of meeting, or when they come near the altar to minister in the holy place; or they will bring guilt on themselves and die. This shall be a perpetual ordinance for him and for his descendants after him.**

The other priestly garments in 28:31–43 have one theme in common. The robe (vv. 31–35) is hemmed with alternating bells and pomegranates; the bells sound when the priest "goes into the holy place before the LORD, and when he comes out, so that he may not die." The turban (vv. 36–38) carries a rosette of pure gold bearing the inscription "Holy to the LORD"; by this means, Aaron takes on himself any guilt incurred in the people's offerings, so that they might find favor before the LORD. Finally (vv. 42–43), under all their other garments the priests wear linen undergarments "to cover their naked flesh," whenever they enter the tent or draw near the altar, "or they will bring guilt on themselves and die." The repeated theme is, to say the least, sobering. Its realism is perhaps recaptured in these words of Annie Dillard:

> I often think of the set pieces of liturgy as certain words which people have successfully addressed to God without their getting killed. In the high churches they saunter through the liturgy like Mohawks along a strand of scaffolding who have long since forgotten their danger. If God were to blast such a service to bits, the congregation would, I believe, be genuinely shocked. But in the low churches you expect it any minute. This is the beginning of wisdom. (*Holy the Firm*)

The general heading under which all this operates is the repeated injunction, "you shall be holy, for I am holy" (Lev. 11:44, 45; 19:2; 20:7; 20:26; 21:6; Num. 15:40). This injunction is rooted in the vocational call in Exodus 19:6, "You shall be for me a priestly kingdom and a holy nation." If the call to be holy has its ground in God's own holiness, it is grounded also in the gravity of Israel's vocation to represent "the whole earth" (19:5) before God. In the Gospels, Jesus is presented as re-interpreting the call to holiness. In Matthew 5:48 he says, "Be perfect [in loving], therefore, as your heavenly Father is perfect"; and in Luke 6:36 he says, "Be merciful, just as your Father is merciful." Does he shift the call from holiness to perfect love and mercy, or does he spell out holiness in these terms? To ponder seriously the sort of claims Jesus makes on us in Matthew 5:43–47 and Luke 6:27–35 is to realize all over again the discrepancy between our own actual condition and the image we are called to conform to. No less than holiness, the issues of love and mercy are issues of life and death. If we are to survive as individuals and as communities until we are perfected in them, we will do well to clothe ourselves in the garments God provides.

THE ORDINATION OF THE PRIESTS
Exodus 29:1–37

29:1 Now this is what you shall do to them to consecrate them, so that they may serve me as priests. Take one young bull and two rams without blemish, [2] and unleavened bread, unleavened cakes mixed with oil, and unleavened wafers spread with oil. You shall make them of choice wheat flour. [3] You shall put them in one basket and bring them in the basket, and bring the bull and the two rams. [4] You shall bring Aaron and his sons to the entrance of the tent of meeting, and wash them with water. [5] Then you shall take the vestments, and put on Aaron the tunic and the robe of the ephod, and the ephod, and the breastpiece, and gird him with the decorated band of the ephod; [6] and you shall set the turban on his head, and put the holy diadem on the turban. [7] You shall take the anointing oil, and pour it on his head and anoint him. [8] Then you shall bring his sons, and put tunics on them, [9] and you shall gird them with sashes and tie headdresses on them; and the priesthood shall be theirs by a perpetual ordinance. You shall then ordain Aaron and his sons.

[10] You shall bring the bull in front of the tent of meeting. Aaron and his sons shall lay their hands on the head of the bull, [11] and you shall slaughter the bull before the LORD, at the entrance of the tent of meeting, [12] and shall take some of the blood of the bull and put it on the horns of the altar with your finger, and all the rest of the blood you shall pour out at the base of the altar. [13] You shall take all the fat that covers the entrails, and the appendage of the liver, and the two kidneys with the fat that is on them, and turn them into smoke on the altar. [14] But the flesh of the bull, and its skin, and its dung, you shall burn with fire outside the camp; it is a sin offering.

[15] Then you shall take one of the rams, and Aaron and his sons shall lay their hands on the head of the ram, [16] and you shall slaughter the ram, and shall take its blood and dash it against all sides of the altar. [17] Then you shall cut the ram into its parts, and wash its entrails and its legs, and put them with its parts and its head, [18] and turn the whole ram into smoke on the altar; it is a burnt offering to the LORD; it is a pleasing odor, an offering by fire to the LORD.

[19] You shall take the other ram; and Aaron and his sons shall lay their hands on the head of the ram, [20] and you shall slaughter the ram, and take some of its blood and put it on the lobe of Aaron's right ear and on the lobes of the right ears of his sons, and on the thumbs of their right hands, and on the big toes of their right feet, and dash the rest of the blood against all sides of the altar. [21] Then you shall take some of the blood that is on the altar, and

some of the anointing oil, and sprinkle it on Aaron and his vestments and on his sons and his sons' vestments with him; then he and his vestments shall be holy, as well as his sons and his sons' vestments.

22 You shall also take the fat of the ram, the fat tail, the fat that covers the entrails, the appendage of the liver, the two kidneys with the fat that is on them, and the right thigh (for it is a ram of ordination), 23 and one loaf of bread, one cake of bread made with oil, and one wafer, out of the basket of unleavened bread that is before the LORD; 24 and you shall place all these on the palms of Aaron and on the palms of his sons, and raise them as an elevation offering before the LORD. 25 Then you shall take them from their hands, and turn them into smoke on the altar on top of the burnt offering of pleasing odor before the LORD; it is an offering by fire to the LORD.

26 You shall take the breast of the ram of Aaron's ordination and raise it as an elevation offering before the LORD; and it shall be your portion. 27 You shall consecrate the breast that was raised as an elevation offering and the thigh that was raised as an elevation offering from the ram of ordination, from that which belonged to Aaron and his sons. 28 These things shall be a perpetual ordinance for Aaron and his sons from the Israelites, for this is an offering; and it shall be an offering by the Israelites from their sacrifice of offerings of well-being, their offering to the LORD.

29 The sacred vestments of Aaron shall be passed on to his sons after him; they shall be anointed in them and ordained in them. 30 The son who is priest in his place shall wear them seven days, when he comes into the tent of meeting to minister in the holy place.

31 You shall take the ram of ordination, and boil its flesh in a holy place; 32 and Aaron and his sons shall eat the flesh of the ram and the bread that is in the basket, at the entrance of the tent of meeting. 33 They themselves shall eat the food by which atonement is made, to ordain and consecrate them, but no one else shall eat of them, because they are holy. 34 If any of the flesh for the ordination, or of the bread, remains until the morning, then you shall burn the remainder with fire; it shall not be eaten, because it is holy.

35 Thus you shall do to Aaron and to his sons, just as I have commanded you; through seven days you shall ordain them. 36 Also every day you shall offer a bull as a sin offering for atonement. Also you shall offer a sin offering for the altar, when you make atonement for it, and shall anoint it, to consecrate it. 37 Seven days you shall make atonement for the altar, and consecrate it, and the altar shall be most holy; whatever touches the altar shall become holy.

The gravity of the ordination service is indicated in several ways. First, there is the washing that enacts cleansing from old ways and the vesting that enacts renewal through the covenant for God's new cosmos as symbolized by the tabernacle (29:4–6). (Compare again Ephesians 4:24:

"clothe yourselves with the new self, created according to the likeness of God in true righteousness and holiness.") Second, there is the anointing with oil (29:7) to be used only for this purpose (30:22–33). Third, there is the threefold action wherein (1) the candidates put their hands on the head of a sacrificial bull and then on two successive rams, (2) each of which is then slaughtered and its blood applied to the altar, and (3) part of the blood of the third ram is applied to the candidate's right ear lobe, right thumb, and right great toe. Fourth, this ceremony continues through seven days, with an atoning sacrifice each day to consecrate the altar.

However foreign the specific character of these rituals, their general significance should come home to us. The utter dedication that the candidates avow by submitting to them is, at the very least, a signpost to the moral and spiritual dedication to which Christians are called by the Christ whom the New Testament speaks of as sacrificially self-offered, in the providence of God, on our behalf. Several times, Paul concludes or initiates his argument with imagery of the tabernacle and its ceremonies applied to Christ or to Christians. Thus, he finds God's solution to universal human sinfulness in the death of Christ as a "mercy-seat" (NRSV, "sacrifice [place] of atonement," Rom. 3:21–26). He finds the possibility of being set "free from the law [or vicious cycle] of sin and death" in God sending his own Son to be a sin offering (Rom. 8:1–4, NRSV margin). Again, the possibility of "new creation" turns on how God has dealt with the sin problem in Christ (2 Cor. 5:19–21). The whole of the Christian's life, as renouncing conformity to this world and being transformed by the renewing of the mind, involves presenting one's body as a "living sacrifice, holy and acceptable to God" (Rom. 12:1–2). It is as we go to school in the Old Testament that we acquire the language that will enable us to understand what Paul and other New Testament writers attempt to say in their presentation of Jesus Christ and the new creation he inaugurates.

CONCLUDING INSTRUCTIONS
Exodus 29:38–31:18

> 29:38 Now this is what you shall offer on the altar: two lambs a year old regularly each day. **39 One lamb you shall offer in the morning, and the other lamb you shall offer in the evening; 40 and with the first lamb one-tenth of a measure of choice flour mixed with one-fourth of a hin of beaten oil, and one-fourth of a hin of wine for a drink offering. 41 And the other lamb you shall offer in the evening, and shall offer with it a grain offering and its drink**

offering, as in the morning, for a pleasing odor, an offering by fire to the LORD. [42] It shall be a regular burnt offering throughout your generations at the entrance of the tent of meeting before the LORD, where I will meet with you, to speak to you there. [43] I will meet with the Israelites there, and it shall be sanctified by my glory; [44] I will consecrate the tent of meeting and the altar; Aaron also and his sons I will consecrate, to serve me as priests. [45] I will dwell among the Israelites, and I will be their God. [46] And they shall know that I am the LORD their God, who brought them out of the land of Egypt that I might dwell among them; I am the LORD their God.

30:1 You shall make an altar on which to offer incense; you shall make it of acacia wood. [2] It shall be one cubit long, and one cubit wide; it shall be square, and shall be two cubits high; its horns shall be of one piece with it. [3] You shall overlay it with pure gold, its top, and its sides all around and its horns; and you shall make for it a molding of gold all around. [4] And you shall make two golden rings for it; under its molding on two opposite sides of it you shall make them, and they shall hold the poles with which to carry it. [5] You shall make the poles of acacia wood, and overlay them with gold. [6] You shall place it in front of the curtain that is above the ark of the covenant, in front of the mercy seat that is over the covenant, where I will meet with you. [7] Aaron shall offer fragrant incense on it; every morning when he dresses the lamps he shall offer it, [8] and when Aaron sets up the lamps in the evening, he shall offer it, a regular incense offering before the LORD throughout your generations. [9] You shall not offer unholy incense on it, or a burnt offering, or a grain offering; and you shall not pour a drink offering on it. [10] Once a year Aaron shall perform the rite of atonement on its horns. Throughout your generations he shall perform the atonement for it once a year with the blood of the atoning sin offering. It is most holy to the LORD.

[11] The LORD spoke to Moses: [12] When you take a census of the Israelites to register them, at registration all of them shall give a ransom for their lives to the LORD, so that no plague may come upon them for being registered. [13] This is what each one who is registered shall give: half a shekel according to the shekel of the sanctuary (the shekel is twenty gerahs), half a shekel as an offering to the LORD. [14] Each one who is registered, from twenty years old and upward, shall give the LORD's offering. [15] The rich shall not give more, and the poor shall not give less, than the half shekel, when you bring this offering to the LORD to make atonement for your lives. [16] You shall take the atonement money from the Israelites and shall designate it for the service of the tent of meeting; before the LORD it will be a reminder to the Israelites of the ransom given for your lives.

[17] The LORD spoke to Moses: [18] You shall make a bronze basin with a bronze stand for washing. You shall put it between the tent of meeting and the altar, and you shall put water in it; [19] with the water Aaron and his sons shall wash their hands and their feet. [20] When they go into the tent of meet-

ing, or when they come near the altar to minister, to make an offering by fire to the LORD, they shall wash with water, so that they may not die. ²¹ They shall wash their hands and their feet, so that they may not die: it shall be a perpetual ordinance for them, for him and for his descendants throughout their generations.

²² The LORD spoke to Moses: ²³ Take the finest spices: of liquid myrrh five hundred shekels, and of sweet-smelling cinnamon half as much, that is, two hundred fifty, and two hundred fifty of aromatic cane, ²⁴ and five hundred of cassia—measured by the sanctuary shekel—and a hin of olive oil; ²⁵ and you shall make of these a sacred anointing oil blended as by the perfumer; it shall be a holy anointing oil. ²⁶ With it you shall anoint the tent of meeting and the ark of the covenant, ²⁷ and the table and all its utensils, and the lamp-stand and its utensils, and the altar of incense, ²⁸ and the altar of burnt of-fering with all its utensils, and the basin with its stand; ²⁹ you shall consecrate them, so that they may be most holy; whatever touches them will become holy. ³⁰ You shall anoint Aaron and his sons, and consecrate them, in order that they may serve me as priests. ³¹ You shall say to the Israelites, "This shall be my holy anointing oil throughout your generations. ³² It shall not be used in any ordinary anointing of the body, and you shall make no other like it in composition; it is holy, and it shall be holy to you. ³³ Whoever compounds any like it or whoever puts any of it on an unqualified person shall be cut off from the people."

³⁴ The LORD said to Moses: Take sweet spices, stacte, and onycha, and gal-banum, sweet spices with pure frankincense (an equal part of each), ³⁵ and make an incense blended as by the perfumer, seasoned with salt, pure and holy; ³⁶ and you shall beat some of it into powder, and put part of it before the covenant in the tent of meeting where I shall meet with you; it shall be for you most holy. ³⁷ When you make incense according to this composition, you shall not make it for yourselves; it shall be regarded by you as holy to the LORD. ³⁸ Whoever makes any like it to use as perfume shall be cut off from the people.

31:1 The LORD spoke to Moses: ² See, I have called by name Bezalel son of Uri son of Hur, of the tribe of Judah: ³ and I have filled him with divine spirit, with ability, intelligence, and knowledge in every kind of craft, ⁴ to de-vise artistic designs, to work in gold, silver, and bronze, ⁵ in cutting stones for setting, and in carving wood, in every kind of craft. ⁶ Moreover, I have appointed with him Oholiab son of Ahisamach, of the tribe of Dan; and I have given skill to all the skillful, so that they may make all that I have com-manded you: ⁷ the tent of meeting, and the ark of the covenant, and the mercy seat that is on it, and all the furnishings of the tent, ⁸ the table and its utensils, and the pure lampstand with all its utensils, and the altar of incense, ⁹ and the altar of burnt offering with all its utensils, and the basin with its stand, ¹⁰ and the finely worked vestments, the holy vestments for the priest

Aaron and the vestments of his sons, for their service as priests, [11] and the anointing oil and the fragrant incense for the holy place. They shall do just as I have commanded you.

[12] The LORD said to Moses: [13] You yourself are to speak to the Israelites: "You shall keep my sabbaths, for this is a sign between me and you throughout your generations, given in order that you may know that I, the LORD, sanctify you. [14] You shall keep the sabbath, because it is holy for you; everyone who profanes it shall be put to death; whoever does any work on it shall be cut off from among the people. [15] Six days shall work be done, but the seventh day is a sabbath of solemn rest, holy to the LORD; whoever does any work on the sabbath day shall be put to death. [16] Therefore the Israelites shall keep the sabbath, observing the sabbath throughout their generations, as a perpetual covenant. [17] It is a sign forever between me and the people of Israel that in six days the LORD made heaven and earth, and on the seventh day he rested, and was refreshed."

[18] When God finished speaking with Moses on Mount Sinai, he gave him the two tablets of the covenant, tablets of stone, written with the finger of God.

The instructions for vesting and ordaining the priests are followed by other instructions, some of which it appears should have come earlier. For example, why is the altar of incense introduced only in 30:1–10 and the bronze basin in 30:17–21? And why are the instructions for making the anointing oil and incense not given before their use is mentioned in 29:7, 21; and 30:1–10? Scholars conclude that some materials (e.g., 30:1–10) were added after the main narrative was established. But why were they placed here? We might have done it differently, but it is worth pondering why the writers and editors did things they way they did. The following suggestions, together with brief comments on the remaining individual units, may help.

Let's begin with 29:38–46. The first priestly ministry mentioned, following the instructions for their ordination, is the "regular" offering of a lamb each morning and a lamb each evening, "for a pleasing odor." This offering's importance lies in its dailiness. The "regular" daily offering means that Israel's presence before God in worship is never simply a thing of the past or something to come. Each day begins and ends in God's presence.

The word "regular" or "regularly" (vv. 38, 42) is pivotal here. The Hebrew word comes from a verb meaning "to extend, stretch, measure," and the word means "continuity, of going on without interruption." It occurs often in Leviticus and Numbers in reference to various "regular" (or continuous) aspects of priestly ministry. (It has occurred in Exodus 25:30;

27:20; 28:29, 30, 38; and will in 30:8.) Significantly, it appears frequently in the Psalms in reference to individual and communal prayers and praises. In these contexts, NRSV translates the word "always, ever, evermore, forever, continually." Depending on the context, it means "on a regular [perhaps daily] basis" or "without so much as a moment's respite." By it, the psalmist can refer to the pain or sin or enemy attack that is "ever" with him or her (Psalm 38:17; 51:3; 74:23) and therefore the prayer and praise that is "continuously" offered to God (Psalm 16:7–8; 25:15; 34:1; 35:27). By it, God can castigate those who think that regular animal sacrifice by itself, unaccompanied by obedience to the moral laws of the covenant, is pleasing to God (Psalm 50:8); by it, the psalmist can vow to keep God's law "continually" (Psalm 119:44, 117). The occurrence in Psalm 40:11–12 is especially noteworthy:

> Do not, O LORD, withhold
> 　your mercy from me;
> let your steadfast love and your faithfulness
> 　keep me safe forever.
> For evils have encompassed me
> 　without number;
> my iniquities have overtaken me,
> 　until I cannot see;
> they are more than the hairs of my head,
> 　and my heart fails me.

Perhaps here the word means not "forever" but "day by day." Like recovering alcoholics, most if not all of us need encouragement, help, and hope "just for today," leaving tomorrow to take care of itself, when it, in turn, will become "today." (Compare Matthew 6:11, 34.)

Psalm 40:11–12 is strikingly echoed in Lamentations 3:22–24:

> The steadfast love of the LORD never ceases,
> 　his mercies never come to an end;
> they are new every morning;
> 　great is your faithfulness.
> "The LORD is my portion," says my soul,
> 　"therefore I will hope in him."

This affirmation celebrates God's side of the "daily" meeting in Exodus 29:38–45. As often as Israel's priests offer the daily morning and evening sacrifice, God will "meet" with Israel (v. 43), to "dwell" (or "tent") among

them and be their God (v. 45). The words "meet" and "tent" are important here. The first means, literally, "to come together at an appointed
time and place." The second gives the picture of camping temporarily at a
given spot before moving on. The fact is that most of us are not continuously conscious of being in God's presence. Most of our time is taken up
with the affairs of daily life. That need not be a defect in our piety, for our
attention to daily affairs, if carried out in the right spirit, can image the
God who each day, after creating this or that specific aspect of the world,
looks closely at it and sees that it is good. Cultivation of the right spirit is
enhanced when we punctuate our daily affairs with "appointed" times,
morning and evening, spent consciously in God's presence. When Paul
writes, "Rejoice always, pray without ceasing, give thanks in all circumstances; for this is the will of God in Christ Jesus for you" (1 Thess.
5:16–18), he does so on the basis of his own practice (Rom. 1:9; Phil. 1:3–4;
1 Thess. 1:2–3; 2:13; see also 2 Tim. 1:3). If that practice has taken on a
new significance for him "in Christ," its foundations were laid in his for-
mative years as a faithful Jew, foundations of "continual" prayer rooted in
Exodus 29:38–46. If Israel lived in the assurance that morning and evening
their priests offered sacrifice to the God who met them in the tent, Paul
came to the assurance that his prayers and those of others were caught up
in the intercession of the Holy Spirit and of the risen Christ (Rom.
8:26–27, 34; compare Heb. 7:23–25).

The daily offering is to be made at the entrance to the tent of meeting
(29:42). Now we move inside the tent, to the altar of incense positioned
"in front of the curtain that is above the ark of the covenant, in front of the
mercy seat that is over the covenant, where I will meet with you" (30:6).
Here, too, the priest is to make a "regular" offering each morning and each
evening (vv. 7–8). Again, the ritual finds its counterpart in the Psalms, for
instance, when the psalmist prays, "Let my prayer be counted as incense
before you, and the lifting up of my hands as an evening sacrifice" (Psalm
141:2). Conversely, when the heart is too heavy to speak or so full of glad-
ness that it cannot find words adequate to its theme, many still find help
in the simple act of burning incense and allowing its pungent rising odor
to carry their unspeakable prayers to God. This would be especially meaningful to Zechariah as portrayed in the Gospel of Luke! As he took his
priestly turn to offer incense in the sanctuary, an angelic visitation answered the prayer of this childless man that may long since have become
only a mute longing (Luke 1:8–17). So startled was he that he remained
mute until the day the answer to his prayer was made good (1:19–20). During this time, he could still allow the incense to speak for him.

But once a year the incense altar also serves another function. On Yom Kippur, the day of atonement (see Leviticus 16), the high priest is to offer "the blood of the atoning sin offering" for the sins of the whole community (v. 10; compare Rom. 3:21–26; 8:1–4; 2 Cor. 5:21; Heb. 9:1–10:18). The issues are profoundly threatening and even more profoundly reassuring: threatening, because the gravity of sin threatens to rupture the relationship irremediably; reassuring, because God makes provision for the rupture to be healed and calls on us to appropriate that provision.

We come now—abruptly—to the half shekel, a tax for the upkeep of sanctuary (30:11–16). A number of elements in this passage are enigmatic, and various interpretations have been offered. In what follows, I shall draw on the studies of others and offer a synthetic interpretation of my own, proceeding from four questions: (1) Why register all twenty years of age and up? (2) Why is there the danger of a plague for such a registration? (3) Why is the passage just here, after 30:1–10? (4) Why is there a tax for the upkeep of a sanctuary built out of strictly voluntary offerings (25:2; also 35:5, 20–29)?

1. If Numbers 1:2–3, 44–47 is a guide, the registration is of those "able to go to war" (excluding Levites; 1:47). What does such a census registration of warriors have to do with the tabernacle, its upkeep, and its services? Why does this incur the risk of a plague unless each person so registered pays a half shekel for sanctuary upkeep?

2. The one place in the Bible where these themes reappear is 2 Samuel 24, where David takes a census of all those "able to draw the sword" (24:9). Why would a war-seasoned general like Joab resist such a move (24:3)? Why does David come to think that he has "sinned greatly" and "done very foolishly" (24:10)? And why does God visit a pestilence or plague on Israel (24:15, 25)? I suggest it is because David has forgotten a fundamental principle of Israel's tradition of Holy War—that Israel's battles with enemies do not turn on its own military power but on God who fights for them. David earlier knew this in his fight against Goliath (1 Sam. 17:45–47). God had Gideon get rid of most of his troops, for "Israel would only take the credit away from me, saying, 'My own hand has delivered me'" (Judg. 7:2). With only his armor bearer, Jonathan routed the Philistines, "for nothing can hinder the LORD from saving by many or by few" (1 Sam. 14:6). This is the tradition of war that Joab grew up with, and that David once knew but now at the end of his life has forgotten, as he imitates foreign kings to establish his kingdom. The plague that God sends is averted when David buys a threshing floor and oxen from Araunah to build an altar and offer atoning sacrifices.

3. But if a census for war is wrong in 2 Samuel, why is it called for in Numbers 1 (and, implicitly, here in Exodus 30, right after verses 1–10)? According to the Priestly tradition, Israel in its march through the wilderness is both God's sacred congregation with the tabernacle at its center and God's sacred army (*ṣaba'*, military "company," Num. 1:3; 10:28) with the ark at its head (Num. 10:1–33). The Levites, we remember, are not registered in that army. They are enumerated and registered separately, to assist the priests in sanctuary service and to carry the tabernacle and its objects after the priests have packed them up for travel. Interestingly, the Levites' "service" of the tabernacle is in Hebrew called *ṣaba'* (Num. 4:3, 23, 30, 35, 39, 43; 8:24–25), the term that elsewhere means military service! This suggests that if registered non-Levitical males are part of God's holy army led by the ark into battle, the Levites' service of the tabernacle is their form of service in God's army. But here is where the danger of the census and registration comes in. As a registration, it underscores that every Israelite male is a member of God's army; as a census, it could be misinterpreted as emphasizing that the strength of that army depends on its human numbers.

As atonement money, then, I understand the half shekel to be an acknowledgment of Israel's tendency to rely on its own strength. As provision for the upkeep of the tabernacle, I understand the half shekel to be an affirmation that Israel's true strength lies not in its own numbers and might, but in the God who tents in the sanctuary and who, enthroned on the cherubim above the ark, fights Israel's battles. In coming right after the provision for the annual Day of Atonement before the ark, this atoning half shekel allows each participant to identify with the priestly action in forsaking the twin idolatries of self-reliance and of fearfulness before merely human enemies.

4. It may seem odd to move from the voluntary offering of materials for the construction of the sanctuary to an annual tax for its upkeep. But if the tax is connected with Israel as God's "sacred army," another theme in the holy war traditions may come into play here. In Judges 5:2 (one of the oldest of the holy war traditions), Israel's warriors are said to "offer themselves willingly." Since the tax is only a half shekel and is the same for rich and poor, I suggest it is the means by which every Israelite of suitable age may symbolically be included in God's sacral army. In ancient and modern times, military status and influence are often directly related to wealth, with the wealthy being able to raise and lead large armies and to dictate national policy, while the poor have nothing to offer but their own bodies in battle. This is another way of assuming that the success of an army turns

on its human resources. By leveling the contribution of every Israelite, this provision is a way of saying that nothing can hinder the LORD from saving by rich or by poor (compare 1 Sam. 14:6).

But what of the women? In most traditional societies, warriors are men. Yet in the Bible there are some noteworthy female warriors, such as Jael who killed Sisera with a tent peg (Judg. 4:17–22), the unidentified woman who was Abimelech's downfall (Judg. 9:50–57), and especially Deborah (Judg. 5:1–16). In that connection, is it significant that, whereas Numbers 1:3 specifies a census of males, Exodus 30:11–16 does not but says, instead, "each one"? This much is clear: The voluntary offerings for the construction of the tabernacle are explicitly said to come from both men and women (Exod. 35:22, 29). Similarly, when Israel makes the idolatrous calf (which I shall argue is a war image), the gold earrings come from the men and the women (32:2). In view of this, I take the Hebrew word "each" in 30:11–16 to allow us to interpret it to include women. In any case, it is interesting that Jesus measures a person's contribution to God's service not by its quantity but by its quality (Mark 12:41–44). When we consider how often we measure the church's strength for its mission by its numbers and by its big-money contributors, perhaps we can appreciate what Exodus 30:11–16, coming right after 30:1–10, is calling us to.

The bronze basin (30:17–21) and the anointing oil and incense (30:22–38) have been mentioned in connection with the provision for ordaining the priests (see 29:4; 29:7, 21) and the provision for the altar of incense (30:1–10). Similarly, I have earlier referred to the divinely gifted artisans who are to make all the parts of the tabernacle and its furnishings, together with the priestly vestments, the anointing oil, and the incense (31:1–11). One further comment on the latter passage is in order. While all these things are to be made by the artisans, they apparently do not assemble them into a completed tabernacle. As Nahum Sarna writes, "When it comes to assembling the parts into an integrated whole, it is Moses personally who performs the task, not they [40:1–33], . . . since only Moses carries a mental picture of the Tabernacle in its completed, coherent form" (*Exploring Exodus: The Heritage of Biblical Israel*, pp. 200–201). The tabernacle arises, then, out of the coming together of (1) the materials offered freely by "all those whose hearts prompt them to give (25:1), (2) the work of divinely gifted artisans in fashioning individual components, and (3) Moses' general oversight and final assemblage. But more than this, it arises out of the coming together of God's initiative and the people's response. As such, it is the architectural embodiment of what is meant by "covenant," the coming together into a relationship that becomes the place out of which the parties to the covenant move together into the future.

This brings us to the climactic passage in God's instructions for the tabernacle: the sabbath law in 31:12–17. Its character as the climax to Exodus 25—31 becomes clear when we remind ourselves that the sanctuary is a microcosm of the whole of creation, and we recall that the six days of creation in Genesis 1 have their climax in the seventh day, which God blesses and sanctifies by resting on it. Just as the rainbow in Genesis 9 is the sign of God's covenant with a world newly created after the flood, so the sabbath is the sign of God's covenant with Israel in a new world architecturally represented by the sanctuary.

The sabbath is presented as a day on which all who have worked during the preceding six days may rest from their labors and be refreshed. The language of 31:17 is in fact quite breath-taking in its graphic boldness. In Genesis 2:1–3 the text says twice that God "rested," using the verb, *shabat*, from which the name sabbath comes. The same verb occurs in Exodus 20:11. But here the text says God "rested [*shabat*] and was refreshed [*yinnaphesh*]." The second verb means "to catch one's breath." Its force is nicely caught in 2 Samuel 16:14: "The king and all the people who were with him arrived weary at the Jordan; and there he refreshed himself." The only other place it occurs in the Bible is in Exodus 23:12, where Israel, having been instructed to allow the land a sabbath every seventh year (23:10–11), hears again, "Six days you shall do your work, but on the seventh day you shall rest, so that your ox and your donkey may have relief, and your homeborn slave and the resident alien may be refreshed." But the noun *nephesh*, on which the verb for "refresh" is based, means more than "breath, soul, living being." It carries also the connotations of "desire, appetite, emotion, passion." Our daughter caught its force perfectly one afternoon when she was four. Overhearing her mother look at a pile of freshly laundered clothes and sigh, "How am I going to iron all those clothes before it's time to make supper?" she said, "Mommy, why don't you make yourself a cup of tea and go watch *Edge of Night?* I can do the ironing—I've got the energy, the breath, and the appetite!" And, she might have added, the morale. In Exodus 6:9, the people are so demoralized by their increased burdens under Pharaoh that when Moses seeks to encourage them, they do not listen, "because of their broken spirit and their cruel slavery." The expression "broken spirit" in this passage uses the word *ruach*, another word for "breath/wind/spirit." The sabbath is instituted in order that we may be renewed in our appetite for life—for the world God has created and the new world for which God has acted to redeem us. As such, 31:14–17 joins 24:9–11 in pointing to the purposes of God that lie beyond what we can imagine.

I noted earlier that the verb "refresh" occurs in both 23:12 and 31:17. These references to the sabbath yoke together in an interesting way two bodies of divine instruction that are distinguishable from one another and can even at times be pitted against one another. Exodus 21:1–23:19 sets forth a lengthy list of laws that largely govern Israel's actual social and economic relations, while 25:1–31:17 sets forth a lengthy list of laws that lay the basis for Israel's ritual life in the sanctuary. In texts like Psalm 50, Isaiah 1:10–20, Amos 5:21–24, and Micah 6:1–8, a sharp contrast is drawn between Israel's scrupulous observance of ceremonial practice and their unscrupulous disregard of the claims of covenant law for justice, especially toward the powerless and the poor. So sharply is the contrast drawn that interpreters have sometimes taken such passages as a repudiation in principle of the sacrificial system.

Such a reading, however, overlooks the fact that the sanctuary with its priestly leadership and ceremonies is a particular form of language, expressing meaning through architecture, ritual, and speech. All forms of language, including human speech, are distinguishable from the realities of which they speak. That is what we mean by language: something that stands in for the meaning or worth of something else. In that sense, money is a form of language. It stands in for real value, whether that real value is real estate, movable possessions, or someone's labor. Money can be debased, devalued, and counterfeited, in which cases it loses its real meaning. But we cannot do without money as such. Where it has been debased or devalued, we seek to reestablish its currency (its real meaning) by making good on the real value that it represents.

So it is, I suggest, with the relation between the laws of 21:1–23:19 as the language of social justice, and the instructions of 25:1–31:17 as the language of sanctuary worship. The fact that they have the sabbath in common suggests that each language is complemented by the other. To worship God in accordance with the provisions in 25:1–31:17 is to speak a language of worship and "new creation" that is given its real value in the sort of social relations called for in 21:1–23:19. Conversely, to live in faithful accord with the covenantal claims of 21:1–23:19 is already to offer implicitly the worship of God that comes to explicit voice in the provisions of 25:1–31:17. But in the latter case, something more also happens, and this something would not be brought into clear focus if it were not for what the tabernacle language says to us.

In 25:8, Israel is invited to make a sanctuary "so that I may dwell [or tent] among them." If the architectural and ceremonial provisions that follow, climaxing in the sabbath, are symbolic language for the covenant relation with God, then faithful pursuit of the covenant laws in 21:1–23:19 will likewise have the effect of shaping Israelite society into a living sanctuary that gives space for the indwelling of God. This is the final motivation for social justice: that human society may become a place where God dwells, a place where God and the people of God, together with the whole creation, may rest to enjoy the fruits of one another's labors.

There is one more point to touch on. In recent years, a number of theologians have become troubled over the tendency in traditional Christian thinking to emphasize the lofty transcendence of God and to neglect God's nearness or immanence. One way in which some have sought to redress this imbalance is to think of God's relation to the world on the analogy of one's relation to one's own body. Thus, for example, Grace Jantzen has written a very stimulating book titled *God's World, God's Body.* There is much in this analogy that is attractive and inviting. Among other things, it can appeal to strands of Christian tradition that have emphasized God's incarnation in Jesus Christ, especially as it is put in John 1:14, "the Word became flesh and lived [tented] among us." Others have resisted the analogy with one's body, fearing a collapse into the sort of pantheism in which everything that exists is God.

I would like to suggest that the tabernacle tradition of Exodus 25—31 and 35—40 offers important clues to how we may think about these things. In human experience, one does not enjoy an optional relation to one's body. From birth to death, we are a psychosomatic unity. There is a necessary connection between what we have traditionally called body and soul. In the tabernacle tradition of Exodus, the relation between God and people through the sanctuary is not a necessary one but rather a relation that is freely entered into as a covenant. The material stuff of creation is freely offered by all those whose hearts make them willing, and the tabernacle that results is a means in and through which God will "tent" with them, as at an appointed place and at appointed times.

The freedom with which Israelites are invited to offer the materials of creation for the sanctuary and in which God meets with them there does not by itself encourage us to think that the world we inhabit is God's body. Yet, insofar as tent and building function as extensions of the body and insofar as the sanctuary is a microcosm of creation as God intends creation, perhaps the tabernacle may be thought of as the point through which the world is called to become God's body and the point at which, at least symbolically, it is in the process of becoming God's body. If the unity of body and spirit is displayed, for example, in the degree to which artistic or athletic intention is embodied in the execution of a piece of vocal or instrumental music or a gymnastic maneuver, then the world becomes God's body as the elements of the world freely conform themselves to God's will and word. In this sense, the tabernacle tradition in Exodus may be taken as a prototype of incarnation. In the New Testament, we may think not only of John 1:14 but also of Luke 1:38, where, in response to the angel's annunciation, Mary says, "Here am I, the servant of the LORD; let it be to me according to your word." We may think also of Colossians 2:9, where Paul or a close disciple writes, "For in him [Christ] the whole fullness of deity dwells bodily"; the cosmic outcome this incarnation promises is sketched in Colossians 1:15–23, an outcome in which the whole of the redeemed creation becomes one with the incarnate, crucified, and risen Christ. Such a vision can, of course, be entertained only through images and pictures, for we have no literal language adequate to it. But such images and pictures as I have been discussing would help us to overcome false divisions between body and soul, spirit and matter, divisions in which we typically have valued and favored one side over against the other. We need to remind ourselves that when God created each of the aspects of the material creation in Genesis 1, God pronounced it good. Such a vision as I have been pointing toward, on the basis of the tabernacle traditions, is another way of affirming God's valuation of matter.

3. Sin, Redemption, Covenant
Exodus 32—34

THE GOLDEN CALF
Exodus 32:1-6

> 32:1 When the people saw that Moses delayed to come down from the mountain, the people gathered around Aaron, and said to him, "Come, make gods for us, who shall go before us; as for this Moses, the man who brought us up out of the land of Egypt, we do not know what has become of him." ² Aaron said to them, "Take off the gold rings that are on the ears of your wives, your sons, and your daughters, and bring them to me." ³ So all the people took off the gold rings from their ears, and brought them to Aaron. ⁴ He took the gold from them, formed it in a mold, and cast an image of a calf; and they said, "These are your gods, O Israel, who brought you up out of the land of Egypt!" ⁵ When Aaron saw this, he built an altar before it; and Aaron made proclamation and said, "Tomorrow shall be a festival to the LORD." ⁶ They rose early the next day, and offered burnt offerings and brought sacrifices of well-being; and the people sat down to eat and drink, and rose up to revel.

The exodus story now takes a calamitous turn. It is Israel's version of the universal human turn in Genesis 2—3. God has acted creatively and redemptively to give and restore life. God has established the conditions within which life may flourish (Gen. 2:16–17; Exod. 20:1–23:19). The result has been a face-to-face communion free from shame or fear (Gen. 2:25; Exod. 24:9–11). Immediately, however, an alien wisdom moves the community to act against the express command of God. The covenant of creation-redemption is broken, innocence is lost, and the community survives only by God's "covering" goodness.

The similarity between Israel's fall and the story in Genesis 2—3 suggests at least two things. First, the Genesis story is not simply an account of what happened once, at the very beginning. It is the story of what happens, again and again, at the very beginning of new beginnings in God's relations with the human community in general, any specific community, or, indeed, any given individual.

Second, if Genesis 2—3 is a story of what again and again goes wrong with new beginnings, it also signifies how all our fallings from early promise have their root in an immemorial past. When we fall, we do so as buying into a mind-set and playing out patterns of behavior that are deeply grooved in the human soul. We cannot simply say, "The devil made me do it," for we are responsible for buying into it. At the same time, there is an effective energy and powerful tendency, not simply originating with us, that works to seduce us into a mind-set and pattern of behavior that amounts to falling short of what we were created and are called to become.

This story of repeated fallings from early promise is disheartening. It is as disheartening, for example, as Vincent Canby's review of Harold Pinter's new stage play *Moonlight* (*New York Times*, Oct. 18, 1995). The play revolves around the bed of a dying husband-father. The review is headed, "Harold Pinter Takes Dysfunction to New Depths" and begins, "Dysfunctional is an inadequate but accurate way to describe the family in Harold Pinter's short, sometimes funny, very melancholy play, 'Moonlight.' . . . There's something almost cosmic about the distances that separate the characters. . . . Though none of them is aware of it, they live only in the fury of the contested memories and impromptu fantasies that keep them forever attached." The difference between Pinter's play and the biblical story, however, is that while both paint a dismal picture of human dysfunction (which we can call dysfunction only if we have some memory or hope of what would be good function), Pinter offers little basis for encouragement—that is, unless encouragement is to be found in the character of the family daughter-sister, Bridget. "She's the only forgiving member of the family, possibly because she's dead and confused." At the very end of the play, Bridget "appears . . . to speak Pinter's benediction." As we shall see, the story of Israel's fall ends more hopefully. But first let us consider how it begins.

Moses has been on the mountain a long time. What has gone wrong? The Hebrew verb translated "delayed" occurs again only in Judges 5:28, where Canaanite women wonder why their husbands "delay" to return from battle. (It turns out they have been defeated.) As we shall see, the people's concern is related to the absence of Moses as their war leader against Pharaoh (and the Amalekites in 17:8–16). It is also related to the status Moses has come to have for them in relation to God.

In 4:1, Moses had introduced the question of whether the people would believe him or listen to him. Though they initially did in 4:30–31, when

Moses offered them encouragement under Pharaoh's increased burdens they did not listen (6:1–9). Again, when they were caught between the sea and Pharaoh's pursuing army they complained against Moses and wished they were back in Egypt (14:10–12). After the deliverance at the sea, they did, indeed, fear the LORD and believe in the LORD and in his servant Moses (14:31), and under Miriam's singing, dancing leadership, they worshiped God with the song at the sea (15:1–21). But the repeated lack of food and water in the wilderness moved them repeatedly to "murmur" against Moses and to wish they were back in Egypt. Significantly, their murmuring against Moses was also a murmuring against God, as they said, "Is the LORD among us or not?" (17:7). When God spoke to Moses on Mount Sinai in the people's hearing, it was so that (as the Hebrew says), "they may believe in you ever after" (19:9).

As the story progresses, the presence of God is increasingly associated with the presence of Moses in their midst (compare 3:12). But if Moses does not come down the mountain, how shall they be assured of the continuing presence of Yahweh to lead them into the land? In place of Moses, "the man who brought us up out of the land of Egypt" (32:1), Aaron and the people fashion a bull calf and cry out, "These are your gods, O Israel, who brought you up out of the land of Egypt!" Clearly, the calf is a replacement for Moses, a visible reassurance of God's presence and activity in their midst. Since they have "believed in the LORD and in his servant Moses," and since God wishes them to "believe in Moses ever after," and since Moses is even spoken of as functioning in some sense "as God" (4:16; 7:1), the calf then can symbolize the presence of both Moses and Yahweh. That they do not mean to worship other gods is clear from Aaron's announcement, "Tomorrow shall be a festival to the LORD" (32:5).

It is customary to describe the ritual on that day as a sexual orgy, which would fit with the bull as a common ancient symbol of sexual fertility. But the bull (especially in its horns; 1 Kings 22:11) also is a common ancient symbol of prowess in battle, and everything in chapter 32 suggests that it is intended as such a symbol here. For one thing, the bull replaces Moses and symbolizes Yahweh who defeated Pharaoh and brought Israel out of Egypt. For another, the "festival" has all the marks of a celebration of military victory, like the celebration at the sea (15:1–21). The burnt offerings and sacrifices of well-being echo those in 18:12 (another celebration of the exodus). The eating and drinking echo the celebration in 24:9–11. The dancing (32:19) echoes the dancing in 15:20. The word translated "revelers" in verse 18 is 'annot, the same word as in 15:21, where it is translated "sang." Finally, from a distance Joshua takes the sounds of the celebration as evidence of "war in the camp" (v. 17). Moses responds that it is not the cry of actual victory and defeat but the sound of those who sing (of victory and defeat) (v. 18). If it is as Aaron says, "a festival to the LORD" (v. 5), we may even imagine the singing to include the song of the sea. Except for the calf, all of this would be "kosher" worship. We may even imagine Moses for a moment being filled with reassurance and delight to think that the people, despite his prolonged absence, would continue in such faithful worship.

There is a double irony in all this, like the double irony in Genesis 2—3. (Ironies always turn on a difference between appearance and reality.) There, the snake leads the couple to go against God's prohibition in hope of becoming wise, better able to deal with the uncertainties of their future in the garden. But (first irony) when they eat they become, not wise, but naked and ashamed. So the snake's words turn out to deliver less than they promised. Then again, in making the garden God had provided more than met the eye (second irony). For all God had said was, "You may freely eat of every tree of the garden," except, of course, for the tree of forbidden wisdom (2:16–17). If they had observed the prohibition and gone about eating freely of the other trees, they would have discovered what they had not been told—that the garden held also a tree of life. The implication is that they exchanged a wisdom of obedience and trust of God's good providence for a wisdom they could seize and use unilaterally to cope with their future in the garden. The question with which the garden story ends is whether the way to the tree of life is now blocked forever (3:22–23), or whether the cherubim who guard it with flaming sword are hopefully connected to the cherubim within the most holy place in the tabernacle, where God seeks to dwell in Israel's midst.

With this in mind, let us consider the ironies in Exodus. Like the tree of life in the garden, God on the mountain has been preparing with Moses a means through which Israel can continue to enjoy God's presence and live. Specifically, God will meet with them at the ark and from between the cherubim will deliver to them all the continuing commandments they will need once Moses is no longer with them to speak in God's name. Moreover, the ark will take the place of Moses and his rod against Israel's enemies in battle (Num. 10:35–36). As with the tree of life, they know nothing of this provision. In their anxiety for the future, they exchange a wisdom of obedience and trust in God's providence for a wisdom widely prevalent in the ancient world. They make the bull calf as a representation of military power.

They could get this image from just about anywhere in the ancient world. Most immediately, they could get it from Egypt. In using such an image, they resort to the very "wisdom" (1:10) under which they have for so long been oppressed, a wisdom based in fear and expressed in overwhelming controlling and coercive force. We may compare this to contemporary understanding of how the victims of long-time abuse, when they come into positions of power, often use that power to become abusers. In effect, they worship the very form of power, and of "wisdom," under which they have suffered. In doing so, they forget that at the sea God overturned such power in the form of Pharaoh's army. Moses' return brings them to an abrupt awakening.

But if the calf is intended to signify the continuing presence of Yahweh in the absence of Moses, and if the ark and the cherubim with their tablets containing the law are to signify God's continuing presence in their midst, how can the ark and cherubim be thought kosher if the calf is a violation of the covenant? Calf and cherubim alike have a long background in ancient religious imagery. My proposal is this: Since the ark contained within it the Decalogue with its provisions against idolatry (25:21), those provisions should safeguard against the ark and cherubim being misinterpreted as an image of God. Instead, it would signal the invisible presence of the God who is beyond all images. Since the calf would not contain the Decalogue, it would be open to misinterpretation as the very image of God— as apparently happened in Israel (e.g., Hos. 8:5–6; 10:5; 13:2).

At one level, then, the golden calf is a violation of the covenant commandments and, as such, is an act of disobedience. But the disobedience arises out of a deeper problem. More grave than the lack of obedience is the lack of trust. Not seeing what provision God has made behind the scenes for their welfare, the first couple in the garden, and Israel at Mount Sinai, act out of anxiety to provide for their own well-being, even if that means to block out of consciousness the fact that their act violates the commandment. In both instances, what has secretly been provided would have become manifest in due course. God has entrusted humans with freedom, either (as the hymn puts it) to "trust and obey" or to try to go it alone by an alternate wisdom. Where God's trust does not win answering trust, the sort of relation into which God seeks to draw us is not possible.

GOD'S WRATH
Exodus 32:7–10

32:7 **The LORD said to Moses, "Go down at once! Your people, whom you brought up out of the land of Egypt, have acted perversely; 8 they have been quick to turn aside from the way that I commanded them; they have cast for themselves an image of a calf, and have worshiped it and sacrificed to it, and** said, 'These are your gods, O Israel, who brought you up out of the land of Egypt!'" 9 The LORD said to Moses, "I have seen this people, how stiff-necked they are. 10 Now let me alone, so that my wrath may burn hot against them and I may consume them; and of you I will make a great nation."

Does "your people, whom you have brought up" (v. 7) and "this people" (v. 9) mean they are no longer God's people, or does it underline Moses' relation to them and his previous actions on their behalf to secure his interest in them even in their present situation? "They have acted perversely." The verb here means "to spoil" and usually takes a direct object indicating what has been spoiled. For instance, the verb occurs in Genesis 6:11–12, where humans have so corrupted the earth that God resolves to sweep away the old creation and start all over again with Noah (6:13–22).

Anyone who has ridden a horse, plowed behind an ox, or tried (as I once did) to wean a three-day-old calf by getting it to drink milk from a pail will appreciate the "stiff-necked" image. It signals an animal's refusal to be steered in a direction it does not want to go, even when (like that weanling calf) the direction would be beneficial. God's burning anger is like that of a "bear robbed of her cubs" (Hos. 13:4–8). What Israel has "spoiled" is the relation God seeks to have with this people. So, as with Noah, God proposes to start over again with Moses, saying, "of you I will make a great nation." Where have we heard this before? Are these not the very words with which God first called Abraham (Gen. 12:2)? Is Moses to become a second Abraham? Is the story of redemption from Egypt and covenanting at Mount Sinai for nothing, just wiped off the slate, erased from memory? Is Moses, who worked so hard to bring the people this far, to take the expression "let me alone" at face value and acquiesce in it? Or do we have a subtle redemptive irony here? Do these very words plant in Moses' mind a possibility for him to seize? Is it possible these words show that God is "of two minds," angered by how everything is so quickly spoiled and yet, at a deeper level, looking for a way through the impasse? (For such a wrestling within God in the face of Israel's covenant violation, compare Hosea 11:8–9 and 14:4).

MOSES' INTERCESSION
Exodus 32:11–14

32:11 But Moses implored the LORD his God, and said, "O LORD, why does your wrath burn hot against your people, whom you brought out of the land of Egypt with great power and with a mighty hand? 12 Why should the Egyptians say, 'It was with evil intent that he brought them out to kill them in the

mountains, and to consume them from the face of the earth'? Turn from your
fierce wrath; change your mind and do not bring disaster on your people.
¹³ Remember Abraham, Isaac, and Israel, your servants, how you swore to
them by your own self, saying to them, 'I will multiply your descendants like
the stars of heaven, and all this land that I have promised I will give to your
descendants, and they shall inherit it forever.'" ¹⁴ And the LORD changed his
mind about the disaster that he planned to bring on his people.

Moses "implores" God. (The Hebrew verb means, literally, "make someone's face sweet or pleasant." I remember the sight of a little child reaching up with her hands to push her mother's angry face into the shape of a
smile.) His prayer is a masterpiece of condensed persuasion. Diplomati-
cally, he first raises his concern indirectly with a twofold "Why?" The first
"why?" nicely turns God's "your people, whom you brought up" (v. 7) back
on God. If God can underscore the people-Moses connection, Moses will
underscore the people-Yahweh connection. Moreover, he emphasizes the
exodus as a demonstration of God's power and mighty hand. The second
"why?" raises the issue of God's motivation in the exodus: Was it with evil
intent? The people make just this accusation in Exodus 16:3; 17:3. Here
Moses gives voice to what they themselves would say if they saw what was
threatened.

Moses now moves to direct confrontation, shifting from his two questions to a series of imperatives: "Turn . . . change your mind . . . do not
bring disaster." The verb that NRSV translates as "change your mind" is
one that with a human subject is translated "repent." In current usage, the
term *repent* implies a past action that one now acknowledges to have been
wrong. This is its most frequent usage in the Bible. Where it occurs with
God as subject in the Bible, it often refers to what God had threatened to
do and then "thinks better of." When Moses says, "Change your mind" or
"Repent," it is as though he says, "Do you realize what you are about to
do? To let anger be the final basis of your dealing with this people is to destroy everything you've done for them—and to call in question your own
integrity as a promiser."

This brings us to the heart of the prayer, the call for God to "remember" the promise and covenant with the ancestors (v. 13). In every previous mention of all three ancestors in Exodus, the reference has been to
Abraham, Isaac, and Jacob (2:24; 3:6, 15, 16; 4:5; 6:3, 8), and so it will be
in 33:1. Only here, in Moses' intercession, is the third ancestor referred to
as "Israel," the name God gave to Jacob after the wrestling and the transformation in the night by the Jabbok (Gen. 32:28). It is as though, in shift-

ing from Jacob to Israel, Moses seeks to bring the present generation under the umbrella of that earlier momentous interaction between the ancestor and God.

Moses next emphasizes the quality of the relationship these ancestors had with God: "your servants." Then he appeals directly to God's promise to them. In doing so, he sounds a theme that will run through the book of Deuteronomy, appearing there in one form or another more than thirty times: It is for the sake of the ancestors and to fulfill the promise made to them that God will bring Israel into the promised land in spite of their ambiguous moral condition.

God heard the cry of the Hebrew slaves and delivered them from Egypt, not simply because they were oppressed, but because of the promise made to their ancestors (2:23–25). So too here, God is asked to hear Moses' prayer for this people, not simply because God has already delivered them from Egypt, but because of the promise made to their ancestors. This point is very important. When the Mount Sinai covenant with its rewards for obedience and punishments for disobedience (Deut. 30:15–20) goes terribly wrong, there is no redeeming clause to save the people from their just deserts. Any hope for them lies outside the framework of Mount Sinai, in an appeal to the prior covenant with the ancestors. The Mount Sinai covenant does not render the covenant with the ancestors obsolete—just the opposite. When the covenant sealed at Mount Sinai gets in trouble, it returns to its roots in the ancestors to get back on track. (Paul makes a similar point in Romans 4 and in Galatians 3. In the latter passage, he argues that one can understand what God has done and is doing in Jesus Christ only by appreciating that it is the Abrahamic covenant that is fundamental, not the Mosaic.)

But Moses' appeal to the ancestors may have a more precise point to it, subtly conveyed in his choice of language. First, the expression "you swore . . . by your own self" occurs in only one other place in the Bible. After Abraham shows his absolute obedience and trust in God, by offering Isaac on the altar, God says, "now I know that you fear God, since you have not withheld your son, your only son, from me" (Gen. 22:12). Then God goes on to say, "*By myself I have sworn* . . . Because you have done this, and have not withheld your son, your only son, I will indeed bless you, and I will make your offspring as numerous [literally, "I will multiply your descendants"] as the stars of heaven and as the sand that is on the seashore. And your offspring shall possess the gate of their enemies, and by your offspring shall all the nations of the earth gain blessing for themselves, because you have obeyed my voice" (vv. 16–18).

Second, the precise expression, "*I will multiply your descendants as the stars of heaven*" occurs for the first time here. In Genesis 12:1–3 God's promise to Abraham arises simply out of God's free goodness and initiative. Following the offering of Isaac, God's promise has a twofold basis: It continues to be grounded most deeply in God, but now it is grounded also in Abraham's unreserved faithfulness and obedience. Thus, when in Genesis 26:1–5 God conveys the Abrahamic promise onto Isaac, the basis of that promise lies partly in Abraham's obedience to God (26:5). It is fitting, therefore, that the promise to Isaac includes, for the second time, the precise expression that first appeared in Genesis 22:17, for Genesis 26:3–4 has God say, "I will fulfill the oath that I swore to your father Abraham. *I will multiply your descendants* [NRSV, "I will make your offspring as numerous"] *as the stars of heaven.*"

Within Jewish understandings of God's continuing faithfulness with the people even when they sin, there is a tradition that understands that faithfulness to rest in part on Abraham's offering of Isaac. That is, when Israel sins and breaks the covenant, God forgives the community and continues with them for the sake of Abraham's faithful covenant obedience in offering Isaac. In some versions of this interpretation, even the sacrificial offerings in the tabernacle and later in the temple derive their efficacy from the offering of Isaac. Moses' intercessory language in Exodus 32:13, by the way it echoes language in Genesis 22, may imply that he also appeals implicitly to Abraham's offering of Isaac as a basis for God's continuing faithfulness to faithless Israel. When he does this, God "thinks better" of the judgment that had been threatened. We shall later encounter further evidence of such an appeal to the ancestors.

At the beginning of the discussion of chapters 32—34, I suggested that there is a deep congruence between the portrayal of the fall in Genesis 2—3 and Israel's fall from covenant loyalty to God through the golden calf. I suggested further, as one lesson from all this, that in every generation and every individual, our wrongful acts are our own responsibility yet also the result of a long and deep heritage of such acts by those in our past. Taken by itself, this can give a very disheartening picture of the human condition and the human prospect. The fact that our situation is not worse, and that it holds within it resources of grace and hope, is owing to the grace of God. But it is owing also to the faithfulness and obedience of those before us who have lived in loyal response to God. In the Old Testament, that loyal response comes to supreme expression in Abraham. In the New Testament, it is embodied in Jesus Christ.

If sin lays down patterns of defective behavior that can bedevil later generations, covenant faithfulness lays down patterns of grace-filled behavior that can bless later generations and provide them with resources of encouragement, communion, and strength. One may think of Hebrews 11:1–12:4 or of the "sincere faith" of young Timothy, "a faith that lived first in your grandmother Lois and your mother Eunice and now, I am sure, lives in you" (2 Tim. 1:5). This last example calls to mind a seminary student who joined a class exercise in which each student worked out his or her "genogram," a diagram of family relations and significant influences. As he presented his genogram and narrated it for us, we learned that his female ancestors and relatives were all women of profound faith and goodness, whereas in nearly every instance his male relatives had problems with addiction to alcohol and drugs. He was the first male in the diagram to embody from childhood the women's pattern of faith. The issues of human legacy come to another form of expression in Exodus 20:5–6 (see comments there). There, the greater weight of good legacies over bad should save us from being disheartened, even within the strictures of the Mount Sinai traditions, and move us to a grateful celebration of the heroines and heroes of faithfulness in our past.

MOSES' WRATH
Exodus 32:15–20

32:15 Then Moses turned and went down from the mountain, carrying the two tablets of the covenant in his hands, tablets that were written on both sides, written on the front and on the back. 16 The tablets were the work of God, and the writing was the writing of God, engraved upon the tablets. 17 When Joshua heard the noise of the people as they shouted, he said to Moses, "There is a noise of war in the camp." 18 But he said,

"It is not the sound made by victors,
or the sound made by losers;
it is the sound of revelers that I hear."

19 As soon as he came near the camp and saw the calf and the dancing, Moses' anger burned hot, and he threw the tablets from his hands and broke them at the foot of the mountain. 20 He took the calf that they had made, burned it with fire, ground it to powder, scattered it on the water, and made the Israelites drink it.

Sometimes in scripture when prayer is offered, God is shown immediately acting in response (for example, in 17:4–6). In the present instance, the narrator tells us that God responds favorably to Moses' intercession

(32:14), but it is not clear that God communicates this immediately to Moses. From the way Moses continues to intercede in chapters 32—33, it is not even clear that God's "change of mind" occurs all at once. It may be that verse 14 gives us advance notice of the outcome of Moses' overall mediation with God, beginning with the pivotal first intercession. We are allowed to imagine that Moses goes down the mountain not knowing what difference his prayer may have made with God.

The narrator now picks up a theme introduced in 24:12 and reiterated in 31:28 at the end of the tabernacle instructions. Whereas in 24:4 Moses had written down all the "words of the LORD" in preparation for the covenant-sealing ceremony, in 24:12 God had spoken of "the tablets of stone, with the law and the commandment, which I have written for their instruction." In 31:18, this shift was even more pointed, as the covenant tablets were said to be "written with the finger of God." Now in 32:16 it is reiterated that "the tablets were the work of God, and the writing was the writing of God." Why is there this emphasis? Is a contrast being made between the calf as "the work of human hands" (Psalm 115:4; 135:15; and often) and the covenant as ultimately coming from the hand of God? (Compare the tabernacle, which is the work of human artisans but ultimately the work of God because the artisans are said to have a spirit of wisdom and skill from God and their work embodies the pattern shown to Moses on the mountain.)

We have already reflected on what Joshua and Moses hear as they come down (32:17–18). When Moses draws closer and sees what is actually going on, his response (like God's in v. 10) is anger. His first experience of God had been the sight of a bush that burned and yet was not consumed. Why was it not consumed? The flame that enveloped the bush was the intense, holy compassion of God for the Israelites in their oppression (2:23–25; 3:7–9), a compassion rooted in God's kinship relation and promise to the ancestors. At the bush, Moses was drawn into that compassion until it overcame his resistance and moved him to act on Israel's behalf. Now he has spent forty days atop Mount Sinai, within the cloud, where "the appearance of the glory of the LORD was like a devouring fire" (24:17). The significance of this fire is spelled out in the Decalogue and the following laws, where it comes to intense focus in the announcement, "I the LORD your God am a jealous God" (20:5). Are the flames of God at the bush and atop Mount Sinai two different flames, or are they two aspects of one and the same flame, as the word "jealous/zealous" suggests (see at 20:5)? Does it suggest to us that zeal for the moral and spiritual integrity of the beloved has its root in compassion for the beloved? Does it indicate that the wrath of God is the shadow cast by the flame of the love of God, when that love is betrayed through fundamental infidelity? As at the bush, so now at Mount Sinai, Moses is drawn into the flame until it moves him to act in its spirit.

First, Moses breaks the tablets written by God's finger. Some propose that Moses, acting on God's behalf, tears up the covenant document to cancel it so that its provisions for dire judgment need not determine God's actions toward the people. That is an attractive interpretation, but Moses' action arises out of his anger, not his compassion. So I take the breaking of the tablets to signify that the covenant has been broken.

Second, Moses destroys the idolatrous calf, burning it with the fire that embodies God's anger and his own. But why does he grind it to powder, scatter it on the water, and make the Israelites drink it? Perhaps we may interpret it against the background of Numbers 5:11–31, which prescribes a test for a wife suspected of sexual infidelity. The test, at its core, has the priest mix dust from the tabernacle floor with holy water, call for the woman to take an oath, and then have her drink the potion. The oath she takes means that, if she is innocent, she will be immune to the water's bitter effects and be able to conceive children; if she is guilty, her guilt will be manifest in her inability to carry a child to term. A Jewish scholar, H. C. Brichto, has proposed that, like this test for adultery, Moses' action at Mount Sinai is a test to ascertain who among the Israelites are the ringleaders behind the making of the calf. If Moses' action is such a test, the outcome will shortly become evident.

AARON'S EXCUSE
Exodus 32:21–24

> 32:21 **Moses said to Aaron, "What did this people do to you that you have brought so great a sin upon them?"** [22] **And Aaron said, "Do not let the anger of my LORD burn hot; you know the people, that they are bent on evil.** [23] **They said to me, 'Make us gods, who shall go before us; as for this Moses, the man who brought us up out of the land of Egypt, we do not know what has become of him.'** [24] **So I said to them, 'Whoever has gold, take it off'; so they gave it to me, and I threw it into the fire, and out came this calf!"**

Before acting on the results of the test in verse 20, Moses confronts Aaron, whose defense, as presented in most (but not all) English translations, looks like a buck-passing appeal to how he and Moses have so often already experienced the people in the wilderness: "they are bent on evil." But in

Hebrew the description is identical to the one in 5:19: "they were in trou-ble." In 5:19, the Hebrew supervisors found themselves and their people in a critical dilemma, full of danger, and they laid this as a charge against Moses. Here, I suggest, Aaron makes a similar plea. The people have found themselves in a fix because Moses, their deliverer, leader, and protector, is gone. In such a case, Aaron was trying to respond with pastoral relevance to the people's anxiety. (But his pastoral response has flown in the face of the theology of the covenant. Let congregations and pastors beware!)

Aaron is often seen as self-excusing in another way. Whereas 32:4 reads, "[Aaron] took the gold from them, formed it in a mold, and cast an image of a calf," in 32:24 Aaron himself says, "I threw [the gold] into the fire, and out came this calf!" The contradiction between the two verses may not be as obvious as the translation of verse 4 suggests. As an NRSV note points out, "Meaning of Hebrew uncertain." Some interpreters take the prob-lematical clause in verse 4 to say, "bound it up in a bag." Aaron then, in verse 24, spells out what happened: He threw this bag of gold into the fire, and the molten gold, as it solidified, took the form of a calf! Brichto points out that, in the ancient world generally, the image of a god was not con-sidered to be the work of human hands but the work of the gods them-selves. He proposes that, under the pressure of the crisis triggered by Moses' absence, Aaron's action was an enacted appeal to God for help. When out of the melted gold "came this calf," Aaron took it as a miracle, a sign from God that the calf would serve as an acceptable replacement for Moses as the embodiment of God's presence. For Brichto, the passage teaches that so-called miracles are not from God when they fly in the face of the Mount Sinai covenant and its laws.

We may compare these two verses about making the calf with the var-ious passages about writing the tablets. In 24:4, Moses wrote the covenant tablets while 24:12, 31:18, and 32:16 emphasize that God wrote them. Similarly, in 32:4 it is said that Aaron made the calf, while in 32:24 Aaron seems to want to imply that God made it. Given that both actions are at-tributed both to a man and to God, what makes the one acceptable and the other unacceptable? No easy answer can be given.

The issue is like the question of true and false prophecy. In Israel, var-ious prophets gave conflicting messages, all claiming to come from God. In some passages, the test is the presence or absence of God's spirit, ap-parently as marked by ecstatic behavior. In some instances, the test is whether the prophecy comes true (e.g., Deut. 18:21–22). In other in-stances, if the prophet announces "a sign or a wonder" (a miracle?) and it comes to pass, it is false if that prophet says, "Let us follow other gods . . .

and let us serve them" (Deut. 13:1–5), for a true prophet walks in the path of the first great prophet, Moses (Deut. 18:15–20). The fact that Israel's true prophets were often persecuted in their day while false prophets were followed is not just an index of the people's "stiff necks," though that is a prominent factor. It is also an index of the difficulty in "discerning the spirits," and in ascertaining what is of God and what is not of God. We typically desire that this difficulty be resolved by some neat formula that will save us the trouble of wrestling with the burning issues of the day. Yet the very neat formula we devise to relieve our anxiety may be an idol, and our very anxiety may be the beginning of a genuine "fear of the LORD," for the anxiety testifies to our awareness that we are not God and that only God will be sufficient for the situation. Such anxieties are to function as a spur to trust and patience, accepting the vulnerability of our situation in the wilderness. Though we may not know it yet, even as we are anxious, God is preparing for us a way forward that is beyond our wildest hopes.

Perhaps the fundamental example in the New Testament is the ascension of Jesus (Luke 24:50–53; Acts 1:1–11). Jesus' departure (and bodily absence) is followed, after several days, by the coming of the Holy Spirit. New Testament writers in various ways portray the Spirit as the new form of Jesus' presence and activity in the church and as the "pledge of our inheritance" (Eph. 1:14; see 2 Cor. 1:22; 5:5), the promise of a future that "no eye has seen, nor ear heard, nor the human heart conceived" (1 Cor. 2:9). It is in the context of such provision and assurance that we are encouraged to wrestle with the ongoing challenge to worship and serve God in spirit and in truth.

JUDGMENT ON THE RINGLEADERS
Exodus 32:25–29

> 32:25 When Moses saw that the people were running wild (for Aaron had let them run wild, to the derision of their enemies), 26 then Moses stood in the gate of the camp, and said, "Who is on the LORD's side? Come to me!" And all the sons of Levi gathered around him. 27 He said to them, "Thus says the LORD, the God of Israel, 'Put your sword on your side, each of you! Go back and forth from gate to gate throughout the camp, and each of you kill your brother, your friend, and your neighbor.'" 28 The sons of Levi did as Moses commanded, and about three thousand of the people fell on that day. 29 Moses said, "Today you have ordained yourselves for the service of the LORD, each one at the cost of a son or a brother, and so have brought a blessing on yourselves this day."

The reference to the people "running wild" has helped to create in many minds a picture of sexual orgy. The Hebrew verb calls for a closer look. Basically, the verb *para'* means "let go, let alone." In several places, it refers literally to "undoing or letting the hair down," and the noun *para'* means "locks, long hair." (In Judges 5:2, those who fight for Yahweh are said to have "long locks.") Elsewhere, the word can refer figuratively to unrestrained behavior. Thus, "Where there is no prophecy, the people *cast off restraint,* / but happy are those who *keep the law*" (Prov. 29:18). What is the precise sense of the word here in Exodus?

If the golden calf is a battle emblem and the people are engaged in a ritual celebration of God as divine warrior, it may be that they have let their hair down like the warriors of Judges 5:2. Moses sees that they have (like the first group in the proverb) acted in unrestrained violation of the *torah.*

It is remarkable that this verb, which does not occur often in the Bible, occurred once before in Exodus, again in connection with Aaron's activity. In chapter 5, where Moses and Aaron seek to persuade Pharaoh to let the people go and worship in the wilderness, Pharaoh accuses them of causing the people to slack off (*para'*) from their work (5:4). In this way they are undoing Pharaoh's authority, encouraging behavior unrestrained by his laws. Now Aaron has allowed the people to undo Yahweh's authority and engage in behavior unrestrained by God's laws. As the proverb says, "Where there is no prophecy, the people cast off restraint." It is not only that Moses the prophet is absent but also there is no mention in chapter 32 of the leadership in worship earlier given by "the prophet Miriam" (15:20). In the contrast between 15:1–21 and chapter 32, we see foreshadowed Israel's long story of worship that seeks to serve Yahweh but goes astray when it fails to heed its true prophets. To put this another way, if Aaron is the prototype for the pattern of Israel's repeated fall into idolatry, Miriam along with Moses is the prototype for the pattern of those prophets who are guardians of true worship. No wonder she is mentioned in Micah 6:1–8.

Now comes a grisly scene, as Israelites put their own friends and neighbors, and even members of their own families, to the sword. The spirit of religious tolerance instinctively cringes in protest. But in regard to the critical nature of the issues at stake, a spirit of lax tolerance will find little comfort in the New Testament. The same Jesus who in Mark 3:33–35 says, "Who are my mother and my brothers?" . . . "Whoever does the will of God is my brother and sister and mother" in Matthew 10:34–36 says (quoting Micah 7:6), "Do not think that I have come to bring peace to the earth; I have not come to bring peace, but a sword. For I have come to set a man against his father, and a daughter against her mother, and a daughter-in-law against her mother-in-law; and one's foes will be members of one's own household." The Greek text in verse 35 is even sharper than NRSV indicates, for its "set . . . against" translates a verb that means "cut in two." The sword Jesus brings will, in some instances, sever the closest of family relations.

Exodus 32:25–29 provides us with an example of a scriptural text that, taken by itself, can be used to sponsor and enforce the worst kind of zealous, fanatical intolerance in the name of God and religion. However, if we follow the biblical story through to its conclusion, we shall see that (like the theme of the sacrifice of Isaac) it will undergo repeated transformations until, under the impact of the teachings and the nonviolent warfare of Jesus on the cross, we will be restrained from acting it out literally. Its continuing importance lies in the graphic picture it gives of the grave crisis introduced into the covenant community by idolatry and the proper place of conflict and judgment, however nonviolent, within the community.

MOSES' SELF-OFFERING
IN ATONEMENT
Exodus 32:30–35

32:30 **On the next day Moses said to the people, "You have sinned a great sin. But now I will go up to the LORD; perhaps I can make atonement for your sin."** [31] **So Moses returned to the LORD and said, "Alas, this people has sinned a great sin; they have made for themselves gods of gold.** [32] **But now, if you will only forgive their sin—but if not, blot me out of the book that you have written."** [33] **But the LORD said to Moses, "Whoever has sinned against me I will blot out of my book.** [34] **But now go, lead the people to the place about which I have spoken to you; see, my angel shall go in front of you. Nevertheless, when the day comes for punishment, I will punish them for their sin."**

[35] **Then the LORD sent a plague on the people, because they made the calf—the one that Aaron made.**

Since Moses' intercession with God atop the mountain, the action has unfolded at the foot of the mountain. Now Moses prepares go back up the mountain. His words to the people suggest that as yet he has no clear idea how God feels about the people's "great sin." What he does hope is that he can "make atonement." On what does he base his hope? The verb *kipper*, "make atonement," is associated with the noun *kapporet*, which in

25:18 is translated "mercy seat." The mercy seat is mentioned again in 30:6, where God instructs that once a year the high priest shall *kipper* ("perform the rite of atonement") on the incense altar before the most holy place. In the instructions for the Day of Atonement (*yom kippur*) in Leviticus 16, the high priest is to enter the most holy place itself and sprinkle sacrificial blood on the mercy seat in atonement for the people's sins. This suggests one way of understanding Moses' proposal in Exodus 32:30. The tabernacle is not yet built, but the mountain itself is the "sanctuary" of God; so Moses proposes to return to its summit (its "most holy place") and do what the instructions in 25:18 and 30:1–10 give him some basis for hoping may be possible. Though he may not yet have a direct response to his intercession, he places his hope in the provision God has previously made to atone for sin.

So Moses goes up the mountain, and again we hear him pray. First, on behalf of the people he confesses the "great sin." Then he asks God to forgive their sin. He goes so far as to propose that, if God is unable or unwilling simply to forgive them, he will undergo God's judgment in their place, by being blotted out of the book in which the members of the covenant community are registered (compare Psalm 87:5–6; Rev. 21:27). In other words, he offers himself as a sacrifice whose blood will atone for the sin of the community. Is he inspired in part by the offering of Isaac in Genesis 22 and his own implicit appeal to that offering in Exodus 32:13?

In response, God agrees to continue with the people as a whole but announces summary judgment on those individuals who have sinned. (This lends support to Brichto's interpretation of verse 20 as a test to find the ringleaders and of verses 25–29 as the judgment on those ringleaders.) Yet the people as a whole are not wholly out from under the cloud. In place of God's direct leadership, we now hear of an angel who will go before them. Moreover, God reserves the right to bring timely judgment on the people—a reminder that the words to the people at Marah (15:26) were not spoken idly.

RESUMING THE JOURNEY
Exodus 33:1–6

> 33:1 The LORD said to Moses, "Go, leave [Hebrew, "go up from"] this place, you and the people whom you have brought up out of the land of Egypt, and go to the land of which I swore to Abraham, Isaac, and Jacob, saying, 'To your descendants I will give it.' 2 I will send an angel before you, and I will

drive out the Canaanites, the Amorites, the Hittites, the Perizzites, the Hivites, and the Jebusites. ³ Go up to a land flowing with milk and honey; but I will not go up among you, or I would consume you on the way, for you are a stiff-necked people."

⁴ When the people heard these harsh words, they mourned, and no one put on ornaments. ⁵ For the LORD had said to Moses, "Say to the Israelites, 'You are a stiff-necked people; if for a single moment I should go up among you, I would consume you. So now take off your ornaments, and I will decide what to do to you.'" ⁶ Therefore the Israelites stripped themselves of their ornaments, from Mount Horeb onward.

The exodus is often portrayed in the Bible by the use of the verbs, "go up/bring up," and "go out/bring out." The first pictures deliverance as being raised from a deep hole or pit (compare 2:10; Psalm 40:1–3; Jer. 38:1–13; Jon. 2:1–6). The second pictures deliverance as being released from a place of confinement (compare Isa. 42:7; 52:11–12). Here, "go up" (Hebrew), together with with "brought up from Egypt," suggests that in making the calf the people have "dug a deep hole" and fallen into it (Psalm 7:15). So, in being called to lead this people "up," as he led them up from Egypt, Moses is being asked to act once again for their redemption. This time, however, the redemption is not from innocent oppression under an evil power but from the entrapping "pit" of their own sin and guilt. The redemption will fulfill God's promise to the ancestors—a further hint to Moses that God heard his intercession in 32:13.

The provision of an angel "before you" to drive out the inhabitants of the land reiterates the promise in 23:20–23. Such a reiteration (like the "land flowing with milk and honey," echoing 3:8), reassures Moses that God's pre-calf agenda is back on track. Yet "I will not go up among you" indicates that Israel's sin distances it from God. This is not simply a punishment, however. It is, at the same time, a gracious means through which God can continue the original agenda without "consuming" the people (32:10).

The people are now called to take off their ornaments, so that God may know what to do with them. Their stiff-neckedness may, of course, lead them (like Pharaoh and like later Israelites) to refuse to listen to this call to repentance, or they may repent and submit to God's call. Only in seeing what they do will God know what to do with them. This is how seriously God respects human freedom (compare Jer. 18:1–17).

The people strip off their ornaments and mourn (v. 4), from Horeb onward (v. 6). In recent years, we have become accustomed to the need for "grief work." (When I was a child, bereaved people no longer wore "widow's weeds," but whenever a Catholic in our town died, family and friends would for six months wear a rectangular black patch sewn or pinned onto their cap, coat, shirt, or dress. The "statement" was not loud, but it spoke in its own way of what lay on these people's hearts.) In addition to grief work, the Bible knows of the need for "guilt work," a process of working through the guilt and shame incurred in betraying a kin or covenant relationship. We see it in Jacob's long exile in Genesis 28—33, in Isaiah 40:2, and in Hosea 3:1–5. In this last passage, the Northern Kingdom, following its destruction, is to remain for a considerable time without the normal institutions of "church and state." This is symbolized in terms of an adulterous wife who is "quarantined" from having any kind of normal sexual relations. What is remarkable is that God is portrayed as similarly observing such a quarantine. In Exodus 33:4–6, guilt work and grief work merge, as the people mourn the loss of the relationship their sin has caused. (Compare William Cowper's hymn, "O for a closer walk with God," which could have been written on this passage.)

PARENTHESIS:
MOSES AND GOD IN THE TENT
Exodus 33:7–11

> 33:7 **Now Moses used to take the tent and pitch it outside the camp, far off from the camp; he called it the tent of meeting. And everyone who sought the LORD would go out to the tent of meeting, which was outside the camp. ⁸ Whenever Moses went out to the tent, all the people would rise and stand, each of them, at the entrance of their tents and watch Moses until he had gone into the tent. ⁹ When Moses entered the tent, the pillar of cloud would descend and stand at the entrance of the tent, and the LORD would speak with Moses. ¹⁰ When all the people saw the pillar of cloud standing at the entrance of the tent, all the people would rise and bow down, all of them, at the entrance of their tent. ¹¹ Thus the LORD used to speak to Moses face to face, as one speaks to a friend. Then he would return to the camp; but his young assistant, Joshua son of Nun, would not leave the tent.**

The step-by-step reconciliation between God and Israel is now interrupted. In an aside to the reader, the narrator describes what used to happen in regard to God's presence with the people. Such a presence ("the LORD used to speak to Moses face to face, as one speaks to a friend," v. 11) contrasts with God's words in verses 3, 5, and sets up Moses' question in verse 18 and God's response in verses 19–23.

There are good arguments for taking this aside as a momentary glance forward to what will happen in the future as the people set out from the mountain, but I take it as referring backward. In that case, the tent would not be the full-blown tabernacle of chapters 25—31 but a more modest tent shrine befitting desert dwellers who practiced a form of kinship religion. It is the sort of religion Moses' father-in-law may well have practiced and that Moses would have participated in as his son-in-law. Also, it would resemble the kinship religion of Israel's ancestors in Genesis 12—50. Following Moses' encounter with the "God of the fathers" at the burning bush, we may suppose that he became the leader in a tent-centered ritual during the trek from Egypt to Mount Sinai. Indeed, some have taken the "tent" in 18:7 to be such a sanctuary (compare 18:12). If, then, 33:7–11 refers backward, we are shown how Moses used to meet with God in such a tent of meeting, on behalf of anyone who "sought the LORD." In such a mediating role, Moses himself would enjoy a "face-to-face" meeting with God, "as one speaks to a friend." Such a note of intimacy would be at home in a kinship relation to God as parent of the family or clan head.

FURTHER INTERCESSION
Exodus 33:12–16

33:12 **Moses said to the LORD, "See, you have said to me, 'Bring up this people'; but you have not let me know whom you will send with me. Yet you have said, 'I know you by name, and you have also found favor in my sight.' 13 Now if I have found favor in your sight, show me your ways, so that I may know you and find favor in your sight. Consider too that this nation is your people." 14 He said, "My presence will go with you, and I will give you rest." 15 And he said to him, "If your presence will not go, do not carry us up from here. 16 For how shall it be known that I have found favor in your sight, I and your people, unless you go with us? In this way, we shall be distinct, I and your people, from every people on the face of the earth."**

Following the parenthetical aside, the narrator picks up the scene from verses 1–6. Moses objects to what God has just proposed by ignoring God's provision of the angel. Hearing God's repeated resolve not to "go up among you" (vv. 3, 5), he asks to know whom God will send with him. It is as though his own past relation with God, on the mountain and in the tent, entitles him to a more immediate presence than the angel. After all, at the bush God had promised, "I will be [*ehyeh*] with you" (3:12), and "I will be [*ehyeh*] with your mouth." The way these two statements had echoed the verb God had used to interpret the divine name "Yahweh" (*ehyeh asher ehyeh*, "I will be who/what I will be"), Moses might well look for a form of divine presence more closely connected with Yahweh's own name.

Of course, in 23:20–21 God had said to Israel, concerning the "angel in front of you" that "my name is in him." But apparently even that is not good enough for Moses. He reminds God, "You have said, 'I know you by name, and you have also found favor in my sight.'" Moses may here be referring to God's initial call to him at the bush, where God said, "Moses, Moses" (3:4). But in the Bible, "knowing" also means "recognizing, acknowledging as legitimate," and such acknowledgment is often signaled by giving God's name to the one known (as in Isa. 43:7; Amos 9:12). If God at the bush showed favor (or grace) to Moses by making known to him the divine name, Moses now would like a similar disclosure as an assurance of God's continuing favor toward him.

Only now does he shift from his own relation with God to the people's relation to God. In 33:1 (as in 32:7) God had referred to them as "your people." Continuing his intercessory efforts, Moses again (as in 32:11) refers them back to God as "your people." God responds, "My presence ["my face"] will go with you, and I will give you rest." (This "rest" is the gift of entry into the land and freedom there from enemy attack [see, e.g., Deut. 3:20; 2 Sam. 7:8–11].) In response, Moses asks, "If *your* presence [literally, "face"] will not go," and then says, "unless *you* go with us," as if to request that God's "face" mean, not just the angel or some other proxy, but God's very own self. In this way Moses and God's people will "be *distinct* . . . from every people on the face of the earth."

Thus Moses implicitly appeals to God's original intent that this people should be a "distinct" people, "a priestly kingdom and a holy nation" (19:3–6). To be sure, their "distinctness" is to be marked by their conformity to wise and just laws such as no other nation enjoys (Deut. 4:5–6, 8). But their distinctness is to be even more clearly marked by the presence in their midst of a God as gracious and responsive to prayer as Yahweh (Deut. 4:7).

GLORY HIDDEN IN MERCY
Exodus 33:17–23

> 33:17 The LORD said to Moses, "I will do the very thing that you have asked; for you have found favor in my sight, and I know you by name." ¹⁸ Moses said, "Show me your glory, I pray." ¹⁹ And he said, "I will make all my goodness pass before you, and will proclaim before you the name, "The LORD";

and I will be gracious to whom I will be gracious, and will show mercy on whom I will show mercy. [20] But," he said, "you cannot see my face; for no one shall see me and live." [21] And the LORD continued, "See, there is a place by me where you shall stand on the rock; [22] and while my glory passes by I will put you in a cleft of the rock, and I will cover you with my hand until I have passed by; [23] then I will take away my hand, and you shall see my back; but my face shall not be seen."

Once again God agrees to Moses' request. So Moses takes matters one step further: "Let me see your glory." What is he asking for? Is it a final sign that the breach opened up by the idolatry of the calf is now completely healed? What would such a sign be? Might it be some form of the sign God gave when the covenant was first sealed? At that point, God had allowed Moses, Aaron, Nadab, and Abihu, and seventy of the elders of Israel to see God without coming to any harm and, in the presence of that amazing sight, to eat and to drink (24:9–11). Moreover, following that, Moses had ascended into the cloud of God's glory and into its consuming fire, without being consumed. If God would again let Moses see his glory, he would know that all was well. This time he asks more than is possible. Given the gravity of Israel's sin, "no one shall see me and live."

It is remarkable how often commentators read verse 20 as a free-standing statement whose universal truth needs no context for its understanding or interpretation. Because the verse is taken as a universal truth, it is then used as a guide to the interpretation of such passages as 24:9–11. But if it is a universal truth, then the human hope of beatific vision is doomed to everlasting disappointment. Then Jesus' beatitude "blessed are the pure in heart, for they shall see God" is empty or reduced to a mere figure of speech. Then the solemn oath of Sir Thomas More loses all of its force when, in the climactic scene of Bolt's *A Man for All Seasons*, he answers the charge of his false accuser with the words, "If what this man says is true, may I never see God in the face." But if "I bore you on eagle's wings and brought you to myself" finds its climax in 24:9–11, then the negatives in Exodus 33:20 are not intrinsic and universal, but circumstantial. A person, a community, that stands in the aftermath of such covenant betrayal cannot see God's face and live.

Yet in spite of the deep hurt and blazing anger that such a betrayal stirs in the heart of God, God does not seek the death of the betrayers but their life—therefore, the response, "I will make all my goodness pass before you." As in English, so in Hebrew, the word "goodness" is the most all-encompassing positive word in the language, including but going

beyond all more specific positive qualities. Paul makes a revealing statement when in Romans 5:6–7 he compares a "good" person favorably to
a "righteous" person. It is better to be righteous than wicked; yet righteousness can fall short of goodness. I remember a "righteous" elderly
couple years ago in a rural congregation. They lived morally impeccable
lives. But their righteousness had a coldly upright character, for they
would have nothing to do with their scapegrace son. He had violated the
laws of God and society, and righteousness called for his banishment
from the farm and from parental communication. Goodness calls for
something more.

So God says, "I will make all my goodness pass before you," by proclaiming before him the name "Yahweh." How will that show Moses
God's goodness? At the bush, in the face of Israel's oppression under the
power of Pharaoh, the divine name meant, "I will be who I will be." Here,
in the face of Israel's penitential mourning under the burden of their own
sin and guilt, that same name is interpreted to mean "I will be gracious to
whom I will be gracious, and will show mercy on whom I will show mercy."
As comparison with the sentence at the bush suggests, this is not a statement about who will or will not receive grace and mercy but a statement
about the gracious and merciful character of God.

In exploring the meaning of the divine name at the bush, I suggested
that God's interpretation of the name to Moses set the name Yahweh free
from limitations that might be imposed upon its meaning through past experiences. If, in the past, God was experienced and known as giver of human and cosmic fertility in situations of barrenness and famine, this
interpretation of the name Yahweh signified that God, while remaining
loyal to past promises, remains free to be whoever God needs to be in any
new situation.

We have seen that Pharaoh, who initially hardened his heart and
would not let the people go, finally came to the place where in his hardened heart he could not let them go. By then, he "couldn't want to." In
spite of easy talk about the need to forgive when one is wronged, deep
down we know how hard if not impossible that is when we have been
grievously wronged. Hurt and anger testify to an injustice that calls for
justice to be done. Not to hold what others have done against them can
amount to condoning the wrong and colluding with the wrongdoers in
it. But then, by degrees, the hurt and the anger can settle into such a firm
disposition that the wronged are no longer free from their hurt and
anger, nor even wish to be. They take pleasure or consolation in nursing
their grievance in the name of a sense of justice. Aggrieved righteousness

then becomes its own prison, destroying the possibility of further relationship. But where the wrongdoer has been so moved to repentance as to "mourn" the wrong and the loss of relationship, moral and spiritual freedom manifests itself in the ability of the one wronged to be gracious and merciful.

If we are honest, we will sympathize with those who said to Jesus, "Who can forgive sins but God alone?" (Mark 2:7). The marvel that is at the center of Exodus 33:19 is that God is free to want to and will do so. Because of the sort of testimony borne in this Old Testament passage, the angel in the New Testament can say of the child born to Mary, "you are to name him Jesus [Yahweh saves], for he will save his people from their sins" (Matthew 1:21).

Yet for all the wonder of such grace and mercy, it is not God's "face," but God's "backside." How is this a positive mercy? Recalling how shame makes us want to hide from the gaze of another or to wish another would turn away from us and not look at us, we may look to Psalm 51:9 for a clue: "Hide your face from my sins, / and blot out all my iniquities." God's "backside" is God's gracious and merciful willingness not to look on us accusingly in our shame and guilt. Still, when God's face and gaze are turned aside in this way, the anxious question may arise as to whether the momentary vision of God and God's glory in 24:9–11 has been irretrievably forfeited. Or does God's turning aside conceal a promise of glory to come, when the problem of sin has been adequately dealt with? That such a veiled promise is realized in Christ is Paul's testimony in 2 Corinthians 3:7–4:6. Such testimony also underlies Romans 5:1–5, when Paul begins by talking about the reconciliation and peace found through the grace of God in Christ, goes on to speak of "our hope of sharing the glory of God," and ends with the conviction that "hope does not disappoint us, because God's love has been poured into our hearts through the Holy Spirit that has been given to us." Such also is the testimony of the writer in 1 John 3:1–3, who begins by saying, "See what love the Father has given us, that we should be called children of God; and that is what we are." This writer then goes on to say, "Beloved, we are God's children now; what we will be has not yet been revealed. What we do know is this: when he is revealed, we will be like him, for we will see him as he is. And all who have this hope in him purify themselves, just as he is pure." Such testimony underscores the conviction that, however seriously sin may affect our relationship with God and our present experience of God's presence, it will not forever cancel out the promise implicit in the brief dreamlike experience of 24:9–11.

STARTING OVER
Exodus 34:1–4

> 34:1 **The LORD said to Moses, "Cut two tablets of stone like the former ones,
> and I will write on the tablets the words that were on the former tablets,
> which you broke. ² Be ready in the morning, and come up in the morning to
> Mount Sinai and present yourself there to me, on the top of the mountain.
> ³ No one shall come up with you, and do not let anyone be seen throughout
> all the mountain; and do not let flocks or herds graze in front of that moun-
> tain." ⁴ So Moses cut two tablets of stone like the former ones; and he rose
> early in the morning and went up on Mount Sinai, as the LORD had com-
> manded him, and took in his hand the two tablets of stone.**

Because verses 6–7 contain the climactic revelation of this section (chapters 32—34), it is easy to hurry over verses 1–4 as a mere introduction. But
the repeated phrase "like the former ones" (vv. 1, 4; literally, "like the
first") suggests that even though the idolatry of the calf was the gravest of
sins, Israel was not left with God's second best but was given a chance to
start all over again by covenanting with God just like the first time.

This passage may be illuminated by comparing it to a human situation
that occurs often, the experience of people previously married and then divorced as they prepare to remarry and thus take the marriage vows a second time. The vows in the previous marriage, in spite of the original
wholehearted intention, did not prove binding "until we are parted by
death," but had been dissolved. How can one presume to vow again "until we are parted by death" when these words, precisely because they sound
exactly "like the first ones," would only echo mockingly in one's own
ears? It is as though one of the most sacred and self-defining of human
powers—the power to bind oneself by a vow and to hold to that vow—
has been called into question and suffered a crippling blow. The sense of
failure, compounded by guilt, has to do with issues of identity and self-
esteem. Better, perhaps, some other vow such as "so long as we are held
in the bonds of our mutual love"? Unless, beyond human self-help, there
might lie the possibility of being restored and healed by God in one's capacity to vow once again, "like the first time," with full intention, knowing more profoundly this time that "I will" is shorthand for "I will, God
being my helper."

Just such a possibility is implied in God's instruction to Moses, and
Moses' compliance, in making two tablets "like the former ones" or "like
the first." In this connection, we may note that several prophets later liken
God's judgment and then redemptive restoration to a divorce and remar-

riage (Isa. 54:4–8; Jeremiah 3; Hos. 2:2–23; 3:1–5). The portrayal in Hosea 2:14–15 is especially interesting. What begins as a final judgment in "the wilderness" (2:3) turns out to be a return to the place of first courtship. There, God will "speak tenderly to her." There, amazingly, "she shall respond as in the days of her youth." When Jesus speaks to Nicodemus about being born "from above/again" (see NRSV text and note), readers have dwelt on the "requirement" aspect of the text ("you *must* be born again/ from above"). A "teacher of Israel" (John 3:10), versed in scripture, should not be surprised at such a call, for it only presses to a radical depth the need to start over from scratch, given such radical indictments as Deuteronomy 32:4–6, 15–18; Isaiah 1:1–4; and Hosea 1:2–9; 5:7, and such despairing assessments of the possibility of change as Jeremiah 13:23; 17:9; Psalm 38:1–8; and especially Psalm 51:5. But if Jesus' words come with the surgical force of a prophetic knife (compare Hos. 6:5; Heb. 4:12–13), they may also be heard as opening up a possibility that lies beyond human powers—the possibility of a new beginning. Such a possibility is in the deepest continuity with God's instruction to Moses to make two tablets "like the first." If 34:1–4 serve as an introduction to 34:5–7, we can appreciate how aptly these verses set the stage.

But does not 33:20, after all, leave us with God's second best? Then again, if the covenant of 20:1–23:19, sealed so wholeheartedly in 24:3–8, could result in the vision of God in 24:9–11, how can the prohibition in 33:20 be everlasting? If new tablets are made "like the first" and a covenant therefore is entered into "like the first," does this not hint that by God's grace this covenant, too, will eventually somehow issue in beatific vision?

WHAT'S HIDDEN IN A NAME?
Exodus 34:5–7

> 34:5 The LORD descended in the cloud and stood with him there, and proclaimed the name, "The LORD." 6 The LORD passed before him, and proclaimed,
>> "The LORD, the LORD,
>> a God merciful and gracious,
>> slow to anger,
>> and abounding in steadfast love and faithfulness,
>> 7 keeping steadfast love for the thousandth generation,
>> forgiving iniquity and transgression and sin,
>> yet by no means clearing the guilty,
>> but visiting the iniquity of the parents

**upon the children
and the children's children,
to the third and the fourth generation."**

In 33:19, to "proclaim . . . the name, 'The LORD,'" was to unpack its meaning by the sentence, "I will be gracious to whom I will be gracious, and will
show mercy on whom I will show mercy." Now, to proclaim the name,
"The LORD," is to follow it with two adjectives from the two verbs in 33:19
and then with a number of phrases that further spell out what those two adjectives mean in the face of human sin. The character of God, as disclosed
in the divine name "Yahweh," consists in mercy and grace, steadfast love
and faithfulness. Such a God responds to human transgression and sin with
a forgiveness that is never to be mistaken for winking at or condoning, let
alone colluding in, the iniquity that humankind is capable of. With this
summary comment, let us now look at the various terms more closely.

The first adjective is Hebrew *rahum*, for which the lexicon gives the primary meaning "compassionate." Like the verb in 33:19 and the related
noun *rahamim*, "compassion," this adjective is formed from the noun
rehem, "womb." Some take these words to refer to "brotherly feeling (of
those born from the same womb)." I follow those who hold that they refer to the feeling a mother has for the children whom she carries and feels
in her womb, then carries in her arms and nurses at her breast, and afterward continues in faithful compassion toward them. As contemporary
studies in mother-child relations suggest, such motherly feeling is the first
context and climate of the infant's experience, an experience that may begin already within the womb (compare Judges 13:7; Psalm 22:9–10), and
remains the child's primary horizon until weaning (in the ancient world as
late as the third or fourth year). Thus the mother's compassion (*rahamim*)
is the continuing matrix (*rehem*) of the child's own nurture and growth in
relational feeling. If such relational feeling is the foundation of morality,
the mother's compassion is the child's first schooling in moral relations.
When the child, then, whether male or female, shows compassion to others, that child is relating to them in a manner learned from the mother. Of
course, children need not have learned this only from their mothers. If all
persons, male and female, have gone to primary school to their mothers or
mother-surrogates, then it is possible for fathers, too—indeed, all members of the family and wider community—to relate to children compas-
sionately and thereby to play a part in their moral and spiritual formation.

Thus, the first adjective, *rahum*, indicates the familial connection of the
affirmation that God is first of all "merciful." Throughout this companion

to the book of Exodus, I have drawn attention to how the exodus story is grounded in God's earlier relation to Israel's ancestors of Genesis 12—50. I have noted how the "kinship" (or family-clan) religion of the ancestors may be distinguished in several respects from the "covenant" (or nation-state) religion of Israel starting with Moses. One feature of this distinction lies in the way relationships are spoken of. The relations of *kinship*, and the religion appropriate to it, are governed by compassion, steadfast love (*ḥesed*, "loyalty"), and faithfulness (*'emet*). The Mount Sinai *covenant* relations are governed by ethical, social, and ceremonial commandment, statute, and ordinance, summed up in the term *torah*, "instruction, teaching, law," aiming at justice. These two sets of moral frameworks need not be opposed, for they both arise out of the same concern for the well-being of human life, but they often have a different feel to them. The first set often has a more personal flavor (of interrelating with those one knows and has feelings for). The second set often has a more impersonal flavor (of interrelating with fellow citizens one does not know personally). Indeed, one positive feature of "equality before the law" is that judicial decisions are not based on personal relationships but on evidence, testimony, and laws that should apply the same way to everyone regardless of who they are or whom they know.

Now, as the exodus story began, God was known primarily in the character of El Shaddai, giver of the blessings of cosmic generativity and of "blessings of the breasts [*šedayim*] and of the womb [*reḥem*]" (Gen. 49:25). Implicit in these blessings would be the blessing of compassion. (It is not accidental that *raḥamim*, "compassion, mercy," makes its first appearance in Genesis 43:14 in association with El Shaddai, and its second in 43:30 [NRSV "overcome with affection" translates "his compassion/mercy became warm"].) If God was also known as Yahweh, this name, too, at that time, was associated with issues of barrenness and famine, fertility and fruitfulness. As we saw in Exodus 1—2, God as known in this way continued to be active in the births of the Hebrew children in Egypt and in the activities of the midwives, Moses' mother and sister, and Pharaoh's daughter. But in the face of a new human crisis—political oppression—the story of divine revelation took a decisive new step. At the burning bush, the name Yahweh was given a new meaning. This development was summed up in Exodus 6:3–8. After that point, the name El Shaddai has not again been encountered in Exodus.

Where has El Shaddai been since 6:3? Is Yahweh no longer a God of field and flock, of breast and womb, of steadfast love and faithfulness? That cannot be, for the very motivation for the exodus, as well as the motivation for compassion in the face of the idolatry of the calf, lies in God's continuing relation to the ancestors (2:23–25; 3:6, 15; 32:13; 33:1). This suggests that God as El Shaddai continues to be present implicitly within God as "I will be who I will be." This becomes evident when God, echoing Exodus 3:14, says to Moses, "I will be gracious to whom I will be gracious, and will show mercy on whom I will show mercy." Moreover, the language of 34:6 does not employ *elohim*, the normal term for God, but the rarer term, *el*. The proclamation thus begins, "Yahweh, Yahweh, *El rahum we-hanun*," "The LORD, the LORD, a God merciful and compassionate." If this whole expression is reminiscent of 3:15, "Yahweh, the God of your fathers," the element *El rahum* is parallel to *El Shaddai*.

The significance of 33:19 and 34:6 is that, in the face of Israel's most grievous covenant betrayal, El Shaddai, as hidden within the divine name Yahweh "flame[s] out, like shining from shook foil" (Gerard Manley Hopkins, "God's Grandeur"), and becomes manifest as El Rahum we-Hanun, "God compassionate and gracious." This is to suggest that El Rahum we-Hanun not only exegetes the divine name Yahweh but also does so in terms of El Shaddai. Other examples of Yahweh "flaming out" in the character of El Shaddai may be seen in Isaiah 49:13–18 and 66:5–13.

What of the second adjective, *hanun*? Unlike *rahum*, this adjective is not built out of a concrete noun but out of the verb *hanan*. In Hebrew this verb means "to yearn toward, long for, be merciful, compassionate, favorably inclined toward." The Hebrew adverb *hinnam* means "freely, without cause, undeservedly." The noun *hen* means "favor, grace." This noun's most frequent occurrence is in the expression "find favor in someone's eyes," an expression that occurs no less than six times in the context of 34:6 (33:12, 13, 13, 16, 17; 34:9). Let us take this expression as a guide to the basic meaning of the *hanan* group of words. What is involved is looking at someone and viewing that person with favor. One may view that person with favor because of qualities seen there (as sometimes in the Bible) or "freely, without cause, undeservedly" in spite of what one sees there. Of course, the first pair of eyes in which every person finds favor is the eyes of that person's mother or mother surrogate. Infants are adored for what they are and for what they may become, but not in a calculating way. The infant is adored because the nature of a "good enough mother" is to adore the child of her own womb. (In so doing, she images the God of Genesis 1, who looks at each created thing and sees it to be good.) Even for the child who has been naughty and must be firmly or even severely dealt with, the mother's enduring favor is the final basis of such action.

I suggested before that every person learns compassion at the mother's breast and also from other older family and community members, male or female, who had learned to receive and show it in their infant relation to their mothers. As an example, I cited Joseph in the reconciliation scene with his brothers in Egypt. This scene illustrates how the "favor/grace" word (*hanan, hen, hanun*) fits into the same context. When Jacob allows the brothers to return to Egypt and take Benjamin with them, he says, "May El Shaddai [God Almighty] grant you mercy [*rahamim*] before the man" (Gen. 43:13). When the brothers arrive in Joseph's presence, and he looks up and sees "his brother Benjamin, his mother's son," he says, "God be gracious [the verb *hanan*] to you, my son!" and he is flooded with a sense of warm compassion (*rahamim*) (43:29–30).

The two adjectives in Exodus 34:6 that gather up the re-interpretation of the name Yahweh in 33:19 are adjectives that disclose the parental heart of God toward the covenant people, even in the face of its most grievous betrayal. Further, the descriptions of God that follow in 34:6–7 are not additional to the first two adjectives but spell out in various ways what those first two adjectives imply. The first elaboration, in verse 6, is "slow to anger." The Hebrew idiom, literally translated, would mean "long of nose." God's anger does not, as we might say, "burn on a short fuse"! This is not to say that God never becomes angry, but the anger is held in check and comes into play only as needed for the sake of the moral quality of the covenant community. Especially in the context of the idolatry of the calf, there is a certain wisdom in giving this reassurance up front.

The second elaboration, also in verse 6, is "abounding in steadfast love [*hesed*] and faithfulness [*'emet*]" The first term, *hesed*, by itself refers to the tie that binds kin together in mutual loyalty and help. The help that *hesed* offers shapes itself to fit the need in a given situation. The second term, *'emet*, refers to what is enduring and reliable. Sometimes it is translatable as "truth," in the sense of being true to a relationship. The yoked phrase, *hesed*-and-*'emet*, "steadfast love and faithfulness," which occurs so very many times in the Bible, refers to a loyalty that is enduring and reliable.

The third elaboration, in verse 7a, continues the positive emphasis of the second, showing how "steadfast love and faithfulness" act in the face of what may go wrong in the covenant relation. They act to "keep" (that is, to observe and thereby preserve) *hesed* to the thousandth generation, by "forgiving iniquity and transgression and sin." The Hebrew word that "forgiving" translates here is revealing. It means, literally, "bearing," presumably in the sense of "bearing with" or "putting up with." But "bearing with" comes at the cost of pain and sorrow to the one who bears, so, in a real sense, the forgiver is the one who bears the sin of the forgiven.

The fourth elaboration, in verse 7b, returns to the theme of anger in verse 6, lest the pronounced emphasis on forgiveness give the impression that God is indifferent to the wrongdoing. As the God of the one who has been wronged, God is also wronged. (Indeed, the lacerated conscience of the penitent in Psalm 51:4 testifies that the wrong done to another is most deeply a sin committed against God.) So for God's own sake and for the sake of the one wronged—but also for the sake of the wrongdoer, who is acting out of character as a child of God—God must uphold the truth of the wrongdoing. Not to do so would be to collude in the wrong and to conspire against the truth. (John's Gospel discusses these matters in terms of darkness and light, as in 1:14 and 3:16–21; see also 1 John 1:5–2:2.) If God's compassion and grace keep justice from becoming harsh and unyielding, God's justice keeps compassion and grace from becoming the kind of softness that indulges children in their peccadilloes until they become self-centered tyrants responsive to nothing but their own whims and appetites. But the imbalance between "the thousandth generation" and "the third and the fourth generation" suggests that God's justice is a component in God's mercy and grace, and not the other way around.

FINAL INTERCESSION
Exodus 34:8–9

34:8 **And Moses quickly bowed his head toward the earth, and worshiped.** **⁹ He said, "If now I have found favor in your sight, O LORD, I pray, let the LORD go with us. Although this is a stiff-necked people, pardon our iniquity and our sin, and take us for your inheritance."**

Moses' final intercession begins with the expression he has already used several times ("if I have found favor in your sight," 33:12, 13, 13, 16), and that God has also used toward him (33:17). In this way, he claims God's regard for him as one basis for his request on behalf of the people. The other basis is God's just-announced promise to forgive iniquity and sin. Supported by these two motives, he makes his request: "Let the LORD go with us" [or "among us" as in 33:3, 5]. But his prayer is also a confession. For his shift from "If *I* have found favor in your sight" to "let the LORD go among *us*" leads him also to say, "pardon *our* iniquity and *our* sin, and take *us* for your inheritance." Such is Moses' solidarity with the people that their sin becomes his sin, and in his confession they make their confession. Moses is that "favored" son of God in whom the people as God's "firstborn son" (4:21–23) confess their iniquity and their sin and seek God's forgiveness. Perhaps this passage helps us enter into the meaning of Paul's words in 2 Corinthians 5:21: "For our sake [God] made [Christ] to be sin who knew no sin, so that in him we might become the righteousness of God" (see also Rom. 8:1–4).

GOD'S AWESOME COVENANT
Exodus 34:10

> 34:10 He said: I hereby make a covenant. Before all your people I will perform marvels, such as have not been performed in all the earth or in any nation; and all the people among whom you live shall see the work of the LORD; for it is an awesome thing that I will do with you.

In 34:1–4, God instructs Moses to prepare two stone tablets, like the first, so that God can "write on the tablets the words that were on the former tablets." In spite of the grave sin of idolatry, God is going to renew the Sinai covenant as originally intended. Now we are told that there is something new about this covenant, something so new that God has to use the verb *bara'*, "create." (The NRSV "perform" is not strong enough.) We have not seen this verb since the creation story in Genesis 1:1–2:4a and references to that creation in Genesis 5:1–2 and 6:7. Its occurrence now implies that what God is promising to do is so marvelous that the only thing with which we can adequately compare it is the beginning of all things in the creation of the world. In what sense is this new beginning a "new creation"?

Let us review what has followed upon 34:1–4. First, God has given a definitive re-interpretation of the divine name Yahweh, in terms of mercy and grace, steadfast love and faithfulness, and a forgiveness of sins that far exceeds and outlasts such judgments as may be called for in Israel's moral and spiritual education. Then Moses has offered a concluding intercession for the people, in which he makes confession of sin on their behalf and claims for them the general provision for forgiveness that God has just made through the revelation of God's character. I agree with those commentators who understand God's promissory covenant in verse 10 to be in direct response to Moses' intercession. This means that the "marvels," such as have not previously been created "in all the earth or in any nation," are God's acts of forgiveness for Israel's sins of covenant breaking through idolatry. This truly is a "new creation," insofar as the relationship that was "dead" because of the idolatry is now brought back to life. The same sense of the meaning of forgiveness comes in Psalm 51, the most penitential of all the psalms: "Create [*bara'*] in me a clean heart, O God, and put a new and right spirit [or, "renew a right spirit"] within me" (v. 10). (The same basic picture is presented in John 3:1–10, where rebirth from above occurs by the same Spirit [3:8] as in Genesis 1:2 swept over the face of the waters just before God said, "Let there be light.")

God then says to Moses, "all the people among whom you live shall see the work of the LORD; for it is an awesome thing that I will do with you." Such profound forgiveness, deeper than the idolatry, is truly awesome. Yet we may wonder whether the claim in verse 10 is exaggerated. Has such forgiveness never been seen in all the earth, prior to Moses? Perhaps the language here expresses not so much an objective fact as the subjective sense of an individual or community under the impact of such an experience of forgiveness.

But verse 10 may touch on a truth deeper than simply the subjective sense of the marvel of forgiveness and restoration. Israel was surrounded by nations and peoples who worshiped many gods and for whom the proper worship of those gods included the making of images to represent them. Israel's covenant understanding, calling for worship of only one God, without the use of images, was a new thing among the nations. Within that covenant, worship of any other God or the use of an image to worship Yahweh was so grave an offense that the analogy for it would be small city-states that revolt against their imperial overlord and make alliance with the overlord's enemies. The ancient world well knew the typical military and political consequences of such revolt. Now, the Hebrew word for such political rebellion is *pesha'* (e.g., 1 Kings 12:19; 2 Kings 1:1). It is significant, then, that this word occurs in Exodus 34:7, where (appearing between "iniquity" and "sin") it is translated "transgression." Such transgression is much more than simply breaking this or that law. One can break a given law and still remain a citizen. But rebels are traitors against their own government and country and are everywhere punished most gravely. The "marvel" God "creates" in the eyes of the nations is that the majesty and overlordship of Israel's God is seen nowhere more vividly than in God's forgiveness of covenant rebellion, where it is confessed and repented of.

This "marvel" in the eyes of the nations is celebrated again in Micah 7:11–20, in reference to the exile. There, too, such forgiveness is characterized as a "marvelous thing" (7:15). There, too, as in Exodus 32—34, it comes on the basis of God's sworn promise to the ancestors, God's "faithfulness [*'emet*] to Jacob and unswerving loyalty [*hesed*] to Abraham" (7:20).

A final comment is needed on the relation between 34:1–4 and 34:10. While verses 1–4 imply that the covenant that is about to be made is the original covenant done over, verse 10 asserts that the covenant is a new thing, as new and unprecedented as the creation of the world. Here we have an important clue to how Christians should view the relation between the Old Testament and the New Testament. Especially in an age when youth is celebrated and the word "old" is at a discount, it is easy to dismiss the Old Testament simply because it is called Old and to concentrate exclusively on the New Testament as in every way obviously "superior." This is a tragic mistake, tragic because it is so harmful. Not only has it fed grievous acts of prejudice and persecution against Jews and their religion but also it has allowed Christians to entertain a distorted understanding of their own religion. As Paul never tires of emphasizing in his letter to the Romans, the only Gospel Gentiles should be interested in is the gospel of God's faithfulness to the Jews—not only to those Jews who preceded Jesus but also to those Jews who continue, and will continue, to understand themselves as children of Abraham and as Benei Berith, children of the Mount Sinai covenant. Augustine may have had in mind the relation between the Old Testament and the New Testament when he coined the interpretive formula "the old is in the new revealed; the new is in the old concealed." But this formula itself is "concealed" already in the book of Exodus. In fact, it is doubly concealed here. First, it is concealed in the relation between the religion of the ancestors and the religion of Mount Sinai, and in the relation between God as El Shaddai and God as Yahweh. Second, within the religion of Mount Sinai itself, the relation between old and new is concealed in the relation between 34:1–4 and 34:10. We cannot say simply "renewed" without needing also to say "new"; yet, as soon as we say "new," the theme of God's continuing faithfulness means that we need to say "new in the sense of renewed."

COMMANDMENTS AND FOREWARNINGS RENEWED
Exodus 34:11–28

34:11 **Observe what I command you today. See, I will drive out before you the Amorites, the Canaanites, the Hittites, the Perizzites, the Hivites, and the Jebusites.** [12] **Take care not to make a covenant with the inhabitants of the land to which you are going, or it will become a snare among you.** [13] **You shall tear down their altars, break their pillars, and cut down their sacred** poles [14] (for you shall worship no other god, because the LORD, whose name is Jealous, is a jealous God). [15] You shall not make a covenant with the inhabitants of the land, for when they prostitute themselves to their gods and sacrifice to their gods, someone among them will invite you, and you will eat of the sacrifice. [16] And you will take wives from among their daughters for your sons, and their daughters who prostitute themselves to their gods will make your sons also prostitute themselves to their gods.

[17] You shall not make cast idols.

[18] You shall keep the festival of unleavened bread. Seven days you shall eat unleavened bread, as I commanded you, at the time appointed in the month of Abib; for in the month of Abib you came out from Egypt.

[19] All that first opens the womb is mine, all your male livestock, the firstborn of cow and sheep. [20] The firstborn of a donkey you shall redeem with a lamb, or if you will not redeem it you shall break its neck. All the firstborn of your sons you shall redeem.

No one shall appear before me empty-handed.

[21] Six days you shall work, but on the seventh day you shall rest; even in plowing time and in harvest time you shall rest. [22] You shall observe the festival of weeks, the first fruits of wheat harvest, and the festival of ingathering at the turn of the year. [23] Three times in the year all your males shall appear before the LORD God, the God of Israel. [24] For I will cast out nations before you, and enlarge your borders; no one shall covet your land when you go up to appear before the LORD your God three times in the year.

[25] You shall not offer the blood of my sacrifice with leaven, and the sacrifice of the festival of the passover shall not be left until the morning.

[26] The best of the first fruits of your ground you shall bring to the house of the LORD your God.

You shall not boil a kid in its mother's milk.

[27] The LORD said to Moses: Write these words; in accordance with these words I have made a covenant with you and with Israel. [28] He was there with the LORD forty days and forty nights; he neither ate bread nor drank water. And he wrote on the tablets the words of the covenant, the ten commandments.

Comparison of verse 27 with verses 1–4 implies that the ten commandments given here are in some sense "the words that were on the former tablets" (v. 1). Clearly, this is not literally true. The fact that there are ten suggests a relation to the "ten words" in 20:1–17. Yet these ten often repeat only the theme of those ten, or repeat commandments given earlier (13:13) or later (23:10–19); or they are unprecedented (e.g., the prohibition of foreign wives).

Once again, we encounter a complex relation between "old" and "new." I make two suggestions. First, the ten given here are to be taken as representing the previously given laws. None of the old laws are abrogated. Second, whereas the ten commandments in 20:1–17 focus first on Israel's relation to God (the first four) and then on relations of Israelites with each other (the last six), the ten given here all focus on Israel's relation to God in worship. This exclusive focus is understandable, given that the sin of the calf was a violation against the first part of the original ten. Clearly, it does not mean that Israelites are now free to dishonor father and mother, murder, commit adultery, steal, bear false witness, or covet what is not theirs. It does emphasize that exclusive worship of Yahweh, as spelled out in these ten ways, is the very foundation of just covenant relations between Israelites.

In this respect, notice how verses 15–16 introduce a "new" provision related to the earlier prohibition of idols and images. The problem with foreign wives is that they will bring with them the gods whom they worshiped among their own people. Here is a good example of how the first table of the commandments is spelled out in relation to those social practices that might lead Israel into idolatry. (The book of Ruth is often celebrated as providing a more open attitude toward foreign wives. Yet two things in this book should be carefully noted. First, the Moabite wives are married while the sons of Naomi are in Moab, so that the gods of these wives are not in danger of introducing idolatrous worship into Israel. Second, when Ruth returns to Israel with Naomi, she adopts Naomi's people as her own and Naomi's God as her own, sealing all of this with an oath in the name of Yahweh [1:16–17].)

The tenth commandment in 34:26b (compare 23:19) looks at first simply like a dietary provision. But its inclusion among provisions for worship in 23:14–20 suggests that here, too, it relates to a matter of right worship. These ten commandments begin (like 20:4) by prohibiting worship of other gods and end with the law found in 23:19, again suggesting that these "new" ten are meant to stand for all the laws in 20:1–23:19.

MOSES' SHINING FACE
Exodus 34:29–35

34:29 **Moses came down from Mount Sinai. As he came down from the mountain with the two tablets of the covenant in his hand, Moses did not know that the skin of his face shone because he had been talking with God.** [30] **When Aaron and all the Israelites saw Moses, the skin of his face was shining, and they were afraid to come near him.** [31] **But Moses called to them; and Aaron and all the leaders of the congregation returned to him, and Moses** spoke with them. ³² Afterward all the Israelites came near, and he gave them in commandment all that the LORD had spoken with him on Mount Sinai. ³³ When Moses had finished speaking with them, he put a veil on his face; ³⁴ but whenever Moses went in before the LORD to speak with him, he would take the veil off, until he came out; and when he came out, and told the Israelites what he had been commanded, ³⁵ the Israelites would see the face of Moses, that the skin of his face was shining; and Moses would put the veil on his face again, until he went in to speak with him.

This is an astonishing passage. We may best approach it by noting its relation to themes we have encountered throughout the book of Exodus.

First, there is the peculiar fact that the Hebrew verb translated "shine" appears to derive from the Hebrew word for "horn." In ancient imagery, an animal horn (e.g., of a bull) is a common symbol of military might. The fact that Moses' face shone with hornlike rays may underscore that Moses is the people's true leader, not the golden calf. In this case, he is the "angel" who is to go before them (33:2; see 23:20–22 and my comments there).

Second, there is the Israelites' reaction. For the first time, they react to him in fear. This is exactly how they reacted when God spoke to them in the ten commandments. Then (20:18–21) the people "stood at a distance" and begged Moses to stand between them and God. Here they keep their distance from Moses himself. Clearly, some of the fearful radiance of God has rubbed off on Moses.

Third, this passage speaks not simply of a one-time experience but of a repeated and ongoing pattern, apparently from Mount Sinai through to Moses' death. As a customary pattern, marking Moses' movement between the people and God, this passage is in some respects similar to 33:7–11. There we are told that Moses would disappear from the people's view, into the tent of meeting, and in the tent God would speak to him "face to face, as one speaks to a friend." When friends speak to one another, their faces do not frown or darken in a scowl. Rather (like the LORD's face in the Priestly blessing of Numbers 6:24–26), their faces shine. Similarly, when in Psalm 34 the psalmist reports God's answer to prayer, the report ends in a call to others to "look to [God], and be radiant; / so your faces shall never be ashamed." So we are invited to imagine such a communion between God and Moses, following the revelation of God's character in 34:6–7, Moses' prayer in 34:8–9, and the recovenanting in 34:10–27. If the people's sin, though forgiven, has its lingering effect in their not being able to see God directly, yet they do see God's face as reflected in the face of Moses whenever he comes back to them from meeting with God.

But now comes an unexpected thing. In various traditional cultures, leaders in worship put on masks in order to represent the deity. Here, and hereafter, when Moses speaks to the people in God's name, he does so "with unveiled face," and only after he is finished speaking in God's name does he put the mask on. Then he keeps the mask on until he goes in to speak with God again, at which point he takes the mask off. What does this mean?

For one thing, it means that the old Moses is a thing of the past. The only Moses the people now know is either an individual whose human face is transformed by shining with the radiance of God or a leader whose own face is hidden behind a mask or veil. Moses in this way becomes like the most holy place, where God's invisible presence is hidden by the curtain, and only once a year is approached by the high priest on the Day of Atonement. But if Moses the individual is now hidden either by the mask or by the radiance of God shining from his face, this suggests that he is significant now as a representative. He represents the radiance of God to the people. And he represents the people as being "in the image of God." In these two respects, the figure of Moses in this passage is thus filled with promise. But it is a promise whose realization continues to turn on Israel's conformity to God's will as expressed through the commandments that Moses continues to convey.

RECURRING THEMES

Now I would like to sketch briefly how some of the central themes in chapters 32—34 reappear in the rest of the Bible, first in the Old Testament and then in the New Testament. The themes I have in mind appear in 33:19, 34:6–7, and 34:29–35.

The characterization of God in 34:6–7 centers in the two adjectives, "merciful and gracious." They carry forward the two verbal statements in 33:19 that reinterpret the divine name Yahweh. These two adjectives (and in some instances the further descriptions in 34:6–7) run through the Old Testament like gold carried by water from a mother lode and deposited at various points along in a stream bed.

I shall survey quickly the major passages in which the selected themes appear, now and then making brief comments.

1. The first occurs in Deuteronomy 4:31, at the end of a passage about the people's future violation of the covenant. Though they will go into exile for their sin, when they repent God will bring them home, "because the

LORD your God is a merciful God [*El raḥum*, as in Exod. 34:6], he will neither abandon you nor destroy you; he will not forget the covenant with
your ancestors that he swore to them." As often in Deuteronomy, the ancestors here are Abraham, Isaac, and Jacob. (With this passage, compare
Psalm 78:38.)

2. The words "merciful" and "gracious" occur together, in one or the
other order, in Psalm 86:15, which quotes all of Exodus 33:6; Psalm 103,
a meditation on Exodus 34, which in verse 8 quotes all of Exodus 33:6;
Psalm 111:4, which (like Exod. 34:10) identifies the LORD's wonderful
deeds as "gracious and merciful"; Psalm 116:5, where God is called "gracious" and "righteous" and "merciful"; Psalm 145:8–9, which quotes Exodus 34:6 and more. (These three terms are also used in Psalm 112:3 to
describe those who "fear the LORD, / who greatly delight in his commandments" [v. 1]; as though those who do so mirror God's character.)

3. In the book of Joel, a call to national repentance and prayer, the call at
one point is "Return to the LORD, your God, for he is gracious and merciful, slow to anger, and abounding in steadfast love, and relents [RSV, repents]
from punishing" (2:13). The last clause is in Hebrew an exact repetition of
Exodus 32:14. In Jonah 3:9, the king of Nineveh calls on his people to repent at the prophet's words of judgment, saying, "Who knows? God may relent [or repent] and change his mind; he may turn from his fierce anger, so
that we do not perish." In a sweet irony, this king does not know that he is
echoing the words of Moses in Exodus 32:12. But he does not have to know
this for his repentance to be effective. What angers Jonah is that God commissioned him to proclaim unavoidable judgment, when, as he says, "I knew
that you are a gracious God and merciful, slow to anger, and abounding in
steadfast love, and ready to relent [or repent] from punishing" (Jonah 4:2).
But the king of Nineveh knows something Jonah seems to have forgotten:
God cannot simply forgive the sins of those who go on sinning with a high
hand. Part of God's grace and mercy consists in the proclamation of judgment that moves to a repentance that can then hear the words of forgiveness. In the case of a nation that persists in its evil ways, the prophet Nahum
can quote Exodus 34 to quite different effect. Omitting the other elements,
verses 1:2–3 emphasize "A jealous and avenging God is the LORD," and conclude, "The LORD is slow to anger but great in power, and the LORD will
by no means clear the guilty." In both Jonah and in Nahum, though in different ways, we see the terms of God's covenant with Israel extended to the
Gentiles. With both Jew and Gentile, circumcised and uncircumcised, God
will be utterly gracious and merciful, but this is no excuse for going on sinning. Those who do so will be brought up short. Jonah's mission is to bring

Nineveh to repentance, and he succeeds. In Nahum's day, Nineveh will not listen to a call to repent and will go down in judgment.

In the New Testament, the themes of Exodus 34:6–7 are, as we would expect, closely associated with the figure of Jesus Christ. I touch on four instances: 1. The Prologue to John (1:1–18) is filled with imagery from Genesis and Exodus. Starting with verse 14 and its tabernacle theme ("the Word become flesh and lived [literally, "tented"] among us"), Exodus imagery flows through to the end. "Glory" picks up the theme of God's manifestation on Mount Sinai (Exodus 24 and 40), while the repeated references to "grace and truth" echo key terms in Exodus 34:6–7. It may be thought that verse 17 draws a contrast between Old Testament "law" and New Testament "grace and truth," but several commentators argue that, for the writer of John's Gospel, the "grace and truth" in Exodus 34 were already manifestations of the preexistent Christ, or at any rate of the divine Word that became incarnate in Jesus Christ. In that case, the contrast is not between Old Testament "law" and New Testament "grace and truth" but between Moses and Jesus. The law was "given" through Moses, but grace and truth, even back then, "came" through the preexistent Christ. As verse 18 puts it, "the only Son," who is "in the bosom of the Father" [RSV], has made known the innermost character of that bosom.

2. The letter to the Romans is Paul's final and greatest attempt to lay out the "gospel of God" (Rom. 1:1). As he repeatedly states, it is a gospel "for the Jew first" and then for the Gentiles. Therefore, he experiences "great sorrow and unceasing anguish" in his heart (9:1–5), over the fact that this gospel does not win wider acceptance among his fellow Jews. So he wrestles with this problem all through Romans 9—11, three of the most difficult chapters in the New Testament. Most significant for our purposes is how he lays the foundation for his reflections. He begins in 9:6–13 with Israel's ancestors, Abraham, Isaac, and Jacob. He takes God's choice of Isaac over firstborn Ishmael and of Jacob over firstborn Esau to show that God's call to salvation does not depend on human deserving or status in the world. Rather, it rests on God's free graciousness. Paul sums this up in 9:15 by quoting Exodus 33:19: "I will have mercy on whom I will have mercy, and I will have compassion on whom I will have compassion." (In connecting Exodus 33:19 intimately with the ancestors, it is as though Paul remembers Moses' intercessory emphasis in Exodus 32:13 and God's response in Exodus 33:1.)

By the way Paul follows the quotation of Exodus 33:19 with his statement in Romans 9:17–18, one could get the impression that he understands the exodus passage to mean God can freely decide to show grace to

some and not to others. That is not Paul's argument. In his view, God
hardens Pharaoh's heart as a means to Israel's salvation. Later, Paul will
speak of God hardening the Jews' heart (11:25), yet this does not mean
their rejection (11:1). Just as Pharaoh's heart was hardened to serve the salvation of the Israelites, now, Paul argues, the Jews' unbelief is the means
God is using to bring the gospel to the Gentiles (11:12). In the end, "all
Israel will be saved" (11:26), for "as regards election they are beloved, for
the sake of their ancestors" (11:28), the ancestors mentioned in 9:6–13.
Just as in Exodus 32:13 God hears Moses' prayer and spares Israel for the
sake of the ancestors, so it is now, argues Paul. And finally, bringing his
long, tortured argument in chapters 9—11 to a conclusion, he shows us
what he really understands Exodus 33:19 to mean: "God has imprisoned
all in disobedience so that he may be merciful to all" (11:30). No wonder
Paul bursts out with a doxology in 11:33–36! If all things are from God
as creator, then all the twists and turns of human history take place
"through," or within the embracing horizon, of the God who provides a
mercy seat (Rom. 3:25) even before the people fall into idolatry and sin.
And if all things are "through" such a God, then we may hope that all
things in the end are "unto God," the God who said to Israel, "I . . .
brought you to myself" (Exod. 19:4).

3. From the twin peaks of the prologue to John, and the letter to the
Romans, we may descend to an ordinary pastoral situation in which Paul
again draws on the mother lode of grace that was proclaimed at Mount
Sinai and enacted for all on Calvary. One of the great texts of consolation
and encouragement in the Bible comes in 2 Corinthians 1:3–7. It deserves
to be quoted in full.

> ³Blessed be the God and Father of our LORD Jesus Christ, the Father of
> mercies and the God of all consolation, ⁴who consoles us in all our affliction,
> so that we may be able to console those who are in any affliction with the
> consolation with which we ourselves are consoled by God. ⁵For just as the
> sufferings of Christ are abundant for us, so also our consolation is abundant
> through Christ. ⁶If we are being afflicted, it is for your consolation and sal-
> vation; if we are being consoled, it is for your consolation, which you expe-
> rience when you patiently endure the same sufferings that we are also
> suffering. ⁷Our hope for you is unshaken; for we know that as you share in
> our sufferings, so also you share in our consolation.

This may be taken as a general statement of what is always true of God
everywhere and for everyone. Yet Paul typically makes his most profound
statements about God in reference to some specific situation in the con-

gregation he is writing to. So it is here. The affirmations he makes in this passage and other affirmations that flow from it (such as 1:19–22) set the stage for him to deal with some very difficult and sensitive problems in the Corinthian church. The first problem he takes up concerns an individual guilty of such grievous behavior that he was subjected to a severe "punishment by the majority" (2:6). Some commentators think he was the same person mentioned in 1 Corinthians 5:1–5. There, a man had been living sexually with his father's wife, and he was so defiantly flagrant about it that Paul finally instructed the congregation to "hand this man over to Satan." It is as though the last hope for the man was that in being excommunicated he might be smitten in conscience by the accuser.

If not this same man, the man in 2 Corinthians 2:5–11 seems to have been in an analogous situation. So successful was the congregation's disciplinary action, that the accuser had succeeded in imprisoning the man within a conscience burning with shame and guilt, and now his "excessive sorrow" threatened to overwhelm him and shut out all sense or hope of God's grace. So Paul urges the congregation to "forgive and console him," by applying to him the consolation so lavishly celebrated in 1:3–7. What is to be noted, now, is that 1:3–7 is an extended unpacking of Paul's opening words, "Blessed be the God and Father of our Lord Jesus Christ, the *Father of mercies* and *God of all consolation.*" The phrase "Father of mercies" is based on a Hebrew phrase current in the synagogue in Paul's day, *'abi raḥamim* ["mercies, compassion"]. The word *raḥamim* is the noun whose verb form we have in Exodus 33:19 and whose adjective form we have in Exodus 34:6. Thus the treatment of this man gives a specific example of how "God has imprisoned all in disobedience, so that he may be merciful to all" (Rom. 11:32). The stream of grace that flows from Mount Sinai flows through Jesus Christ in whom all, Jews and Gentiles alike, are its beneficiaries.

4. A final note on how Paul's treatment of Exodus 34:29–35 relates to 2 Corinthians 3:1–4:6, where he applies the theme of Moses' mask to the experience of Christians. He begins by speaking of the Corinthian Christians as "a letter of Christ," written not on tablets of stone but on tablets of human hearts. Already this reminds us of the covenant of grace and mercy God has had Moses write in Exodus 34. Nevertheless, that covenant still has harsh things to say about disobedience, and, so long as it remains written only on stone and not on the heart, it kills by its judgments (2 Cor. 3:6). As Paul says elsewhere (Rom. 8:1–4; Gal. 2:19–20), it is only through the inner transformation worked by the Spirit of Christ that the covenant will achieve its aim of bringing life and not death.

But Paul sees in his fellow Christians just such a transformation, so that they are now a "letter of Christ" bearing good news to all who will read them. Indeed, he says, they are like Moses who, when he "went in before the LORD" (Exod. 34:34), the veil on his face was removed. Like him, their own faces are transformed by their encounter with the grace of God. Their experience, like Paul's, is that "it is the God who said, 'Let light shine out of darkness,' who has shone in our hearts to give the light of the knowledge of the glory of God in the face of Jesus Christ" (2 Cor. 4:6). To look at Christ crucified and risen is to look at the one in whom the Father of mercies is finally and fully disclosed, not simply as a bare example to follow but as one who will give us his Spirit to transform us so that we are enabled to follow in his steps. As a result, "all of us, with unveiled faces, seeing the glory of the LORD as though reflected in a mirror, are being transformed into the same image from one degree of glory to another" (2 Cor. 3:18). Who is the mirror? Christ? No doubt. Perhaps it is also other Christians, whom we are now to see as the created and redeemed image of God. As Paul says later (5:16–17), "From now on . . . we regard no one from a human point of view; even though we once knew Jesus Christ from a human point of view, we know him no longer in that way. So if anyone is in Christ, there is a new creation; everything old has passed away; see, everything has become new!" Just as Israelites once knew Moses from a human point of view but then knew him either as veiled or as with open face radiating God's glory, so now Paul sees Christ, and all who are in Christ, either as hidden with him in God (Col. 3:1–3) or radiating the image into which they are called to be transformed.

4. Preparing a Place for Presence
Exodus 35—40

The book of Exodus ends with an extended description of Moses constructing the tabernacle in accordance with God's instructions. Within the limits of this volume, there is not space to explore the passage to the extent to which we explored the giving of those instructions in chapters 25—31, but much of this last section repeats those chapters and there is no need to do so. Nevertheless, there is great meaning in this repetition, and we will do well to reflect on the repetition as such. First, however, I shall comment on features of the text that are novel.

We should note that the order of the text is different. To give only the most important instance, whereas in the instructions the call to observe the sabbath comes last, here it comes first. Why is this? The importance of this injunction, prior to the beginning of work on building the tabernacle, is connected to the fact that the tabernacle is to be understood as a miniature cosmos, or as the cosmos in miniature. More specifically, the tabernacle is a miniature model of the cosmos *as God would have it be.* As such, it becomes a symbolic prototype of what some later Old Testament prophets, Jewish apocalypticists, and New Testament writers will call "a new heaven and a new earth." Now, in the original creation in Genesis 1:1–2:3, God is portrayed as creating the world in six days and resting on the seventh. Here, before the tabernacle building is even begun, Moses emphasizes the need to observe the sabbath, so that even in the building of the tabernacle Israel will image God. Israel's loyalty to the covenant, through obedience to its laws, is to bring into being a "priestly kingdom and a holy nation" (19:6) that will serve God on behalf of all kingdoms and nations until (in the words of the book of Revelation) they "become the kingdom of our Lord and of his Messiah" (Rev. 11:15). The sabbath that is to symbolize the completion of that "new creation" is to mark Israel's life from now on, beginning with its work of building the tabernacle. In that way, each sabbath celebrated within time gives a foretaste of the sabbath that will come at the end of time.

The second thing to note is the emphasis the narrative of completion places on the willingness with which everyone, men and women alike, bring material offerings in abundance (35:4–29). So abundant are their offerings that finally they have to be restrained from bringing any more (36:2–7).

The third thing to note is the way in which the completion of the tabernacle is reported. Nahum Sarna (*Exploring Exodus*, pp. 213–214) points out a series of correspondences between Exodus 35—40 and Genesis 1:1–2:3:

1. The summarizing formula of Genesis 2:1, "Thus the heavens and the earth were finished," has as its counterpart, "In this way all the work of the tabernacle of the tent of meeting was finished" (Exod. 39:32)
2. Put another way, the statement that "God finished the work" (Gen. 2:2) is echoed in "Moses finished the work" (Exod. 40:33).
3. Just as God at the end "saw" (or inspected) all that had been made and pronounced it "very good" (Gen. 1:31), so Moses at the end "sees" that all that has been made is in accordance with God's command (Exod. 39:43).
4. Just as God marked the completion of the creation of heaven and earth with a blessing (Gen. 2:3), so Moses too marked the completion of the tabernacle with a blessing (Exod. 39:43). The refrain, "just as the LORD had commanded," which recurs more than a dozen times toward the end of chapters 35—40, provides the clue to why these chapters are not just summarized but, instead, spell out in such repetitive detail how the tabernacle was built. It is the narrator's way of assuring the reader of the step-by-step quality control with which Israel carried out God's plans. As such, we might say, it is a sermon for building contractors. But if the tabernacle is a symbolic miniature of the new heaven and new earth God will bring about through God's covenanted co-workers, it is a sermon for all of us!

Finally, we may note how, when the tabernacle is completed, the cloud that had covered Mount Sinai for the giving of the tabernacle instructions (24:15–18) now covers the tent of meeting, and the glory in which Moses was there enveloped now fills the tabernacle (40:34). This sign of the presence of God amid the people of God (25:8) will go with them, marking each day's movement through the wilderness until they arrive in the promised land (40:36–38).

The picture of the glory of God filling the tabernacle matches the cry of the seraphim in the temple, in Isaiah 6:3, as they call out, "Holy, holy, holy is the LORD of hosts; / the whole earth is full of his glory." The seraphim enjoy a vision of the new heavens and the new earth in which the glory of God fills not only the tabernacle but also the whole restored cosmos. The same vision, which Isaiah glimpses only momentarily, immediately fills him with a sense of how far he falls short of the glory of God (6:5; see Rom. 3:23). It is only when the judging-atoning coal from the altar touches his lips that he is able to serve God with those lips. It is not surprising that it is this prophet who announces the rise of a royal figure who will so establish the peace of the whole creation that "the earth will be full of the knowledge of the LORD as the waters cover the sea" (Isa. 11:9). And it is not surprising that it is within the prophetic collection associated with this prophet's name that the theme of new heavens and new earth takes its rise (e.g., 65:17–25; note how 65:5 quotes from 11:6–9 and echoes Genesis 3:14).

In the meantime, the theme of the daily presence of God along the journey is echoed in, for example, Matthew 28:20, where Jesus, having commissioned his disciples to their worldwide mission, says, "Remember, I am with you always [literally, "all the days" or "every day"], to the end of the age." In this way, and through these words of Jesus, the final words of the book of Exodus continue with us as part of our Bible companion.

Works Cited

Alter, Robert. *The Art of Biblical Narrative.* New York: Basic Books, 1981.

Aulén, Gustaf. *Christus Victor: An Historical Study of the Three Main Types of the Idea of the Atonement.* New York: Macmillan, 1909.

Bolt, Robert. *A Man for All Seasons.* New York: Random House, 1962.

Brichto, H. C. "The Worship of the Golden Calf: A Literary Analysis of a Fable on Idolatry," *Hebrew Union College Annual* 54 (1983): 1–44.

Brown, Francis, Driver, S. R., and Briggs, Charles A. *A Hebrew and English Lexicon of the Old Testament.* Oxford: Clarendon Press, 1957.

Buber, Martin. *Moses: The Revelation and the Covenant.* New York: Harper & Row, 1958.

Childs, Brevard S. *The Book of Exodus: A Critical, Theological Commentary.* Philadelphia: Westminster Press, 1974.

Cross, Frank Moore, Jr. "George Ernest Wright: A Tribute to him at his death." *Harvard Divinity Bulletin* 5 (October 1974): 4.

Daly, Mary. *Pure Lust: Elemental Feminist Philosophy.* Boston: Beacon Press, 1984.

Dillard, Annie. *Holy the Firm.* New York: Harper & Row, 1984.

Durham, John I. *Exodus.* Word Commentary. Waco: Word Books, 1987.

Gaster, T. H. "Sacrifices and Offerings, OT," in G. A. Buttrick (ed.): *Interpreter's Dictionary of the Bible*, vol. 4. New York: Abingdon Press, 1962.

Frost, Robert. *Collected Poems, Prose, & Plays.* Edited by Richard Poirer and Mark Richardson. New York: The Library of America, 1995.

Heidegger, Martin. *Being and Time.* London, SCM Press, 1962.

Hillman, James. *Insearch: Psychology and Religion.* New York: Charles Scribner's Sons, 1967.

Hopkins, Gerard Manley. *Poems of Gerard Manley Hopkins.* London: Oxford University Press, 1948.

Jantzen, Grace. *God's World, God's Body.* Philadelphia, Westminster Press, 1984.

Levenson, Jon. *The Death and Resurrection of the Beloved Son: The Transformation of Child Sacrifice in Judaism and Christianity.* New Haven: Yale University Press, 1993.

Lidz, Theodore. *The Person: His Development throughout the Life Cycle.* New York: Basic Books, 1968.

Lohfink, Norbert. *Great Themes from the Old Testament.* Edinburgh: T. & T. Clark, 1982.

MacIntyre, Alasdair. *After Virtue: A Study in Moral Theory.* Notre Dame: University of Notre Dame Press, 1981.

MacLeish, Archibald. *The Collected Poems of Archibald MacLeish.* Boston: Houghton Mifflin Co., 1962.

Mann, Thomas W. *Deuteronomy.* Westminster Bible Companion. Louisville: Westminster John Knox Press, 1996.

Mays, James L. *Psalms.* Interpretation: A Bible Commentary for Teaching and Preaching. Atlanta: John Knox Press, 1989.

Moberly, R. W. L. *The Old Testament of the Old Testament: Patriarchal Narratives and Mosaic Yahwism.* Minneapolis: Fortress Press, 1992.

Sarna, Nahum. *Exploring Exodus: The Heritage of Biblical Israel.* New York: Schocken Books, 1987.

Sheehy, Gail. *Passages: Predictable Crises of Adult Life.* New York: E. P. Dutton, 1976.

Sprinkle, Joe M. *The Book of the Covenant: A Literary Approach.* Sheffield: JSOT Press, 1994.

Stockwell, Eugene L. "Latin American Protestants: Open and Closed." *The Christian Century* (March 22–29, 1995): 317–19.

Toombs, L. E. "Lampstand," in *The Interpreter's Dictionary of the Bible,* vol. 3. New York: Abingdon Press, 1962.

Valliere, Paul. *Holy War and Pentecostal Peace.* New York: Seabury Press, 1983.

Wright, George Ernest, and Fuller, Reginald H. *The Book of the Acts of God.* Garden City: Doubleday & Co., 1957.

The hymn "When God of Old Came Down from Heaven" is by John Keble, and is found in *The Book of Common Praise: 1938* of the Church of England in Canada. Oxford: Oxford University Press, 1938.

The hymn "How Sweet the Name of Jesus Sounds" is written by John Newton and is found in *The Hymnal: 1982* of the Episcopal Church. New York: The Church Hymnal Corporation, 1982.

The hymn "Praise, My Soul, the King of Heaven" is written by Henry

Francis Lyte and is found in *The Hymnal: 1982* of the Episcopal Church. New York: The Church Hymnal Corporation, 1982.

The hymn "Ye Holy Angels Bright" is written by Richard Baxter and is found in *The Hymnal: 1982* of the Episcopal Church. New York: The Church Hymnal Corporation, 1982.

The hymn "O For A Closer Walk with God" is written by William Cowper and is found in *The Hymnal: 1982* of the Episcopal Church. New York: The Church Hymnal Corporation, 1982.

The hymn "Take the Name of Jesus with You" is written by Lydia Baxter and is found in the *United Methodist Hymnal.* Nashville: United Methodist Publishing House, 1989.

For Further Reading

Brueggemann, Walter. *The Book of Exodus.* The New Interpreter's Bible, vol. 1. Nashville: Abingdon Press, 1994.

Croato, J. Severino. *Exodus: A Hermeneutics of Freedom.* Maryknoll, N.Y.: Orbis, 1978.

Fretheim, Terence E. *Exodus.* Interpretation: A Bible Commentary for Teaching and Preaching. Atlanta: John Knox Press, 1985.

Please note that the following abbreviations are also used throughout the text:

KJV, *King James Version* (Nashville, Tenn.: Thomas Nelson Inc., Publisher, 1982).

RSV, *Revised Standard Version* (New York: Division of Christian Education of the National Council of the Churches of Christ in the U.S.A., 1913).

Printed in the United States
203421BV00003B/91-114/A